Interpreter-Mediated Interactions of the Courtroom

STUDIES IN LANGUAGE, CULTURE AND SOCIETY
Edited by Łucja Biel, Andrzej Kątny and Piotr Ruszkiewicz

VOLUME 14

PETER LANG

Agnieszka Biernacka

Interpreter-Mediated Interactions of the Courtroom

A Naturally Occurring Data Based Study

PETER LANG

Bibliographic Information published by the Deutsche Nationalbibliothek
The Deutsche Nationalbibliothek lists this publication in the Deutsche Nationalbibliografie; detailed bibliographic data is available online at http://dnb.d-nb.de.

Library of Congress Cataloging-in-Publication Data
A CIP catalog record for this book has been applied for at the Library of Congress.

This publication has been co-financed from the funds of the University of Warsaw Foundation.

UNIVERSITY
OF WARSAW
FOUNDATION

ISSN 2195-7479
ISBN 978-3-631-67429-1 (Print)
E-ISBN 978-3-653-06834-4 (E-Book)
E-ISBN 978-3-631-70177-5 (EPDF)
E-ISBN 978-3-631-70178-2 (MOBI)
DOI 10.3726/978-3-653-06834-4

Peter Lang – Berlin · Bern · Bruxelles · New York · Oxford · Warszawa · Wien

This publication has been peer reviewed.

www.peterlang.com

Acknowledgments

I wish to extend my heart-felt gratitude to Professor Małgorzata Tryuk for reading the first draft of my study, her continuous support, help in limiting the field of my research, and spreading her immense knowledge.

I would like to express my sincere thanks to Professor Łucja Biel for reading the first draft of this book, sharing her valuable experience, and providing scientific advice.

Any shortcomings remain my own.

Contents

Abbreviations

C	Counsel
CA	Conversation Analysis
CR	close rendition
D	Defendant
EN	English version
ER	extended rendition
ES	Spanish version
FPP	first pair part
I	Interpreter
IT	institutional talk
J	Judge
NR	non-rendition
P	Prosecutor
PL	Polish version
RR	reduced rendition
SBR	substituted rendition
SL	source language
SMR	summarized rendition
SPP	second pair part
TCU	turn constructional unit
TL	target language
TMR	two-part or multi-part rendition
TRP	transition relevance place
W	Witness
ZR	zero rendition

The use of an Interpreter in the courtroom increases the complexity of the communication and adds an element of unpredictability [...].

– Sabine Fenton

Introduction

Court interpreting understood as services provided for court stakeholders (institutional clients) and the court's private clients (brought before the court by those) seeking justice is a subdiscipline which has emerged, as other varieties of public service interpreting, or dialogue interpreting, and independently of conference interpreting, as a separate area of investigation within Interpreting Studies (Pöchhacker 2001, 2012, 2015; Tryuk 2004, 2006). Despite the key importance of the interpreters' assistance in the courtroom as guarantors of the right to a fair trial, as well as the legal provisions and the ethical principles that are in force on them – as is the reality in the case of Polish court interpreters, the services rendered before the courts are still underestimated. As Repa indicates, court interpreting is "the Cinderella of interpretation: an unglamorous girl […]" (1991: 595), while court interpreters do not enjoy a high reputation of the profession, and their services are unappreciated, both prestigiously and economically (Hale 2007: 108; Katschinka 2013: 9; Biernacka 2014a: 49). This, along with the highly reduced availability of research data, contributes to the still scarce research into court interpreting as compared to other types of interpreting. According to Hale, "[m]uch of what is written or said on the topic […] is of a very prescriptive or anecdotal nature, rarely based on empirical evidence" (2004: xv). This, certainly, deepens the stereotypes of court interpreting as shrouded in secrecy and wreathed in aura of mystery, and of court interpreters as in-betweens who cannot be trusted. As Colin and Morris state, "[…] many people who work in legal settings (…) treat interpreters with suspicion, distrust and a lack of respect for the skills which they bring to the job" (1996: 15). Hence, a *non-party approach* (Berk-Seligson 1990/2002; Morris 1995; Mason and Stewart 2001) is postulated through the studies promoting interpretation as a text-based activity, and court interpreters as text producers; de Jongh emphasizes the need to "standardize equivalent foreign language terms" (1992: 117) while Poznański (2007) points out the necessity to work out glossaries of legal terms. Such an approach may be a consequence of ignoring the fact that court interpreters are entitled to occupy a certain physical place; thus, their activities are reduced to the functions perceived as either non-existing, somebody or something supposedly present in the interaction between main speakers but that actually retains *invisible presence* (Apostolou 2009; Torikai 2009), or "a polyglot who is also an automatic language converter" (Gentile, Ozolins, and Vasilakakos 1996: 65).

As pointed out by the scholars who regard court interpreters as more than text producers, there is a huge discrepancy between such an understanding of an act of communication with the participation of an interpreter and the reality. As Gentile, Ozolins, and Vasilakakos put it, "a gulf exists between reality and the perception of the interpreter's clients" (1996: 65). Thus, in accordance with the wish expressed by Harris of the need to discuss such indicators of the interpreting profession as "accreditation, training, remuneration, research" (1995: 2), the 1990s witnessed the flourishing of the descriptive trend in studying community interpreting in all settings, including courts (although the research in court interpreting in line with the prescriptive tradition has been continued).

While the research in court interpreting has been enjoying prominence at an international level, there are still areas which need discovering. As Wadensjö indicates, "there is still much to explore concerning institutional interaction, and not least when it comes to the peculiarities and particularities of dialogue interpreting" (2012: xi). When it comes to the Polish bilingual courtroom, scholarly studies concerning court interpreters are far from being able to give a comprehensive perspective on the subject as regards both Polish courts and Polish as one of the languages of the pair. Apart from the studies based on recommendations regarding professional issues (Jopek-Bosiacka 2006, 2010, 2014; Kierzkowska 2007/2008; Kościałkowska-Okońska 2010; Matulewska 2014), there are only a few (Biernacka 2008a, 2008b, 2009, 2010a, 2010b, 2014a, 2014b, 2016; Nartowska 2013a, 2013b, 2015; Stawecka 2010; Tryuk 2010), which form part of the empirical path marked out by the scholars contributing to the *First Critical Link Conference* in 1995 who integrated court interpreting analysis to community interpreting studies, as well as further works within public service interpreting.

This book is aimed at fulfilling the neglected area of qualitative research into court interpreting in Poland, and in particular, where the Polish-English and Polish-Spanish (to a lesser extent and mainly for illustrative purposes) language pairs are involved.

This study pertains to the descriptive research into court interpreting where the interpreter is perceived as an active participant in the interaction (Roberts 1997: 13–14). As Wadensjö puts it, "[i]f we look at interpreting as interaction, (…), it is evident that interpreter-mediated talk forms a particular type of encounter, with its own specific organizational principles" (1997: 203). Such an approach, where the interpreter is considered "as a third interlocutor" (Gentile, Ozolins, and Vasilakakos 1996: 31) within the bilingual communicative events ("courtroom triadic exchanges", Kang 1998; "triadic speech events", Jacobsen 2008), has its roots in the sociological theory of interaction (Garfinkel 1967,

Goffman 1956, 1967), according to which all interactants, even though involved in symmetrical and asymmetrical relationships (Goffman 1967), cooperate in order to maintain the communicative act.

The product-oriented, small-scale qualitative study, based on naturally occurring, "recorded spoken data" (Dörnyei 2007: 19), is a logical consequence of the adopted ethnomethodological paradigm fueled by interactions taking place at institutional communicative settings. The material for the Conversation Analysis (CA) of the interpreter-mediated interactions, obtained during a seven-month search query conducted between December 2013 and June 2014 at the Civil and Economic Divisions of the Regional Court in Warsaw, Poland, constitutes bilateral real-world communicative events ("real-life interpreter-mediated encounters", Wadensjö 1995: 50), in which court interpreters working with Polish-English and Polish-Spanish language pairs assisted.

On the assumption that the interpreters leave their footprint on bilingual interactions of the courtroom, the research questions of this study are as follows:

(1) How do the interpreters[1] interact with primary parties (the court stakeholders or the court's private clients) at the level of the communicative act?
   (a) is it the primary parties who make the interpreters submit to the mechanisms of interaction, or
   (b) is it the interpreters who impose an order of the interaction on the original speakers?
   (c) is a question-rendition-answer-rendition pattern of bilingual interaction (understood as the one, in which after each primary party's turn the interpreter speaks to render the original utterance) followed, or are any irregularities detected as regards the turn-taking system according to which the interactants change?
(2) What renditions of the original utterances produced by primary speakers provided by the interpreters can be identified?
(3) In what way can these renditions be considered as manifestations of complying, on the part of the interpreters, with the ethical principles of accuracy and impartiality required in the bilingual communicative events of the courtroom?

---

1 Throughout the entire book, for the purposes of this study, after Jacobsen, "an interpreter is referred to as she, and any other participant as he, unless specifically identified as female" (2003: 236).

(4) What patterns in deploying interpreting techniques, depending on a particular interaction mechanism to which the interpreter is a component, can be observed?

The book encompasses two parts. Part I provides insights into a theoretical background for the research into court interpreting and includes two chapters. Chapter 1 contextualizes court interpreting. First, it describes this variety of interpreting within community, or, public service interpreting, and discusses the principles of ethics as one of the crucial characteristics of the profession; furthermore, it focuses on the Polish perspective: legal and ethical framework, historical issues affecting the profession at present, as well as challenges faced to make court interpreting a full-fledged profession. Chapter 2 reviews the ethnomethodological paradigm developed by Garfinkel (1967) and Goffman (1967) as applied in the studies concerning court interpreting, specifies the features of institutional talk (IT) in interaction, and presents the findings of scholarly investigations conducted thus far in the field of court interpreting understood as interpreter-mediated institutional talks. Part II comprises an empirical study of episodes of interpreter-mediated interaction in the Polish courtroom. Chapter 3 concentrates on methodology: collecting data for qualitative research into court interpreting, data processing for CA, as well as presents a proposal for integrating the CA of interpreter-mediated court interactions with the study of the interpreters' renditions. Chapter 4 analyzes the turn-taking system in the interpreter-mediated talks, where the interactants are selected by the current speaker, but also self-select to speak. Chapter 5 focuses on the interpreter's (non-)participation in the gap and overlap mechanisms, the former being perceived as opportunities for the interpreter to talk, and the latter as considerable obstacles to performing interpreting responsibilities. Chapter 6 is devoted to adjacency pairs as those components of bilingual interactions, which enable the active participation of the interpreters. Chapter 7 aims at investigating pre- and post-expansions in bilingual communicative acts, and Chapter 8 presents insert-expansions at institutional talk of the courtroom; both concentrate on the interpreters' inclusion in these mechanisms. Chapter 9 analyzes repairs as responses to problems in bilingual interactions. It is in Chapter 10 where the overall results of the analyses performed in the empirical part of this book are discussed and re-contextualized within previous scholarly research. Moreover, this final chapter puts forward recommendations for further research into court interpreting.

Part I Theoretical Background for the Research into Court Interpreting

1 Court interpreting: contextualization

Court interpreters render their services in the courtroom. Apart from being the "oral interpretation of speech from one language to another" (Edwards 1995: xv), and not the translation of documents issued by the court, as well as taking place in a particular setting, **court interpreting** (Hale 2004; Gamal 2009: 63) or **courtroom interpreting** is characterized by "complex ritualized interaction and power hierarchies" (Morris: 2015: 91). Another term, **legal interpreting**, is also applied to refer to the interpretation before the court, nonetheless, it is a broader concept than **court interpreting**; according to Hertog, **legal interpreting** is carried out through the entire legal procedure (2016). In the same vein, *ISO/DIS 20228 Interpreting services – Legal interpreting – Requirements* (under development)[2], the document prepared by the International Organization for Standardization in order to establish standards of legal interpreting, proposes that this cover all law-related settings. Furthermore, the term **tribunal interpreting** is used, but limited to refer to interpreting done for the needs of ad hoc international courts to judge war criminals (Takeda 2015: 424).

1.1 Court interpreting within the context of community interpreting

Court interpreting is contextualized within oral communication, but further allocating to either community or legal interpreting is problematic.

Pursuant to *ISO 13611:2014 Interpreting – Guidelines for community interpreting*[3], a document establishing the criteria and recommendations for community interpreting, the term also includes court interpreting. On the one hand, the document defines community interpreting as the one that enables access, *inter alia*, to services provided at police stations, courts and prisons, but on the other hand it respects a national context of different countries, where court interpreting can be considered a separate variety of interpreting.

Some scholars claim that court interpreting is a specific type of community interpreting (Roberts 1997: 9; Garber 2000: 14; Apfelbaum 2004: 32; Tryuk

---

2 *ISO/DIS 20228 Interpreting services – Legal interpreting – Requirements* https://www.iso.org/standard/67327.html (October 1, 2017).

3 *ISO 13611:2014 Interpreting – Guidelines for community interpreting* https://www.iso.org/standard/54082.html (October 1, 2017).

2006: 25; Biernacka 2010b, 2014a; Kościałkowska-Okońska 2010) and highlight its bilaterality, need for transmitting the message sentence by sentence without taking notes, as well as modifying the original utterances by expressing opinions, summarizing or shifts in register (Dąmbska-Prokop 2000). In *ISO 113611:2014* a bidirectional nature of community interpreting is also emphasized, while Tryuk, making reference to a similar nature of both types of interpretation, uses an expression "an interpreter in a court setting" (2006: 101; transl. by the author)[4]. Similarly, Wadensjö (1998: 51) and Pym (1999: 265) state that court interpreting is one of the varieties of community interpreting.

The characteristics exhibited by both court and community interpreting include: **unequal status of participants**, **confidentiality** of interpreter-mediated talks, personal **context**, and **modes** of interpreting (Tryuk 2006).

As regards **unequal status of participants**, according to a guidance document *ISO/DIS 20228 Legal Interpreting*, the participants in the act of communication include "(…) persons deprived of liberty, suspects, accused, defendants, plaintiffs, claimants, complainants, witnesses, victims, (…)", that is, the interpreter's private clients, and "(…) judges, lawyers, prosecutors, (…)" who are the interpreter's institutional clients embodying the judiciary; both parties, in the event there is an individual in the courtroom who does not understand the language of the court, "(…) require interpreting services (…)"[5]. Hence, an interpreter is situated somewhere in-between an institutional client (the court) and a private client (a suspect, an accused, etc.) and her responsibilities include enabling these parties to communicate. The lack of balance between the participants (with the judge being the most powerful figure (Morris 2015)) in the interaction results not only from the fact that they represent different backgrounds (Shackman 1984), do not speak the language or do not know the culture of the other party, but is also related to the power and the shifts of control over the interpreted event. These relations of inequality may affect the way the interpreter's job is carried out (Tryuk 2006).

As far as **confidentiality** is concerned, it is defined in the Act on the Profession of Sworn Translator[6] of November 25, 2004[7] as an obligation to keep

---

4 "tłumacz w środowisku sądowym" (all translations in this book are mine, unless otherwise indicated).

5 https://dgn.isolutions.iso.org/obp/ui#iso:std:iso:20228:dis:ed-1:v2:en (July 4, 2018).

6 An issue of taxonomy for the profession of sworn translators and court interpreters is discussed in Sections 1.4.1 and 1.4.2.

7 Ustawa o zawodzie tłumacza przysięgłego z dnia 25 listopada 2004 r. (Dz.U. z 2015 r. Nr 487) https://bip.ms.gov.pl/pl/rejestry-i-ewidencje/tlumacze-przysiegli/ (October 28, 2017); all quotations from the English version of the Act on the Profession

any sensitive information obtained in relation to the interpreting services provided in secret. Sensitive information includes the personal data of the parties to the proceedings, as well as the data regarding the object of the proceedings. It also determines that if an interpreter takes notes during a trial, these should be destroyed just after the interpretation so that they did not fall into the wrong hands (Kierzkowska 2005: 79). Confidentiality arises from a personal context of the courtroom; private clients of the court do not appear before the judge because they want to; instead, they are summoned because a dispute or a conflict cannot be amicably resolved, or because someone committed a crime. Neither of the situations is pleasant; on the contrary, the clients of the court find themselves in dramatic situations which become even worse if they do not understand the language of the court. Furthermore, Nagao (2005: 3) and Gentile, Ozolins, and Vasilakakos (1996: 30–31) point out that court interpreting is one of these types of community interpreting that is done for the clients whose life depends on the interpreter. Also, Nagao (2005) and Katschinka (2000) discuss an issue of the importance of services provided by court interpreters; they compare court interpreting to conference interpreting and claim that viewed within the context of personal tragedies, for a foreign language speaking witness or accused it is much more important to be understood by other parties to the proceedings through the professional interpretation than it is in the case of conference settings. Therefore, the personal context of the interaction: means a great (both professional and personal) liability of an interpreter; channels an interpreter who is to deal with emotionally charged communicative acts individually (there is no teamwork in the courtroom); also, may make an interpreter feel involved in the interaction due to a short physical distance between the interpreter and main speakers.

As to the **modes** of interpreting, in the courtroom, short, (question-answer) dialogues or a bit longer fragments are interpreted consecutively (at the examination stage, when a witness is being heard by a judge). Moreover, whispered interpreting is provided when a judge is hearing a witness and they both speak the same language, but still, there are other parties to the proceedings, who are not involved in the trial at the moment, who do not speak the language of the court. Sight translation is also applied, when a judgment is delivered at the final stage of the entire court proceedings and the interpreter is provided with

---

of Sworn Translator come from the translation of the entire Act by Setkowicz-Ryszka available at: http://www.mc-tlumaczenia.pl/files/file/PolishSwornTranslatorAct%2827_1_2005%29.pdf (October 20, 2017).

a written document to be interpreted into a language understood by the client. The application of the above modes is conditioned by an important feature of court interpreting that is a bi-directionality meant as transmitting the information from and into a foreign language. An issue relating to the modes is a use of note-taking. Heimerl-Moggan and John observe that note-taking is an important memory aid for public service interpreters contributing to precise and correct rendering of long, emotionally loaded, and redundant original utterances, in particular when primary speakers change pace and use specific terminology (2007). Nonetheless, in spite of its undisputable advantages, the use of note-taking in public service interpreting is scarce (Tryuk 2006). This may be a result of the fact that note-taking is underappreciated and considered useless in the settings where interpreters transmit dialogues (Allen 2014).

Yet another issue discussed in attributing court interpreting to community interpreting is the **scope of competences** required in both varieties. Zimman (1994), who refers to community interpreting, proposes a catalog of competences regarding interpreters, which includes: language, culture, common knowledge, knowledge of social systems, knowledge of a topic of the encounter, as well as an ability to make interpreting decisions that are the fundamental skills. Furthermore, Kaczmarek (2008) proposes a descriptive model of community interpreter competence recognizing its three-fold nature structured by: the individual system (knowledge, skills and motivation), episodic system (variables considered during a particular episode of interaction), and relational system (based on the protracted observations of interpreter-mediated encounters with participation of the same interlocutors). As regards the competences of court interpreters, Bednarek emphasizes textual and discourse competences, claiming that they are subject to dynamic modifications due to implementing new EU legislation[8] binding for court interpreters (2014a, 2014b). The most recent list of competences relating to court interpreters, suggested by Hertog is extremely detailed; court interpreters are supposed to possess pre-requisite and specific competences. Pre-requisite competences include: general language competence; listening, speaking, reading and writing skills; interpersonal skills and attitudes; and knowledge of relevant countries and their cultures. Specific competences cover: knowledge of legal systems and legal language; knowledge of resources and information retrieval; interpreting and oral sight translation skills; as well as

8 The legal basis for the interpreter's assistance in court proceedings is referred to in Section 1.4.

knowledge of the professional code of conduct and guidelines to good practice (2016).

In general, court interpreting is lined up with interpretation for the needs of other public institutions or for the needs of persons who do not know the language of the country in which the trial they are involved in takes place; such interpretation enables full and equal access to these institutions (Mikkelson 2004).

1.2 Historical dimension of court interpreting

It is impossible to indicate the precise moment when the profession came into existence; however, court interpreters have been providing their services ever since the judicial power was implemented. Repa (1991: 595) points out that "[f]rom time immemorial, an untrained bilingual person was brought into the court to help with the understanding of evidence given by a foreigner" which makes it obvious that representatives of different cultures speaking different languages needed to communicate. Court interpreters were not necessarily professional interpreters and, as Kierzkowska indicates, their status, at least in English speaking countries of the British Empire of the nineteenth century, was rather low and limited, as exemplified by the interpreters who transferred "elements of a rich Anglo-Saxon culture to inferior cultures with a feudal obedience to an author" (1991: 66)[9]. Other scholars (Tryuk 2006: 54–56; Giambruno (Miguélez) 2008: 29–32; Tryuk 2012a: 16) maintain that it was in particular in the Age of Exploration and Discovery when the importance of the profession of court interpreters as cultural mediators enabling communication between representatives of various cultures and languages began to increase. Alonso and Payàs (2008) emphasize the role of interpreters in the border regions of thirteenth- and fourteenth-century medieval Spain and the sixteenth-century New Spain, where they were officially appointed professionals who had their own code of ethics and whose hybridized services—not limited only to interpreting—were highly appreciated by their clients.

In the twentieth century, the period after the Second World War was a turning point for the profession, "when a role of interpreters in deciding on people's lives grew in value in the history of the profession[10]" (Kierzkowska 1991: 66; transl. by the author). The profession of court interpreter developed

9 "element[y] bogatej kultury anglosaskiej kulturom niższym z feudalnym posłuszeństwem wobec autora".

10 "kiedy rola tłumaczy w rozstrzyganiu o ludzkich losach nabrała przełomowego znaczenia w dziejach ich zawodu".

in the twentieth century parallel to the profession of conference interpreter; during the Nuremberg Trials (held from December 9, 1946 to August 13, 1949), in which Nazi war criminals were judged, the proceedings were interpreted simultaneously with the aid of special equipment. Interestingly, the Trials are considered a milestone in the development of conference (!), and not—court interpreting (Repa 1991: 595; Gentile, Ozolins, and Vasilakakos 1996: 8; Gaiba 1998; Tryuk 2006: 101; Tryuk 2015). The Tokyo War Crimes Trials (from April 29, 1946 to November 12, 1948) before the International Military Tribunal for the Far East (Takeda 2007; Tryuk 2012b: 51–51, 55–58; Tryuk 2015), as well as, in Poland, trials before the Supreme National Tribunal (from June 21, 1946 to July 10, 1948) were held almost concurrently (Tryuk 2015: 105); during these trials interpreting services were also provided. Moreover, interpreters participated in two other trials of Nazi criminals after the Second World War in Jerusalem: the trial of Adolf Eichmann in 1961–1962 and of Iwan Demjanjuk, the cases of which were heard in 1987–1988 (Shlesinger 1991a: 148), and afterwards in Munich in 2009–2011[11].

At present court interpreters render their services during trials in national criminal and civil courts of all instances, as well as before international courts of justice, e.g. the International Criminal Tribunal for the former Yugoslavia (1993) and the International Criminal Tribunal for Rwanda (1994) established by the UN Security Council (Izydorczyk and Wiliński 2004: 17–18); the International Criminal Court in the Hague (1998) governed by the Rome Statute (Keating 2005) and the Special Tribunal for Lebanon (2009) established by virtue of the resolution of the UN Security Council. Moreover, in administrative proceedings regarding EU citizens, it is the European Court of Human Rights in Strasbourg that makes use of interpreting services (Jopek-Bosiacka 2006: 215).

Individual countries have their own national legislations pursuant to which they guarantee the assistance of an interpreter in the event a party to the proceedings does not speak the language of a given jurisdiction (Hale 1997a: 201; Tryuk 2006: 57–58).

1.3 Principles of ethics in court interpreting

Court interpreters are unconditionally obliged to observe principles of ethics which is a consequence of the nature of the legal process, and which distinguishes court interpreting from other varieties of interpreting (Gamal 2009: 63). Such a

11 http://news.bbc.co.uk/2/hi/europe/8385577.stm (October 28, 2017).

viewpoint is in complete agreement with the comprehensive approach to professionalism; even though there are countries in which the code of ethics does not exist, "the welfare of the client demands ethical practices" (Gentile, Ozolins, and Vasilakakos 1996: 57). Moreover, it proves, that in those countries in which there is no requirement of training before becoming a professional interpreter, ethics provides guidelines for practicing court interpreting (Hale 2007: 103).

Codes of ethics are a source of knowledge of all the principles that should govern court interpreters' approach to their activities. Moreover, the codes help identify a profession in order to enable to share knowledge and experience (Corsellis and Fernández 2001: 77), from which it can be inferred that codes of ethics not only assume a function of guidelines for court interpreters, but play a vital role in consolidating the profession as well.

Historically, it is, among others, a seventeenth-century set of documents known as "Recopilación de Leyes de los Reynos de las Indias" that proves the significance of court interpreters as professionals. This is a collection of legal provisions governing all aspects of political, economic, social and cultural life in American and Filipino colonies belonging to Spain. In 1681, the King of Spain Charles II ordered them to be published in 4 volumes divided into 9 books comprising 6385 legal provisions included in 218 titles, out of which Title 29 titled "About interpreters" covers 14 laws passed from 1529 to 1630. The laws touched upon such legal and ethical aspects of the profession as: guaranteeing the court interpreter's assistance, criteria for the selection and certification of interpreters, high quality of interpretation services, the interpreter's impartiality, confidentiality, as well as the accuracy of the interpretation (Giambruno (Miguélez) 2008: 37–47). Hence, it is hard not to appreciate the importance of these laws for the development of the profession; it is safe to say that the collection is an early form of the professional code of ethics for interpreters (Giambruno (Miguélez) 2008: 34) whose standards are included in all modern documents of this type. Moreover, the laws provide for certain obligations of interpreters, such as e.g. the obligation to appear before the court, which even today considerably exceeds the standards envisaged in the codes of professional ethics.

It is undoubtedly an exceptional need for an ethical conduct of court interpreters that contributed to the attempts to outline deontological guidelines for those interpreting in the courtroom. Another historical example showing the importance of establishing the principles of court interpreting is the case of seven interpreters who in 1820 rendered their services during the divorce proceedings of Caroline of Brunswick and King George IV and whose impartiality was subject to criticism:

> Then Giuseppe Bianche was called in, and sworn through the interpretation of the Marchese di Spinetto. Mr. Deuman objected to the evidence being given through the interpretation of the Marchese di Spinetto, not on the ground that he had not interpreted truly, but that he was informed he had seen the witness before, and had interpreted the examination taken out of court by the attorney on the part of the prosecution; he conceived, therefore, that the rehearsal of the evidence which had taken place before, might in some degree affect the mode in which the evidence might be given now (Worth 1821: 449–450).

Therefore, it was imperative that interpreters be excluded from the activities that might have affected their interpretation.

The significance of the interpreter's neutrality is also highlighted as regards the *Amistad* Case, a chronologically subsequent trial, which took place in 1839. Fifty-three African captives who revolted, took over the *Amistad* ship during the voyage from Havana to Port Principe, and managed to arrive at Long Island, New York, were arrested. After three trials they were announced to have been kidnapped from West Africa; as not guilty, they returned to Africa in 1842. From the first trial, in order to enable a communication between them and the court, the Africans (who all spoke the Mendi language) had been assisted by two court interpreters, James Covey and Charles Pratt, who were Mendi natives and freed slaves. These interpreters had been recruited through a meticulous process during which their qualifications, including complying with the principles of ethics, were evaluated (Zaragoza 2015).

Currently, as investigated by Hale (2007) who compared 16 codes of ethics binding in 9 countries (Australia, Austria, Canada, British Columbia, Indonesia, Ireland, Great Britain, Spain and USA), the principles that most frequently appear in these codes are: confidentiality (13 codes, 81.25 percent), accuracy (12 codes, 75 percent), and impartiality (11 codes, percent). Hale puts these three principles under the heading of the "interpreters' responsibility to the authors of the utterances" (2007: 108). In addition, Hale distinguishes two other groups of principles, i.e. those which include "interpreters' responsibility to the profession" (2007: 108) (solidarity), and those covering "interpreters' responsibility to self as a professional" (2007: 108) (professional development, working conditions and role definition).

Two of the aforementioned principles—**accuracy** and **impartiality**—are of particular importance as they directly refer to the interpretation in the courtroom, and what is more, the (non-)compliance with them can directly and (adversely) affect the proceedings and judgments.

Accuracy means that the interpretation should be "faithful to the original" (Hale 2007: 109), which is understood as the interpreter's abstaining from summarizing original utterances, adding or omitting information ("embellishing", Framer: 2005: 4), as well as altering (Hewitt 1995). Mason and Stewart developed a definition of accurate interpretation by observing that court interpreters are obliged to translate accurately and only what was actually said (2001: 52–53). Jacobsen observes that not only accurate, but the literal interpretation of an original text becomes a requirement in court interpreting (2002: 62); this is due to a favor shown by lawyers to such interpretation as interpreters who are not able to provide a word-for-word interpretation are perceived as those who want to hide information (Laster 1990: 18). Mikkelson also highlights a conflict between the lawyers' expectations of a verbatim interpretation and accurate interpreting (1999). Hale is of an opinion that it is in such situations that the interpreters have to use common sense (2007: 129–130) as it is not true that the interpreter who provides literal renditions would be able to place the primary parties to the communication event in the same position; in other words, even though the interpreter might interpret word by word, the message lacks precision and fidelity in relation to original information (1997a: 201). To support this view, Hale states that the codes of ethics do not recommend literal renditions, perceived as "machine-like, unthinking performance" (2007: 109). What is more, what non-professionals consider accurate interpreting, is not necessarily accurate, and vice versa; as Hale explains it, "[t]he interpreted version must not only convey the 'general idea' of the message, but also the speaker's intention" (1997a: 202) in order to produce the same reactions in both the SL and TL listeners. Interestingly, in some codes, the concept of accuracy is defined as being contradictory to literal interpretation; e.g. according to the "Code of Ethics and Guidelines for Professional Conduct of the Association of Visual Language Interpreters of Canada", accuracy in interpreting allows adaptations, which make the original utterance be "felt" (Hale 2007: 112) in the target language.

In the same vein the International Criminal Tribunal for the Prosecution of Persons Responsible for Serious Violations of International Humanitarian Law Committed in the Territory of the former Yugoslavia in its decision of September 27, 2007 in the case no. IT-05-87-T concerning a motion to compel the registry to provide a verbatim transcript of proceedings, expresses a full understanding of the fact that "synthesizing" is a legitimate interpretation technique (Lukić *Decision* 2007: 2).

The aforementioned opinion stands in contradiction with the point of view shared by representatives of the judiciary who generally claim that only a verbatim interpretation is justified (Mason 1999: 150). Edwards goes one step further and claims that accuracy means not only faithfulness to the text, but also to the voice tone (1995: 81). On the one hand, although the interpreter should render, or even copy, the tone of the original statement, such intonation is something additional, in particular when the pace of the original speech is high; if this is the case, the interpreter may ignore the intonation in favor of a precise rendition of significance and the speed of the utterance. On the other hand, however, a precise interpretation also comprises transmitting the tone of voice. Nevertheless, in many instances it happens, that the interpreter's rendition is "dispassionate and unexpressive" (Morris 2008: 42). According to Shlesinger, an interpreter may "use intonation to dissociate himself from the propositional content of his own rendering" (1991a: 152) in order to stress that she is an active participant in the interaction instead of being just an impassive device that repeats the utterances of the main speakers. There is a danger, however, that even when an interpreter transmits information in an emotional way, it is never known whether emphasis is put on a given fragment of the main speakers' original utterance or it is produced by the interpreter herself.

Not surprisingly, Edwards states that faithful and accurate interpreting means transmission of the words (1995: 82–83); such an approach is justified by the content of an oath taken by court interpreters in the United States: "I will convey the true meaning of the words, phrases and statements of the speaker (…)" (Edwards 1995: 188), which means that the original utterances should be reproduced in the TL not only on the level of sentences and expressions, but also words: "[a] reply of 'Huh?' should be repeated as 'Huh?'" (Edwards 1995: 87). Exactly the same opinion is shared by representatives of the judiciary, as in the following examples:

(1) "The Court: Madame Interpreter, I want you to just interpret literally everything that is said" (Edwards 1995: 94);
(2) "Adwokat do tłumacza: A to proszę przetłumaczyć dosłownie" [The lawyer to the interpreter: And this, please, should be interpreted literally] (Biernacka 2008a: 187);
(3) "[…] just translate word-for-word what he's saying" (Mikkelson 2010: 4).

In light of the quoted recommendations, it is not astonishing that the principle of accuracy is understood by court interpreters rather freely:

(1) "In my opinion I should translate in the way it was said. If the witness's answer is 'Yhy', then I translate it as 'Yhy' because it depends on a judge whether he understood it or he would ask additional questions to understand a sense of the answer" (Biernacka 2014a: 56; transl. by the author)[12];

12 "Uważam, że tłumaczyć należy tak, jak to zostało wypowiedziane: Kiedyś osoba

(2) "According to the ethical rules I should stick absolutely to the letter" (Wadensjö 1998: 251);
(3) "I communicate to the bitter end, I get involved to explain the situation. A foreigner has to know what is going on. Representatives of the judiciary also approach this issue in this way, so we exchange opinions" (Biernacka 2014a: 114; transl. by the author)[13].

These opinions show that there is no unanimity as regards implementing the principle of a faithful interpretation. The approach presented by interpreters may be a consequence of what Shlesinger and Pöchhacker call "[...] the idealization of [a naïve notion of] *accuracy*" (2008: 2–3); this underlines that defining accuracy is either impossible or that the whole range of definitions should be provided.

Jacobsen pays attention to yet another aspect of accuracy claiming that the discussion on this principle excludes such issues as "linguistic (...) [and] cultural differences, [...] ambiguity [and] non-explicitness" (2002: 64), which can affect the meaning of the original utterance in the event it is interpreted verbatim (Hewitt 1995: 200). By this, interpreters are admonished against literal interpreting, which can possibly modify the sense of the original statement. Nevertheless, Shlesinger notices that the requirement of accuracy is so fluid that it "leaves considerable discretionary power to the interpreter" (1991a: 153), although such an approach may be questioned in the case of court interpreting. Indeed, what in conference interpreting has gained the name of "interpreters' creative behavior" (Horváth 2012: 123–148) or errors (Kopczyński 1984; Kempiński 1986; Łyda and Gumul 2008), in court interpreting is unambiguously perceived as inaccuracy (Hale 2004), or "misinterpretations and interpretation errors" (Torstensson and Gawronska, 2009). Moreover, Morris observes that court interpreters, even though obliged to follow the principle of accuracy, cannot be perceived as unthinking echoes of the original speakers, or a "transparent non-presence" (1993: 3). Furthermore, it is even emphasized that an ideal interpreter who literally transmits all the elements of the utterances produced by the main speakers does not exist at all (Berk-Seligson 1990/2002; Wadensjö

---

zeznająca w sądzie na pytanie czy zna obwinionego odpowiedziała 'Yhy' i tak też przetłumaczyłem, gdyż to od osoby rozmawiającej z osobą, której wypowiedzi tłumaczę, zależy czy zrozumiała czy też zada dodatkowe pytania, aby zrozumieć sens wypowiedzi".

13 "Ja się komunikuję do skutku, angażuję się w celu wyjaśnienia sytuacji. Cudzoziemiec musi wiedzieć, co się dzieje. Pracownicy instytucji wymiaru sprawiedliwości też raczej tak do tej kwestii podchodzą, więc wymieniamy opinie".

1998) mainly due to imperfection, which characterizes linguistic communication (Tryuk 2006: 88). Nonetheless, as Kempiński notes, "a subjective feeling of the Recipient and/or of the Addressee that the process of communication is carried out smoothly does not mean that the interpreter acts correctly"[14] (1986, 52–53), which in the event of court interpreting means that accuracy needs to be defined from both interactional and linguistic perspective.

Therefore, and as the interpreters are said to be "the only person[s] in the courtroom with a full command of both languages being used" (Edwards 1995: 63), in order to protect the clients of the court from those interpreters who abuse their power of language, Matulewska recommends that the courts ensure two interpreters, each verifying the other as to the precision in interpreting (2014: 110–112). Such a viewpoint is known in the history of court, or, more specifically, tribunal interpreting, where at the International Military Tribunal for the Far East (1946–1948) the verification policy based on "the three-tier structure of interpreting system", composed of interpreters, monitors and language arbiters, was to guarantee a fair trial through balancing power and control (Takeda 2007: 32).

All in all, the codes of professional ethics do not equate accuracy and literal interpreting; however, the same codes recommend that interpreters not intervene in the content and form of utterances in the source language. Therefore, from a prescriptive point of view, accuracy means: preserving a style and register, grammatical forms, interpreting all the elements of the source text along with vulgarisms; as well as prohibiting any comments and additions to the utterances of the main speakers.

Impartiality is an ethical principle to which interpreters assign a great importance and strive towards refraining from expressing their own opinions or judgments (Edwards 1995: 64–65; Ostarhild 2001: 28) as unbiased interpreters are "essential to the integrity of the judicial system" (Najarro Smith 2005: 163). As regards a definition of impartiality, Framer indicates that the court interpreter's neutrality[15] also means "prohibition against giving advice, legal or otherwise, and

---

14 "subiektywne odczucie O lub/I N, że proces komunikacji, w którym uczestniczą odbywa się bez zakłóceń, nie oznacza, że tłumacz działa bezbłędnie".

15 In this study the terms **impartiality** and **neutrality** are used interchangeably in the meaning of the interpreters' not taking sides or expressing their personal opinions, although there is a discussion concerning the difference between these two concepts (Donald 2003; the *Proclamation of the Fundamental Principles of the Red Cross* https://www.icrc.org/eng/resources/documents/misc/fundamental-principles-commentary-010179.htm (December 10, 2017)).

the inappropriateness of ever advocating for one side or the other" (2005: 4). Tryuk observes that the interpreters working during the Nuremberg Trial had a difficult task not to give in to the pressure resulting from the fact that the accused—who understood and spoke the languages used during the entire proceedings—often commented on the way the interpreters were working and what they were saying; therefore, the neutrality and impartiality of interpreters was jeopardized (2006: 101; 2012a; 2015)[16]. According to Cal-Meyer, impartiality is also defined as a balance ("equilibrium", 2013: 1) between information provided in the SL and information in the TL. González, Vásquez and Mikkelson understand impartiality as prohibition to make assumptions as to the intentions of original speakers (1991: 314).

All of the above ethical principles should be readable enough to let the interpreter solve moral dilemmas without any fear that she could be imputed infringing the principles guiding the profession.

Nonetheless, interpreters are confronted with situations involving human tragedies and influenced by their own incapability (Biernacka 2014a, 2016; Tryuk 2015). According to Hale (2007: 116), the reasons for interpreters' moral dilemmas include: conflicts of interest, lack of competences, contradictory requirements and expectations of the clients, bad working conditions, overlaps, as well as cultural and personal issues. The principles arising out of the codes of ethics cannot provide a ready solution to these problems, hence, the interpreters must frequently intuitively decide on how to proceed in a given situation. Furthermore, court interpreters, on the one hand, claim that the code of ethics is a bible which constantly reminds them of the principles binding upon them; on the other hand, however, they maintain that the only recommendation they receive from the code is the one of a necessity to use a common sense; yet others believe that the code is completely useless (Hale 2007: 101–102). Najarro Smith takes the view that court interpreters should know that it is the code of ethics that is a determinant of all activities carried out in the courtroom, but at the same time it is a "common sense, knowledge and experience in the field" (2005: 166), which need to be used. What is more, it is indicated that as the candidates to the profession gain experience and become comfortable and

16 Such an image of the interpreter—although already in modern times—who is put under pressure, is portrayed in "La Traductrice" [The Interpreter] (2006). The film directed by Elena Hazanov features Julia Batinova as an interpreter who cannot be impartial during the interrogation as she has to follow the lawyer's instructions to the content of her renditions.

confident, then they are able to assess the situation on a case-by-case basis and to use common sense, which enables the interpreters to "uphold the spirit of the canon of ethics" without becoming "entangled in following the letter of the rules" (González, Vásquez and Mikkelson 1991: 474).

In general, the codes of ethics are an indispensable tool in the interpreter's work serving as a point of reference for what is permitted and what is prohibited. Hale notes certain "[o]ver-reliance on a code of ethics" (2007: 114); this is further explained as a strong belief on the part of interpreters that the codes provide for the highest ethical standards to be obeyed. Nevertheless, she warns that the codes are not precise as to how interpreters should understand their role, perceive the interpreting process and get over the difficulties to achieve precision in interpreting. Interestingly, Hale even points out that it frequently appears that the code is of no help as "by its very nature, a code of ethics needs to be prescriptive", no matter if it recommends that the interpreter should be "an advocate or […] a faithful renderer of the utterances" (2008: 101). In consequence, interpreters are to make continuous choices that expose their own conviction of acting according to the prescribed ethical norms to a risk. In other words, despite the existence of such norms, the interpreters act on their own, and can count on their intuition, which is a derivative of their competences based on knowledge and experience.

Hence, all codes of professional ethics are to be "[…] a guide for resolving real ethical issues" (Najarro Smith 2005: 161), nonetheless, they are not detailed enough to provide simple answers to all complicated situations faced by interpreters. Despite the fact that the codes provide for an idealistic, far from the reality, courtroom context where everything what is said is interpreted by unbiased professionals, the ethical principles undoubtedly help the interpreters maintain a moral integrity. Indeed, the principles included in the codes are not able to predict all, sometimes difficult and dramatic, situations. In such cases the interpreter can (and she frequently does so) decide that facilitating communication prevails over the principles set forth in the code of ethics (Tate and Turner 1997/2002: 376).

1.4 Interpreters and the right to a fair trial: Polish perspective

In Poland, the right to a fair trial is guaranteed in numerous international and national documents[17]. From among the international legal acts, it is the

17 See Kierzkowska 2005 (180–192) for a full index of legal acts concerning the assistance of a sworn translator in judicial and administrative proceedings in Poland.

Universal Declaration of Human Rights of 10 December 1948[18], the European Convention for the Protection of Human Rights and Fundamental Freedoms of 4 November 1950[19], the Charter of Fundamental Rights of the European Union (2000/C 364/01)[20], and Directive 2012/13/EU of the European Parliament and of the Council of 22 May 2012 on the right to information in criminal proceedings[21] which attach outstanding importance to the equal rights of all people to be protected by law understood as, among others, the right to the assistance of the court interpreter. According to the European Association for Legal Interpreters and Translators (EULITA) the principles set forth in these legislative acts "demonstrate the key role of legal interpreters and translators in the search for truth and how their work may affect the life and rights of others"[22]. Indeed, if a person cannot communicate with the court, "[…] then justice cannot be delivered" (Lowney 2005: 9) which leads to a direct violation of this fundamental human right.

The national legal provisions also ensure the right to understand and to be understood. The assistance of an interpreter in the proceedings before Polish courts is provided for in the Polish Code of Civil Procedure (*Kodeks postępowania cywilnego*) and the Code of Criminal Procedure (*Kodeks postępowania karnego*). Pursuant to Article 265 §1 of the *Code of Civil Procedure* "[…] the court may cite an interpreter if a witness does not speak Polish"[23] (Fijałkowski 2001: 55; transl. by the author), and Article 204 §1 of the *Code of Criminal Procedure* envisages that "[…] the court shall cite an interpreter if it is necessary to interrogate (…) a person who does not speak Polish"[24] (Criminal Code (*Kodeks karny*) 2005: 264; transl. by the author). Hence, in the case of the civil procedure the court may,

18 Universal Declaration of Human Rights of 10 December 1948 http://www.ohchr.org/EN/UDHR/Documents/UDHR_Translations/eng.pdf (September 4, 2017).

19 European Convention for the Protection of Human Rights and Fundamental Freedoms of 4 November 1950 http://www.coe.int/en/web/conventions/full-list/-/conventions/rms/0900001680063765 (September 4, 2017).

20 Charter of Fundamental Rights of the European Union (2000/C 364/01) http://www.europarl.europa.eu/charter/pdf/text_en.pdf (September 4, 2017).

21 Directive 2012/13/EU of the European Parliament and of the Council of 22 May 2012 on the right to information in criminal proceedings http://eur-lex.europa.eu/legal-content/EN/TXT/?qid=1503417979735&uri=CELEX:32012L0013 (May 22, 2017).

22 http://eulita.eu/wp/code-ethics/ (November 6, 2017).

23 "[d]o przesłuchania świadka nie władającego dostatecznie językiem polskim sąd może przybrać tłumacza".

24 "[n]ależy wezwać tłumacza, jeżeli zachodzi potrzeba przesłuchania (…) osoby niewładającej językiem polskim".

but is not obliged, to cite an interpreter (e.g. if a judge speaks the language of a defendant or witness)[25]; while in criminal procedures, a citation of the interpreter is obligatory even though a judge speaks a foreign language (Pieńkos 1999: 132–133).

What is more, by way of the implementation of Directive 2012/29/EU of the European Parliament and of the Council of 25 October 2012 establishing minimum standards on the rights, support and protection of victims of crime[26], the Polish Code of Criminal Procedure was amended in 2013[27]; it now gives an auxiliary prosecutor (*oskarżyciel posiłkowy*) (Article 56a) and a private prosecutor (*oskarżyciel prywatny*) (Article 60a) the right to interpretation and translation, i.e. not only the witness provides explanations or the accused gives testimony through the interpreter.

1.4.1 Past legislation concerning court interpreters in Poland

In the Polish legislative tradition relating to court interpreters, they have been referred to as sworn translators (*tłumacze przysięgli*), which is an umbrella term for officially appointed professionals who render both translation and interpreting services[28]. Although the historical legislation concerning sworn translators in Poland was already referred to in earlier works (Kierzkowska 2005: 126–131; Kubacki 2012: 19–24), taking the aim of this study into account, it seems necessary to give sharp focus to reflect on court interpreters as a heterogeneous group, from the point of view of acquiring the right to practice the profession.

After the period of partitioned Poland (1772–1918), the Ordinance of the Minister of Justice on the remuneration of witnesses, experts and translators in criminal proceedings of August 7, 1920[29] was the first legal instrument binding

---

25 Moreover, in accordance with Article 265 §2 of the *Code of Civil Procedure* it is the functionary of the judicial institution who may fulfill the obligations of the interpreter (Fijałkowski 2001, 57).

26 Directive 2012/29/EU of the European Parliament and of the Council of 25 October 2012 establishing minimum standards on the rights, support and protection of victims of crime http://eur-lex.europa.eu/legal-content/EN/TXT/?uri=CELEX%3A32012L0029 (May 22, 2017).

27 Bednarek (2015) provides a comprehensive analysis of the linguistic consequences of these amendments.

28 This issue is further discussed in detail in 1.4.2.

29 Rozporządzenie Ministra Sprawiedliwości w porozumieniu z Ministrem Skarbu z dnia 7 sierpnia 1920 r. w przedmiocie wynagrodzenia świadków, znawców i tłumaczów w

upon sworn translators passed by the Polish authorities. The document referred to the Ordinance of the Austrian Minister of Justice of March 20, 1901 in the Austrian partition of Poland. From the Polish document it results that translators were obliged to provide both translation and interpretation services for the courts, however they were not called *sworn*.

A chronologically subsequent document binding upon Polish sworn translators was the Ordinance of the Minister of Justice of December 24, 1928 on sworn translators[30] whose §1 sets forth the criteria to be satisfied by those who wish to enter the profession, i.e. "(…) a sworn translator may be the one who possesses Polish citizenship, enjoys civil and citizens' rights, is of good character and demonstrates a knowledge of the language for which they are to be appointed as a translator"[31] §3 of the same document provides for the translator's obligation to take an oath before the President of a competent District Court, of the following content: "I swear to the Almighty and Omniscient God that I shall fulfill the responsibilities delegated to me with all diligence. So help me God"[32]. §4 specifies that "(…) in case of being called to a court in the capacity of an interpreter, a sworn translator shall not take an oath unless the acts concerning court proceedings provide otherwise"[33]. It is precisely in §4, where the legislator identifies a sworn translator with a court interpreter, which is key to understand the specificity of the Polish context of the profession. What is more,

postępowaniu karnem (Dz. U. z 1920 r. Nr 67, poz. 453) http://isap.sejm.gov.pl/DetailsServlet?id=WDU19200750515 (May 21, 2017).

30 Rozporządzenie Ministra Sprawiedliwości z dnia 24 grudnia 1928 r. o tłumaczach przysięgłych (Dz. U. z 1928 r. Nr 104, poz. 943) http://isap.sejm.gov.pl/DetailsServlet?id=WDU19281040943 (July 22, 2016).

31 "[t]łumaczem przysięgłym może być ten, kto posiada obywatelstwo polskie, korzysta w pełni z praw cywilnych i obywatelskich, jest nieskazitelnego charakteru i wykaże znajomość języków, dla których ma być mianowany tłumaczem".

32 "Przysięgam Panu Bogu Wszechmogącemu i Wszechwiedzącemu, że powierzone mi obowiązki tłumacza spełniać będę z całą sumiennością. Tak mi, Panie Boże, dopomóż". Tryuk (2015, 129–131) indicates that the interpreters who rendered their services before the Supreme National Tribunal in the post-war Poland (1946–1948) had to take the following oath: "I do solemnly swear in front of God the Almighty and All-knowing, that I will execute the interpretation tasks assigned to me with utmost conscientiousness and impartiality, so help me God."; the wording of this oath is almost the same as the one included in the discussed Act of December 24, 1928—it differs only in that the ethical principle of impartiality appears.

33 "(…) w razie wezwania do sądu w charakterze tłumacza, tłumacz przysięgły nie składa przysięgi, o ile ustawy postępowania sądowego nie stanowią inaczej".

the Ordinance anticipates the modern legal provisions in that in §14 it stipulates for an annual publication of a list of sworn translators in the Official Gazette of the Minister of Justice (*Dziennik Urzędowy Ministra Sprawiedliwości*).

The subsequent document—the Ordinance of the Minister of Justice of December 9, 1953 on sworn translators[34], repeats the 1928 provisions concerning the eligibility criteria to be fulfilled by a sworn translator, identifies a sworn translator with a court interpreter, as well as provides for the translator's obligation to take an oath before the President of a competent Provincial Court, of the following content: "Being aware of my words and responsibility before the law, I solemnly swear that I shall fulfill the responsibilities of the translator delegated to me with all diligence and impartiality"[35]. An ethical implication that arises from the text of the oath is that not only a very general notion of *diligence*, but also a concept of *impartiality* is thereby introduced. Also, the Ordinance imposes an obligation to keep a register of sworn translators on the President of a competent Provincial Court (§15).

The Ordinance of the Minister of Justice of August 19, 1968 on sworn translators[36] lays out more details than the previous document. Firstly, it adds two new criteria: a sworn translator shall be of at least 25 years of age and shall guarantee the due fulfillment of the translator's responsibilities. Moreover, §2 provides for specific information on how a candidate should prove their knowledge of the language: either by way of presenting a diploma of completion of relevant higher education philological or foreign language studies, or by submitting a diploma of completion of a higher education school, or a certificate of completion of a general secondary education school if a foreign language was lectured in such schools; in the latter case, a candidate shall in addition pass an examination (organized by a competent Provincial Court) in translation, with a special emphasis put on the translation of legal texts. It is also possible to prove knowledge of a foreign language by way of passing an examination in that language, including the ability to translate. In exceptional cases, a candidate

34 Rozporządzenie Ministra Sprawiedliwości z dnia 9 grudnia 1953 r. w sprawie tłumaczów przysięgłych (Dz. U. z 1953 r. Nr 51, poz. 256) http://dziennikustaw.gov.pl/du/1953/s/51/256 (July 22, 2016).

35 "Świadomy swych słów i odpowiedzialności przed prawem, przyrzekam uroczyście, że powierzone mi obowiązki tłumacza wykonywać będę z całą sumiennością i bezstronnością".

36 Rozporządzenie Ministra Sprawiedliwości z dnia 19 sierpnia 1968 r. w sprawie tłumaczy przysięgłych. (Dz. U. z 1968 r. Nr 35, poz. 244) http://isap.sejm.gov.pl/VolumeServlet?type=wdu&rok=1968&numer=035 (July 22, 2016).

shall prove knowledge of a foreign language by way of presenting a diploma or a certificate other than those mentioned above. As to an oath taken before the President of a competent Provincial Court, its content is identical to the one provided for by the previous Ordinance of 1953 (§6). Similarly to the Ordinances of 1928 and 1953, sworn translators are authorized to prepare certified translations of documents as well as to appear before the court to provide their services (§7). The Ordinance confirms an earlier obligation of the President of a competent provincial Court to keep a register of sworn translators (§20).

The Ordinance of the Minister of Justice of June 8, 1987 on legal experts and sworn translators[37] fails to specify any criteria to be satisfied by candidates for the profession, from which it it follows that the requirement of examining graduates from non-philological studies has been nullified. However, §4 of the Ordinance provides for taking an oath before the President of a competent Provincial Court that envisages fulfilling the responsibilities of the translator with all diligence and impartiality.

1.4.2 The Polish Act on the Profession of Sworn Translator

At present in Poland, it is the Act on the Profession of Sworn Translator of November 25, 2004[38] that is the only national legal document that governs the profession of sworn translators. The Act sets forth, among others, the criteria to be satisfied by the candidates for the profession. Pursuant to Article 2.1 of the Act, a candidate shall pass an examination which is a two–stage procedure consisting in verifying both translation and interpretation skills from Polish into a foreign language and from that foreign language into Polish. Due to exacting examination requirements "[t]he Act is one of the most demanding among similar legislative instruments passed by other European states"[39]. According to Article 7.1 thereof, the newly appointed sworn translators are bound by the following oath taken with the Minister of Justice:

---

37 Rozporządzenie Ministra Sprawiedliwości z dnia 8 czerwca 1987 r. w sprawie biegłych sądowych i tłumaczy przysięgłych (Dz. U. z 1987 r. Nr 18, poz. 112) http://isap.sejm.gov.pl/DetailsServlet?id=WDU19870180112 (July 22, 2016).

38 Ustawa o zawodzie tłumacza przysięgłego z dnia 25 listopada 2004 r. (Dz.U. z 2015 r. Nr 487) https://bip.ms.gov.pl/pl/rejestry-i-ewidencje/tlumacze-przysiegli/ (October 28, 2017; transl. by Setkowicz-Ryszka available at: http://www.mc-tlumaczenia.pl/files/file/PolishSwornTranslatorAct%2827_1_2005%29.pdf) (October 20, 2017).

39 http://www.tepis.org.pl/index.php/tepis-o-sobie/dzialalnosc-pt-tepis/the-polish-society-of-sworn-and-specialized-translators (May 22, 2017).

> Being aware of the significance of my words and my liability before the law, I do solemnly affirm that I will perform the tasks of sworn translator and interpreter entrusted to me with due diligence and impartiality, keeping state secrets and other secrets protected by the law, as well as following, in my conduct, the rules of honesty and professional ethics[40] (transl. by Setkowicz-Ryszka).

A significance of the oath consists in that it provides a definition of the sworn translator as a professional who follows the ethical principles of diligence, impartiality and confidentiality, while the importance of the entire Act of November 25, 2004 derives from the fact of anticipating the provisions of Directive 64/2010/EU of the European Parliament and of the Council of 20 October 2010 on the right to interpretation and translation in criminal proceedings[41] which defines a quality interpreting in legal settings as enabling the parties to the proceedings to be provided with the information about possible allegations against them and about the rights they have. Hence, in compliance with Article 6.1 of the Act, successful candidates are entered onto the list of sworn translators kept by the Minister of Justice which satisfies the provisions of Article 5.2 of Directive 64/2010/EU that introduces a concept of adequacy of interpretation (and translation) which can be followed only by independent and competent professionals. In addition, Article 5.3 thereof provides for the principle of confidentiality as one of the criteria conditioning high quality interpreting.

1.4.3 The Polish sworn translator's code

Court interpreters in Poland have the **code of ethics** at their disposal, the first version of which was published in 1991 as *Kodeks tłumacza sądowego* [*Code of the Polish Court Translator and Interpreter*] by TEPIS (Polskie Towarzystwo Tłumaczy Przysięgłych i Specjalistycznych [Polish Society of Sworn and Specialized Translators]) and commented by practitioners and academics; afterwards, in 2005 *Kodeks tłumacza przysięgłego z komentarzem* [*The Sworn Translator's Code with a Commentary*] was prepared to then be verified by representatives of Polish authorities and universities and published as *Kodeks*

40 "Mając świadomość znaczenia moich słów i odpowiedzialności przed prawem, przyrzekam uroczyście, że powierzone mi zadania tłumacza przysięgłego będę wykonywać sumiennie i bezstronnie, dochowując tajemnicy prawnie chronionej oraz kierując się w swoim postępowaniu uczciwością i etyką zawodową".

41 Directive 2010/64/EU of the European Parliament and of the Council of 20 October 2010 on the right to interpretation and translation in criminal proceedings http://eur-lex.europa.eu/legal-content/EN/TXT/?uri=celex:32010L0064 (January 10, 2017).

tłumacza przysięgłego [*The Sworn Translator's Code*] in 2011. The principles of professional ethics covered by the *Code*, along with the guidelines laid down in the sworn translator's oath, are to serve as a point of reference in the implementation of the profession. The two main principles directly relating the interpretation provided in the courtroom are: **accuracy** and **impartiality**.

According to §68 of the *Sworn Translator's Code*, **accuracy** means not only that "[t]he sworn translator shall translate statements made by foreigners exactly in the form in which she heard them, rendering the whole content, without omitting, adding or modifying anything" (Kierzkowska 2011: 11; transl. by the author)[42], but also commenting on what has been said if such a procedure contributes to a better understanding of the original utterance. Hence, there is acquiescence to a multitude of interpretations of the term of accuracy because:

> [...] a perennial dilemma to choose between "word by word" translation/interpretation considered by non-professionals as "faithful" and a "free" translation/interpretation understood as departure from "accuracy", can be only correctly solved by a professional translator/interpreter (Kierzkowska 2005: 26; transl. by the author)[43]

Thus, it is assumed that if a court interpreter is professional, then she is undoubtedly capable of solving any interpreting problems.

Impartiality is referred to in §3 of the Polish *Sworn Translator's Code* as the prescription that "[t]he sworn translator shall perform the entrusted tasks with impartiality, shall not express personal opinions or represent the views of the client or persons concerned or involved" (Kierzkowska 2011: 3; transl. by the author)[44]. In the 2005 version of the *Code* the principle of impartiality is also referred to as neutrality, which means that in carrying out the obligations the sworn translator shall not "[...] speak arbitrarily, comment, gesticulate or in

---

42 "[t]łumacz przysięgły powinien tłumaczyć wypowiedzi cudzoziemców dokładnie w takiej formie, w jakiej je usłyszał, oddając całą treść wypowiedzi, niczego nie ujmując, nie dodając i nie zmieniając".

43 "[...] odwieczny dylemat wyboru między tłumaczeniem "słowo w słowo", uznawanym przez nieprofesjonalistów za "wierne", a tłumaczeniem "wolnym", traktowanym przez nich za odejście w ich rozumieniu od "wierności", może być poprawnie rozwiązany tylko przez zawodowego tłumacza".

44 "[t]łumacz przysięgły wykonuje powierzone mu zadania z bezstronnością, nie wyraża w żaden sposób swoich osobistych poglądów i nie reprezentuje ani stanowiska zleceniodawcy, ani osób, których tłumaczenie dotyczy, ani też tych, których wypowiedzi tłumaczy".

other visible way react to the course of the proceedings without the consent of the presiding person" (Kierzkowska 2005: 27; transl. by the author)[45].

Interestingly, even though Polish sworn translators can be proud of having a point of ethical reference, not only the principles compiled in the code of ethics guideline their professional conduct; it is also their own moral code applicable in all areas of life, as well as the Decalogue and common sense (Tryuk 2004: 180, 288–289).

1.4.4 Professional associations of sworn translators in Poland

There are two professional associations of sworn translators in Poland. The Polish Society of Sworn and Specialized Translators (Polskie Towarzystwo Tłumaczy Przysięgłych i Specjalistycznych TEPIS) has been since its establishing in 1990 the first professional organization of which the main aim is "to satisfy the urgent need to consolidate and train specialist translators and interpreters in order to meet the demands of the rapid political and economic changes in Poland after 1989" as well as "to represent the interests of legal translators and court interpreters and enhance their status by its actions as a public benefit organization, entitled to cooperate with the government to perform public tasks"[46].

In 2017, the Trade Union of Sworn Translators in Poland[47] (transl. by the author) (Związek Zawodowy Tłumaczy Przysięgłych w Polsce) was established "to ensure the best possible working conditions and remuneration for sworn translators"[48].

Of these two professional associations, TEPIS is a member of EULITA (European Legal Interpreters and Translators Association), an organization which promotes quality in legal interpreting and translation[49].

---

45 "[…] samowolnie zabierając głos, komentując, gestykulując lub w inny widoczny sposób reagując na przebieg postępowania bez zezwolenia osoby je prowadzącej".

46 http://tepis.org.pl/the-polish-society-of-sworn-and-specialized-translators/ (January 5, 2017). A whelm of information concerning the activities of the Society is available on the website of TEPIS (http://tepis.org.pl), as well as can be found in Kubacki (2012).

47 Związek Zawodowy Tłumaczy Przysięgłych w Polsce http://www.zztp.pl/ (December 15, 2017).

48 "zapewnienie tłumaczom przysięgłym jak najlepszych warunków pracy oraz płacy" http://www.zztp.pl/ (December 15, 2017).

49 Information about EULITA is available at eulita.eu (March 2, 2018).

1.4.5 Sworn translator's training in Poland

In Poland, training courses for sworn translators are available at the level of postgraduate studies, with the Interdisciplinary Postgraduate Studies in Translation and Interpreting at the Institute of Applied Linguistics, University of Warsaw, being the first program of this type, established in 1998 to offer a comprehensive 360-hour training course in legal translation and court interpreting[50], as well as in the form of life-long learning training offered firstly by TEPIS. In this way, § 7 of the Polish *Sworn Translator's Code*, according to which "[t]he sworn translator is obliged to continually upgrade her skills in translation, language and those pertaining to the content [...]" (Kierzkowska 2011: 3; transl. by the author)[51], is satisfied[52].

Interestingly, Polish court interpreters indicate various sources of their knowledge: specialized literature, dictionaries, experience gained 'on the spot', parallel texts, Internet, training courses, and help provided by lawyers; interpreters also point out that they expect an open attitude on the part of their more experienced colleagues who could share their experience, but at the same time declare that "interpreters are a hermetic clan, nobody has ever given me advice, I don't know why [...]" (Biernacka 2014a: 41)[53]. Also Skorek claims the need for training prospective court interpreters by their experienced colleagues, indicating however, that this issue has been broadly discussed and afterwards rejected "by the experts" (2014: 263). These comments prove that in spite of the existence of professional organizations, interpreters do not feel that they form a group whose members are linked by a common interest. Such a situation may adversely affect fostering knowledge sharing and working out coherent principles of ethics consciously applied by court interpreters.

1.5 Conclusions

Court interpreting has obtained the status of a separate variety of community interpreting which is due to legal developments relating to the need to make interpreting services available in all public settings, and to the necessity for

---

50 A comprehensive study of the program can be found in Jopek-Bosiacka (2014).

51 "[t]łumacz przysięgły jest zobowiązany do stałego doskonalenia swoich kwalifikacji translatorskich, językowych i merytorycznych [...]".

52 The issue of trainings available to sworn translators, as well as to the candidates for sworn translators, is described in Tryuk (2006), Kubacki (2012), Solová (2013).

53 "tłumacze to taki zamknięty w sobie klan, nikt nigdy nie udzielił mi żadnej porady, nie wiem tylko, dlaczego [...]".

professionalization of interpreting. Court interpreters contribute to achieving a goal that is one of the indicators of a fair trial: the right to understand and to be understood. It is undoubtedly the legal and ethical framework that creates the conditions, which enable a high quality interpretation and constitutes a point of reference for court interpreters, as well as a measure of their professionalism.

The provisions of both the EU and Polish legislative acts, firstly, highlight the need to guarantee a fair trial as the fundamental human right, and secondly, provide for the concept of the qualified court interpreter defined as the one who ensures adequacy of interpretation, remains impartial, as well as maintains the confidentiality of the proceedings. What is more, the legal requirement of a quality interpretation in the courtroom is fulfilled not only on the basis of the EU legal acts, but is heavily embedded in the Polish tradition. Nonetheless, nowadays in Poland, one of the consequences of a large number of former regulations relating to admitting candidates for the profession, and, in particular, these concerning (not) examining candidates for sworn translators, is that not only court interpreters whose competences were verified in the course of harsh examinations, but also those who obtained permission to interpret in the courtroom on the basis of completion of higher education philological or foreign language studies and had never been trained to render court interpreting services, are entered onto the list of sworn translators and can exercise their profession. Therefore, it can be stated that not all court interpreters in Poland are highly qualified specialists, and as Kierzkowska puts it, only an "adequately qualified court interpreter" (2005: 21; transl. by the author)[54] is able to assure a quality interpretation understood as the one provided by the competent interpreter. What has already been dome within the legal framework is that the national legislation provides for the criteria to be fulfilled by the candidates for the profession: court interpreters in Poland are, firstly, required to possess specific competences, and secondly, obliged to satisfy the principles of professional ethics[55]. As far as the specific competences of Polish sworn translators are concerned, it is *Ordinance of Minister of Justice of January 24, 2005 on Particulars*

54 "odpowiednio wykwalifikowany tłumacz sądowy".

55 These two factors can be discussed only with reference to court interpreters and court interpreting in those countries which can boast of having the relevant national legislation and the codes of ethics. Such is the case of court interpreters in Poland, while in other countries, different legal provisions concerning the admission to as well as the implementation of the profession may be binding upon (or they do not exist at all).

of Performing the Examination for Sworn Translators and Interpreters[56] which provides for a catalog of categories on the basis of which both a written and an oral part of the examination for sworn translators is assessed; these are: (i) accurate rendition of the original message, (ii) use of terminology and idiomatic expressions, (iii) correct grammar and vocabulary, (iv) appropriate register and (v) correct intonation, pleasant pace and diction. Hence, what is expressly assessed is the content and form of the renditions, while the remaining competences covering linguistic, cultural and legal knowledge establish a background for the interpreter's admission to the profession. However, on the spot, the evaluation criteria suggested in the *Ordinance* are insufficient as what counts in the courtroom is also an ability to speak in public, to talk with people and to manage stress.

Furthermore, two other stages of professionalization[57]: developing a professional association and organizing training courses, would, at least partially[58], give court interpreting in Poland the status of a prestigious profession; nonetheless, court interpreters are not full-time employees, but provide their services on the basis of contracts for professional services.

---

56 Rozporządzenie Ministra Sprawiedliwości z dnia 24 stycznia 2005 r. w sprawie szczegółowego sposobu przeprowadzenia egzaminu na tłumacza przysięgłego http://isap.sejm.gov.pl/DetailsServlet?id=WDU20050150129 (January 11, 2017).

57 E.g. Wilensky (1964) proposes five stages of professionalization: "(1) making the occupation full-time; (2) establishing formal training; (3) developing a professional association; (4) pushing for legalized protection; and (5) adopting a code of ethics" (Grbič 2015: 322).

58 Court interpreters in Poland complain about unpunctual and poor payments for their services (Biernacka 2014a). See also Hale 2007, Katschinka 2013.

2 Interpreters as active participants in the communicative events: literature review

It is Lang who, in an empirical discussion on community interpreting based on his research in the activities, position[59] and roles of court interpreters in Papua-New Guinea carried out in 1978, pays attention to the necessity of considering court interpreting from a perspective of interaction with the active participation of an interpreter (Mason 1999: 147). According to Lang's findings, court interpreters do not mindlessly repeat utterances in the source language, but strive for being a participant in a communication event in order to enable main speakers understand each other:

> Although his official role is that of a passive participant as far as the origination of primary conversation is concerned, the realization of that role depends on the active co-operation of his clients and the extent to which they wish to include him as an active participant not only linguistically but also gesturally, posturally and gaze-wise. Likewise it is the interpreter who can by these means actively involve himself, or abstain from such involvement (Lang 1978: 241).

Although the above description is of a trial with the participation of unprofessional interpreters in the country where the interpreter's assistance is not incorporated into a legal framework, the importance of this research consists in showing that, firstly, the court interpreter is more than just a passive observer of a communication event between main speakers; and that, secondly, it is necessary to investigate court interpreting not only from the point of view of the

---

59 The terms *position* and *positioning*, as defined by Giddens (1984), are alternatives for Goffman's concept of *role*. Interlocutors bring a certain social identity associated with their specific rights and obligations to an interaction; they make gestures such as e.g. positioning of their bodies by which they show other parties to the interaction *who they are* and thus, *what other parties can expect* from them. As Baraldi, with reference to dialogue interpreting in intercultural communities, states, "[t]he definition of positions of individual participants is a relevant cultural presupposition of communication" (2009: 6). In the courtroom everyone knows that the figure who takes a seat behind the long table situated by the wall and under the emblem of the Republic of Poland is the judge. The parties get to know that the interpreter is in the courtroom with the passing of the trial, when the judge refers to the interpreter and asks for her identity document (Biernacka 2008a: 180–181).

interpreters' compliance with the ethical principles, but also from the perspective of real-world events.

2.1 Ethnomethodological insights into court interpreting

In interpreting studies, the ethnomethodological theory of interaction as a practice by which the communication between interlocutors is maintained, has been applied to investigate the importance of the interpreter's active position within the act of communication, as well as to contrast the interpreter's real performance with the prescriptive model of interpreting submitted to legal framework and ethical principles guiding the profession in all kinds of settings, be it legal, medical or police settings (Wadensjö 1998: 72):

> [t]he traditional, if idealized view of the (professional) interpreter as a highly skilled (and specially trained) information or message transmitter between speakers of different languages is contrasted with the figure of the culturally competent intermediary who acts to promote mutual understanding between communicating parties at a level beyond that of language (Pöchhacker 2008: 22).

In other words, the interpreter is perceived as a communicative link between the main speakers. Logically, in order to translate information that exceeds the level of speech, she needs to become incorporated into the context and to gain the same interlocutory rights as the primary parties. Although it is noted that bilingual interactions differ from monolingual communicative events (Wadensjö 1997: 203), certain patterns of verbal and non-verbal expression binding upon the participants are applied by the parties to an interpreted event.

2.1.1 Garfinkel's approach to interaction

Ethnomethodology assumes that a spontaneous dialogue as a manifestation of human communication is a basic form of the social action; it thus investigates everyday methods used by social actors in their communication (Garfinkel 1967). All activities carried out by participants in interactions are dictated by their need to communicate, that is, to understand the information obtained and pass on information created by them. Therefore, the participants in the interaction behave in a certain way because they want to communicate and not because they apply the imposed norms. Thus, it is the language that is the tool for creating the reality, while all provisions and regulations are of a secondary function. What is more, it is not the social structures that impinge on social actors, but individuals who create social structures at the moment of carrying out everyday routine activities and interacting with other people. The social structures are a kind of reality; every individual creates their own reality and social order.

To better understand the nature of the act of communication, Garfinkel proposes a distinction between two notions: the *product* and the *process* where the former means "a shared agreement on substantive matters", while the latter "consists of various methods whereby something that a person says or does is recognized to accord with a rule" (1967: 24–25). Furthermore, Garfinkel formulates the rules of interaction: (1) the parties to the interaction understand what they are talking about although they do not expressly refer to these issues; (2) the parties understand what they are talking about thanks to both what is said and what is 'left unspoken'; (3) the parties understand what they are talking about on the basis of a sequence of utterances; (4) the parties understand each other because they both refer to a basic state of the art and common knowledge; (5) the parties refer to what has already happened in the interaction; and (6) each party waits for the other party's turn in order to obtain information on what has already been discussed (1967: 39–40). In other words, for the successful interaction it is important *how* the participants understand their utterances (*what the parties talk about*) and not *what* is actually said (*what the parties say*) (Garfinkel 1967: 25, 27). To this end, the parties to the conversation constantly carry out an analysis of what is said; such analysis can continue indefinitely due to the possible adding of subsequent referents as being interpretations of signs. This means that signs can create extensive catalogs of referents; thus, each act of communication runs on several levels and can be understood in various ways. It manifests in these moments of the conversation when a party, in order to state what the other participant means by saying something, introduces a verb of thinking. This proves that the observers of the act of communication are never sure *what* the talk is about. In order to establish the meaning of what is said in the conversation, participants need to resort to their common knowledge, their shared experience and understandings (Garfinkel 1967: 27). On the assumption that the act of communication in the courtroom is a spontaneous social interaction, ethnomethodological model covers by analogy to "social structures of everyday activities" (Garfinkel 1967: 32), the court interpreter-mediated bilingual talks.

Hence, an analysis carried out by the court interpreter during an interpreted event in the courtroom is also an indefinite process. However, taking the time constraints of the trial (de Jongh 1992: 36)[60], as well as relatively fast pace of a dialogue between main speakers (Mikkelson 1999) to which the interpreter has

60 Potential clients are also advised that an "interpreted conversation takes longer than a regular one", as stated on a website of a Canadian Social Enterprise CISOC (Cultural Interpretation Services for Our Communities) cisoc.net (December 13, 2017).

to adjust into account, such an analysis of signs and adding referents to them is rather abridged. Therefore, the interpreter's understanding of the main speakers' utterances is based on the first associations and the easiest and most popular referents to the signs. This means that the target message produced by the interpreter is only one of the choices, which might be multiplied depending on a number of referents; it is the interpreter who, being aware of the context, decides on the meaning of a particular original utterance (Linell 1997: 55). Moreover, the parties to the courtroom interaction assume that, first, what others say results from their competences as native speakers of a particular language, and secondly, the speakers follow the rules of expressing themselves "honestly, openly, candidly, sincerely, and the like" (Garfinkel 1967: 27). These virtues are comprised by the ethical principles of accuracy and impartiality guiding the behavior and activities of court interpreters. What is more, Garfinkel's model is of crucial importance for the understanding of the gist of the interpreter's task. The interpreter is not to say *what the primary parties said* in the SL but what *the primary parties talked about*. This means that in order to understand the message, the interpreter needs a particular context (de Jongh 1992: 61), but even though this requirement is satisfied, a full understanding of the intended meaning is impossible (Morris 1993: 100).

2.1.2 Goffman's ritualized face–to–face interactions

In the ethnomethodological knowledge that people talk to fulfill their inherent need for communication, Goffman investigates **face-to-face interactions** defined as "[…] the syntactical relations among the acts of different persons mutually present to one another" (1967: 2) and claims that even a short and seemingly trivial event, in which persons situated in the same place and time interact, can be an object of a sociological analysis. To describe the interactions, he uses a term **social gathering** meant as "[…] a shifting entity, necessarily evanescent, created by arrivals and killed by departures" (1967: 2). The individuals who participate in these events are referred to as interactants, whose main goal is to establish and maintain, be it consciously or unconsciously, the act of communication. Face-to-face interactions have a potential to take place during all kinds of gatherings, be it private or public. Interactants communicate within naturally coherent units of dialogue called **interaction episodes** which are separated and independent situations in which a conversation is carried out.

By analogy to Garfinkel, Goffman also acquiesces in the application of the concept of face-to-face interaction to various fields of study by listing together different social gatherings and prompting that the concept itself is "[…] stripped and cramped to suit the sociological study of conversation, track meets, banquets, jury trials and street loitering" (1967: 3).

Furthermore, face-to-face interactions can be divided into symmetrical and asymmetrical. In the symmetrical interaction, an individual has certain obligations towards and expectations from other parties to the communicative act, but is also authorized to expect that these other parties shall have their obligations towards and expectations from such an individual. This balance is preserved by way of equal rights of all the participants in the interaction as to asking and answering questions, listening to the others' utterances, taking the floor, interrupting and remaining silent; in all these instances where the interactants show respect towards the choices made by the individual and do not force the interlocutor to make a different choice which might be more suitable for them – they do not violate the interaction rules. Contrary to that, in the asymmetrical interaction the obligations and expectations of the parties differ; all participants have the right to listen to the others, but not all of them enjoy the right to speak, interrupt monologues or remain silent (Goffman 1967).

Apart from symmetrical and asymmetrical rules governing interpersonal relations, there are also the ones that can be denoted as formal and informal. Goffman suggests that the former are fundamental and cover legal provisions and ethical principles, while the latter are of secondary importance and refer to etiquette (1967: 53–54).

In a legal discourse, these two types of relationships can be distinguished between senders and receivers (Trosborg 1995: 1997) on different levels of social structure. According to Jopek-Bosiacka, the *asymmetrical* relationship exists between the lawmaker and the citizens, where the legislative power (law-maker) has the authority to make rules for citizens to obey them in order to maintain law and order (2010: 63), while in the courtroom the *asymmetrical* model of interaction results from "hierarchization of procedural roles and the authority [of the judiciary]" (Jopek-Bosiacka 2006: 222; transl. by the author)[61]. This unequal status of participants in institutional settings is expressed in various ways: the design of the courtroom and the location of the seats occupied by the judge and the parties to the proceedings (Atkinson and Drew 1979; Tryuk 2006; Biernacka 2014a). Moreover, the asymmetrical relationship can be discussed from a point of view of **ritualization of communication** of the courtroom. Jopek-Bosiacka pays attention to the existence of an "algorithm of the proceedings (code of civil,

61 "hierarchizacja ról procesowych oraz (…) autorytetu władzy [sądowniczej]".

criminal or administrative proceedings)" (2006: 222), which governs the courtroom interaction, and which must be observed by the parties.

2.1.3 Institutional talk

In their studies concerning interactions, Garfinkel (1967) and Goffman (1967) referred to mechanisms of casual conversations, however, their invitations extended to carry out research not only in informal, but also formal settings, laid the foundations for the analysis of institutional talks. In particular, Atkinson and Drew (1979: 195) claimed a need for further research in the field of courtroom interactions, with special focus given to studying the organization of activities in the course of the proceedings.

Institutional talk, as opposed to casual conversation, is produced in a particular setting. However, it is not the place (or, the setting), which allows to describe the talk as institutional, but the interactants themselves and their identities (Liddicoat 2011: 345). This definition is contrary to what Drew and Heritage (1992) propose in their discussion on the features of institutional talk, as they maintain that not only a physical location, but also attributing certain identities to the interactants does not make the interaction institutional; they rather intend to denominate those which cannot be called casual conversations as institutional talk. Moreover, Maynard and Clayman are of the opinion that describing the settings as courtrooms, police stations or classrooms "can obscure much of what occurs within those settings" (1991: 406–407), by which they recommend that determining the physical location of a particular talk is not of importance for its analysis. Silverman (2001) also observes that it cannot be assumed that institutional talks are generally structured differently from casual conversations, however, in the courtroom the turn-taking sequence is well-established and any deviation from court order can be considered as contempt of court. Bednarek indicates that institutional talk in the courtroom is shaped by both the setting and the context, nevertheless, it is used by institutional stakeholders only (2015: 49).

As a consequence, there are several factors that characterize institutional talk. Atkinson (1982) lists the following: one topic; a *question-answer* sequence, where one party only asks and the other only answers the questions; and, the absence of spontaneous reactions of one party to the utterances of the other. Drew and Heritage also distinguish three characteristics of institutional talk: the parties want to achieve a certain goal in their conversation by following a pattern of behavior that lets them fulfill the institutional tasks assigned to them; the talk is limited by certain conventions that may vary depending on the setting in which the talk takes place; and, the parties to the conversation interfere or reason in a specific way (1992: 22–25).

As regards courtroom talks – described by Atkinson and Drew (1979: 194) as "more closely ordered environment" – their misleading nature arising out of its diversity of forms depending on the stage of the proceedings (dialogue prevail during the judge's examination of the witnesses or defendants, while judge's instructions to the examined parties and prosecutor's speech are monologues) is indicated (Atkinson and Drew 1979: 34–35). Furthermore, they maintain that there is not just one kind of talk in a court setting, depending on the speaker and the stage of the proceedings (1979: 34–35). Nonetheless, they point out the restrictions as to the turn-taking system in the courtroom: (1) in spite of a large number of people being present in the courtroom, the number of actual participants is limited, (2) only those expressly asked to do so can speak, (3) talk is coordinated so that it is conducted according to certain order, (4) the order in which the participants speak is predetermined (Atkinson and Drew 1979: 35, 179). In other words, the turn-taking system in the courtroom talk is pre-established as regards the performance of such activities as opening and closing the talk, or asking and answering questions. Moreover, according to the findings based on the study of the inquisitorial procedure of the Polish monolingual courtroom, Bednarek confirms the question-answer sequence of the talk, the rigid order of turn-taking, and the dialogical form of the talk (2014a: 139).

As regards turn-taking system of the courtroom, it is indicated that it contributes to ritualization (Fenton 1997). This, in turn, is established also on the basis of *who* asks questions and *who* answers them, and moreover, according to the registers used by particular primary parties (Jopek-Bosiacka 2006). As far as the register used in the courtroom is concerned, it is indicated that one of its features strictly connected with ritualization is a system of address forms (Zgółka and Zieliński 2003: 189) characterized by formality (Zieliński 1999: 66), which helps maintain a considerable distance between interlocutors (Zieliński 1999: 66)[62]. This ritualized context of the courtroom makes the participants deploy pre-established address terms, which ensure impartiality and reflects the majesty of the court: (1) expressions such as "Your Honor", "Counselor", (2) impersonal "did the witness see…?", and (3) "the Court decided…" (Zieliński 1999: 66).

62 Other linguistic features of the Polish institutional talk of the courtroom can be found in Rzeszutko 2004.

In general, institutional talk is characterized by (1) sharing the same physical environment, (2) maintaining a physical distance between particular participants in the interaction, which underlines the hierarchy of the courtroom, (3) satisfying an obligation to verbalize questions and answers, without using non-verbal communication due to recording verbal communication, (4) abstaining from interrupting when other participants are speaking, and (5) speaking only when allowed, and only on the topic imposed by the questions (Heffer 2005: 46–47).

2.2 Shift from a conduit metaphor to active participation

A perspective from which the activities of court interpreters were perceived as transmitters which had originated in the theory of **conduit metaphor** proposed by Reddy (1979) where only two parties—a sender and a recipient, who were situated in a kind of social emptiness—participated in the act of communication no matter if it was carried out through an interpreter, was challenged by the developments in the research into public service interpreting started in the 1990s. To illustrate this mechanical approach to bilingual communicative events, Gentile, Ozolins, and Vasilakakos report that according to a sentence of an Australian court in Gaio v. R. (1960), the interpreter was a " 'translating machine', a bilingual transmitter" (1996: 103), while Fenton, referring to the same case, describe the interpreter's as "a conduit pipe, a mere machine, transmitting the message in one direction in one language and in the other direction in the other language, like an electrical instrument overcoming a long distance" (1997: 30). The interpreter who is treated like a mechanism which can be switched on and off upon request and that will produce utterances in any language is discussed by Martin and Ortega Herraéz (2010) who describe the way in which "the judge advised one of the witnesses: "*Use el traductor de árabe*" ["*Use the Arabic translator*"] and, on another, made a request to the sound technician "*Póngale el sistema de traducción*" ["*Connect him to the translation system*"]".

The *conduit metaphor* perspective has been challenged by those scholars who opt for perceiving the interpreter as an "intelligent participant" (Morris 1993: 1), whose interpreting services consist in making constant lexical and grammatical choices (Fenton 1997: 33), as well as transmitting not only words, but also extralinguistic elements of speech, such as "intention, context, form, gist, gesture, tone, relations of power" (Angelelli 2000: 580). In line with this approach, Hardy discusses an example of the act of communication between English- and Spanish-speaking interlocutors, where a lexical choice made by the interpreter (using a calque) leads to confusion and a lack of understanding: "[…] words do not always translate simply on a one-to-one basis. *Molestar* in Spanish does not mean 'to sexually molest', as one might expect, but simply 'to bother' " (2004: 4). Similarly, Mason presents an example that illustrates the fact that verbatim is not always accurate interpretation (1999: 150–151).

Hence, Tryuk recommends a need to discuss the perception of the profession, which does away with an idealistic concept of the machine-like interpreter who transmits the entire message in the target language, and instead, proposes a more human approach, according to which the interpreter can actively participate in the communication (2006: 31). Inghilleri expresses a parallel opinion, highlighting the fact that target utterances produced by interpreters need to be socially and ideologically contextualized in order to present "inform communicative behavior" (2012: 83).

Even interpreters demonstrate two viewpoints: they either picture themselves as 'text producers'—which results from the fact that pursuant to the legal provisions interpreters are reduced to that function—prevails not only among judges and lawyers, but also among interpreters themselves who perceive their services as just producing the text; and this is due to their conviction that they constantly have to isolate other people's utterances from the context to formulate the other version of the utterances in a target language (Wadensjö 1998: 9), or manifest their need to become active participants in the interaction situated in a particular context:

> Sometimes it happens that I kindly apologize to the judge, the prosecutor, the policeman, that my temporary reflection is not a consequence of my ignorance but results from the necessity to find a proper lexical equivalent in order to translate more precisely. In such a moment I refer to the fact that I have to think and speak simultaneously in two languages (Biernacka 2014a: 75; transl. by the author)[63].

The above opinion expressed by one of the 87 respondents to the survey regarding court interpreting in Poland proves that court interpreters prefer to be considered as rightful participants in the communicative act rather than mere providers of source text.

Indeed, it is confirmed that court interpreters, even though unintentionally, leave their mark on the proceedings (Morris 2008: 37–38) in order to ensure what Pöchhacker calls "successful communication" (2002: 97), consisting in achieving

63 "Czasami zdarza mi się uprzejmie przeprosić sąd, prokuratora, policjanta, że moje chwilowe zastanawianie się nie jest skutkiem niewiedzy, ale powodem jest konieczność znalezienia właściwego ekwiwalentu słownego, aby dokładniej przetłumaczyć. W takim momencie powołuję się na fakt, że muszę myśleć i mówić jednocześnie w dwóch językach".

the goal of understanding between the participants. Similarly, Angelelli defines a communication event with the participation of the interpreter not only as a text, but also an action; thus the interpreter is a visible partner in a multicultural conversation and a co-author of the interaction (2003: 16).

Linell indicates that to make verbal communication understandable for all the participants, it is necessary to situate it in a particular social and cultural context; individuals are situated in a context or setting, and the interaction to which they are parties is called a **situated action** (1997: 54).

The above approach confirms the findings of Wadensjö who distinguishes between a **talk as text** and a **talk as an activity**, where the former means that the focus is on processing and translating texts, irrespective of the context in which the utterances are produced, while the latter highlights utterances as activities contributing to interactions between interlocutors (1998: 21–23). Furthermore, Wadensjö proposes to classify interpreter utterances into **implicitly coordinating interpreters' utterances** and **explicitly coordinating interpreters' utterances**, where the former is explained by the assumption that the interpreter's all utterances are aimed at coordinating an interaction, while the latter are those which originally come from the interpreter and are not a reproduction of the primary speaker's talk (ibid 109). Moreover, **explicitly coordinating interpreters' utterances** are further divided into **text orientated utterances**, which include the interpreter's asking for explanations and time to provide interpreting, and **interaction orientated interpreter utterances**, which cover asking for observing turn-taking system, as well as asking to start, continue or stop talking (ibid 109–110).

When making an attempt to combine a sociological and cultural layer with a linguistic level, with reference to a situated action, it is necessary to consider the real activities of an interpreter in a communication event, in which the same words or even utterances may be understood differently in various interactions. This means that participants in the communication event are not exactly sure whether the words they use are precise equivalents of the objects that they describe. It may appear that there are areas of only partially shared meanings. Participants in the interaction are usually satisfied if they manage to achieve a provisional meaning; they hope it will be sufficient to continue a successful communication. In the event in which the parties to a communication event face a problem consisting in the lack of comprehension, then they attempt to search for other meanings and investigate the possible points in which they did not understand each other. This is possible due to a continual interaction between the parties to the communication event and the context; this makes them build a sense of the utterance (Linell 1997: 53).

As regards the mechanisms in interpreter-mediated talks, of special interests are those which, when used by primary speakers, make it impossible for the interpreter to take her turn and speak, that is, to provide interpretation as prescribed by ethical principles. In particular, the research in overlaps is subject to the studies as at interpreter-mediated institutional talk the episodes of interaction in which the interlocutors speak at the same time and with a dizzying pace are naturally a problematic element of the communicative event. Contrary to idealistic recommendations that everything what is said in the courtroom should be interpreted, and the interpretations should be performed in real time in order to immediately deliver the message (Mikkelson 1999), Roy finds out that there is a physical impossibility to consecutively interpret overlapping utterances produced simultaneously by several main speakers, nevertheless the interpreters try to solve the problem of potential misunderstanding of those instances where overlapping appears in the following ways: (1) they interrupt one speaker to let the other speak, (2) they ignore overlapping utterances by interpreting one of them, and then, proceed to interpret the other as precisely as the interpreter's memory permits, (3) they ignore all overlapping utterances, (4) they ignore the utterance that is produced as the second one, interpret the first, and then ask for the repetition of the second utterance (2000: 85). According to Hale, such choices are evident and used on a regular basis by interpreters who are to cope with overlapping utterances produced by the witnesses and lawyers representing the parties to the proceedings who struggle to obtain and maintain control over the speakers and the content of their talks (2007: 75).

2.3 Visibility of the interpreter involved in the trilogue

Even though the interpreters are bound in a special way by the principles arising from the code of professional ethics, they are perceived as rightful and "very visible verbal participants" in the courtroom interactions (Fenton 1997: 32). Pym indicates that it was the criminal trial of O. J. Simpson in 1995, which, apart from being converted into an "international cultural event" (1999: 265), contributed to viewing court interpreters as not only linguistically, but also socially and culturally involved participants in the communicative event. Angelelli also considers the interpreters' participation in the interaction in terms of their **visibility**, which in turn is defined as:

1. Alignment with parties
2. Establishing trust with/facilitating mutual respect between the parties
3. Communicating affect as well as message

4. Explaining cultural gaps/interpreting culture as well as language
5. Establishing rules of communication during the conversation (2003: 17).

Hence, visibility is a direct reference to an active role of the interpreter in the act of communication. On the other hand, Tryuk emphasizes that the interpreter's invisibility, understood as her anonymity or neutrality, may appear to be ineffective (2010: 23).

Moreover, the term **three-cornered interpreting**, which, in turn, is one of the designations of community interpreting, as well as **trilogue** (Tryuk 2006: 146), are both the illustrations of a socio-cultural dimension of the act of communication in which an interpreter takes part. In the courtroom, the interpreter is mobile as she changes her position depending on the sender and the recipient of the message (Edwards 1995; Poznański 2007). Nevertheless, the trilogue does not so much refer to a physical situation of individual participants of the act of communication as it presents the interaction in which three rightful individuals—the sender, the recipient and the interpreter—participate regardless of the place they occupy; only such a model fully renders a dynamics of the interpreted situation.

A communication event with the participation of an interpreter is a triad, or "triadic intercultural communication" (Shisheng and Shuang 2012: 160) in which the interpreter is probably the only person who understands all utterances (Linell 1997: 55) and is aware of possible communicative problems (Kelly 2000: 137). This issue is also raised by Taylor Torsello (1997: 173) who believes that in a communication process, the text is created between an institutional client and a private client, between an interpreter and an institutional client and between an interpreter and a private client. Due to the fact that participants in the interaction do not know each other's languages, it is the interpreter who is the only person capable of maintaining communication and, in case of any problems, making repairs. As Roy observes in more technical terms, "if interpreters are resolving overlap, offering turns, and taking turns [through their knowledge of the linguistic system, the social situation, and how each participant used language to say what they meant], they are active at a level of participation" (1990: 85). In consequence, the interpreter may affect the communicative event as regards the direction and the outcome (Roberts 1997: 10–11), which adds to perceiving the interpretation process as interaction between interlocutors and highlights its "interpersonal dimension" (Pöchhacker 2008: 12).

Furthermore, as Malheiros-Poulet remarks, the trilogue with the participation of the interpreter does not have a fixed structure, which can be affected by modifications depending on the competences of the particular participants.

Firstly, the interpreter's competences[64]; secondly, the interpreter's linguistic and cultural competences as compared to these competences presented by each main speaker (this means that in the case of one of the speakers, the interpreter and this particular speaker share the same language of communication while in the other case—it is the same native language and the same culture); thirdly, the main speakers share a common knowledge, which happens to be partially or totally unknown to the interpreter as a non-professional in a given field; fourthly, there are differences (culture, different goals, social status) in a hierarchy between the main speakers; and, finally, there are differences between the main speakers at the linguistic level—speakers may know, their respective languages, to a certain degree (1995: 136). This means that each participant in the act of communication possesses their *own* knowledge that is a consequence not only of the field of expertise but also of the experience and general knowledge.

2.3.1 The interpreter's active participation as manifested by asking and answering questions

At institutional talk in the courtroom, it is the judge who stands higher than the other interactants: as the master of ceremony and the president over the proceedings who rules and passes a sentence. As Bednarek notices, in the interaction, it is the judge who allows the particular parties to the proceedings to talk (2014a, 2015). Such an approach is well discussed by Edwards, who warns the interpreters that should the need arise to ask the examined party for clarification, this must be done "with the permission of counsel" (1995: 65).

Among the activities that make court interpreters actual interlocutors in the interaction is e.g. asking questions on their own when a problem arises, "it is through the very nature of their job that they must at times step forward, interrupt the flow of the proceedings and draw attention to themselves" (Fenton 1997: 33). Some scholars discuss asking questions not only in terms of the interpreter's active participation in the communicative event, but also from the point of view of the principle of neutrality. According to Rudvin (2002: 223), by asking questions interpreters confirm that they cannot be fully neutral and invisible. Mikkelson emphasizes that the interpreters who do not just reproduce the original utterances in the TL, but communicate with the parties to the proceeding on their own, are consider as biased because they "establish a rapport" (2008: 83) with the primary interlocutors. Such a relationship, or even emotional *bond*, which results from the fact that the interpreter is "the only one who understands" (Valero Garcés

64 The interpreter's competences in public service interpreting are referred to in Chapter 1.

and Dergam 2003: 264)[65] may affect the interpreter's attitude towards her clients and shake their confidence in her neutrality. Anderson also declares that the interpreter holds an edge over the primary parties due to the fact of being the only bilingual participant in the interaction and by this, exercising the linguistic control over the communicative act; he also indicates that such an attitude is a rejection of the recommended principle of neutrality (1976/2002: 218).

Fowler emphasizes that it is the main speakers who have conflicting expectations towards interpreters; on the one hand, the interpreters are recommended to remain impartial while on the other, the lawyers want them to establish "the 'warm' and 'helping' relationship with the defendant" (1997: 196). Indeed, in the context of the courtroom it is necessary to refer to a position of the parties to the court proceedings in the interaction, and in particular, to a picture of the interpreter based on treating her by representatives of justice with superiority and mechanically (Fenton 1997), while the interpreter herself must remain impartial and neutral.

Furthermore, it is pointed out that pursuant to the legal provisions, only the evidence, which can be confirmed, e.g. by the eye witnesses of the event, shall be admitted; if the evidence is adduced by a person who does not know the event 'first hand', then it cannot be admitted and is considered as merely hearsay evidence (Fenton 1997: 30). Also according to the Polish law the interpreter is not a source of evidence but a medium through whom the court is able to communicate with the parties being heard (Pieńkos 1999: 133). This means that the interpreter only serves as an information transmitter between the primary parties out of whom it is the lawyers (including the judge) who share three powers being the three features of the courtroom interaction: the power of language, the power of lawyers and the power of ritual (Fenton 1997: 30–33). Indeed, it is the judge who opens the trial and who speaks out first in order, but then, it is the lawyers who use the language to achieve their own goals (Maley and Fahey 1991: 3; Hale 2001).

The power of language is the consequence of an assumption that it is a primary party who is initiating an interaction or the one who is talking at a given moment, and, in general, the one who is controlling the course of the interaction (Fenton 1997: 30). In a situation where the representatives of the judiciary use the interpreter's services to communicate with a foreigner, their control over the trial can shift. This process is due to the fact that the lawyer and the foreigner are not direct interlocutors in the interaction; it is an interpreter from whom the

---

65 "el único que le entiende".

foreigner receives questions, which are originally asked by the lawyers. Thus, the lawyers are supposed to *give up* a part of their control to the interpreter (Fenton 1997: 30–31) which, obviously, cannot be done because of the "jurists' distrust of interpreters" (Morris 2008: 40) in the courtroom that refers to a double understanding of the concept of interpretation; English *interpreter*, French *interprète* or Spanish *intérprete*, all meaning *oral translator* come from a Latin *inter partes*, which means *mediator between the parties* or *inter-pretium*, which means *mediator in communication between cultural values* (Tryuk 2007: 15). Therefore, by definition, the interpreter's task is to interpret, i.e. to choose the corresponding meaning; this in turn contradicts a common belief shared by lawyers for whom court interpreters are only translators[66] (Morris 2008: 40).

To contradict a popular opinion on the huge responsibility assumed by court interpreters, Mason points out that in the interpreter-mediated communicative event the main interlocutors may either accept or reject lexical choices made by the interpreter, as well as perceive these choices as if they were made by other primary parties (1999: 153–154). However, an opposite attitude is also observed on the part of primary speakers who, instead of addressing their interlocutors, ignore them and refer to the interpreter (Mason 1999: 149).

With reference to another kind of power, the power of lawyers, this belongs to those who ask questions (Lane 1985: 196). In the trial, the lawyers as well as the parties to the proceedings (if permitted by the judge) ask questions. Hale gives a huge importance to the questions as an element of the strategy adopted by the representatives of judiciary (2003: 21). What is more, not only the content of the question, but also the way (e.g. the tone and pace) it is asked, is important and is to serve a certain goal. It seems that irrespective of *what* the interpreter does—whether she precisely transmits all the elements of the question, including the tone and the pace, or she intervenes in the source text—the primary party will hear and understand the utterance formulated by the interpreter. If the questions are transmitted by the interpreter, then, additionally, as in the case of the power of language, it is the interpreter who is perceived as one of the representatives of the judiciary. Thus, also in this case, the power is subject to a shift, which consists in sharing the power, or "prestige" (Mason 1999: 149) between the judge and the interpreter (Fenton 1997: 31).

66 Cronin observes that the interpreter's responsibilities are belittled; he provides an example of "The Interpreter" by Sydney Pollack (2005), the film in which one of the characters addresses the interpreter: "[...] 'With respect, you are only an interpreter' [...]" (2006: 118).

If it comes to the power of ritual, all participants in the trial have the rights and obligations imposed by the legal provisions. As already observed, it is the judge who monitors the course of the trial. Taking account of the dichotomy of the courtroom where the legal proceedings are monitored by the judge, but according to the ethnomethodological approach the trial is an interaction, the power of ritual exercised by the judge covers only an area of the trial as a legal event, while within the area of the trial as an interpreted event, it is the interpreter who controls the course of the communicative act, by which she *deprives* the judge, and also other representatives of the judiciary, of certain prerogatives (Fenton 1997: 31). Moreover, this particular position of the interpreter as an in-between linking the two cultures and languages underlines other forms of the interpreter's power manifested in the communicative event (Mason 1999: 159).

Furthermore, according to Wadensjö (1997: 204), techniques of asking questions aimed at obtaining information from non-Swedish speaking suspects do not serve the function they are expected to perform in the interaction without the participation of an interpreter. One of such techniques, consisting in turning somebody's words against them, does not bring an expected effect due to an obvious deceleration resulting from the necessary assistance provided by an interpreter. Nonetheless, only thanks to the interpreter, the suspect is able to understand and answer the questions. Hence, it is the interpreters who can ensure an understanding between the parties to the act of communication. It is also pointed out that when the interpreter asks questions, it is not always because she wants to gain power in the courtroom, but due to bad audibility or not having understood what the primary party says.

2.3.2 Additions and omissions introduced in the interpretations

The active participation of the interpreter in the act of communication can be manifested through: adding new elements, which do not appear in the original speakers' utterances[67], or, contrary to that, omitting the components of the original utterance.

---

67 Gumul proposes a different classification of the elements added by conference interpreters and translators in the process of transmitting the message from one language to the other, and provides a list of sixteen types of **explicitation** (namely: adding connectives, categorical shifts of cohesive devices, shifts from referential to lexical cohesion, shifts from reiteration in the form of paraphrase to reiteration in the form of identical/partial repetition, reiterating lexical items, filling out elliptical constructions, adding modifiers and qualifiers, inserting hedges and discourse organizing items, adding a

As regard additions, in spontaneous talks of the courtroom, interpreters enrich their renditions. Jacobsen (2003: 227–228) provides a detailed classification of the additions introduced by court interpreters and proposes three main categories:

(1) "additions with no impact on the semantic and/or pragmatic content of the source text" including: repetitions, silent pauses, voice-filled pauses and false starts. Interestingly, Jacobsen assigns no importance to these elements as being a regular realization of the principle of accuracy;
(2) "additions with minimal impact on the semantic and/or pragmatic content of the source test" comprising: repetitions, fillers, paralinguistics, as well as explicating and elaborating additions;
(3) "additions with significant impact on the semantic and/or pragmatic content of the source test" covering: emphasizing, down-toning and new-information additions.

As far as omissions are concerned, professional ethics provides for an absolute and complete transfer of the message, without summarizing or omitting any element of the original utterance (Gentile 1991: 30–31). If the contrary happens, that is, "[i]f someone is speaking and the interpreter's mouth is not moving, there is a problem. If someone makes a lengthy statement and the interpretation is a few words, or vice versa, there is a problem" (Kenigson Kristy 2009/2010: 3).

Nonetheless, during the trial, in opposition to the ethical requirement of interpreting everything that is said in the courtroom, there are fragments, which are either omitted by the interpreter in her renditions or even completely neglected. Sometimes it is the representatives of the judiciary who tell the interpreter not to render those fragments that are not addressed to the foreign language speaking party (Wadensjö 1992: 238–239). There are also occasions where the interpreter chooses to remain silent rather than to literally render such utterances in order to protect her face and not to be perceived as "stupid or incompetent" (Berk-Seligson 1990/2002: 65).

Another element of the interaction that might take place in the courtroom which is never interpreted, mainly in order not to profane the majesty of the court, is procedural and/or technical issues discussed by the judge and the lawyers and/or the interpreters (Fowler 1997: 195).

---

proper name to a generic name, lexical and meaning specification, distributing the meaning, replacing nominalizations with verb phrases, disambiguating metaphors, and including explanatory remarks (2010: 97–99).

2.3.3 Modifications of the main speakers' styles

From the point of view of the interaction ritual, a shift in a grammatical person is an effect of the general attitudes of the participants in all sorts of interactions. Interlocutors use the personal pronoun *I* to put themselves within the context of the story they are telling, to be perceived as someone "who belongs to the world that is spoken about, not the world in which the speaking occurs" (Goffman 1981: 147). The *I* form is reserved to original speakers who express their own, individual and personal views and opinions. Therefore, it is the judge or other legal representatives, who may refer to themselves by using the *I* form. Meanwhile the interpreter, obliged to obey the rule of neutrality, at the moment of asking her own question, is supposed to use the third-person singular (e.g. the interpreter wants to ask if…); in this case such a form is typically impersonal (Edwards 1995: 83). Also, the interpreter who changes a grammatical form gives to understand that she does not belong to a described scene, she isolates and separates herself from the main speakers and does not identify with them linguistically; by doing so, the interpreter emphasizes her independence in the interaction (Shlesinger 1991a: 152).

Furthermore, Shlesinger explains omitting expressions of courtesy, such as address forms, by the lack of time and the need to interpret in a short time the utterances produced by primary parties; at the same time, however, she is aware of the fact that such omissions "pose a no-win conflict between the obligation not to *use up* the precious time of the court on superfluities and that of abiding by the *accuracy* pledge" (1991a: 151). To illustrate an extent of modifications in style introduced by the interpreter, Shlesinger provides an example of a complete softening of the style used by the witness by replacing the original phrase "the guy with the bald head" with "a title (Dr.) and a full name" (1991a: 153).

As regards interpreting address terms between Polish and English, it is problematic for the interpreter to render formal forms. Polish has five polite forms for saying *you*: *Pan* (singular, masculine), *Pani* (singular, feminine), *Państwo* (plural, mixed), *Panowie* (plural, masculine), and *Panie* (plural, feminine). When the English *you* is rendered into Polish directly as *ty*, it situates the interlocutor in an uncomfortable situation ("face-threatening situation", Bartłomiejczyk 2016: 136) due to pertaining this form to informal style used between socially and hierarchically equal speakers[68].

68 Issues of symmetry and asymmetry as reflected in the Polish address terms are discussed by Marcjanik (2007: 36–50).

Berk-Seligson (1988), who analyzed two stylistically different versions of the interpretation of the witness evidence to the members of the jury, notices that address forms used in the courtroom are of huge importance for the course and the result of the trial. According to Pöchhacker (2001: 418), any alteration of the style seriously affects the way in which all participants in the proceedings and the judge assess the credibility of the speaker. Tryuk (2006: 105–106) adds that representatives of the judiciary are more indulgent when they hear that polite forms are deployed.

Interestingly, Berk-Seligson (1988, 1999), Hale (1997b, 2007), and Mason and Stewart (2001) indicate that interpreters (of English and other languages) change (raise, copy or lower) the register and the level of formality depending on whose words and into which direction they interpret.

Yet another issue involving the style as interpreted in the courtroom is shifts from direct into indirect, and reversely, style. The interpreters are obliged to transmit the utterances directly and without changing the grammatical person (Framer 2005: 4). Berk-Seligson comments that the court staff themselves refer to the interpreters instead of addressing main speakers, and gives the following examples of such attitude on the part of the judges: "Ask him what his name is" "Would you ask her if she understands?" "Is she pleading guilty or not guilty?" (1990/2002: 55). Kenigson Kristy adheres to this viewpoint by indicating that the interpreter's distancing from the content of the utterances (by using indirect instead of direct style) is actually initiated by the main speakers who address the interpreter by saying: "Ask him if… or He says that…" (2009/2010: 3).

The court interpreters consider such behaviors outrageous and report that "an interpreter is not a mediator and she cannot describe the judge's question; instead, she is supposed to faithfully translate the content of both the question and the answer" (Biernacka 2014a: 88; transl. by the author)[69].

It seems that the recommendations to use a certain grammatical form concerning a particular person are not clear to interpreters: on the one hand the interpreters want to show their neutral position, on the other hand however, they are aware of the fact that they are not the primary speakers. Hence, a shift that the interpreters frequently apply is the use of the third-person singular instead of the first singular (or plural): they use reported speech (*He says he feels good*) or quote (*He says 'I feel good'*) (Wadensjö 1998: 248, 252; Stawecka 2010: 106). Another modification applied by the interpreters in order to establish who is

69 "tłumacz nie jest pośrednikiem i nie wolno mu opisywać pytania sądu, a jedynie wiernie tłumaczyć treść pytania i odpowiedzi".

speaking and who did what is replacing personal pronouns with proper names. As Wadensjö puts it, interpreters introduce such changes in order to make it clear to the primary interlocutors, *who* is speaking (1997: 204).

Certainly, verbatim interpretation is also deployed. Wadensjö gives an example of a dramatic event in which an interpreter of Spanish participated who was identified by the main speaker as representing the authorities who want to deport him from Sweden: "[w]e have decided not to give you permission to stay in Sweden", says the police officer. I translate: "We have decided not to give you permission to stay in Sweden". The man rushes up to me and shouts in anger and despair: "And me, I always thought you were my friend!" (1998: 239). In other words, a *faithful* rendition of the policeman's words, with a full preservation of the grammatical person, appeared to be the key to understand the policeman's statement.

Indeed, to equate an accurate interpreting with verbatim interpreting may lead to unintentional results (Obenaus 1995: 248). Morris indicates that an interpreter is to solve an internal conflict, which is a consequence of her affiliation to two linguistic communities: she knows both languages spoken during an interaction and by this is able to recognize those features of the speaker's utterance that could possibly "distort a communication process" (1993: 14).

One of such problematic features deployed by the speakers is figurative meanings. Roberts suggests that in the event of facing such challenges, the interpreter should either apply an equivalent in the TL with the same figurative meaning, or interpret verbatim and explain the figurative meaning, or tell the judge that the client has used expressions with a figurative meaning (1990).

When Edwards discusses the issue of the interpretation problems resulting from the use of idiomatic expressions by the original speakers, she uses the examples of the Spanish 'no' which is an equivalent of the English pragmatic marker 'well, ah', and of the Spanish expression 'como no' in English meaning 'of course, naturally' (1995: 96). Wadensjö also discusses the possibility of a lack of understanding between the parties to the communication process relating to the meaning, use and interpretation of the affirmative interjection 'yes' as the negative particle 'no' is illustrated by the following example, in which—during an interpreted hearing—the judge speaks Swedish and the suspect speaks Russian:

Judge: So you don't confess the theft.
Interpreter: That is you don't confess the theft.
Suspect: Yes.
Interpreter: No. (1998: 23)

Wadensjö further explains that 'yes' expressed by the suspect and interpreted as 'no' could lead to a conclusion that the interpretation is not accurate, or, better to say, that the interpreter committed a fatal error. Nonetheless, such a procedure can be considered an error in translation only when we look at an isolated fragment of an interaction, without taking the entire situation in which the interpretation is provided into account. Having not only a social and cultural context in mind, but also a multiple meaning of 'yes' in Russian, in the described example, the suspect, by saying 'yes', does not answer the judge's question; instead, he makes an introduction to his further statements and confirms that he understands what he being is asked about. What is more, an equivalent of the Russian 'yes' used in such a meaning is the Swedish 'no'. Thus, it is obvious that the interpreter does not make an error; on the contrary, the interpretation is accurate and reflects what the suspect actually says (1998: 23–24). This confirms the need for "constant negotiation" (Mason 1999: 149) of meaning.

Moreover, as regards the style, Shlesinger observes a common tendency on the part of court interpreters, which she refers to as **grammaticizing** ungrammatical utterances, as in the following example:

Back-translation of the Hebrew original:

> "[...] to this moment not an iota connected with these twenty identifications, I beg your pardon, these twenty non-identifications."

The English simultaneous interpretation thereof:

> "[...] till this very moment, not so much as a grain of information pertaining to these non-identifications" (1991a: 150).

By sanitizing[70] the original utterance, the interpreter imposes her style in the interaction thus ignores ungrammatical utterances, repetitions, and false starts characteristic of the act of communication.

Vulgarisms form a separate group of elements involving the style which interpreters find difficult or impossible to render (Biernacka 2008b: 303). Edwards claims that the interpreter should transfer all the statements of the main speakers without evaluating as to the degree of their vulgarity; this is due to several reasons: firstly, a degree of offensiveness depends on a personal

70 In this study the terms *grammaticizing* and *sanitizing* are used interchangeably, however, the former is used by Shlesinger (1991a) with reference to oral interactions in the courtroom, while the latter relates to translation universals first described by Baker (1993), and applied by Biel in her comprehensive research into the Polish Eurolect (2014).

sensitiveness of a particular speaker, secondly, different languages have different thresholds of vulgarity, and finally, the interpreters are to interpret what the main speakers say and are not supposed to identify with the opinions expressed by them (1995: 99). What is more, Edwards provides ready recommendations as to how the interpreter should deal with vulgarisms: (1) to provide "an equally offensive" term, (2) to interpret literally the original utterance, or (3) to repeat the original utterance (1995: 100). Even under the assumption that the interpreter is not a real sender of the vulgar message, it seems that the above approach is idealized. From the studies concerning Polish court interpreters, it results that court interpreters feel uncomfortable with vulgarity as they have the impression that main speakers are not always aware of the fact that it is their interlocutors, and not the interpreter, who are the actual authors of possible vulgar expressions. Another interesting finding is that interpreters are reluctant to render vulgarisms because they may sound artificial as they do not fall within the real time of a given interaction and may lose their impact. What is more, a vulgar expression produced by the interpreter sounds different than the one provided by the primary party: the interpreter sometimes finds it difficult to translate it literally and instead uses a description, comments that a vulgar expression has been used and that it corresponds to this or that equivalent in the target language, sometimes interpreters soften such words or simply reject translating them (Biernacka 2014a: 94).

2.4 Conclusions

Viewing the trial from the perspective of the interaction, in which a picture of the court interpreter as a conduit is challenged, helps: (1) investigate the communicative acts of the courtroom in the knowledge that the relationships between individual primary parties do not belong to the same level and there is a clear indication that one participant in the interaction is (or wants to be) more important than the other; (2) explain the linguistic choices made by court interpreters; (3) justify their behavior before the court; (4) discuss over the interpreter treated as an element of the trilogue; and (5) analyze the interpreter's (un)biased position towards the primary parties to the communicative event.

The courtroom interactions bring unexpected developments, which require spontaneous reactions on the part of the interpreter. It is only the active court interpreter participating on an equal basis along with primary parties, who is able to successfully render not only messages, but also emotions and underneath shades hidden in the original utterances.

Part II Empirical Study of Episodes of Interpreter-Mediated Interactions in the Polish Courtroom

3 Methodology and preliminary constraints in the research into interpreter-mediated courtroom talks

This chapter provides a methodological approach to the analysis of "real-life interpreter-mediated encounters" (Wadensjö 1995: 50) of the bilingual courtroom. First, main assumptions of a qualitative research as a "context-sensitive *micro-perspective*" (Dörnyei 2007: 29) as applied to this empirical study are discussed; secondly, issues concerning collecting, processing and classifying data are presented; and finally, underlying methodological issues of this integrated study comprising Conversation Analysis (CA) of episodes of interaction and the interpreter's renditions are explained.

3.1 Collecting data for qualitative research in court interpreting

Collecting data for qualitative research in court interpreting is a challenging task (Jacobsen 2004; Biagini 2012; Biernacka 2014a; Nartowska 2015) as the material for CA consists of naturally occurring talks (Silverman 2001; Dörnyei 2007; Rancew-Sikora 2007; Rapley 2007; Liddicoat 2011; Creswell 2014), which are situated in particular and real contexts (Sacks et al. 1974: 699). The scarce availability of the resources which can be submitted for analysis, contributes (especially in the event of the court communicative events in which Polish is one the languages of the interaction) to the fact that a detailed study within the paradigm of qualitative research is needed due to a superficial knowledge (Dörnyei 2007: 39; Creswell 2014: 29) of interpreter-mediated interactions. On the other hand, it is a consequence of **confidentiality** restrictions resulting from the very nature of legal proceedings involving personal issues. Unlike in translation studies and the research within corpus-based translation studies (Biel 2014: 123–124), and contrary to what Bartłomiejczyk elsewhere (2016: 43–44) states as regards collecting data on simultaneous interpreting that the studies are significantly facilitated by the on-line availability of resources on which observational research can be based, obtaining the data for the analysis of bilingual court interactions constitutes the first and most **time-consuming** stage (Dörnyei 2007: 42). Nonetheless, as courtroom interactions are conditioned situationally, socially, and culturally, it is qualitative, unlike quantitative, research that enables to analyze the context and possible factors affecting communicative events (Dörnyei 2007: 36).

What can hinder the study is both the institution's natural reluctance to provide access to the data and the interpreters' uncompromising attitude towards being them and their services an object of any research. Nevertheless, obtaining the material, which reflects real verbal and non-verbal behaviors, is always a precondition for the study of the courtroom interactions with the participation of interpreters.

In this study, a key methodological decision was to ask[71] the Court for ready–to–use recorded material instead of applying for permission to carry out a field study consisting in observing the interactions during the trials and recording the acts of communication[72]. Apparently, this can be regarded as the main research limitation resulting from the data collecting method: neither on-site observations nor follow-up interviews with the interpreters can be conducted[73]. Nevertheless, this helped avoid the circumstances relating to the observer's paradox (Labov 1972) according to which the presence of the investigator who collects speech samples affects the way the interlocutors talk to one another; it does not mean that their language and behavior is artificial as compared to their 'normal' talks but they are certainly less spontaneous than in those interactions that are not the object of a scientific study (Goffman 1967; Goodwin 1981; Heffer 2005; Rancew-Sikora 2007). Such a behavioral pattern is also confirmed in interpreting studies:

> [...] accessing "naturally occurring" data in SI is particularly difficult because practicing interpreters are usually reluctant to be recorded, especially by their colleagues and for research purposes, and conference organizers may reject the idea for reasons of confidentiality or simply because they fear the recording process may create an additional hassle and jeopardize the flow of the interaction (Diriker 2004: 51).

---

71 Ethical issues relating to obtaining naturally occurring data for the purposes of qualitative research are widely discussed e.g. in Goffman (1967), Silverman (2001), Rancew-Sikora (2007).

72 As regards a field study in the courtroom, Heffer claims that, as far as the English courtroom is concerned, first, it is difficult for the researcher to obtain information about dates and types of trials, and secondly, potential observers are not allowed to make their own recordings (2005: 53).

73 The methodology varies depending on the aim of the study. In the studies concerning conference interpreting, according to two extreme views, it is either advisable to combine both product- and process-oriented research to which aim both recording the interpretations and interviewing the interpreters are applied (Diriker 2004), or, it is claimed that the process-oriented research consisting in interviews or retrospective protocols is unnecessary (Bartłomiejczyk 2016).

In other words, even though the interpreters' awareness of the existence of the facilities recording the course of the trials is unknown (this being a possible object of further studies in the field), it is believed that the presence of a researcher in the courtroom can affect the interpreter's renditions.

Furthermore, the researcher's presence in the courtroom has a potential to obstruct the pursuit of objectivity of the analysis. It is noted that in the course of a field study the researcher may become an "insider" (Heffer 2005: 53; Dörnyei 2007: 38) involved in the observed situation to the degree that it adversely affects possible academic findings.

The above perspective allows the study to be limited to a product-oriented analysis. Following the call of Pym, the interpreters are not interviewed about the reasons for their particular positioning or renditions (1999). The most important reason for that was a time span between the dates on which the trials took place and the data was collected (at least several months in each case), which was a consequence of a choice of the type of material (audio and video recordings of selected trials made for the monitoring purposes of the courts). For the researcher this means that an 'on–the–spot' access to the interpreter before, during, and after the trial, was impossible. A consequence of that, and another reason, is that interviewing the interpreters as regards their participation in the trial (which they had attended a few months earlier and might have forgotten much of it) seems to be pointless. Yet another reason, claimed by the researchers (Bahadir 2001; Diriker 2004; Hale 2007; Biernacka 2014a) is that the interpreters are often not aware of what they actually did or said during the interpretation, and thus their answers to research questions posed in questionnaires or survey include a set of impressions rather than memories of how they interpreted.

The above is also the reason for not applying a quantitative method for this study, although in the research carried out in court, and, more generally, in legal or community interpreting, this method has been used (Hearn 1981; Garber and Mauffette-Leenders 1997; Kadrić 2000; Pöchhacker 2000; Tryuk 2004; Martin and Martí 2008). In Poland, surveys which investigated the condition of Polish community interpreters (Tryuk 2004: 2006) and court interpreters (Biernacka 2009, 2010a, 2010b, 2014a) were also conducted. However, e.g. the response rate of the latter (87 out of 900 copies distributed among sworn translators of various languages) proves that, firstly, the interpreters (although anonymously) are overwhelmingly not interested in participating in scientific undertakings, and secondly, that many sworn translators (being sworn to both certify translations and interpret before the court) have in fact never appeared in any judicial institutions (Biernacka 2014a) due to the fact that they are newly appointed, have never been called by the court, or they always reject appearing before the court[74].

3.1.1 The Court's permission

In order to obtain permission for access to the recordings of oral court proceedings, a request dated December 10, 2013 was submitted to the President of the Regional Court in Warsaw.

In the application it was specified that the request includes access and the possibility to copy fragments of the trials, in whatever division of the court, be it civil, family, economic or criminal, attended by interpreters of Spanish and/ or English for the purposes of research into court interpreting. Moreover, it was assured that the recordings would only be used for academic purposes and with full respect of the protection of personal data, that the recordings should never be made available to third parties, and that all personal data should be changed so that any identification of the parties, places, events, etc. would never be possible.

As a result, on February 11, 2014 the President of the Regional Court in Warsaw issued the Authorization, which entitled to "get acquainted with the material" requested, however, with certain limitations and exclusions, namely: (1) the recordings could be transcribed only in the Files Reading Room and with the use of a special program already installed on the library computer of the Regional Court; in other words, the use of any external systems (or computer software, Nartowska 2015), that could have helped transcribe the recordings was prohibited, thus the preparation of transcriptions appeared to be both a challenging and time-consuming task; (2) access only to the recordings of particular cases, conducted by the Civil Divisions and the Economic Division of the Regional Court, the file numbers of which were expressly indicated in the Authorization, was obtained; (3) the data made available could be used exclusively for scientific purposes concerning interpreters and interpreting in court proceedings; (4) publishing the results of the study could not lead to the identification of the persons involved in the cases; and (5) the authorization did not cover a permit for access to the files of a particular case. Moreover, the Authorization was valid until April 30, 2014 and was subject to a renewal upon a subsequent application until June 30, 2014 when the search query was completed.

The timelines of the query as imposed by the Court's permission have become one of the pre-limitations of this study and was one of the factors that affected

74 These are ethical issues related to the profession of sworn translator and a mission which they are supposed to fulfill, and which requires further research.

the sample size. Nonetheless, in the course of collecting the material, it was also **saturation**, defined as a moment when "gathering fresh data no longer sparks new insights or reveals new properties" (Creswell 2014: 189) leading to repetitiveness of occurrences (Dörnyei 2007: 127), which contributed to completing this early stage of the research.

As regards other pre-limitations of this study relating to the Court's permission, these include two issues revealed at the early stage of the research.

First, it was decided to address the Regional Court in Warsaw, and only one court of justice. The decision was conditioned by a previous consideration to use ready recordings, i.e. the ones officially made during the trials. At the time the research was carried out (2013–2014) it was in the Regional Court where the trials were recorded for monitoring purposes[75]. What is more, it was in the Regional Court where the ratio of cases in which a non-Polish (English- or Spanish-) speaking party participated had a potential to be the highest as compared to other courts. Therefore, at the preliminary stage, the rationale behind the assumption that qualitative research would be conducted was a small number of trials assisted by interpreters of either English or Spanish.

Secondly, the external limitation of the study was imposed by the Court's authorities; the permission expressly indicated the civil and economic cases as those, which can be subject to the analysis. In this way, all other, be it criminal or family cases had to be excluded; this also partially contributed to a shift from the lexically-oriented study to the interaction-oriented research. Interestingly, focusing on civil and economic cases has become the strength of this study: Morris, when mentioning the study of Abel (2009) as one of these, which focus on interpretation in civil proceedings, claims that research into the interpreters' participation in criminal proceedings prevails (2015: 91); it is proven by the studies carried out by Jacobsen (2003, 2004, 2009), Hale (2007), and Nartowska (2013a, 2013b, 2015).

In general, it is **flexibility** (Dörnyei 2007: 40) or "**emergent design**" (Creswell 2014: 186) that is characteristic of qualitative research which made it possible to modify the initial plan for this study.

3.2 Data processing for CA

In line with the research into the discourse of monolingual court interactions carried out by Atkinson and Drew (1979), CA is perceived as a natural approach

75 The recordings are made pursuant to Article 157 §1 of the *Code of Civil Procedure*.

to analyze the collected material from the perspective of the interpreter's active participation in the communicative events of the courtroom.

CA is based on three assumptions: 1) **structurally-organized interaction**, 2) **contextual and sequential organization of a talk**, and 3) **empirically grounded analysis** (Heritage 1984: 241–244), all of which are inherent characteristics of court interactions.

A structurally-organized interaction means that the talk is composed of organized patterns, which "stand independently of psychological or other characteristics of particular speakers" (Heritage 1984: 241). This means that CA focuses on the procedures deployed by interactants and what they talk about, and not on the psychological conditions resulting from the individual characteristics of particular speakers.

For the CA research into court interactions this means that it is unnecessary to identify interpreters[76] in order to ask follow-up questions regarding their performance. Hence, for the purposes of this study, even though it was feasible to obtain the personal data of particular interpreters, focusing on the product, that is, the structure of a given interaction was decided (Silverman 2001).

The contextual and sequential organization of a talk refers to its two features: the talks are context-shaped and context-renewing. According to Heritage (1984), context is indispensable for the analysis of a particular talk. What is more, the context is necessary for the interactants, who by observing what other speakers say and do in the interaction, are able to create a record of information obtained during the talk. The interactants can consciously follow the trajectory of the talk and respond to the developments in the conversation only thanks to the context. Furthermore, as Lyons states, there are two types of the context: situational and situational-linguistic, thus exclusive of the context, which is "purely linguistic" (1972: 60). That is why the talk is context-renewing: the interactants need to process the information to have a current view on the topic of the talk (1984: 242). The "shared understanding" (Goodwin and Goodwin 1992) stands in opposition to the original ethnomethodological perspective on

---

76 As stated in Chapter 1, today, Polish sworn translators have to undergo examination procedures to be admitted to the profession, however, those professionals who became sworn translators at earlier stages of the development of court interpreting in Poland, thus had never attended any training courses or been examined at the Ministry of Justice, still appear before the court. Therefore, a limitation of this study, resulting from obtaining the data already recorded by the court, is that the exact professional profiles (such as professional experience or competences) of the interpreters involved remain unknown to the researcher. Nonetheless, such information is irrelevant for the CA.

the context, according to which understanding can only be "sufficient" due to the backgrounds of the particular interactants who may have different life, professional, and other, experience. Garfinkel observes that in renewing the context, the interactants also take advantage of "ad hoc considerations" (1967: 21), that is, the pieces of information created during the talk. As regards the sequential organization of the talk, Schegloff (1991: 1995) claims that it should be considered from the point of view of what the interactants actually do and not from the perspective of what they say. Thus, supremacy of interaction as a turn-taking system over the content of the talk is emphasized.

As far as interpreting is concerned, Pöchhacker underlines the importance of the context for the fulfillment of the requirement of quality in interpretation, which is the "*successful communication* among the interacting parties" (2002: 97). As regards the bilingual courtroom, Jacobsen mentions three factors which characterize the context, namely: "immediacy of the encounter", which means that the participants in the communicative event are in the same place; "physical presence" of the participants who can see and hear one another, and "sensitive nature" of the trial (2002: 128).

An empirically grounded analysis means that the information conveyed by the transcripts of the talk subjects for analysis is a "bottom-up approach" (Silverman 2000: 139) where naturally occurring conversations and "the empirical conduct of speakers" (Heritage 1984: 243) are a point of departure for investigating forms of talk.

A pre-condition for an empirically grounded analysis within CA as formulated by Sacks (Sacks et al. 1974), and further developed by Atkinson and Drew (1979), Jefferson (1983), Heritage (1984), and Atkinson and Heritage (1984), is to describe procedures applied by interactants to create orderly social interactions (Rancew-Sikora 2007: 25, Gavioli 2016: 186) on the basis of real-life episodes of interaction, in which the investigation focuses on spoken language and comes from ethnomethodological assumptions concerning talk-in-interaction[77].

CA has been deployed as a method to study dialogue interpreting and the role of the interpreter in bilingual encounters. The interpreter-mediated talks in medical settings are the best analyzed encounters, having been studied by Angelelli (2004, 2007, 2012), Davidson (2000, 2002), Gavioli (2012), Niemants

77 A comprehensive contribution to the interdisciplinary research in monolingual courtroom discourse while applying the CA approach is a comparative study of Polish and American discourse of institutional stakeholders during criminal trials (Bednarek 2014a).

(2013), and Pasquandrea (2011), as well as (Wadensjö 2001) in therapeutic encounters. In particular, Bolden (2000) proved that the interpretation provided in medical settings is bound primarily by the rules of interaction, and only secondarily by the interpreting task, by which the research into monolingual talks (Schegloff 1991: 1995) has been confirmed. Roy (2000) and Davitti (2012) have proven the active participation of the interpreter at encounters in educational settings. Interpreter-mediated talks in refugee settings have been studied by Keselman, Cederborg, and Linell (2010). As regards police settings, the CA method allowed Wadensjö (1998) to investigate the role of the interpreter as a coordinator of the bilingual encounter, as well as show the contrast between an ideal image of dialogue interpreting and the real performance of the interpreters.

As far as court interpreting is concerned, Jacobsen carried out an empirical study of additions deployed by interpreters (2002, 2003, 2004) and elaborated on the roles of court interpreters (2009), Biernacka (2014a, 2016), in line with Goffman's theory of interaction classified the activities of court interpreters according to the roles they assume in the episodes of interaction, while Nartowska (2015) showed the biases to which the interpreters are submitted in criminal proceedings.

3.2.1 Transcribing the recordings

Audio-video recordings prepared by court technicians are accompanied by the minutes of the trial which, however, are not word-for-word records of the proceedings. This means that there are no ready-to-use transcriptions, but written documents drawn up during the trial, which, pursuant to Article 158 of the Polish *Code of Civil Procedure*, include such information as: the name of the court, place and date of the trial, case number, names and surnames of the judges, the court recorder, the parties and their legal representatives, as well as a reference to the presence of the interpreter. Therefore, the minutes are a summary of the proceedings rather than a literal reflection of the trial; they contain the information revealed in the course of the trial, but not in a genuine form; the information is filtered by the judge who repeats what the interlocutors have said and only this data is put in the minutes by the court recorder.

For the researcher it means that there is no transcription of naturally occurring data, which can be used in the study. Apart from an evident disadvantage of the necessity to devote much time to listen and write down the acts of communication (thus a serious time-limitation should be considered), preparing transcriptions has an advantage of having an opportunity to listen the recording as many times as required to draw all the details enabling meticulous CA from the conversations:

> (...) linguists know what to listen for in a conversation. They listen for topic initiations, topic recycling, response strategies, interruption patterns, intonation markers, pause lengths, speech event structure, speech acts, inferencing, ambiguity resolution, transcript accuracy and many other things. (...) Linguists understand the significance of context in the search for meaning in a conversation (...) (Shuy 1996: xviii)

From the above it results that transcripts are subjective (Heffer 2005: 58) and can be a consequence of individual choices of the transcriber who decides on the importance of elements of a particular interaction and thus includes or excludes certain components of communicative events in the written material subject to further analysis[78].

For the purposes of this study, all episodes of interaction have been transcribed using transcription conventions, while preserving a standard orthography.

The transcription conventions used for the interactions subject to the analysis in this empirical study are a compilation of symbols, presented in Tab. 3.1 below, originally proposed for the CA of monolingual talks (Sacks et al. 1974; Jefferson 1983, 2004), and afterwards adopted and applied for the purposes of the research in the field of interpreting studies (Wadensjö 1998; Jacobsen 2002, 2003, 2004; Biernacka 2014a, 2014b).

3.2.2 Quality of the collected material

The material to which access was obtained was in the form of audio-video recordings. In each case a camera was fixed either above the judge's desk and covered the image of the benches where the parties to the proceedings together with their legal representatives were sitting, or on the side wall of the court-room, in which case the view also included the judge and the court clerk. Thus, the interpreter was also visible; her position changed according to where the

78 Apart from subjectivity, and elaborating on the validity of the transcript data, Heffer (2005: 58), indicates other characteristics of transcriptions prepared by the official court reporter and afterwards made accessible to the researcher which may either limit a qualitative analysis, namely: (1) neglecting "phonetic, prosodic [and] paralinguistic features", (2) omitting non-verbal items; or help carry out the study, i.e. (3) including all lexical items.

Tab. 3.1: Transcription symbols (Sacks et al. 1974; Jefferson 1983, 2004; Wadensjö 1998; Jacobsen 2002, 2003, 2004; Biernacka 2014a, 2014b)

Symbol	Meaning
Judge:	Current speaker
?:	Speaker is unknown
a:::	Long vowel (the longer the sound, the higher the number of colons)
...	Open-ended intonation
.	Falling intonation
,	Slightly rising intonation
?	Rising intonation
!	Enthusiasm
court	Words spoken with emphasis
°court°	Words spoken quietly
>the court<	Words spoken faster than the surrounding talk
<the court>	Words spoken slower than the surrounding talk
h	Breathiness
-	Cut-off of the current sound
=	No discernible interval between the units of talk
[	Overlaps
(.)	Micro-pause (very short silence)
(0.5)	Half second pause
(2.0)	Two second pause
(xxx)	Inaudible words due to technical problems or chuchotage
[(xxx)]	Overlap with inaudible words
(the court)	Author's best hearing of the talk
((looks up)) ((knocking))	Non-verbal element of the talk or information added by the author

non-Polish speaking party sat or stood. The camera was immovable so it was impossible to zoom in on a particular interlocutor. Moreover, although in the majority of trials the image was not sharp enough to see a facial expression of a particular participant in the interaction, a gaze could be caught during some talks, and it was possible to get an overall idea as to who was present in the courtroom and who was who in the interaction in all the proceedings[79]. Hence, the

79 The constraints imposed by the type and quality of the collected material are discussed by Ford and Thompson (1996: 142).

study focuses on verbal aspects of the interaction, nevertheless, whenever possible, the analysis includes non-verbal communication[80]. Furthermore, as to the sound quality, it varied depending on who was speaking; the judge's questions as well as the utterances of those who spoke into the microphone were clearly audible; unfortunately, the interpreter, as not the primary party to the proceedings, could not count on a microphone for her exclusive use. Thus, technically, she had either to bow towards a microphone used by the non-Polish speaking party (when she interpreted for the judge and the lawyers) or she spoke right to the ears of the non-Polish speaking party (when she interpreted for that party); logically, only the fragments produced out to the public were heard, while (the rare episodes of) whispering remained a secret of both the interpreter and the non-Polish speaking client.

The use of ready audio-video recordings poses a serious limitation to the study consisting in the fact that only what the camera was able to record can be heard and observed when watching the material, hence many details of the interaction, mainly those concerning the body language, are left hidden and remain out of the analysis. At the same time, however, the camera zoom focused on the actual interactants helps the researcher not to be distracted by the activities possibly carried out by other actors in other parts of the courtroom.

Furthermore, in spite of the advantages of having an opportunity to transcribe the recordings, there is also a considerable limitation resulting from the naturalness of the obtained data. A preliminary analysis of the material collected for the purposes of this research shows that there are chains of overlapping turns taken by the main speakers (which cannot be rendered by the interpreter). In three cases of all the revealed overlaps, the interpreters fail to render them at all. In one of these cases (152 seconds) the interpreter decides not to interpret an exchange of views between the parties' lawyers who have provoked their reciprocal allegations that their questions are framed in a leading way. In another case (190 seconds), during the entire trial the interpreter does not render a discussion concerning procedural issues between the judge and the lawyer representing one of the parties. In yet another example (193 seconds), where the parties' lawyers exchange ideas, the interpreter resorts to intensive gazing at the judge's decision to make the interactants stop talking to allow the interpreter to speak. All three episodes of interaction prove that the interpreter takes a decision not to interpret long overlapping talks in which she cannot separate, understand and render

80 A comprehensive study of non-verbal elements of communication in dialogue interpreting during parent-teacher interactions can be found in Davitti (2012).

Tab. 3.2: Collected material: sample size and languages

	Number of cases	Number of trials	Number of hours	Number of interpreters	Languages
	9	13	37	12	English
	2	3	5	3	Spanish
Total:	11	16	42	15	English or Spanish

talk units. The researcher also cannot process such data, hence these instances, even though deemed interesting from the point of view of scientific investigation, can be only described as taking place, however, are impossible to transcribe and submit to a detailed analysis.

3.2.3 Collected material: sample size and languages

During the search query, and as presented in Tab. 3.2, access to forty two hours of recordings (thirty seven hours of which were trials attended by the interpreters of English, and five hours were trials, in which the interpreters of Spanish participated) was obtained. These numbers translate into nine *English* and two *Spanish* cases; however, as cases are not equivalents of particular trials[81], the number of trials is: thirteen for English (assisted by twelve interpreters) and three for Spanish (assisted by three interpreters).

As regards the small **sample size** obtained for the purposes of this study, this is due to at least two reasons. The first is strictly connected with ethics and in particular with confidentiality, which is the main obstacle to obtain extensive data. The second concerns the fact that qualitative research is "very labour-intensive" (Dörnyei 2007: 38), thus obtaining the data comparable in size with these processed within quantitative research is impossible. These two issues explain the sample size collected for the purposes of ealier studies conducted by Hale (2004), Torstensson and Gawronska (2009), Nartowska (2013a, 2013b, 2015), Biernacka (2014a); these studies also confirm that a small-scale research (owing to its **exploratory** nature) into court interpreting based on a small number of trials and where the material for the analysis is collected in one court, has a potential to map new "uncharted areas" (Dörnyei 2007: 39) of academic interest.

81 A case is defined as a legal action, especially one to be decided in a court of law https://en.oxforddictionaries.com/definition/case while a trial is a formal examination of evidence by a judge (…) in order to decide guilt in a case (…) https://en.oxforddictionaries.com/definition/trial (December 10, 2017).

As regards **validity** of the sample size, the number of trials (sixteen in total) and of interpreters (fifteen in total) assisting in the trials subject to this study contribute to **triangulation** of sources of information (Creswell 2014: 201).

Furthermore, in spite of a considerably smaller size of the Polish-Spanish material as compared to the Polish-English resources, an analysis of the fragments of interactions with the participation of the court interpreters of Spanish was decided, however, only for illustrative purposes and not in order to investigate possible differences between the interactions with English–Polish and Spanish–Polish language pairs.

Thus, the distribution of languages is due to an overwhelming number of cases, the parties of which are English–speaking participants (either native speakers or those who indicate English as the language in which they want to communicate during the trial) as compared to the available cases with the participation of Spanish interpreters (unlike in the event of English, if a Spanish–speaking party appears before the court, he is always a native speaker; cases for which a party indicated Spanish as the language of communication with the court while not being a native speaker of the language are not reported and thus unknown to the author).

As to a language profile of the main speakers, it is important to indicate that the interpreters' institutional clients (judges and other representatives of the judiciary) are Polish speaking parties who, often, pretend to speak English (and never–Spanish), the consequences of which are shown in the empirical part of this study, where the parties examined speak basic English at a communicative level. The interpreters' private clients (witnesses, defendants, respondents) are non-Polish speaking parties, some of them having a passive knowledge of Polish, which in this study means that they roughly understand Polish—as shown in the examples that follow. Except for one case, the English–speaking parties are native speakers of English; only one witness is not a native speaker, but indicated English as the language for communication with the court. As stated above, in the event of Spanish–speaking parties, all are native speakers of the language.

As to the language profile of the interpreters, they are sworn translators of either Spanish or English, respectively, with Polish as their mother tongue.

The choice of the language pair[82] has been limited by the researcher's language profile, whose mother tongue is Polish, Spanish is an active (B) language, while English is C (working) language. This language configuration conditions, first,

82 As reported by the court staff in the course of the search query for the purposes of this study, a number of trials with the participation of interpreters of Russian, Ukrainian and Belarusian is incomparably higher than a number of cases in which interpreters of

the choice of the language of the analysis, and secondly, ensures self-sufficiency as regards the full understanding, transcribing, and analyzing the collected data.

Furthermore, owing to "**space limitations**" (Dörnyei 2007: 56) of this book, it has been impossible to include, analyze and discuss the entire material collected for the purposes of this study. Therefore, interaction **sampling** has been based on selecting the communicative events, which show the most remarkable possible variety of interaction mechanisms and the interpreters' renditions; as Dörnyei indicates, "the main goal of sampling is to find individuals who can provide rich and varied insights into the phenomenon under investigation so as to maximize what we can learn" (2007: 126). Therefore, a possible lack of **representativeness** (Dörnyei 2007: 126), understood as a disinterest in exploring trends with a simultaneous emphasis put on single incidents and a "focus on individual meaning" (Creswell 2014: 4), is one of the features of qualitative research.

3.2.4 Data presentation

All the transcriptions are cut into small fragments of interactions, these being single acts of communication that are transmitters of meaningful information. Hence, the length of the fragments vary depending on whether it is possible or not to understand what the interpreter does or does not do in a particular episode of interaction. The majority of fragments include episodes where private clients of the court are examined however these episodes are not identified as such, as it is not the aim of this study to analyze the procedures performed in the courtroom[83]. Only in some cases are the fragments described as belonging to a particular stage of the proceedings.

All the episodes of interaction are denominated as Extracts and numbered in ascending order throughout the entire empirical part of this book.

In each Extract, an original PL/EN or PL/ES talk is presented on the left side, while the author's verbatim translation into English is on the right side, written in italics and put in square brackets. The author's verbatim translations into English are added only for informative purposes for those readers who do not speak Polish or Spanish, and are not supposed to be attempts to correct or instruct the interpreters in terms of prescriptive guidelines as to how they *should*

---

other languages are summoned, owing to a huge immigration from Eastern European countries to Poland.

83 As regards the procedures and language of the Polish courtroom, a broad study can be found in Rzeszutko (2003).

or *should not* interpret before the court[84]. For the same reasons a discussion over the lexical aspects is reduced to a minimum and conducted only insofar as it helps explain interactional issues.

Some Extracts are classified as belonging to two or more categories and are thus discussed at least twice. This is due to the complexity of the interaction in which the interlocutors use all the available mechanisms to participate in the act of communication[85]. Such a double classification of particular episodes might prove a hindrance to attempts to quantify the CA data.

3.3 Integrated research in interpreter-mediated court interactions

For the purposes of this study an integrated approach to the research in interpreter-mediated interactions of the courtroom is proposed. The three dimensions of the research are as follows:

1) the interpreter's participation in the turn-taking system at institutional talk,
2) the interpreter's renditions of institutional talk, and
3) the interpreter's impartiality as an expression of complying with ethical standards (whenever, based on a particular episode, this aspect is detectable).

Hence, the interpreters' activities are subject to analysis from the point of view of interaction, text-processing and, possibly, ethical attitudes.

3.3.1 Classification of the collected material according to the mechanisms in interaction

All the episodes of interaction are classified according to the mechanism in interaction to which the interlocutors are submitted, as well as according to the interlocutor in whose talk a particular mechanism occur. It is noticeable that particular stages of court proceedings appear in a given mechanism – such is the

84 Hence, if, for example, grammatical mistakes appear in the interpreter's or other interlocutors' talks, they are copied in the author's verbatim translation, which is supposed to give an overall idea of a pragmatic meaning of the interpreter's rendition, and not to correct the interpretation.

85 For example, a post-first insert expansion can be produced by the speaker in the case of a problem of hearing; as a consequence, a repair mechanism is implemented in order to maintain the interaction (Schegloff et al. 1977).

case of examining the parties, where a pledge is given by the witness, unless the judge exempts him from doing so (Rzeszutko 2003: 133).

The mechanisms presented below do not constitute a full catalog of possible procedures deployed by the interactants, however, at the preliminary stage when the material for this study has been pre-selected they have been identified as those occurring in the interpreter-mediated talks of the courtroom. Therefore, the division of the collected material reflects the three tiers which create the court talk. The first tier which is fundamental for the design of the conversation covers the **turn-taking** system, within which **gaps** and **overlaps** can be isolated as the elements disturbing a flow of communication. The second tier comprises **adjacency pairs** and **expanding sequences**, which contribute to constructing the talk as a complex sequence of turns. The third tier consists of the **repair** system which works as a safety net in case the procedures used by the participants in the interaction fail.

The **turn-taking** system is fundamental for all talks as speakers need to change in order to maintain a conversation. As regards monolingual casual conversations, Sacks et al. (1974) claim the existence of two techniques employed by interactants within the system: either **the current speaker selects the next speaker** or **the speaker** who wants to take a turn **self-selects**. In both cases the speakers need to know when to start speaking, thus they look for a **turn constructional unit** (**TCU**) to be completed by a current speaker at a **transition relevance place** (**TRP**), that is, a point in the current speaker's turn where a possible completion occurs. The next speaker knows that the TCU is completed on the basis of their linguistic competences and because s/he is immersed in the context of a given talk. As Ford and Thompson indicate, it is syntactic, intonational and pragmatic features of the talk that help the interactants manage the turn-taking mechanism (1996: 134–184). Thus, it is a TRP where the next speaker is supposed to start speaking.

Overlaps and **gaps** (**silences**) occur in conversations as spontaneous manifestations of the interactants' need to speak or remain silent, and occur as varieties of a transition space (Sacks et al. 1974, Jefferson 1986), that is, the instances between particular turns of particular speakers. In other words, in taking turns the speakers break the rules of waiting until the current speaker completes their TCU: they start speaking before that point of interaction (an overlap is produced), or, once the current speaker completes their TCU, they do not take their turn (a gap is created). These two phenomena disturb an ideal pace of the talk, but are inherent features of conversations. In particular, overlaps, which are basically the instances in interaction where the current and next speakers' talks are produced, partially or totally, at the same time, and more specifically, longer overlaps, are considered interruptions and can be problematic for the interlocutors (Liddicoat 2011: 113). What is more, in casual conversations, not all overlaps interrupt a conversation or violate the rules of interaction; instead, they may be a manifestation of the parties' interest in the subject of the talk (Díaz-Campos, Geeslin, and Gurzynski-Weiss 2017: 290). Furthermore, episodes in which silences understood as pauses in verbal interaction occur can be filled in with non-verbal communication where the parties use body language instead of speaking ("**unspoken activity turns**", Atkinson and Drew 1979: 194). In other words, non-verbal communication is not supplementary to what interactants say, but it rather replaces the talk. According to Borg, interlocutors' gestures credibly convey attitudes (2011: xviii), while Liber adds that gestures are a manifestation of speakers' actual involvement in the conversation through which their real relationship to a subject of the conversation is revealed (2012: 138). Diamond confirms that participants in formal settings: exchange glances, keep an eye contact, and use gestures as well as other ways of non-verbal expression to show their emotions and opinions (1996: 71); what is more, it is specifically the non-verbal channel that is used when the interactants want to preserve certain information off the record, in other words, some details of what is said are hidden from other participants in the interaction (1996: 72).

Adjacency pairs are turns which form basic sequences at a talk (Sacks et al. 1974; Schegloff 1991; Schegloff and Sacks 1973), such as: question-answer, summons-answer, telling-accept, greeting-greeting (Tomaszkiewicz 1993: 105, 107, 113; Liddicoat 2011: 140). A basic structure of the talk within the adjacency pairs is built up of the first, opening, turn (**first pair part, FPP**) and the second (**second pair part, SPP**). When the FPP occurs, it requires a specific SPP; at an institutional talk, when the judge, in his FPP, asks the witness about his age, the witness is expected to produce a SPP containing a precise answer to the judge's FPP. These **relevance rules** (Schegloff and Sacks 1973) ensure that the talk follows the pattern until the closing of the conversation. Furthermore, at institutional talks, these pairs are considered as **preferred**; it is supposed that only one interlocutor (the judge or other representatives of the judiciary, depending on the stage of the proceedings) asks questions and the other (the witness, plaintiff, claimant, defendant, etc.) responds. More specifically, Atkinson and Drew observe that in the court examination, summons and accusations are FPPs, while justifications and excuses are SPPs (1979: 49). In other words, at both casual and institutional talks, ideally, each FPP requires an SPP to ensure the flow of the talk. However, this trajectory can be broken by one of the speakers in case they announce a **problem** (of whatever nature) by producing a **counter** (Liddicoat 2011: 142), which adopts a form of either asking an extra question or requesting for repeating the message transmitted by a previous speaker, or by remaining silent. Moreover, the responses within adjacency pairs can be **dispreferred**, in the event of which SPP is e.g. a refusal or a disagreement to FPP (Pomerantz 1984; Liddicoat 2011). Furthermore, the parties to the interaction may cooperate to produce adjacency pairs which are **assessments**: in that case the next speaker refers to the elements of the current speaker's talk. According to Pomerantz (1984), when one speaker deploys an assessment, only this may provoke the next speaker to elaborate on the assessment in the event they agree to such an evaluation. Furthermore, Pomerantz (1984) divides such cooperatively built assessments into three categories: **upgrades**, **same evaluations** and **downgrades**, by which the next speaker intensifies, copies, or alleviates, respectively, a particular assessment included in the TCU produced by the current speaker. Within the category of upgrades a separate mechanism has been detected at the stage of classifying the obtained material, namely, it has been noticed that the interpreters, instead of proposing a verbatim interpretation of short one-particle *yes* or *no* answers offered by the witness, provide elaborated statements. Wahlster et al., who based their findings on the research into artificial languages, denominate such upgrades as *over-answering yes-no questions* defined as "generating extended responses that provide additional information" (1983: 643).

Expansions form a category of procedures used by the speakers to develop the interaction and are divided into pre-, insert, and post-expansions. The division runs according to the place in a sequence occupied by a particular expansion. **Pre-expansions** preface the sequence. They are produced by the current speaker when they address the next speaker – at court talk it is addressing the judge with *Your Honor*, after which an actual TCU is produced, but can have also other forms (e.g. pragmatic markers *well, so*) to begin a particular TCU (Schegloff 2007). **Insert expansions** separate a FPP from a SPP and develop the internal talk within the main trajectory. They are divided into post-first insert expansions (they refer to a FPP after which they occur), and pre-second insert expansions (referring to a SPP before which they occur) (Schegloff 2007). **Post-expansions** occur after a possible completion of a sequence (Schegloff 1990) and can be minimal (one word: *oh, okay*) or non-minimal (when the next speaker repeats the TCU produced by the current speaker to indicate a repairable) (Schegloff 2007).

Repairs are procedures deployed by speakers when they detect a problem, or a difficulty, in conversation (Liddicoat 2011: 208). These difficulties are referred to as **repairable** or **trouble source** (Jefferson 1987, Schegloff et al. 1977), however, cannot be identified with errors (Liddicoat 2011: 209). Furthermore, Schegloff et al. (1977) propose a classification of repairs: **self-initiated self-repair**, where the current speaker identifies a repairable and makes a repair; **self-initiated other-repair**, where the current speaker identifies a repairable, but it is the next speaker who makes a repair; **other-initiated self-repair**, where the next speaker identifies a repairable, and the current speaker makes a repair; and **other-initiated other-repair**, where the next speaker identifies a repairable and makes a repair.

3.3.2 Interpreter's renditions and interpreter's utterances: evolution of the model

Wadensjö (1998) applied CA to investigate real interpreted events in police and medical settings. The fundamental finding of her study is an idea of the contrast between ideal interpreting and actual performance (1998: 103). For bilateral interpreting, she proposed a model in which she considered the interpreter's utterances from two perspectives: translating and coordinating. As regards the former, interpreting is viewed as a translating task, where the original speakers' and interpreter's utterances are analyzed from the point of view of their compatibility ("mutually compatible types of short texts", 1998: 106); while the latter assumes that interpreting is understood as coordinating the interaction between the main speakers.

In line with the above division and as far as the interpreter's translating task is concerned within the talk-as-text approach (Wadensjö 1998: 21–22), the term **rendition**[86] is suggested to be used to describe the act of producing, on the part of the interpreter, a new version of what the primary party has said (Wadensjö 1998: 107).

Accordingly, the renditions are divided into: **close**, **expanded**, **reduced**, **substituted**, **summarized**, **two-part** or **multi-part**, **non-**, and **zero renditions**, as presented in Tab. 3.3:

In other words, **close renditions** are those, which are referred to by codes of ethics as accurate, precise, or faithful to the original. In the remaining types

---

86 While a discussion concerning strategies and techniques has had a long academic tradition in the research into conference interpreting (Kalina 1992; Gile 1995; Moser-Mercer 1997; Riccardi 1998; Bartłomiejczyk 2004; Gumul 2010, 2015; Tryuk 2007), in bilateral interpreting it is Wadensjö who proposed a classification of **renditions** to cover the patterns followed by the interpreters in public service settings.

Tab. 3.3: Classification of renditions (adapted from Wadensjö 1998: 108)

Type of rendition	**Definition**
Close rendition	Rendition, which is equal as to its content and style to an original utterance
Expanded rendition	Rendition, which includes more information than an original utterance
Reduced rendition	Rendition, which includes less information than an original utterance
Substituted rendition	Rendition, which is a mixture of expanded and reduced renditions
Summarized rendition	Rendition, which is an interpretation of utterances expressed by various speakers, including the interpreter
Two-part or multi-part rendition	Rendition, in which the interpreter splits the original utterance and transmits the information the form of two or more utterances
Non-rendition	Utterance, which is originally produced by the interpreter, but have not appeared in the primary speakers' talk
Zero rendition	Untranslated instances of primary speakers' talk

(**expanded, reduced, substituted, summarized, two-part** and **multi-part renditions**) modifications introduced by the interpreter can be traced. In the event of **zero renditions** the changes become omissions of (the elements of) the original utterances, while **non-renditions** are voluntary comments or requests expressed by the interpreter[87].

For the purposes of this integrated analysis, a modification of a denomination of one of the renditions proposed by Wadensjö (1998) is introduced; in this study, the term **expanded rendition** is replaced by the term **extended rendition** to be understood as equivalent of which the aim is to avoid confusing taxonomy – as explained above in this chapter, the concept of **expansion** is used in CA to denominate an interactional mechanism of adding extra turns to the main trajectory of the conversation.

87 As a "type of translatorial action" (Koskela, Koskinen, and Pilke 2017: 474), close renditions are also denominated **duplicating,** defined as "producing full content" (ibid 474). Moreover, the authors distinguish **summarizing**, described as "condensing the gist" (ibid 477), and **expanding**, which "challenges the definition of translation" (ibid 479) as it consists in making spontaneous translation choices infringing the ethical principle of accuracy.

3.3.3 Integrating the results: correlation of interaction mechanisms and interpreter's renditions

The classification of the material collected during the search query follows the division into interaction mechanisms comprised by the three tires and proposed within the CA. It is believed that such a categorization of the episodes of interaction highlights the instances in the communicative acts featured with potential difficulties for the interpreters to position themselves within the talk as both active participants and oral translators of the primary parties' talks. Once the episodes are attributed to a particular mechanism in interaction as applied by the interpreter and primary speakers, they are further described as pertaining to a particular category of the interpreter's renditions of original utterances. In other words, each extract is firstly analyzed as presenting a particular mechanism, and secondly, within this mechanism, as exemplifying a particular rendition pattern. Moreover, as rendition patterns – which by themselves comprise a strong element of a debate regarding accuracy in interpreting – inevitably lead to considering ethical issues as an inherent feature of court interpreting, some episodes will be discussed from the point of view of the interpreter's impartiality.

Hence, the interpreters' activities are subject to analysis from three perspectives: interaction, text-processing, and ethical attitudes. Such an approach reflects the findings concerning the nature of the act of communication to which the interpreter is a party as much more complicated than what the code of ethics provides for (Hale 2007: 114; Dybiec-Gajer 2013: 277; Biernacka 2014a: 40), mainly due to a complexity of the interactions taking place at the same time between different interlocutors (Gentile, Ozolins, and Vasilakakos 1996: 31).

The results of the study are presented as diagrams of interaction patterns in the courtroom. As far as the **quantification of data** in CA is concerned, Schegloff (1993) finds it difficult and Heritage (1995) opposes to quantifying the CA data due to the impossibility to count the instances in which a particular mechanism occurs. Instead, to analyze "open-ended, non-numerical data" (Dörneyi 2007: 24) collected for the purposes of qualitative research non-statistical methods are applied, where vague adjectives such as *regularly*, *typically*, *commonly*, *overwhelmingly* (Liddicoat 2011: 11) are used to describe the interaction phenomena. This confirms that, unlike within quantitative research, it is the researcher who becomes a "measurement device" (Miles and Huberman 1994: 7) or a "key instrument" (Creswell 2014: 185). What is more, the "**in-depth analysis**" (Creswell 2014: 14) of samples covers not only regular features of the interaction, but also any irregularities resulting from the differences between particular talks (Heritage 1984: 244). These irregularities cannot be a point of departure for the **generalizability of results** as single occurrences has rather a potential to push boundaries of the knowledge of a phenomenon; therefore, in qualitative research the awareness is raised against "over-reading" of the findings (Yates 2003: 224). What is more, it is **particularity** (instead of generalizability) that is the "hallmark of good qualitative research" (Creswell 2014: 204).

As regards this study, some episodes are included under two or more headings thus mathematically they constitute one instance to be counted, while in CA they present a range of interactional issues. Furthermore, with reference to categorizing and describing the interpreters' renditions Wadensjö repeats the constraints imposed on this analysis, claims that it is impossible to quantify the results, but highlights that they serve qualitative research in that they demonstrate an "elementary variety of textual structures" (1998: 108) and explore the "functions of this variability" (ibid 108).

Taking all the hindrances to the quantification of data into account, the results of the study as correlatives of interactions and renditions are presented in the form of tables which integrate the qualitative data into quantifiable patterns[88]. Nonetheless, caution is urged in evaluating such an approach as it is impossible to quantify the qualitative, thus the results can be considered as approximate and partially subjective. Hence, any numbers which appear in the tables serve illustrative purposes rather than are mathematical reflections of the results of the study.

3.4 Conclusions

Qualitative research is characterized by the features, which enable analyzing the interpreter-mediated interactions of the courtroom. First, it requires small sample size. Secondly, the data are collected to describe a phenomenon and possibly, to discover irregularities, thus qualitative research is exploratory in terms of outlining new areas of potential studies. Thirdly, the data is collected until the moment of saturation. Fourthly, flexibility of qualitative research enables to introduce changes to the plan adopted before the beginning of the query. Finally, particularity supersedes generalizibility of data, which means that the in-depth analysis of the samples is recommended in qualitative research.

---

88 Similar solutions can be found with regard to quantifying, on the basis of CA, treatment of patient-generated direct questions in same-language and interpreted visits in medical setting (Davidson 2000) or counting, within DA, the interpreters' renditions of particular elements of original utterances (Hale 2007).

The naturally occurring data serve as a point of departure for investigating interpreter-mediated communicative events of the courtroom. In this study, an integrated study is proposed. Therefore, the episodes of interaction are analyzed from the perspective of both Conversation Analysis and the interpreters' renditions, with an additional assessment of the ethical principles satisfied by court interpreters.

Both Conversation Analysis and the interpreter's performance within bilateral interpreting events have its implications in terms of taxonomy. Thus, for the purposes of this study, interaction mechanisms are denominated after Schegloff and Sacks (1973), Sacks et al. (1974), Schegloff et al. (1977), Atkinson and Drew (1979), Schegloff (1990, 1991, 2007), Wahlster et al. (1983), Jefferson (1986, 1987), Pomerantz (1987), Ford and Thomson (1996), and Liddicoat (2011). Furthermore, as regards the description and classification of the interpreters' performances, the concept of *renditions* introduced by (Wadensjö 1998) has been restored. Thus, any other denominations of the mechanisms or renditions deployed by the interactants are not applied to this study, which is due to the intention to provide a clear framework by avoiding "proliferation of terminology" and "parallel criteria"[89], as elsewhere explained by Dörnyei (2007: 57).

89 Dörnyei (2007) comments on the double taxonomy of quality criteria, nonetheless his opinion gives food for thought as regards classifications created in other fields.

4 Interpreters as participants in the turn-taking system of courtroom talks

This chapter deals with the system of turn-taking through which the interpreter-mediated interaction in the courtroom is coordinated by its participants. In particular, the following issues, on which the focus is intended to help find a reply to the research questions of this study, are analyzed:

(1) how and by whom are the next speakers selected,
(2) who (primary parties or interpreters) are the next speakers,
(3) in what way the interactants self-select as next speakers, and
(4) what types of renditions of the elements of utterances, which contribute to selecting the next speaker or self-selecting as the next speaker, are provided by the interpreter?

For the purposes of this analysis, the episodes of interaction, following the classification proposed by Sacks et al. (1974) for monolingual casual conversations, are attributed to two main categories, one of them including the examples of the **next speaker being selected by the current speaker**, and the other covering the extracts, where the **next speaker self-selects**.

4.1 The next speaker selected by the current speaker

In the institutional talk of the courtroom, the technique of selecting the next speaker by the current speaker is naturally deployed by the judge who allocates the turns or by other representatives of the judiciary who address the examined parties. In other words, the speaker who asks a question is also privileged to select the next speaker.

4.1.1 The primary party selected as the next speaker

Extract 4.1 below shows an instance, in which the judge asks the parties or their representatives if they deem an oath necessary:

(4.1)	**Original PL/EN talk**	**Author's verbatim translation into EN**
Judge:	panie mecenasie (.) co do przyrzeczenia:?=	*[Mr. Counselor, in terms of the oath?]*
Lawyer I:	=dziękuję...	*[Thank you]*

(4.1)	Original PL/EN talk	Author's verbatim translation into EN
Judge:	(.) pani mecenas (.) co do przyrzeczenia?=	*[Ms. Counselor, in terms of the oath?]*
Lawyer II:	=dziękuję	*[Thank you]*
Interpreter:	(0.3) no oath	

The judge addresses his question to the counselor by indicating to whom he is speaking (*Mr. Counselor* and *Ms. Counselor*, respectively). The counselor immediately responses to the judge's utterance and the judge asks the same question to the other counselor, who, also immediately, rejects the possibility of taking an oath by the parties to the proceedings. In other words, it is the judge who selects the next speaker by asking the question combined with the address form. The interpreter does not interfere in the question-answer episode of the interaction, which may be caused by the fact that she is not the one who is expressly addressed by the judge, thus the interpreter's possible interruption would be considered as violation of interaction rules. Hence, **the interpreter summarizes** the substance of the talk between the judge and legal representatives of the parties to the proceedings by announcing *no oath* which informs the witness that he is not required to give a pledge before the court.

Similarly, in the following episode of interaction, the judge asks about an oath:

(4.2)	Original PL/ES talk	Author's verbatim translation into EN
Judge:	(.) co do przyrzeczenia…?	*[In terms of the oath?]*
Lawyer I:	hmm: (.) bez przyrzeczenia.	*[Without an oath.]*
Lawyer II:	(.) dziękuję wysoki sądzie.	*[Thank you, Your Honor.]*
Interpreter:	((to the witness)) (0.2) puede declarar sin juramento.	*[You are allowed to declare without an oath.]*

In Extract 4.2 the judge asks a question, but he does not mention the name or position of the addressee. In terms of the CA, anyone can be the next speaker. However, in the context of the courtroom, it is procedurally justified that it is the parties' lawyers who are implicit recipients of such questions. Thus, both lawyers, subsequently, respond to the judge's question. The interpreter does not transmit the judge's question and lawyers' answers concerning a possible oath after each of them completes their turn. Only at the end does she inform the witness of the result of the talk, hence a **summarized rendition** is provided. However, unlike in Extract 4.1, the interpreter produces a fully grammatical statement, which in addition is an affirmative sentence; this certainly creates the witness's positive attitude to the trial and to the necessity to interact with the judge and other lawyers.

Furthermore, during the examination of the defendants or witnesses, the judge deploys an address term to indicate whom he expects to answer his questions.

Extract 4.3 shows the interaction in which the judge selects the petitioner as the next speaker:

(4.3)	**Original PL/EN talk**	**Author's verbatim translation into EN**
Judge:	czy są jakieś problemy y::: związane z y:: (0.2) wykonywaniem kontaktów z dzieckiem przez powoda?	*[Are there any problems with the child being seen by the petitioner?]*
Interpreter:	((gazing at the petitioner)) (0.2) are >there any problems< with the child being seen by the petitioner?	
Petitioner:	(0.3) not that I know.	
Interpreter:	(0.2) nic mi na ten temat nie wiadomo…	*[Not that I know of.]*

The judge begins this episode of interaction by addressing the petitioner with a question concerning possible problems in contacting his child. In a monolingual talk it would thus be the petitioner selected as the next speaker. However, logically, in a bilingual talk, it is the interpreter who, although not expressly indicated as the next speaker, is tacitly expected to intervene just after the judge completes his turn. Hence, the interpreter begins her turn after an appreciable pause (0.2) and, preserving the level of formality of the original utterance (a 3rd person singular address term *the petitioner*), provides a **close rendition** of the judge's question. As the camera is zoomed at the interpreter's and the petitioner's faces, it can be presumed, that the addressee of the question knows that it is he who is supposed to respond not necessarily because he identifies himself as the petitioner but that the interpreter gazes at the petitioner when rendering the question. Irrespective of whom the judge is looking at (be it the petitioner or the interpreter), the petitioner knows that he is selected as the next speaker thanks to the interpreter's gazing at and speaking to him. In other words, the interpreter contributes to selecting the next speaker.

In the subsequent example the judge also deploys a formal address form to select the next speaker:

(4.4)	**Original PL/EN talk**	**Author's verbatim translation into EN**
Judge:	co według strony powodowej było celem tej umowy?	*[What was the goal of this contract according to the plaintiff?]*
Interpreter:	((gazing at the plaintiff)) (0.5) what was the goal of this contract (.) according to the plaintiff?	
Plaintiff:	(0.2) we were contracted to provide advi::ce… to X...	
Interpreter:	(.) naszym celem było…	*[Our aim was to…]*
Plaintiff:	0.4) if this contract could be:: hmm: (.) introduced in Poland…	
Interpreter:	(0.3) mieliśmy doradzać (.) czy ten kontrakt może być hy:::m::: wypełnio:ny (.) być zrealizowany…	*[We were to provide advice… if this contract could be… fulfilled, be executed.]*
Judge:	czy może być zrealizowany pod jakim wzglę:dem?	*[Could be executed in which aspects?]*
Interpreter:	(0.2) the settlement of (.) what (0.3) what was >your advice<? <I me::an> y::: under which >terms and conditions<?	

In Extract 4.4 the judge is even more precise than in Extract 4.3 to select the next speaker: he expressly selects an addressee of his question by requesting his opinion (*what, according to the plaintiff…*). The interpreter attempts to provide a **close rendition** of the judge's question; however, she needs an appreciable pause (0.5) to begin to render the message. It may prove that the interpreter finds it problematic to 'take over' the turn which is actually assigned to the plaintiff.

Extract 4.5 shows that it is the counsel who selects the next speaker:

(4.5)	**Original PL/EN talk**	**Author's verbatim translation into EN**
Counsel:	((gazing at the interpreter)) czy świadek uczestniczył e:: w odbieraniu przez powoda (.) dziecka (0.2) z mieszkania obecnej partnerki?	*[Did the witness take part in picking up the child by the plaintiff from the present partner's apartment?]*
Interpreter:	((gazing at the witness)) (.) did you take pa::rty::: (0.5) were you present (.) in picking up the child (.) from the present partner's flat?	
Witness:	= ye:s. =	
Interpreter:	= tak.	*[Yes.]*

The counsel expressly addresses the witness with his question, but gazes at the interpreter. This ambiguity is resolved by the interpreter who, firstly, directs her gaze to the witness, and secondly, makes the counsel's question less formal by substituting a direct form *you* for the address form *the witness*. By applying an **extended rendition**, the interpreter not only gives the interactants to understand that according to her the pronoun *you* indicates who the next speaker is, but also shortens the distance between the counsel and the witness. Although the content of the message is rendered, the level of formality of the interpretation differs from the one of the original utterance. Thus the interpreter, through her contribution to assigning the next speaker, can unconsciously distort the main speaker's actual intentions as to maintaining and marking the fact of the lawyers and the witness belonging to two distinct groups of interactants.

The example that follows shows that the judge selects the next speaker by deploying an address term characteristic for casual conversations:

(4.6)	**Original PL/EN talk**	**Author's verbatim translation into EN**
Judge:	czyli chodziło o to: (0.2) że pani uniemożliwia kontakty z y:: córką?	*[So, did you mean that you made contact with… your daughter impossible?]*
Interpreter:	(0.2) so::: (0.3) does it mean that *the claimant* makes the contacts with yo:::ur (.) your contacts (0.2) with the child (0.3) impossible?	
Defendant:	and my experience so far well (0.2) she's already told you everything (.) you need to know (0.4) no contact (0.2) that's her wish (.) no contacts. =	
Interpreter:	= a moje doświadczenie jest takie (0.2) tak jak ona powiedziała (0.3) tłumaczę dosłownie (.) czyli tak (.) jak powiedziała (0.5) prze:d (0.2) >przede mną< (0.3) żadnych kontaktów…	*[And my experience is like she's already said, I'm interpreting literally, that is, like… she's said… before… before me, no contact…]*

The interpreter takes a turn when the judge completes his question addressed to the claimant, and attempts to provide a close rendition of the message contained in the judge's question. However, she upgrades the register; the judge addresses the claimant with *you* (in Polish this is a polite form of the third-person singular: *Madam* [*pani*] used in the formal, but not necessarily institutional talks), while the interpreter introduces the term *claimant* which leads to achieving a higher level of formality. In other words, the judge asks a commonly comprehensible question free from any formal register, and the interpreter, by applying an **extended rendition**, fogs the issue that may result in the claimant not being that eager to answer the judge's questions.

4.1.2 The interpreter selected as the next speaker

It is presumed that the interpreter is obliged, and is competent to know when to speak (understood as her obligation to render the primary speakers' utterances) without being selected as the next speaker. Nonetheless, there are instances in which the judge or other lawyers expressly select the interpreter to speak.

Such is Extract 4.7, where the judge indicates the interpreter as the next speaker:

(4.7)	**Original PL/EN talk**	**Author's verbatim translation into EN**
Judge:	pan przychodzi do czytelni i czyta akta (0.5) pytanie sądu jest (.) czy zna język polski w związku z tym? (0.2) proszę zapytać (.) czy pan sam czyta akta? =	*[You come to the reading room and read the files. The question of the court is whether he therefore knows Polish? Please, ask, if he reads the files himself?]*
Interpreter:	= so:: (0.2) do you read the files by yourself in Polish?	
Witness:	no::: (.) what I do is this (0.2) I take a smartphone (.) I take pictu::res (.) ye:s… ((gazes at the interpreter)) (1.0) I want this on protocol.	
Interpreter:	(.) czyli pan chciał (.) żeby to było zapisane w protokole y:: (.) że pan robi zdjęcia akt (.) robi zdjęcia akt.	*[So he wants to have it recorded in the minutes that he takes the photos of the files, takes the photos of the files.]*

In his turn, the judge produces several TCUs, the last being addressed to the interpreter (*please ask if he reads the files himself, proszę zapytać czy pan sam czyta akta*). By deploying the next-speaker selection technique addressed to the interpreter, the judge positions the interpreter among active participants in the interaction: she becomes a noticeable interlocutor. As a consequence, the interpreter feels justified to provide a **reduced rendition** of the judge's two questions. This example shows however, that that the judge veils his selecting the interpreter as the next speaker by the use of an immediately preceding TCU (*the question of the court is, pytanie sądu jest*); by doing so the judge announces that it is his question that will be asked in a moment and that the interpreter is only a transmitter of that question.

In Extract 4.8 the judge also addresses the interpreter to speak:

(4.8)	**Original PL/EN talk**	**Author's verbatim translation into EN**
Judge:	((to the Interpreter)) proszę zapytać (.) o co sąd pytał (0.2) czyli o tę sobotę... (0.2) jaki był plan na tę sobotę?	*[Please ask about what the court has asked, meaning about that Saturday. What was the plan for that Saturday?]*

(4.8)	Original PL/EN talk	Author's verbatim translation into EN
Interpreter:	plea:se (.) tell the court exactly the plans for Saturday.	

The judge selects the interpreter as the next speaker by deploying a pre-expansion *please ask about what the court has asked* (*proszę zapytać o co sąd pytał*). The question, however, also includes an extra element: from the pre-expansion it results that the judge does not give the interpreter a free hand as to the content of the question, but specifies what the interpreter is allowed to ask the witness: it is *what the court has asked*. This limitation is also repeated twice: when the judge, after an appreciable pause (0.2) expands on the pre-expansion (*meaning about that Saturday, czyli o tę sobotę*), and when, after another appreciable pause (0.2), he asks a direct question addressed to the witness. Although the judge expressly selects the interpreter to speak, by limiting the interpreter's right to speak makes her reproduce the level of formality and by the same, maintain the majesty of the court (*please tell the court*), and then transmit the actual question. As a result, a **reduced rendition** is provided.

The next example shows that the judge selects the interpreter to speak without any pre-expansions preparing for such request:

(4.9)	Original PL/EN talk	Author's verbatim translation into EN
Judge:	((to the Interpreter)) pan (0.2) proszę zapytać (0.2) czy pan pozwany wynajmuje mieszkanie (.) jeśli tak (.) to jakie to jest mieszkanie (0.3) duże? (0.4) gdzie ono jest y::: położone? (0.2) czy jest wyposażone w pełni we wszystkie sprzęty?	*[You, please, ask, if the defendant rents an apartment, if so, then what kind of apartment is it, big? Where is it… located? Is it fitted with all the equipment?]*
Interpreter:	(.) do you rent an [apartment?	
Defendant:	[yes.	
Judge:	((silence)) (3.0)	

The judge asks a question about the defendant's renting an apartment, the size of the apartment, where it is located and about the possible equipping of the flat. Nevertheless, the next speaker's selection technique deployed by the judge reveals that it is not the defendant who is a recipient of the question. Even though the first pre-expansion confirms that the judge addresses the defendant (*you, pan*), then an appreciable pause (0.2) occurs when the judge rethinks the recipient, and produces the other pre-expansion *please ask* (*proszę zapytać*), in which the interpreter is told to ask the defendant. The judge's selecting the interpreter as the next speaker triggers a mechanism described in Extract 4.7 above: the interpreter preserves only the general question (hence provides a **reduced rendition**) whether the defendant does or does not rent an apartment, but omits all other questions concerning the details of a possible flat. The interpreter's failure to transmit all the information included in the original question leads to a substituted rendition. This is proven by the fact that when the defendant provides an affirmative response (*yes*), the judge's turn contains a marked pause (3.0) which is an equivalent of his surprise that the answer to detailed questions is the one that can be expected only in the event of asking general questions.

In the subsequent example, the judge selects the interpreter as the next speaker and reaffirms his selection:

(4.10)	Original PL/EN talk	Author's verbatim translation into EN
Judge:	((to the Interpreter)) proszę panu przetłumaczyć (0.2) proszę panu wyjaśnić (.) że…	*[Please translate to him, please explain to him that…]*
Interpreter:	((gazes silently at the judge, waiting for the question))	
Judge:	(xxx)	

The judge deploys two pre-expansions separated by an appreciable pause (0.2): *please translate to him* (*proszę panu przetłumaczyć*) and *please explain to him* (*proszę panu wyjaśnić*), in which he expressly refers to the interpreter as the participant in the interaction whose main tasks are firstly, to translate, and secondly, to explain. Hence, the judge, by addressing the interpreter instead of referring directly to the party to the proceedings, gives an understanding that he perceives the interpreter as a missing link in the act of communication. In response to that, the interpreter looks at the judge to communicate non-verbally to him that she is waiting for the question; hence a **zero rendition** is provided.

Similarly, the example below shows a double next-speaker selection which occurs in the judge's talk:

(4.11)	Original PL/EN talk	Author's verbatim translation into EN
Judge:	((to the interpreter)): proszę powiedzieć (0.2) zapytać (.) czy pan pracuje? (0.3) jeżeli tak (.) to gdzie: (.) i w jakich godzinach? =	*[Could you say… ask, if he works. If so, then where and during what hours?]*

(4.11)	Original PL/EN talk	Author's verbatim translation into EN
Interpreter:	do you work? (.) if so (0.2) where and what are your hours?	
Defendant:	(.) my hours are US hours. =	
Interpreter:	= so (.) that's according to US time or...? =	
Defendant:	= fifteen to twenty four.	
Interpreter:	(.) o:ke:y (0.3) więc pan pracuje tutaj zgodnie z godzinami amerykańskimi (0.2) czyli jakby według naszego czasu od piętnastej do dwudziestej czwartej.	*[OK. So he works here according to US time, that is sort of according to US time from 3:00 pm to 12:00 am.]*

The judge deploys two pre-expansions separated by an appreciable pause (0.2): *could you say* (*proszę powiedzieć*) and *ask* (*zapytać*), both addressed to the interpreter. The latter pre-expansion is actually a repair of the former: the judge first requests the interpreter to *say*, and only then reflects (0.2) that the interpreter is not supposed to substitute the defendant for speaking. Thus the judge repairs the pre-expansion and requests the interpreter to *ask* the defendant. Only then is an actual detailed question asked. The interpreter provides a **reduced rendition** of what the judge tells him to ask. Nonetheless, the judge's selecting the interpreter as the next speaker affects the interpreter's attitude towards the judge's question. The interpreter shortens the distance and partially *takes over* the judge's power; she perceives the judge's pre-expansions as permission to select the next speaker. It is now the interpreter who asks the defendant the additional questions, adds—in the last rendition—new elements (pragmatic markers *OK*, *so*, *sort of*), as well as changes the grammatical form from 1st to 3rd person singular.

4.2 The next speaker self-selects

In the interactions the next speaker can select themselves to take a turn in the episodes of interaction in which the current speaker has not selected the next speaker. In bilingual interactions, the interpreter ideally takes a turn after the current primary speaker completes his turn to render his message, and afterwards, listens to the next primary speaker to interpret his utterances, and the sequence repeats. In other words, the interpreter naturally self-selects to speak in order to transmit the information provided by the primary speakers. However, even though the interpreter physically speaks, she is not considered the primary speaker in the conversation as her task is to reproduce the message revealed by the original speakers. Hence, as stated above, the interpreter needs to wait until the main speaker completes his turn and only then interpret the information provided by that speaker.

4.2.1 The interpreter self-selects

The episodes of interaction in which the judge informs the witness about his legal liability in the event of giving false testimony show the interpreter's self-selecting as the next speaker: the interpreter takes a turn just after the judge to render his instructions. Nonetheless, the instances showing a deviation from this pattern can also be observed.

Extract 4.12 shows the interpreter's turn occurring immediately after the judge's instructions:

(4.12)	**Original PL/EN talk**	**Author's verbatim translation into EN**
Judge:	pouczam pana (0.2) >o obowiązku mówienia< prawdy (1.0) za zeznanie nieprawdy (0.5) zatajenie prawdy przed Sądem (0.2) grozi odpowiedzialność karna pozbawienia wolności do lat trzech (1.0) na podstawie przepisu artykułu dwieście trzydzieści trzy kodeksu karnego. =	*[I instruct you about an obligation to tell the truth. You shall be made liable to prosecution of up to 3 years imprisonment according to the provision of Article 233 of the Criminal Code for providing false testimony, concealing the truth before the Court.]*
Interpreter:	= there is a duty to tell the truth (1.0) there is a criminal liability for false testimony up to three years of >custody in sentence< according to article two hundred thirty three of the Criminal Code.	
Witness:	((nodding))	
Interpreter:	((nodding and gazing at the judge))	

The interpreter selects herself as the next speaker and begins interpreting immediately after the judge completes his turn. The interpreter, in the knowledge of the importance of this fragment of the trial, which is to foster the witness's awareness about the consequences of providing possible false testimony, the interpreter knows that it is her turn to talk to maintain the non-Polish party linguistically present (Gentile et al. 1996: 98). To preserve the level of formality of the judge's utterance *I instruct you to tell the truth*, the interpreter changes the form to an impersonal *there is a duty to tell the truth*, by which the majesty of the Court is transmitted. The judge's use of active voice results from the fact that he has the right to say so because he personalizes the system of justice. By altering the form, the interpreter, providing a **reduced rendition,** distances herself from the figure of the judge and from what he is stating; indeed, it is the judge and not the interpreter, although both are present and visible in the courtroom, who instructs the witness.

Similarly, the next example shows the interpreter's self-selecting as the next speaker:

(4.13)	Original PL/EN talk	Author's verbatim translation into EN
Judge:	pouczam pana o obowiązku mówienia prawdy (0.5) za fałszywe zeznania grozi odpowiedzialność karna do trzech lat pozbawienia wolności.	*[I instruct you about the obligation to tell the truth. You shall be liable to prosecution of up to 3 years of imprisonment for providing false testimony.]*
Interpreter:	(.) you are instructed to say <truth> (0.3) only truth (2.0) otherwise you: (.) can be punished >with up to three years< of imprisonment.	
Witness:	((nodding))	
Interpreter:	((looking at the judge))	

The interpreter selects herself as the next speaker; she needs a micro-pause to begin her turn. As in Extract 4.12, she changes the judge's active statement (*I instruct you about an obligation to tell the truth*) into a passive expression (*you are instructed to say truth*). In addition, a modality *can be punished* (meaning: it is possible that you will be punished) is used instead of an originally deployed categorical *shall be liable*. The shift in modality from an obligation to a possibility makes the interpreter's rendition soften as compared to the judge's utterance. As to the content of the message, a **substituted rendition** is provided.

The subsequent example also shows the interpreter self-selecting as the next speaker:

(4.14)	Original PL/EN talk	Author's verbatim translation into EN
Judge:	pouczam pana o obowiązku mówienia prawdy (2.5) za fałszywe zeznania grozi odpowiedzialność karna do trzech lat pozbawienia wolności.	*[I instruct you about the obligation to tell the truth. You shall be liable to prosecution of up to 3 years of imprisonment for providing false testimony.*
Interpreter:	(.) tiene la obligación de decir la verdad (2.0) por prestar una declaración falsa puede ser castigado con tres años (0.2) hasta tres años de cárcel.	*[You have an obligation to tell the truth. You can be liable to prosecution of up to 3 years of imprisonment for providing false testimony.]*
Witness:	((silence))	
Interpreter:	((silence))	

The interpreter begins her turn after a micro-pause. She introduces two modifications as compared to the judge's original utterance. The first one consists in changing a perspective: the judge puts himself as the subject of the statement—by this, the witness is solemnly advised of his liability. In the interpreter's **substituted rendition**, it is the witness who is the subject of the statement and the judge, as representing the judicial institution, is not mentioned. What is more, the interpreter shifts a modality: from a strong *shall be punished* in the judge's instructions to a mild and calming down *can be punished*. Indeed, in this and in the previous Extract 4.13, the interpreters act as tranquilizers giving the witness a sense of security, which, as presumed, is not the judge's goal during the trial, however, can contribute to the witness's eagerness to answer the judge's questions.

Extracts 4.15 shows that there are instances in which, after the interpreter self-selects as the next speaker, the witness may unexpectedly self-select as the next speaker:

(4.15)	**Original PL/EN talk**	**Author's verbatim translation into EN**
Judge:	pouczam pana o obowiązku mówienia prawdy (0.2) ponieważ w przeciwnym wypadku (.) może być pan ponownie przesłuchany po odebraniu przyrzeczenia.	*[I instruct you about the obligation to tell the truth because otherwise you may be interrogated again under oath.]*
Interpreter:	(.) so: (0.2) I <u>instruct</u> you to tell the truth (0.2) because otherwise (.) you will be interrogated under oath. =	
Witness:	= okey.	
Interpreter:	((silence)) (2.0)	

When the judge completes his turn in which he instructs the witness about his legal liability, the interpreter, after a micro-pause begins her rendition, in which she preserves the *I* form deployed by the original speaker. Nevertheless, the interpreter chooses to make her rendition differ from the original utterance by replacing the original modality *you can be questioned* by a more categorical statement expressed by *will be interrogated*. This shift in modality probably contributes to the witness's self-selecting as the next speaker (*okey*), although neither the judge's nor the interpreter's utterances have invited a possible turn by the next speaker. The witness, even though in a short and humble TCU, feels obliged to respond. A **zero rendition** is provided by the interpreter.

Extract 4.16 shows that the interpreter self-selects as the next speaker although she is not expected to do so:

(4.16)	Original PL/EN talk	Author's verbatim translation into EN
Judge:	w tym miejscu tłumacz (0.3) >na zarządzenie< przewodniczącego (0.3) opuszcza salę rozpraw. to wszystko. może pan opuścić salę rozpraw.	*[Here the interpreter... by an order of the presiding judge shall leave the courtroom. That is all. You can leave the courtroom.]*
Interpreter:	(.) you can go.	
Witness:	((nodding to the interpreter and to the judge, and going out))	
Interpreter:	((gazes at the judge and goes out))	

The judge announces that the interpreter is allowed to leave the courtroom as she is no longer needed for the further development of the proceedings. The judge communicates this message twice. For the first time, when he dictates the adequate information to the court clerk who is drawing up the minutes of the trial (*here the interpreter... by an order of the President shall leave the courtroom*), and for the second time, when he addresses the interpreter (*that's all (0.2) you can leave the courtroom*). Although, in response to the judge's permission to go, the interpreter is supposed to leave the courtroom, she chooses to refer to the witness. To this end she applies the **non-rendition** of the judge's utterances in order to inform the witness that the examination has ended and thus he can go out. What is more, from what the judge says, it results that it is the interpreter who is permitted to go, while the witness, although no longer examined, is allowed to either go out or stay. By intervening where she does not have to, the interpreter selects the witness as the next speaker, who responds with body language: he nods to confirm that he understands the interpreter and leaves. So does the interpreter. The difference is that the interpreter goes out as a consequence of the judge's direct permission, while the witness's response is caused by the interpreter, not the judge.

As stated above in this chapter, a self-selecting pattern for the interpreter-mediated interaction is the one in which the interpreter waits until a primary party completes his turn and only then does she take her turn consisting in reproducing this party's utterance. Nonetheless, there are instances which prove that although the interpreter self-selects as the next speaker, she does not do so to render the primary speaker's utterances, but to replace that speaker in the interaction.

Extract 4.17 shows the instance in which the interpreter skips the defendant's turn by self-selecting as the next speaker:

(4.17)	Original PL/EN talk	Author's verbatim translation into EN
Judge:	czym się pan zajmuje?	*[What's your occupation?]*
Interpreter:	(.) your occupation?	
Defendant:	(0.2) I work as a:: hm::: eh::: contractor.	
Interpreter:	(0.2) czyli pan pracuje: na zlecenie tak naprawdę…	*[So he works as a contractor actually…]*
Judge:	(0.3) czy:li rozumiem (0.2) że ma pan umowy z firmami różnymi? =	*[So I understand that you have contracts with various companies?]*
Interpreter:	tak (0.2) wygląda że z trzema różnymi.	*[Yes, it seems that with three different.]*

The judge begins the episode of interaction by asking the defendant about his occupation. As soon as the interpreter renders the question, the defendant, after an appreciable pause (0.2) responds in a hesitant way; there are three vocalic fillers in his turn (*a:: hm::: eh:::*) indicating that he is not sure about the answer. In reply, the interpreter does not only add a particle *so* [*czyli*], but also an adverb *actually* [*tak naprawdę*], by which she wants to implicitly provide the judge with the information that the defendant works on the basis of a particular type of the contract. The judge elaborates on the defendant's answer by asking a detailed question. It is now the interpreter's turn in which she reproduces the judge's question to let the defendant respond. However, the interpreter replaces the defendant in answering the question, hence she provides a **non-rendition**. As a consequence of reducing the number of turns, the judge becomes a recipient of the information originally provided by the interpreter and not the primary speaker's message. The interpreter's failure to maintain an orderly institutional talk may be a manifestation of her biased attitude towards her clients; she is evidently eager to cooperate with the judge with whom, in addition, she speaks without preserving an official style (*it seems that…*).

The next episode shows that the original speaker's question which may be confusing for the interpreter:

(4.18)	Original PL/EN talk	Author's verbatim translation into EN
Counsel for the Defense:	pytanie jest takie (0.2) czy świadek powiedział (.) że w grudniu to było: (.) że te raty były uzgodnione w grudniu? (.) czy były uzgodnione wcześniej?	*[The question is this – did the witness say that this took place in December, that these installments were agreed upon in December or were they agreed upon earlier?]*

(4.18)	Original PL/EN talk	Author's verbatim translation into EN
Interpreter:	(0.2) raty były uzgodnione w lipcu. (0.4) świadek powiedział (.) że raty były uzgodnione w lipcu (.) a że datę spotkania lipcowego pamięta wyraźnie (.) dlatego że była ona również wymieniona (0.2) ta data (0.3) w protokole grudniowego spotkania (0.2) tak (.) przepraszam pomyliłem się (0.3) chodziło mi o sierpień.	*[The installments were agreed upon in July. The witness has said that the installments were agreed upon in July, and that he remembers the date of the July meeting because very well because, that date, it was also mentioned, in the minutes of the December meeting… yes, sorry, I made a mistake, I meant August.]*

It is the counsel who begins this episode of interaction. He deploys two pre-expansions. The first one (*the question is this, pytanie jest takie*) is impersonal and includes an announcement that the counsel is going to ask a question. Then, after an appreciable pause (0.2) the counsel continues by asking *whether the witness said that… (czy świadek powiedział, że…)*. The 3rd person singular is used to maintain a formal style of the question, but results in a misleading selection of the next speaker. As the counsel does not expressly refer to a particular interlocutor, the question may be understood as addressed either to the witness, in which case it is supposed to be rendered by the interpreter, or to the interpreter, in which case she would be expected to respond. Evidently, the interpreter chooses the latter and provides a **non-rendition**: she feels selected as the next speaker, hence takes a turn and answers the question on the basis of her own knowledge of the case and probably what she has memorized from the proceedings so far. This example proves that if in a bilingual talk the current speaker is ambiguous about selecting the next speaker, it is the interpreter who identifies herself as the next speaker (understood as not the one to render the primary parties' utterances, but the one who replaces that primary party in speaking).

Furthermore, there are instances in bilingual interaction of the courtroom, in which the interpreter self-selects as the next speaker irrespective of the trajectory of the current communicative act. In other words, when the judge examines the witness through the interpreter, she immediately self-selects as the next speaker in order to announce a problem:

(4.19)	Original PL/EN talk	Author's verbatim translation into EN
Interpreter:	((addressing the judge)): dochodzi dwunasta. ja muszę już iść.	*[It's almost twelve. I have to go.]*

(4.19)	Original PL/EN talk	Author's verbatim translation into EN
Judge:	(0.3) pani musi już iść? =	*[You have to go already?]*
Interpreter:	tak (.) muszę (0.2) bo umówiłam się z moim pracodawcą. ja dzwoniłam do sądu (0.3) i pytałam (0.2) do której trwa rozprawa i powiedziano mi że do dwunastej.	*[Yes, I do because I'm meeting with my employer. I called the court and asked until what time the court session would last and I was told that until 12.]*
Judge:	(0.4) wystarczy nam dziesięć minut.	*[10 minutes is enough for us.]*
Interpreter:	(.) to dobrze (0.2) dobrze...	*[It's good, good.]*

Extract 4.19 is a typical episode in which a **non-rendition** appears. It is the interpreter who begins this episode of interaction: she informs the judge that she will have to leave the court in a short time due to her professional responsibilities at her workplace. The judge, surprised by the interpreter's announcement, echoes the interpreter's words with a rising intonation. The interpreter then elaborates on her first turn and provides more details to justify her need to leave. The judge, by projecting the time necessary to close the examination, implicitly informs her that he consents to her requests. The interpreter confirms that she is grateful for the judge's decision. Strikingly, the interpreter's attitude to the judge's majesty is contrary to what could be expected at an institutional talk. Firstly, it is she who begins the episode of interaction. Secondly, it is she who initiates the closing of the interpreter-mediated interaction, while all pre-closing sequences characterize the judge's talk. Thirdly, she does not use any address terms corresponding to the courtroom talk. Fourthly, neither the first nor the second of her turns includes a trace of request: they are affirmative sentences which announce plans and facts concerning the interpreter. Furthermore, from the point of view of the obligation to keep the non-Polish speaking witness informed, the technical matters that are discussed between the judge and the interpreter cannot be rendered. Moreover, even afterwards, the interpreter does not have time to provide the witness with an interpretation or a summary of her talk with the judge as the trial is continued by the judge.

4.2.2 The primary party self-selects

Extract 4.20 shows that the witness self-selects in response to the interpreter's natural self-selecting as the next speaker:

(4.20)	Original PL/EN talk	Author's verbatim translation into EN
Judge:	uprzedzam pana o obowiązku mówienia <u>prawdy</u>.	*[I advise you of the obligation to tell the truth.]*

(4.20)	Original PL/EN talk	Author's verbatim translation into EN
Interpreter:	(.) you must >tell the truth<. =	
Witness:	((gazing at the interpreter)) = what?	
Interpreter:	(.) you must say the truth.	
Witness:	(.) ye:s…	
Interpreter:	((silence))	

The interpreter self-selects as the next speaker. After a micro-pause she transmits the judge's utterance containing the warning about an obligation on the part of the witness to tell the truth. Nonetheless, the judge uses a set phrase regularly applied on such occasions, while the interpreter resorts to the use of the modal verb *must*. Although the witness is informed of his obligation resulting from the legal requirement, the style of the judge's statement has been altered, a shift from *I* to *you* is introduced, by which a perspective slightly changes: in the interpretation the judge no longer speaks about himself and about his warning addressed to the witness, but about the witness's responsibility. Hence, the interpreter's rendition is straightforward and shortens the distance between the judge and the witness. This encourages the witness to self-select as the next speaker, although he is not expected to take a turn: he addresses the interpreter with a short TCU (*what?*), which also manifests that the witness might have not heard the interpreter's rendition. In reply to that, the interpreter repeats the rendition, hence providing a **zero rendition** of the witness's question, but this time replacing the verb *tell* with *say*, by which a lexical error appears in the interpretation. The error, however, does not unable the witness to understand the rendition which is confirmed by the witness response (*yes*).

Extract 4.21 shows that it is the defendant who self-selects as the next speaker:

(4.21)	Original PL/EN talk	Author's verbatim translation into EN
Defendant:	((to the Judge, very impatiently)) Okey (0.5) may I say something?	
Interpreter:	(.) czy może pan co[ś powiedzieć?	*[Could he say something?]*
Defendant:	[I'm aware of cultural issues in Poland…	
Interpreter:	((addressing the judge)) (xxx)	

The defendant selects the judge as the next speaker to impatiently address him with a nonchalant question. By doing so, the defendant puts the interpreter in a position to render his, and not the judge's question. Moreover, the question is inappropriate in terms of style (deploying a stressed pragmatic marker *okey* at the beginning of the turn, and emphasized *I say* to expressly indicate that now it is his turn to speak). Therefore, when the interpreter naturally self-selects as the next speaker, she attempts to transmit the information that it is not she who has self-selected as the next speaker but the defendant who asks *whether he could say something*; a **reduced rendition** is provided.

Extract 4.22 shows a similar episode of interaction, where it is the respondent who self-selects as the next speaker:

(4.22)	Original PL/EN talk	Author's verbatim translation into EN
Defendant:	(.) anything <u>else</u> (.) stupid to say?	
Interpreter:	((with her mouth open to start interpreting)) (5.0)	

The respondent self-selects as the next speaker to ask a question. However, due to an aggressive style deployed by the respondent inappropriate as for an institutional talk, the interpreter decides to provide a **zero rendition.**

In Extract 4.23 the primary party also self-selects as the next speaker:

(4.23)	Original PL/EN talk	Author's verbatim translation into EN
Witness:	<u>who is</u> the petitioner?	
Interpreter:	((Interpreter makes a head movement to point out an adequate party to the proceedings)) (0.3)	

The witness self-selects as the next speaker to request the interpreter to tell him who the petitioner is. This is probably a consequence of the witness's feeling of being excluded from the interaction as no-one has informed him about the identities of the parties assisting the examination. The interpreter, under the assumption that her explanations could interrupt the trajectory of the proceedings, deploys non-verbal communication to answer the witness's question. As a result, a **non-rendition** is provided.

4.3 Conclusions

The analysis of the turn-taking system at an institutional talk of a bilingual courtroom has shown that the turns are allocated by either the current speaker who selects the next speaker or by the next speaker who self-proclaims as such.

As regards the mechanism of **selecting the next speaker by the current speaker**, it is the judge, as the current speaker, who, by deploying an address form, indicates the next party to speak. If the lawyers are indicated to speak, they immediately respond by taking their turn. In such instances, the interpreter does not interrupt the interaction and takes her turn only when she considers the episode of interaction as completed. Hence, summarized renditions are provided. If the judge (or other representatives of the judiciary) addresses the non-Polish speaking parties, it is the interpreter who takes turn to transmit the message. Hence, although the interpreter is not the next speaker expressly selected by the current speaker, she assumes that she is to speak at a particular instance of the interaction. What is more, as the original self-selecting technique has a potential to fail (in the instances where the judge gazes at the interpreter and not at the selected next-speaker, or the judge selects the next speaker by using court-specific address terms such as: petitioner, defendant, plaintiff, with which a non-Polish speaking party might not identify), it is the interpreter who co-participates in selecting the next speaker. On such occasions, close or extended renditions are provided. When the judge (or the lawyer who examines the witness) expressly selects the interpreter as the next speaker, then reduced or zero renditions are provided, which prove that the interpreters find it problematic when they are requested *to explain* or *translate* the information. Nonetheless, the examples show that the instances, in which the primary parties address the interpreter to speak, are actually the points in the interaction in which the interpreter is to speak anyway, irrespective of her selecting as the next speaker.

The mechanism of selecting the next speaker by the current speaker with the types of renditions attributed to each episode is presented in Tab. 4.1[90]:

As regards the interpreters' renditions, from the above cumulative breakdown it follows that the discussed mechanism does not allow for substituted, two- or multi-part, or non-renditions, while all others can be identified.

90 In the Tables included in Chapters 4 to 9, the types of the interpreters' renditions are shown for each discussed Extract. In the first column a serial number of a given Extract is provided, in the second column the interactant with whom the interpreter co-participates in a particular episode of interaction is indicated. In the subsequent columns the renditions are marked (namely: CR – close renditions, ER – extended renditions, RR – reduced renditions, SBR – substituted renditions, SMR – summarized renditions, TMR – two-part or multi-part renditions, NR – non-renditions, and ZR – zero renditions), all of them, as defined in Chapter 3. If '1' is inserted, it means that a particular rendition has been noted when the interpreter interacted with a party indicated in the second column. E.g. in Extract 4.3 '1' is inserted under CR (close rendition), which means that the interpreter provided a close rendition of the judge's utterance. At the bottom line of the table a total number of particular renditions is shown; '0' indicates that no such rendition was observed during the analysis of the Extracts (Dörnyei 2007: 270).

Tab. 4.1: Next speaker selected by the current speaker

Extract	Renditions / Interactant	CR	ER	RR	SBR	SMR	TMR	NR	ZR
4.1	Judge	0	0	0	0	**1**	0	0	0
4.2	Judge/Lawyer	0	0	0	0	**1**	0	0	0
4.3	Judge	**1**	0	0	0	0	0	0	0
4.4	Judge	**1**	0	0	0	0	0	0	0
4.5	Counsel	0	**1**	0	0	0	0	0	0
4.6	Judge	0	**1**	0	0	0	0	0	0
4.7	Judge	0	0	**1**	0	0	0	0	0
4.8	Judge	0	0	**1**	0	0	0	0	0
4.9	Judge	0	0	**1**	0	0	0	0	0
4.10	Judge	0	0	0	0	0	0	0	**1**
4.11	Judge	0	0	**1**	0	0	0	0	0
Total:		**2**	**2**	**4**	**0**	**2**	**0**	**0**	**1**

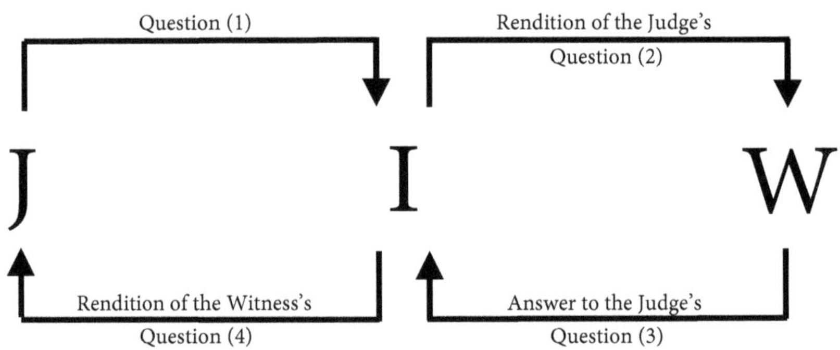

Fig. 4.1: Interaction with close, extended, and reduced renditions

The most commonly followed interaction, appearing when close (Extract 4.3), extended (Extracts 4.5 and 4.6), and reduced (Extracts 4.7 and 4.8) renditions are provided, is as shown in Fig. 4.1[91]:

After each original utterance the interpreter's rendition comes: the judge asks the question, which is rendered by the interpreter to the witness, who answers the question, which in turn is rendered by the interpreter to the judge; the sequence

91 In the Figures included in Chapters 4 to 9, the following abbreviations are applied: C – Counsel, D – Defendant, I – Interpreter, J – Judge, P – Prosecutor, W – Witness.

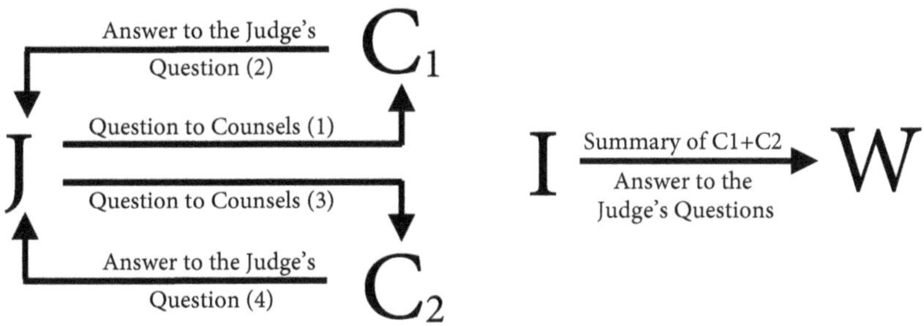

Fig. 4.2: Interaction with summarized renditions

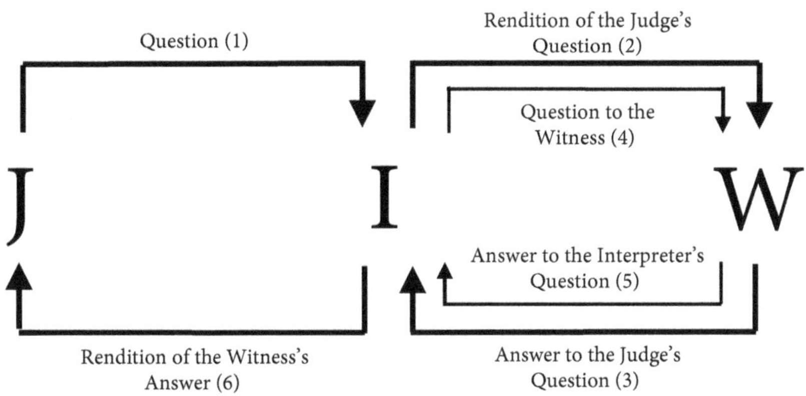

Fig. 4.3: Interaction with reduced renditions

can repeat. Hence, it is a communicative event, where all primary speakers are interactionally and linguistically present, and where the interpreters' renditions are close to the original utterances.

The next in number, appearing when summarized renditions are provided (Extracts 4.1 and 4.2), is the following pattern (Fig. 4.2):

The judge asks the question to one of the counsels and receives an answer, and the same sequence takes place with the other counsel. The interpreter provides the witness with the summary of what the lawyers talk about.

Also, there is one episode with a reduced rendition provided (Extract 4.11), where the pattern of interaction is as follows (Fig. 4.3):

The interpreter renders the judge's question and receives the witness's answer but decides to ask an additional question to the witness; only when the witness

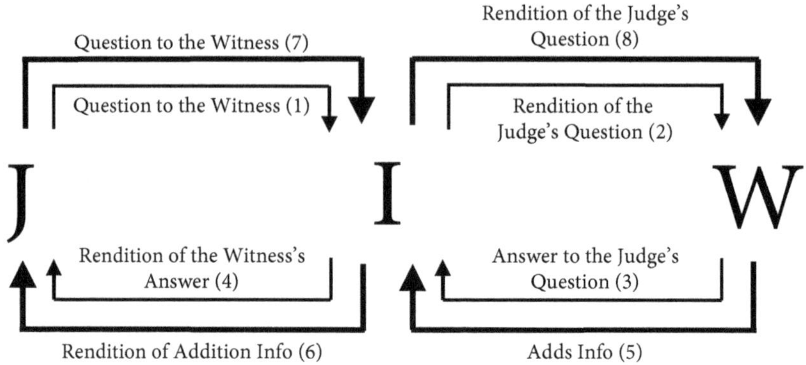

Fig. 4.4: Interaction with close renditions

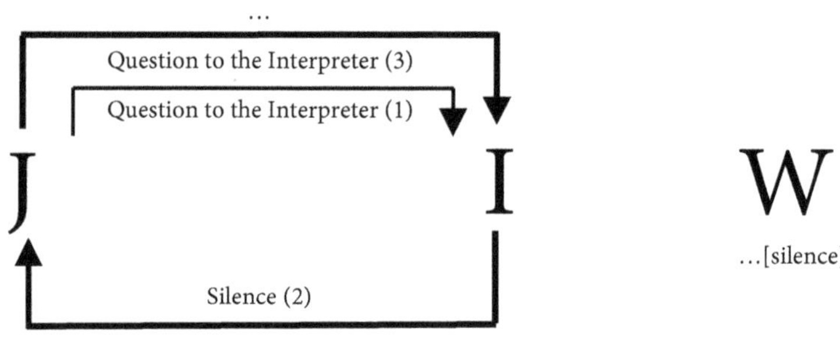

Fig. 4.5: Interaction with zero renditions

answers the interpreter's question, does she render the witness's answer to the judge.

Moreover, three other patterns appear in single episodes, each showing a different rendition. When a close rendition (Extract 4.4) is provided, the following pattern of interaction can be identified (Fig. 4.4):

When the judge expressly selects the plaintiff as the next speaker, the plaintiff is eager to give explanations. That is why he adds information to his previous TCU. However, this also triggers the judge's next question.

When a zero rendition appears (Extract 4.10), the interactants follow the pattern as shown in Fig. 4.5:

The judge does not ask the question; instead, he addresses the interpreter with pre-expansions, to which she responds by remaining silent and only looking at

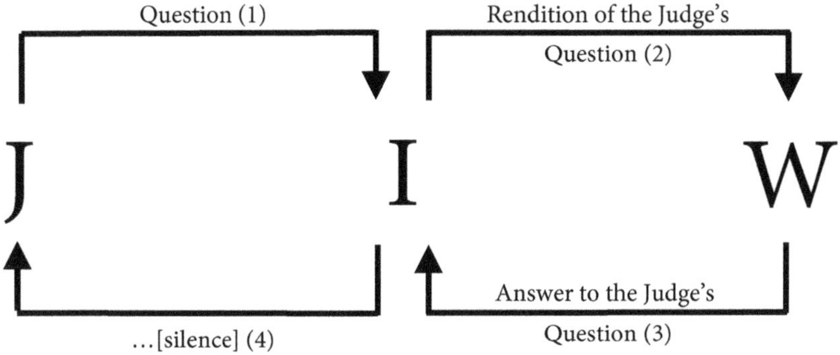

Fig. 4.6: Interaction with reduced and zero renditions

the judge, and waiting for his utterance. Only then does the judge ask a proper question.

Yet another pattern, which appears with reduced renditions (Extract 4.9), and also within the mechanism of the next speaker being self-selected, where a zero rendition is provided (Extract 4.15), is as follows (Fig. 4.6):

This pattern would be a typical question-rendition-answer-rendition interaction if the interpreter rendered the witness's answer to the judge's question. Nevertheless, the interpreter fails to do so under the assumption that either the judge understands the witness's utterance or the judge should not know what the witness is saying due to his rudeness or any other reason relating with the content of the witness's answer.

As far as the mechanism of **self-selecting the next speaker** is concerned, it has been shown that the interpreter naturally selects herself as the next speaker which results from her inherent legal and ethical obligations to facilitate the communication between the primary parties. There are also instances in which the interpreter self-selects as the next speaker according to the question-rendition-answer-rendition order assumed for bilingual interactions, but from what she says, it results that she does not take a turn as the interpreter but that she replaces the primary speaker in answering questions. Even though these instances are caused by the main speaker's fault to unambiguously select the next speaker, the interpreter's responses manifest her partiality. In the episodes where the interpreter self-selects, reduced, substituted, zero, and non-renditions are provided. Where the primary party selects themselves as the next speaker, this is always unexpected and poses an obstacle in the trajectory of the interaction, leading to reduced, zero, or non-renditions; hence they occur when the primary party

Tab. 4.2: Next speaker self-selects

Extract	Renditions / Interactant	CR	ER	RR	SBR	SMR	TMR	NR	ZR
4.12	Judge	0	0	**1**	0	0	0	0	0
4.13	Judge	0	0	0	**1**	0	0	0	0
4.14	Judge	0	0	0	**1**	0	0	0	0
4.15	Judge	0	0	0	0	0	0	0	**1**
4.16	Judge	0	0	0	0	0	0	**1**	0
4.17	Judge	0	0	0	0	0	0	**1**	0
4.18	Counsel	0	0	0	0	0	0	**1**	0
4.19	Judge	0	0	0	0	0	0	**1**	0
4.20	Witness	0	0	0	0	0	0	0	**1**
4.21	Defendant	0	0	**1**	0	0	0	0	0
4.22	Defendant	0	0	0	0	0	0	0	**1**
4.23	Witness	0	0	0	0	0	0	**1**	0
Total:		**0**	**0**	**2**	**2**	**0**	**0**	**5**	**3**

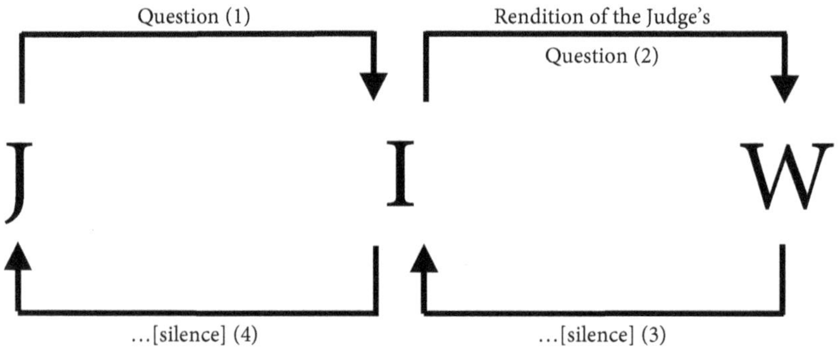

Fig. 4.7: Interaction with reduced, substituted and non-renditions

self-selects to announce inappropriate messages, or when the interpreter's turn includes non-verbal communication. The results are synthesized in Tab. 4.2:

Within the mechanism of the next speaker being self-selected, no instances of close, extended, summarized, or two- or multi-renditions have been detected.

Single episodes, where reduced (Extract 4.12), substituted (Extracts 4.13 and 4.14), and non-renditions (Extract 4.16) are provided, follow the interaction pattern as shown in Fig. 4.7:

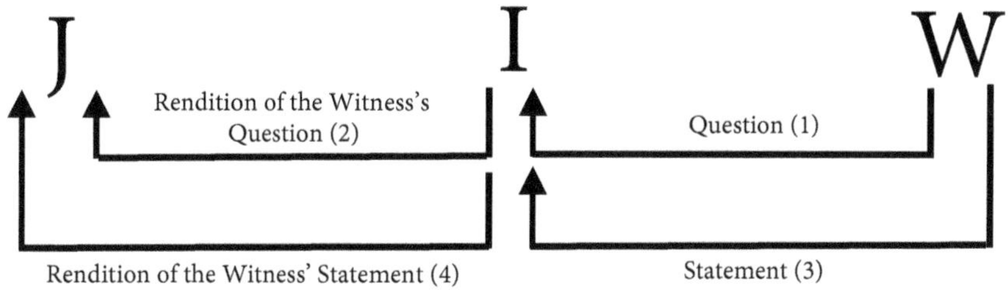

Fig. 4.8: Interaction with reduced renditions

The interpreter renders the judge's utterance, but both the witness and the interpreter, as projected next speakers, do not speak; instead, they nod – the witness to show his approval of what the judge has said, and the interpreter, who in addition looks at the judge, to ensure that he has nothing against them remaining silent. Such a pattern appears in the instances where the judge does not ask (thus no response is required), but instructs the witness about his obligation to tell the truth before the court.

In the remaining seven episodes within the mechanism of next speaker being self-selected, seven different patterns of interaction appear. When a reduced rendition (Extract 4.21) is provided, the interaction is carried out as follows (Fig. 4.8):

The witness asks the question to the interpreter, who passes it to the judge, however, the witness, without waiting for the judge's permission, provides a statement, rendered by the interpreter. This pattern reveals that the interpreter is interactionally submitted to the witness, but his reduced renditions confirm that she dominates the linguistic and cultural aspect of communication.

When non-renditions (Extracts 4.17–4.19, and 4.23) are provided, four different patterns have been identified.

In Extract 4.17 the interaction presents a question-rendition-answer-rendition pattern (Fig. 4.9) until the second question asked by the judge, when the interpreter decides to provide the answer to the question without rendering it to the witness.

In Extract 4.18 the counsel asks the question, it is the interpreter who answers it, without transmitting the message to the witness who is the target recipient (Fig. 4.10).

In Extract 4.19 the interaction shows the instance, in which the interpreter discusses the issues relating to her appearance before the court with the judge,

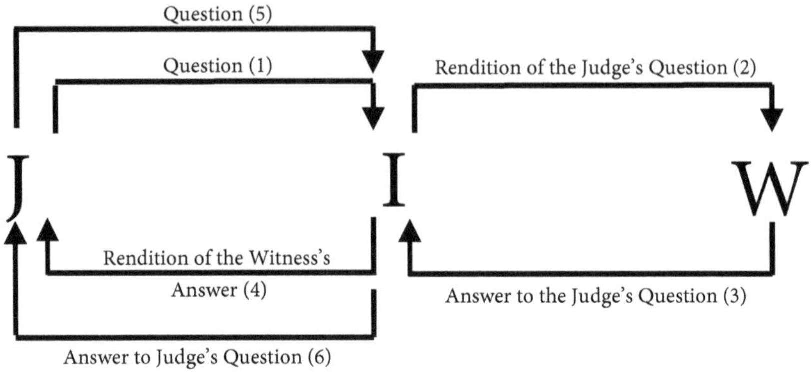

Fig. 4.9: Interaction with non-renditions

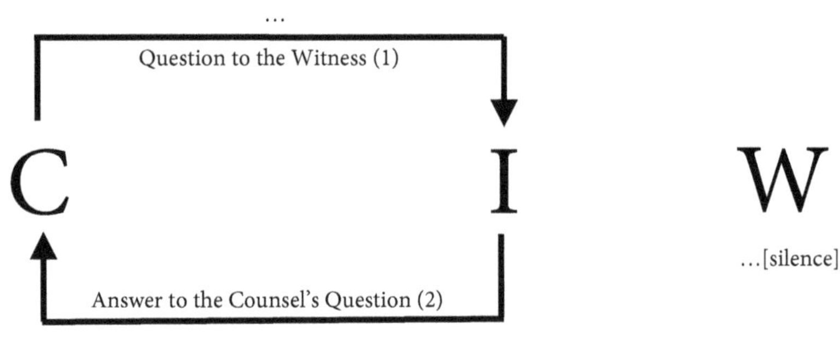

Fig. 4.10: Interaction with non-renditions

while the witness remains excluded from both the interaction and the communicative act (Fig. 4.11).

In Extract 4.23 the witness asks the question to the interpreter who answers by nodding while remaining silent. The judge is not informed by the interpreter about the content of the witness's question (Fig. 4.12).

As regards the interaction patterns with zero renditions, two of them have been detected. In Extract 4.20 the pattern is as shown in Fig. 4.13:

The interaction shows that the witness asks an additional question to the interpreter, and only when she answers it, does the witness answer the judge's original question. If the interpreter does not render this answer, it is not because she fails to do so, but because she deems it unnecessary (as is in the case of short answers: *yes*, *okey*) in the hope that the judge would understand it.

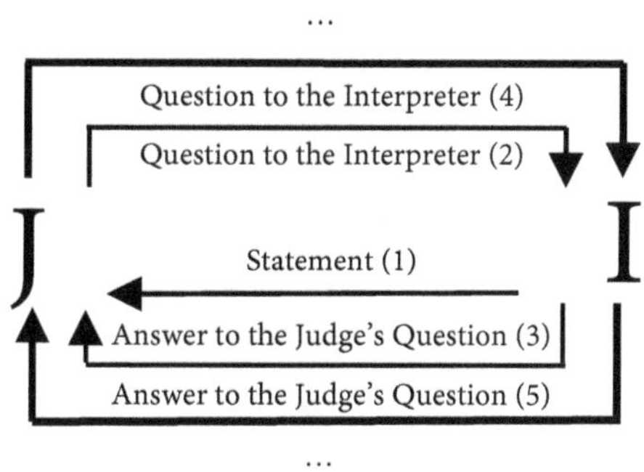

Fig. 4.11: Interaction with non-renditions

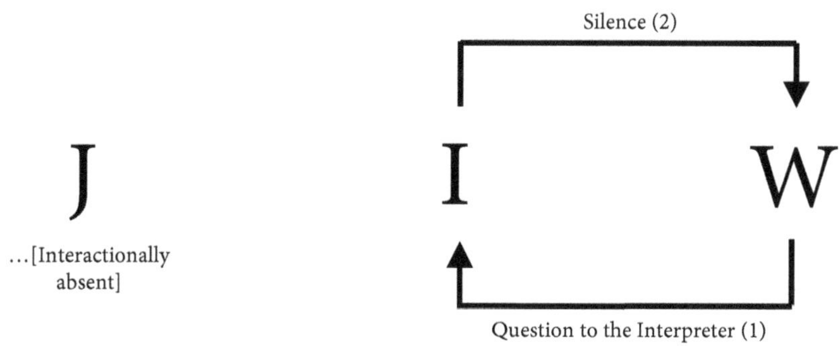

Fig. 4.12: Interaction with non-renditions

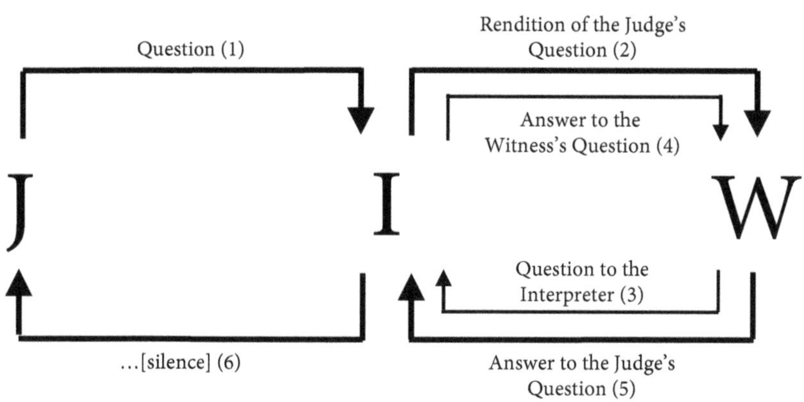

Fig. 4.13: Interaction with zero renditions

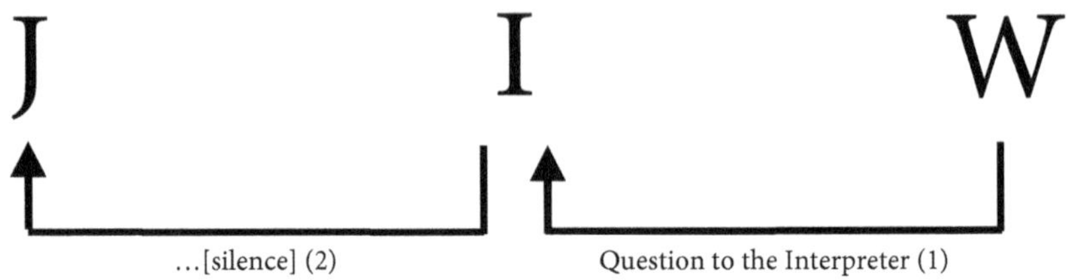

Fig. 4.14: Interaction with zero renditions

In Extract 4.22 the pattern is as shown in Fig. 4.14:

The interpreter's silence is due to the content of the witness's question, which, according to the interpreter, shall not be provided to the judge as inappropriate for the courtroom.

In general, the patterns of interaction for the mechanism of next speaker being selected by the current speaker and next speaker being self-selected are not convergent except in one model. Within the former mechanism, six different patterns have been detected, the most numerous being a bilingual interaction, in which the interpreter's rendition appears after each original utterance. Within the latter, nine patterns have been identified, the largest in number being the interaction in which the interpreter remains silent as reflecting the witness's silence. In this category, an interesting phenomenon appears where non-renditions are provided; these are instances in which the order of speaking is disturbed, it is the witness or the defendant who begins the episode, and on such occasions the interpreters feel alerted and usually non-renditions appear in the communicative event. Therefore, it can be summed up that the findings show that the turn-taking system in the bilingual courtroom is subject to dynamic modifications.

5 Overlaps and gaps in the interpreter-mediated interactions

The analysis proposed in this chapter is aimed at discussing the instances in the courtroom bilingual interactions in which **overlaps** and **gaps** appear. The following are of special interest:

(1) to determine whether they occur in the main speakers' talk, or within the turns taken by the interpreter, or both,
(2) to find out if overlaps and gaps which occur in the main parties' talk are considered as an obstacle to the communicative act by the interpreter and thus the interpreter feels interactionally obliged to intervene to eliminate gaps or overlaps,
(3) to explain the reasons for the possible occurrence of overlaps and gaps in the interpreter's talk, and
(4) to determine what renditions the interpreters provide to tackle overlaps and gaps.

The discussion concerning these issues will contribute to establishing the origin and function of overlaps and gaps in the bilingual interaction, as well as finding out in what way the interpreters actively participate in the communicative event when overlaps and gaps appear.

5.1 Overlaps

As regards overlaps, for the purposes of this study they are classified as **interpreter-included overlaps** and **interpreter-excluded overlaps**, depending on the interpreter's participation or non-participation in the episodes of interaction in which they occur.

5.1.1 Interpreter-included overlaps

In Extract 5.24 the judge starts speaking long before the interpreter completes her turn:

(5.24)	Original PL/EN talk	Author's verbatim translation into EN
Judge:	czy: y::: w międzyczasie (.) pan wyjeżdżał do Stanów czy::: czy:::: czy: jest nieprzerwany (.) cały czas pobyt tutaj?	*[Did you go to the States in the meantime or… or… or is there an uninterrupted stay for the whole time here?]*
Interpreter:	(0.5) so y:: (.) [did you go in the meantime…	
Judge:	[jakieś dłuższe okresy…	*[Any longer periods…]*
Interpreter:	(0.4) to the US in the longer periods o::r (0.3) >did you stay< in Poland permanently?	
Defendant:	(1.0) y:: the only time I left Poland (.) was to go to London for 10 days.	
Interpreter:	(0.2) y::: (0.3) jedynym razem (.) kiedy:: właściwie wyjechałem (.) to było do Londynu na dziesięć dni.	*[The only time I actually left was to go to London for 10 days.]*

The judge initiates this episode of interaction. His TCU consists of a question addressed to the witness as to whether he traveled to the US. The intonation of the question indicates that the TRP is situated exactly when the judge finishes his turn. The interpreter considers the intonation rise as the moment in which she is supposed to take a turn. She starts her rendition with a pragmatic marker *so* produced louder than both the previous speaker's talk and the interpreter's remaining part of the rendition. By this, she not only puts a line between the judge's question and her interpretation, but also emphasizes that she is starting her turn. Nevertheless, as the interpreter stretches the initial part of her turn (*(0.5) so y:: (.)*), the judge takes advantage of a slow pace of the interpreter's talk and overlaps. In the judge's turn, the TCU then appears containing a new element: the judge wants the witness to limit his answer only to the information about the longer periods of his stay in the US. This information is then interpreted as the first, and only then the interpreter goes back to the information included in the FPP. The judge, by adding a new detail to his question asked when the interpreter had already begun her turn, makes the interpreter lose her train of thought. This leads to a slight shift in the meaning (*an uninterrupted stay* vs. *permanent stay*). However, the witness chooses not to provide a projected either *yes* or *no* answer. Instead, he informs the judge where he went and for how long. Apparently, the witness treats the judge's question as a pre-request by which the judge might not want to know whether the witness went abroad, but rather, when and where he went. As regards the interpretation, a **multi-part rendition** is provided.

In Extract 5.25 it is the witness who does not let the interpreter complete rendition:

(5.25)	Original PL/EN talk	Author's verbatim translation into EN
Judge:	krótko (0.2) pytanie >jest na razie< krótkie (0.2) czy cofa pan (.) czy pan je podtrzymuje? =	*[Briefly, the question is brief for the time being, do you withdraw or do you uphold it?]*
Interpreter:	do you withdr[a::w …	
Witness:	[it was withdrawn.	
Interpreter:	(.) pan twierdzi (.) że już to °wycofał°.	*[He states that he has already withdrawn it.]*

The judge requires that the witness shortly answer the question *whether he is withdrawing (his demand) or not.* The interpreter takes turn immediately after the judge completes his question, but manages to say only *do you withdr-*, when the witness starts speaking: he produces an overlap, in which he announces that *it was withdrawn*, and which is probably a consequence of the fact that the witness at least partially understands Polish, thus he does not wait until the end of the interpretation, but answers the question as quickly as possible, in an apparently nonchalant style manifested by the use of passive voice and intonation, in which he stresses the verb *was*; this makes sound the reply *it was withdrawn* as if the witness rejected answering the questions. By this, the witness expresses his anger of finding himself in an uncomfortable situation of the courtroom. The interpreter's reaction to the witness's behavior is that she provides a repair – which forms an **extended rendition** – in order to distance herself from his answer; she achieves this by deploying an indirect style which enables her indicate a real speaker.

In the episode that follows, it is the interpreter who does not wait until the judge completes his turn:

(5.26)	Original PL/EN talk	Author's verbatim translation into EN
Judge:	tak (.) to prawda (0.2) byłem prezesem strony powodowej. (0.2) jak wyglądała realizacja umowy z X dotycząca kontraktu…	*[Yes, it's true, I was the plaintiff's chairman. What did an implementation of the agreement with X regarding the contract look like?]*
Interpreter:	(1.0) what was (0.2) the execution of the contract… =	

(5.26)	Original PL/EN talk	Author's verbatim translation into EN
Judge:	dotycząca kontraktu z marca dwa tysiące siódmego roku: na przygotowanie i przeprowadzenie przetargu na (.) wieloletni kontrakt e:: pilotażowy (0.2) [na zarządzanie i utrzymanie dró::g oparty na wskaźnikach…	*[… regarding the contract of March 2007 for preparing and carrying out a tender for a multi-year pilot contract involving the management and maintenance of roads based on indicators...]*
Interpreter:	[for the performance of the proje:ct of y:: the road buildi:ng (.) based on indexes (.) that's >the name of the< who:le project (0.3) how was the settlement of this project done.	

In Extract 5.26 the judge's turn consists of four TCUs: *yes, it's true*, *I was the the plaintiff's chairman*, and *what did the implementation of the agreement with X regarding the contract look like*. The first three TCUs constitute the text which the judge dictates to be included in the minutes written by the court clerk, and only the fourth is addressed to the witness. Logically, the interpreter attempts to render only the last TCU. The judge—assured by the interpreter's intonation and suspended rendition that it is his turn to speak—takes the next turn to continue asking the question. The interpreter, hearing that the judge's question would be complex, overlaps with her rendition, certainly in order to manage to keep up with the information provided by the judge. This, however, makes the interpreter confuse an original *agreement with X concerning the contract* with *the contract*. As a result, a **reduced rendition** is provided.

The next episode is an example of the judge's and interpreter's reciprocally produced overlaps:

(5.27)	Original PL/EN talk	Author's verbatim translation into EN
Judge:	czego >nie jest w stanie samo[dzielnie załatwić<?	*[What is it that she is not able to take care of by herself?]*
Interpreter:	[help is needed for [what things?	
Judge:	[ale chodzi mi o żonę (0.3) czego żona nie jest w stanie zał[atwić samodzielnie?	*[But I am referring to your wife, what is it that your wife is not able to take care of by herself?]*
Interpreter:	[what >are the activities that your wife is not able to do<? =	
Judge:	na przykład planowanie zakupów… =	*[For example planning shopping…]*
Interpreter:	= is she able [to plan shopping?	

(5.27)	Original PL/EN talk	Author's verbatim translation into EN
Judge:	[ale samodzielnie (0.3) czy żona może w ogóle samodzielnie wyjść na: dwór (0.2) i samodzielnie wrócić do domu?	*[But by herself. Is your wife, in general, able to go outside by herself and come back home by herself?]*
Interpreter:	(.) is your wife (.) is [she…	
Judge:	[sama. =	*[By herself.]*
Interpreter:	= capable of going out and (.) coming back home by herself?	

In Extract 5.27 the judge asks the question in which he explicitly refers to the witness's wife (*what is it that* **she** *is not able…*). The interpreter starts interpreting before the judge completes his turn which is due to the fact that she is able to project what the ending of a current TCU would be. Nonetheless, at the moment the interpreter begins rendition, the judge inserts expansion (*ale samodzielnie, but by herself*) in his question. It is unexpected by the interpreter who interprets the judge's question without the inserted information. This makes the judge overlap to attract the interpreter's attention to the missing word which for this episode of interaction is important as the judge has to become acquainted with the current situation of the parties to the proceedings. In her next turn, the interpreter includes all the information for which the judge has asked in his turn. Next, the judge, with no appreciable pause, expands his sequence by giving an example (*planning shopping*) of an activity which he is asking about. The interpreter renders the judge's question, but the judge does not let her finish and overlaps twice with her turns where he again underlines the word *independently* by which he indicates that this is the key concept in his questions. In this extract, the judge produces his talk as if there was no interpreter, no non-Polish speaking witness, and no need to interpret the questions; for the judge it is not the act of communication but the question that is an end in itself. Nonetheless, the interpreter – by way of a **multi-part rendition** manages to transmit all the information included in the judge's questions to the witness.

Similarly, the next example shows a situation of overlapping produced collaboratively by the judge and the interpreter:

(5.28)	Original PL/EN talk	Author's verbatim translation into EN
Judge:	i czy dzisiaj (0.2) jeszcze raz (0.3) po raz trzeci (.) sąd pyta (0.2) [proszę powiedzieć.	*[And today once again, for the third time, the court asks, could you say.]*

(5.28)	Original PL/EN talk	Author's verbatim translation into EN
Interpreter:	[and today (.) you are asked for the third time [if you...	
Judge:	[i ostatni... =	*[And the last one...]*
Interpreter:	= and the last (.) if you withdraw.	

The interpreter starts her turn at the moment of the first possible completion of the judge's TCU (*the judge asks*) as she cannot project that the judge would expand the sequence by adding *could you say*. Then, the judge starts his next turn when the interpreter has not yet completed her talk. In response to that, the interpreter, with no gap between the judge's and her own turn, starts interpreting the judge's overlapping utterance. This episode of interaction is a battle—between the judge and the interpreter—for taking a turn. The judge wrongly understands the interpreter's taking a turn as her attempt to interrupt, nonetheless, she starts interpreting because she is convinced that the judge has already completed his turn. Another explanation for the judge's overlaps is that he speaks English which enables him to follow the interpretation and ask about these elements which he considers necessary and which have not been included in the rendition. Yet another explanation is that the judge decides to ask about another element but the interpreter has already begun interpreting; hence, there is no other way out but to interject in order to add a new detail. As a consequence, the overlaps between the interpreter's and the judge's utterances appear, and the interpreter provides a **two-part rendition**.

The episode below shows the overlaps produced collaboratively by the witness and the interpreter:

(5.29)	Original PL/EN talk	Author's verbatim translation into EN
Witness:	(.) <u>operational</u> problems.... =	
Interpreter:	= proble[my operacyjne...	*[Operational problems...]*
Witness:	[because [of delays of flights...	
Interpreter:	[z powodu:::...=	*[...due to...]*
Witness:	= ye:s. =	
Interpreter:	ta:k (0.3) problemy operacyjne polegające na: opóźnieniach lotów.	*[Yes..., operational problems consisting of flight delays.]*

The witness produces a TCU consisting of an explanation of the current situation: it is *operational problems* that are raised in this turn. The interpreter perceives the witness' suspending of his voice as a possible completion of his turn, thus she renders the turn. However, the witness expands his sequence by adding a post-expansion in which he elaborates on his explanations regardind a reason for the problems referred to in the FPP. The interpreter does not let the witness finish his turn, probably because she projects that the witness's TCU will be short. Although the witness interrupts her turn to say *ye:s.*, she is not confused and continues interpreting in the next turn. In other words, both speakers are cooperating with each other: the witness produces very short utterances to make the interpretation task easier for the interpreter who provides a **multi-part rendition**. However, contrary to the parties' intentions, the original message is modified: *operational problems due to flight delays* vs. *operational problems consisting of flight delays.*

5.1.2 Interpreter-excluded overlaps

Extract 5.30 is an example of overlaps produced collaboratively by the judge and the counsel:

(5.30)	**Original PL/EN talk**	**Author's verbatim translation into EN**
Judge:	a chodzi o ogrzewanie (.) [tak?	*[This refers to heating, yes?]*
Counsel:	[nie (0.2) o gotowanie.	*[No, cooking.]*
Judge:	(.) aha::: (.) o gotowanie (0.3) rozumiem (.) że pan nie gotu[je?	*[Aha, cooking. I understand that you cook?]*
Counsel:	[czy pan gotuje samodzielnie?	*[Do you cook by yourself?]*
Interpreter:	(xxx)	

The episode begins with the talk between the judge and the counsel. The judge requests confirmation of his understanding of the information that he received in the previous episode of interaction (*this refers to heating, yes?*), where the post-expansion *yes* occurs after a micro-pause. The counsel projects the completion of the TCU before he can hear the post-expansion, thus he overlaps with his turn, which is a dispreferred no-answer, unexpected by the judge. Interestingly, in the next turn the judge admits his failure to properly understand the information about the activity (*heating* vs. *cooking*) by the pre-expansion *aha* and post-expansion *I understand that you cook?* In his next turn, the counsel reiterates in overlapping the judge's question. In this episode of interaction, the interpreter is completely absent from the act of communication, which can be due to two reasons. Firstly, both the judge and the counsel speak simultaneously and dynamically, and secondly, the balance is shaken between the judge's and counsel's behavior: the counsel is arrogant towards the judge who stays calm and seems not to notice the counsel's curt tone. As a consequence, the interpreter chooses not to interfere. This fragment of the interaction is never rendered by the interpreter (a **zero rendition** is provided).

In the example below the interpreter also steps aside when the primary speakers argue:

(5.31)	Original PL/EN talk	Author's verbatim translation into EN
Petitioner's lawyer:	proszę pana (0.2) mówiąc o zdradach rzekomych pana X (.) powiedział pan (.) że o jednej dowiedział się od Y (.) o jednej od Z. =	*[Sir, when you speak about the alleged infidelity of X, you said that you learned about one from Y, and about another one from Z.]*
Respondent's lawyer:	= nie – (0.2) o jednej się dowiedział od partne:ra (.) [tak powiedział.	*[No, he learned about one from the partner, he said so.]*
Petitioner's lawyer:	[czy od partnera (.) przepraszam (.) a o innej że (.) trzeciej jakby (0.2) że widział inną (0.3) co mam >przez to rozumieć<? =	*[Or from the partner, I'm sorry, and about another one, that, the third one, that he saw another one. How should I understand this?]*
Interpreter:	= when you said about Z cheating (0.2) you said that one you learnt from your partner (.) one from X and one you witnessed?	
Witness:	yhm.	
Interpreter:	what do you mean by that?	
Witness:	e::::: (.) the one I witnessed?	
Interpreter:	((nodding)) o tej (.) którą widziałem (0.2) tak. =	*[About the one I saw, yes.]*
Witness:	= yes.	
Interpreter:	tak.	*[Yes.]*

The interpreter patiently waits until the petitioner's and respondent's lawyers finish their argument which interactionally covers three turns. The transition space between the first turn in which the petitioner's lawyer speaks and the second belonging to the respondent's lawyer is reduced to a minimum, while an overlap occurs between this second turn and the next produced again by the petitioner's lawyer. Evidently, the main speakers do not leave space for the interpreter to take her turn. Therefore, the interpreter patiently waits for such a space, which occurs after the petitioner's lawyer's completion of his TCU, when he asks *how should I understand that*. This question is logically addressed to the witness, hence the interpreter starts her turn, but the problem is that both lawyers discussed many details so the interpreter feels obliged to include all of them in her rendition. She achieves that goal by proposing a hybrid of what she can conclude from both lawyers' talks. Evidently, she takes over the responsibility to question the witness about the details and establish an identity of the persons the participants are talking about. Moreover, the lawyer's attitude towards the interpreter's position, as well as a humbling response on the part of the witness (*yhm*) causes the interpreter not to hesitate to expand her talk with the witness. She does so when she asks the witness *what he means by yhm*, and when she changes the intonation of the witness's answer: the witness uses an increasing, question-type intonation with a clearly audible question mark at the end, while the interpreter's rendition is affirmative as to the intonation. Also, the interpreter adds a particle *yes* to the rendition of the witness answer, which contributes to an impression that the witness is pretty sure of his answer, which is a direct opposite of what the witness actually says. As regards overlaps, a **summarized rendition** is provided.

5.2 Gaps

The discussed episodes of interaction present **interpreter-created gaps**, **primary party-created gaps**, as well as **multiple gaps**.

5.2.1 Interpreter-created gaps

In the following episode the judge asks the lawyers representing the parties to the proceedings whether they want an oath given by a witness who is to be questioned/examined in a moment:

(5.32)	**Original PL/EN talk**	**Author's verbatim translation into EN**
Judge:	co do przyrzeczenia…?	*[In terms of the oath?]*
Lawyer 1:	(.) dziękuje[my.	*[Thank you]*
Lawyer 2:	[dziękujemy.	*[Thank you]*
Judge:	bez przyrzeczenia…	*[Without an oath]*
Interpreter:	((silence)) (7.0)	

In Extract 5.32 the lawyers, in overlapping utterances, respond to the judge's question. What is more, they both use the we-inclusive form, which is a probable reason for the interpreter's failure to interpret: she remains silent as from the point of view of the interaction she is not covered by the concept of *us*, comprising only the two lawyers. The interpreter thus is implicitly excluded (a **zero rendition** is provided) from the interaction, and she grants her consent to that by not saying anything.

Similarly, in Extract 5.33 the interpreter remains silent when the witness responds to the judge's explanations:

(5.33)	**Original PL/EN talk**	**Author's verbatim translation into EN**
Judge:	(0.3) <przepraszam> (.) ale to jest ważne dla ustalenia <u>tego</u> (.) czy pan jest osobą <u>bliską</u> dla którejkolwiek ze stron postępowania.	*[I am sorry but it is important to determine if you are a close relative to the parties to the proceedings…]*

(5.33)	Original PL/EN talk	Author's verbatim translation into EN
Interpreter:	(.) I'm sorry for this question (.) but this is necessary to determine if you are closely related to any of the parties?	
Witness:	((nodding)) thank you.	
Interpreter:	((silence)) (5.0)	

The judge begins his turn with an appreciable pause (0.3), after which he expresses his sorry for having asked the witness a delicate question. Astonishingly for the circumstances of an institutional talk, the judge emphasizes his possible embarrassment even more visibly when he produces the second TCU, considerably longer than the first one, which confirms that the judge, as a party to the interaction, feels uncomfortable as regards the type of questions he I asking. Nevertheless, the interpreter has no problem with rendering the judge's question; there are no appreciable pauses in her talk, instead, two micro-pauses occur, which only separate the TCUs and determine a regular pace of her turn. Afterwards, the witness' turn consists of thanking the judge for his attitude towards him (*thank you*), after which the interpreter's completely silent turn occurs. The reason for providing a **zero rendition** of the witness's turn is that either the interpreter considers the witness's words completely comprehensible to the judge, or the interpreter assumes that the witness's response is irrelevant – she is surprised by the witness's reaction, which is not as straightforward as it would be by only nodding or nodding and providing a short affirmative response *okey*.

The following episodes show that when one of the parties deploys universally known words, the interpreter remains silent in the assumption that all interactants understand these elements of the talk.

Such is an example where the defendant responds to the judge's question by using a particle *okey*:

(5.34)	Original PL/EN talk	Author's verbatim translation into EN
Judge:	i teraz sąd pana wysłucha w przedmiocie dwóch pana wniosków.	*[And now you will be heard concerning your two motions.]*
Interpreter:	(.) and now you will be heard and asked questions about your two motions. =	
Defendant:	= okey.	
Interpreter:	((silence))	

In the extract … the judge begins the communicative act by informing the witness *that he will be heard as regards his two motions.* The interpreter renders the message twice: first she says that the witness will be heard, and then she becomes more specific and says that the witness will be asked questions about his two motions. The defendant, who has just been informed, thus the judge does not expect any response on his part, says *okey*. The interpreter remains silent (hence, provides a **zero rendition**), which may be due to the interpreter's assumption that, firstly, the judge does not wait for any response, and secondly that even without the interpretation, the judge understands the defendant's answer. Yet thirdly, the interpreter could presume that the interjection *okey* is inappropriate at an institutional talk, especially when deployed by interlocutors others than the judge.

Similarly, the subsequent example shows the witness who responds *okey* to the judge's question, and the interpreter who fails to render it:

(5.35)	**Original PL/EN talk**	**Author's verbatim translation into EN**
Judge:	zrozumiał pan?	*[Did you understand?]*
Witness:	(.) okey	
Interpreter:	((silence))	

In Extract 5.35 the judge asks the witness whether he understood (what has already been said). The witness (who apparently understands Polish), without letting the interpreter take her turn, responds *okey*, and the interpreter does not interfere (provides a **zero rendition**) as the party uses internationalism, already well-rooted in Polish.

The interpreter also remains silent when other generally known elements appear in the party's talk:

(5.36)	**Original PL/EN talk**	**Author's verbatim translation into EN**
Judge:	kim pan jest z zawodu?	*[What's your profession?]*
Interpreter:	(0.2) <u>so</u> - what's your profession?	
Defendant:	(.) I work for X.	
Interpreter:	((silence))	

The judge asks the defendant about his profession. The interpreter renders the questions after an appreciable pause (0.2) and a particle *so*, which probably serves as a confirmation of the interpreter's comprehension of the judge's question. When the defendant responds, the interpreter, probably under the assumption that the judge is following the defendant's answer and knows the name of the company for which the defendant works, remains silent (provides a **zero rendition**).

The episodes which follow include the interpreter's silences, which are filled with non-verbal communication.

In Extract 5.37 below the interpreter remains silent in the instances of interaction in which she is supposed to speak:

(5.37)	**Original PL/ES talk**	**Author's verbatim translation into EN**
Judge:	wiek pana? (.) ile pan ma lat?	*[Your age, how old are you?]*
Interpreter:	((gazing meaningfully at the witness, but remaining silence))	
Witness:	(0.2) trzydzieści sześć (.) treinta y seis =	*[Thirty three, thirty three]*
Interpreter:	(5.0)	
Judge:	= zawód?	*[Profession?]*
Interpreter:	(.) profesión? =	*[Profession?]*
Witness:	= ingeniero =	*[Engineer]*
Interpreter:	= inżynier	*[Engineer]*

The interpreter fails to render the judge's question about the witness's age (hence, provides a **zero rendition**). The Spanish-speaking witness, however, who apparently speaks basic Polish, answers the question: the first numeral is provided in Polish, and then in Spanish. The judge's next question about the profession and the witness's answer transmitted by the interpreter are close renditions. In this particular interaction, the interpreter's silence is not a manifestation of her lack of competence; it is rather her knowledge that the witness understands Polish that makes her not translate the judge's question. Only then, however, does she recall that she is in the courtroom to provide interpreting services irrespective of the witness's level of Polish. Thus, subsequent turns are rendered immediately and with no hesitation.

Extract 5.38 shows that the interpreter is on the verge of starting interpretation, but she resigns from proceeding:

(5.38)	**Original PL/EN talk**	**Author's verbatim translation into EN**
Respondent:	(.) anything <u>else</u> (.) stupid to say?	
Interpreter:	((with her mouth open to start interpreting)) (5.0)	

The respondent asks a question to which there is no interactional response on the part of the interpreter who remains silent although immediately after the respondent completes his turn, the interpreter is evidently ready to render the question. Nonetheless, she resigns from interpreting (a **zero rendition** is provided) which might be caused by several factors. Firstly, the interpreter might assume that the respondent's question is inconsistent with the nature of the trial, that is, that the issue raised in the question deviates from the main trajectory of the trial. Secondly, the interpreter might decide that in the courtroom, the respondent is supposed only to answer the questions, while it is the judge's and other representatives' of the judiciary privilege to ask questions. Thirdly, and most importantly, the interpreter perceives the respondent's question as improper for the formal interaction of the courtroom.

In Extract 5.39, the interpreter also remains silent when her turn comes:

(5.39)	**Original PL/EN talk**	**Author's verbatim translation into EN**
Witness:	who is the petitioner?	
Interpreter:	((Interpreter makes a head movement to point out an adequate party to the proceedings)) (0.3)	

In the above episode of interaction, it is the witness who asks the interpreter to tell him who the petitioner is. It results from the fact that the witness may feel confused with his very obligation to appear before the court, and thus, he might not be aware of the identities of the participants in the proceedings. The interpreter, focused on listening to the interaction between the judge and the lawyers, in order not to become distracted or probably to spare time, discreetly indicates the person who is the petitioner (an unspoken **non-rendition** is produced).

5.2.2 Primary-party created gaps

Extract 5.40 shows the gap naturally produced by the witness:

(5.40)	**Original PL/EN talk**	**Author's verbatim translation into EN**
Judge:	co było przyczyną wyprowadze:nia albo te:ż (.) e::: rozstania stron?	*[what was the reason for moving out or [the parties'] splitting up?]*
Interpreter:	(.) what was the reason why one of them (.) moved out o:r split up?	
Witness::	(0.5) X got a girlfriend. =	
Interpreter:	= X miał dziewczynę.	*[X had a girlfriend.]*

The judge asks about *the reason for one of the party's moving out or splitting up.* When the interpreter's turn to speak comes, she needs a micro-pause to think of the rendition. When the witness is to take his turn to answer the question, he starts speaking after a long (0.5) pause. The witness's silence is produced out of the necessity to reveal his friend's secret, which might have been a possible reason for the breakdown of his friend's marriage. The interpreter renders the witness's response immediately after it occurs, providing a **close rendition**; by doing so, she shows her neutrality which makes her distance herself from the witness's talk.

Similarly, in the example below the witness who produces a silence which is not reproduced in the interpreter's rendition:

(5.41)	Original PL/EN talk	Author's verbatim translation into EN
Judge:	czy pan wie (.) od kiedy powód >spotykał się z inną kobietą<? =	*[Do you know for how long the petitioner was seeing another woman?]*
Interpreter:	= do you know for how long (.) the petitioner was seeing another woman?	
Witness:	(1.0) he met her (.) when e:: we were on holiday in November that year e::h:: (0.2) I would say (.) <probably> one month (0.2) month and a half?	
Interpreter:	(.) poznał ją jak y:: byliśmy: na <wakacjach> w listopadzie >prawdopodobnie tego roku< tak że prawdopodobnie parę miesię:cy.	*[He met her when we were on holiday in November probably that year, yes, so probably for a couple of months.]*

The judge asks the witness *how long the petitioner was seeing another woman* and the interpreter starts her turn immediately after the judge completes his turn. The witness needs time (1.0) to begin answering the judge's question. The silences in the witness's detailed response, composed of two TCUs (*he met her when we were on holiday in November that year* and *I would probably say one and a half months*), are justified by his need to recall the corresponding information. What is more, these silences are enriched with vocalic fillers (*e::* and *e::::h::*) and a modality *I would probably say* to express his uncertainty as to the exact period of time. In the interpreter's talk there are no appreciable pauses: the interpreter's turn begins with a micro-pause after which she reproduces the witness's response: she repeats an adverb *probably* twice, where the first use is an equivalent of *I would* while the second one is a **close rendition** of the witness's words.

Extract 5.42 is yet another example in which the silence in the witness's talk is absent in the interpreter's rendition:

(5.42)	Original PL/EN talk	Author's verbatim translation into EN
Judge:	czy łączy pana z którąkolwiek ze stron stosunek równorzędny (0.2) stosunek małżeński (.) związek partnerski? =	*[Are you in an equivalent relationship, matrimonial relationship, registered partnership with any of the parties?]*

(5.42)	Original PL/EN talk	Author's verbatim translation into EN
Interpreter:	= do you have an intimate relationship with any of the parties?	
Witness:	(0.3) e::::: (0.2) I'mh:::: no:::::... =	
Interpreter:	= nie.	*[No.]*

The judge refers in his question to a list of three possible ways in which the witness can be linked with any of the parties to court proceedings. The interpreter begins her turn immediately after the judge completes his turn. However, what the interpreter says is not a close rendition of the judge's talk, but a summary of the list proposed by the judge: she puts all the kinds of relationships under an umbrella term of *an intimate relationship*. The use of a summary makes the interpreter's TCU considerably shorter than the original question. The witness seems to be surprised that the TRP has come so quickly: before he produces a negative answer, a series of interactional elements occur: an appreciable pause (0.3), a vocalic filler *e:::::*, the second appreciable pause (0.2), and the second vocalic filler *I'mh::::*. Only then does the witness provide a possible answer (*no:::::...*), which, however, is weak and suspended; this proves that either the witness is still thinking of the answer, or he actually does not know anything about the persons' relationship, or, he does not want to publicly reveal the facts concerning other people's lives. The interpreter begins her rendition just after she realizes that the suspension is a TRP, that is, a point in the witness's turn where a possible completion occurs. She renders a short and categorically sounding *no* response, thus providing a **close rendition** even though she is far from the witness's hesitation.

Extracts 5.43–5.44 include filling the silences in the witness's turn in response to the interpreter's rendition:

(5.43)	Original PL/EN talk	Author's verbatim translation into EN
Judge:	proszę usiąść...	*[Please sit down]*
Interpreter:	(0.2) yhm... let's sit down.	
Witness:	((takes a seat))	
Interpreter:	((takes a seat))	

The judge's request (*please sit down*) is impersonal hence is perceived as addressed to those standing. The interpreter changes the grammatical form of the judge's request (*let's sit down*), however softened by the use of *we–inclusive*. As a result, the non-Polish speaking witness receives a clear indication as to *what* he is supposed to do (an **extended rendition** is provided). Nonetheless, the interpreter's rendition may be considered a lack of impartiality on her part: she includes herself within what is called *a private client of the Court* thus she explicitly positions herself on one of the sides. Paradoxically, when the interpreter identifies with the non-Polish speaking party as shown in this extract, she helps the interaction to achieve its aim: the witness takes a seat.

Similarly, the example below shows a silence as a reaction to the interpreter's substituted rendition:

(5.44)	**Original PL/EN talk**	**Author's verbatim translation into EN**
Judge:	okey… (.) dobrze (0.2) rozumiem (0.3) do:brze (.) o ubezwłasnowolnienie (0.2) dobrze (.) dziękuję panu (.) na razie.	*[OK. Good, I understand, good, about incapacitation, good, thank you for now.]*
Interpreter:	((sitting down)) (0.2) please (0.2) take a seat…	
Witness:	((takes a seat))	
Interpreter:	((takes a seat))	

The judge announces the closing of the talk with the witness. The first signal can be found in the TCU which opens his turn: *okey…* does not belong to a formal register required from the judge in institutional talks, thus in this instance its use is supposed to disengage the judge from the talk. Secondly, the judge repeatedly confirms that he has understood the message passed to him in a previous episode of interaction. Only then the last TCU in the judge's turn occurs: *thank you for now*. The beginning of this TCU projects that the closing is definite, however, when, after a micro-pause, the judge adds *for now*. It proves that a closing of one particular episode of interaction, can also announce an opening of the next episode of interaction, which is not however specified as to the time and, possibly, the date. The interpreter does not render the judge's words. She completely omits the judge's first six TCUs (*okey, good, I understand, good, of incapacitation, good*) and reads the judge's seventh and eight TCU (thank you as for now) as permission to disengage from the turn-taking. Hence, she takes a seat and sums up the judge's utterance whose words *thank you for now* are considered by the interpreter as the end of the questions referred to the witness. In response to that, the witness takes a seat; he does so not because the judge expressly has said what to do, but as a consequence of the interpreter's **non-rendition**.

5.2.3 Multiple gaps

Silences can be produced collaboratively by interactants who are involved in non-verbal activities. In Extract 5.45 the gaps are filled in by both the witness's and interpreter's body movement:

(5.45)	Original PL/EN talk	Author's verbatim translation into EN
Judge:	(.) czy >jakiś dowód< tożsamości? =	*[Any identity document?]*
Interpreter:	= any identity card (.) passport?	
Witness:	((the witness gives the passport to the interpreter)) (1.5)	
Interpreter:	((the interpreter takes the passport from the witness, comes to the judge's table, gives the document to the judge)) (15.0)	
Judge:	(0.2) hm::: okazuje paszpo:rt…	*[He presents a passport…]*
Interpreter:	((takes the passport back from the judge and [gives it back to the witness)) (5.0)	
Judge:	[wiek pana i zawód?	*[Your age and your profession?]*

The judge opens the episode of interaction: he asks the witness for his identity document. The interpreter begins her turn immediately after the judge completes his question: in her services she wants to be attentive to the degree that she eagerly specifies a whole range of possible documents, which might be helpful with establishing the witness's identity. In response to the rendition of the question, the witness does not react verbally; instead, he gives the passport to the interpreter. In her next turn, the interpreter takes the passport from the witness, comes to the judge's table and gives the document to the judge. The judge confirms the presentation of the document, after which the interpreter takes the passport back from the judge, and, when he gives it to the witness, the judge begins his turn where he asks the witness about his age and profession. All the three gaps (lasting 1.5, 15.0, and 5.0, respectively) occur in the witness's and interpreter's turn. In addition, it is the witness who begins the silent turns in the interaction, and the interpreter responds by deploying the same channel of communication (**non-renditions** are provided). The judge interrupts the silence (*hm::: he presents a passport*), but this is not interpreted; the interpreter probably assumes that the judge's words are supposedly addressed to the court clerk who is taking the minutes of the trial. Again, it is the judge who intends to recover the verbal interaction by asking the question about the witness's age and occupation.

A similar interaction is shown in Extract 5.46, but this time there is a balance between the verbal and non-verbal communication, thus the silences are episodic but still, when they occur, they are appreciable pauses:

(5.46)	Original PL/EN talk	Author's verbatim translation into EN
Judge:	chciałam zapytać świadka o godność, (0.3) czy ma pan jakiś dokument tożsamości? =	*[I wanted to ask the witness for their name, do you have any identity document?]*
Interpreter:	what is your name? do you have any identification document?	
Witness:	(xxx) I have got a: passport. =	
Interpreter:	= ma [paszport.	*[He has a passport.]*
Witness:	[((the witness gives the passport to the interpreter)) (1.0)	
Interpreter:	((the interpreter takes a document from the witness and presents it to the judge)) (9.0)	

The judge initiates the episode of interaction by asking the witness about his name and identity document. The interpreter renders the judge's question. The witness answers the question and the interpreter interprets it. Before the interpreter completes her turn, the witness gives her his passport. The interpreter takes it and presents to the judge. These two turns (lasting 1.0 and 9.0, respectively) create pauses in the interaction. Both gaps are needed for the witness's and the interpreter's handling of the witness's passport (**non-renditions** appear). The interpreter's silence when she takes the document from the witness and provides it to the judge may result from her lack of comfort which is manifested by a grammatical shift from *I* to *he* when she renders the witness' statement that he has a passport. By doing so, the interpreter lets the witness to understand where she is positioning herself: she belongs to the judicial institution and thus she deepens a distance between herself and the witness.

In the example that follows there is also a gap which is produced collaboratively by the witness and the interpreter:

(5.47)	Original PL/EN talk	Author's verbatim translation into EN
Witness:	(.) y después lo máximo que tuvimos que pagar era lo más cerca a X ezlotys. =	*[And then the highest price that we had to pay was X zlotys.]*
Interpreter:	= a jeśli dobrze pamiętam (.) najwyższą ceną jaką musieliśmy <zapłacić> (.) najwyższa cena to było: (.) e::: X złotych. =	*[And as far as I remember, the highest price that we had to pay… The highest price it was eee… X zlotys.]*
Witness:	((smiling to the interpreter)): = około… (2.0)	*[… about…]*
Interpreter:	((smiling at the judge, and then, laughing nervously)) (1.5) °mniej więcej°	*[… more or less]*

In the second turn of the above extract, the interpreter attempts to provide a close rendition of the witness's answer, with one exception: the witness provides an approximate amount of money while the interpreter omits this element and gives an exact sum. The Spanish-speaking witness, who evidently understands Polish, prompts the interpreter with the omitted preposition (*about*) just after she completes her rendition. The interaction evidently becomes dramatic to the interpreter. This is so due to the fact that the witness is not only able to trace the detail that has been lost in the interpretation, but also provides the Polish equivalent of the term *as well*. The tension is manifested by the interpreter's response to the witness's turn: she firstly smiles to the judge as if she is apologizing to him for either the witness's behavior or her lack of ability to provide a close rendition, and secondly she laughs nervously, which is only then followed by a quiet rendition of the element that has been omitted. Most likely, in order to create an impression that she is an independent professional who is capable of working out the interpretation, she does not repeat the equivalent provided by the witness; instead, she gives a synonym (*more or less*) of that word, thus a **close rendition** is provided.

The following extract is yet another example of the interaction during which technicalities are discussed hence, from the non-Polish speaking witness's perspective, the entire episode is silence:

(5.48)	**Original PL/EN talk**	**Author's verbatim translation into EN**
Judge:	(.) i dostała pani wezwanie? (0.2) i pan też dostał wezwanie?	*[And you were called in? And you also were called in?]*
Interpreter II:	(0.2) również zostałem wezwany...	*[I was also called in.]*
Interpreter I:	((to III)) ah::: (.) czyli pan dostał wezwanie z urzędu?	*[A…, so you were summoned ex officio?]*
Judge:	a pani jest… yyy:::…	*[And you Miss are… yyy…]*
Interpreter I:	tak. ja jestem tak jakby: wezwana przez pana...	*[Yes, I am sort of summoned by him.]*
Judge:	(0.4) a-<u>ha</u>:… yyy:::…	*aha*
Interpreter I:	tylko że ja nie wie:m (.) jak długo potrwa dzisiejsze: yh::: posiedzenie: i ja mogę zostać tylko tak do: za dwadzieścia dziesiąta,	*[But I don't know how long today session is going to take… and I can stay only up to about twenty to ten.]*
Judge:	to pan zostanie te:ż... no bo myśmy pani nie wzywali (0.2) wzywaliśmy pana (.) >jak naj<u>bardziej<</u> zapraszamy <u>oczywiście</u>… (0.2) i państwo obydwoje z listy? (.) tak? (0.2) tłumaczy?	*[Then you will also stay. Because we did not summon you, ma'am. We summoned him, indeed, we invite you, of course… And you both from the list, yes, of translators?]*
Interpreter II:	(0.1) tak...	*[Yes.]*

(5.48)	Original PL/EN talk	Author's verbatim translation into EN
Judge:	((reading a document, an authorization, presented by one of the interpreters)) (3.0) pan na pewno: jakby:: tak (0.2) co do pani? (.) yhmy:: (0.2) dobrze (.) dziękuję bardzo (0.2) najwyżej >państwo się zmienią< (.) jak już będzie pora (.) kiedy pani będzie musiała wy:jść.	*[You for sure f, yes… As to you, ma'am? Yhm. Good, thank you very much. If need be you can switch when it is time for you to leave.]*

The above episode of interaction is 1 minute long (from minute 05:14 to minute 06:13 of the trial) and is a consequence of summoning two interpreters for the same trial. The judge is to explain the situation and decide which of the two interpreters will be assisting during the trial. Hence, he prompts both interpreters to confirm their identities. The difference between the ways the two interpreters participate in the conversation is visible. Interpreter II is withdrawn; he only answers the judge's questions. The interpreter not only answers the judge's questions but also comments on interpreter II's answers without being allowed to do so by the judge. What is more, she evidently feels encouraged to talk by the judge's silence (0.5) followed by a suspended hedge *a-ha:…* and a stretched vocalic filler *yyy:::…*. She considers the judge's appreciable pause and his hesitation as a TRP hence she begins her own turn to describe the problem that she has: she has to leave at a certain time. The judge answers her question: he permits her to leave when she has to do so. The judge's answer may be perceived as a submission to interpreter *I*'s will. In spite of that, it is the judge who dominates the interaction: he informs interpreter II that they did not summon her. By doing so the judge deploys his power of ritual: it is he who manages the trial. Although the above extract does not include any instances of the interpreters' renditions, still, it is an example of the main parties' (and the interpreters') attitude towards the non-Polish speaking party to the proceedings. Although there are two interpreters in the courtroom, the witness is left uninformed (a **zero rendition** is provided) about the substance of the monolingual talk between the judge and the two interpreters, who are both involved in explaining their appearance before the court.

5.3 Conclusions

The analysis carried out in Chapter 5 allows to establish that both overlaps and gaps in bilingual interactions are not monolithic mechanisms, but can be divided according to the interpreters' participation in creating these instances.

As regards **overlaps**, the interpreters find it difficult, if not impossible, to render the instances, when the primary speakers want to outshout one another, striving for making an impression on, or a conviction of, other interactants that it is their views that supersede the opponents' opinions. In particular, court interpreters are exposed to dealing with overlaps resulting from arguments between the parties or their legal representatives, discussions between various participants in the interaction, as well as the episodes in which the judge expands his sequence to obtain explanations. In such interactions, when overlapping utterances, i.e. statements, comments, questions and answers, which are expressed by two or more speakers simultaneously are produced, the interlocutors are actually confused and they do not understand anything from what is said, thus the act of communication collapses until one of the parties (ideally the primary party) withdraws from the field to let the others speak. Only then is the interpreter able to intervene. In some instances of overlapping, the interpreter is not capable of taking a turn at all, but this does not mean that she completely withdraws from the interaction. On the contrary, she gazes at the judge to select her as the next speaker. In other words, she requests the judge to help her find a place within the interaction where she could render the current speakers' utterances. In all these cases zero or summarized renditions are provided. Furthermore, and overwhelmingly, there are episodes, during which the interpreter's renditions interlace with the primary party's turns. In all such instances it is the primary speakers who do not let the interpreter complete her turn; they interrupt, correct, and supplement the interpreter's utterances. As a consequence, TMRs are overwhelmingly provided, but there are also single episodes with extended, reduced, summarized and zero-renditions, as shown in Tab. 5.1:

The most frequently followed pattern of interaction is that deployed by the parties when the interpreter provides a two-part or multi-part rendition (Extracts 5.24, 5.27, and 5.28), as shown in Fig. 5.1:

Before the witness is able to answer the judge's question, the interpreters have to split the message into parts to gain space for their renditions.

With multi-part renditions (Extract 5.29) within the mechanism of overlaps, and when the interpreter provides a close rendition (Extract 5.47) within the mechanism of gaps, the following pattern of interaction is possible (Fig. 5.2):

The interpreter renders the witness's answer to the judge's question, the witness continues answering, and the interpreter renders the subsequent parts of the witness's answer.

Within the mechanism of overlaps, four more patterns can be detected.

Tab. 5.1: Overlaps

Extract	Renditions / Interactant	CR	ER	RR	SBR	SMR	TMR	NR	ZR
5.24	Judge	0	0	0	0	0	**1**	0	0
5.25	Witness	0	**1**	0	0	0	0	0	0
5.26	Judge	0	0	**1**	0	0	0	0	0
5.27	Judge	0	0	0	0	0	**1**	0	0
5.28	Judge	0	0	0	0	0	**1**	0	0
5.29	Witness	0	0	0	0	0	**1**	0	0
5.30	Lawyers	0	0	0	0	0	0	0	**1**
5.31	Lawyers	0	0	0	0	**1**	0	0	0
Total:		**0**	**1**	**1**	**0**	**1**	**4**	**0**	**1**

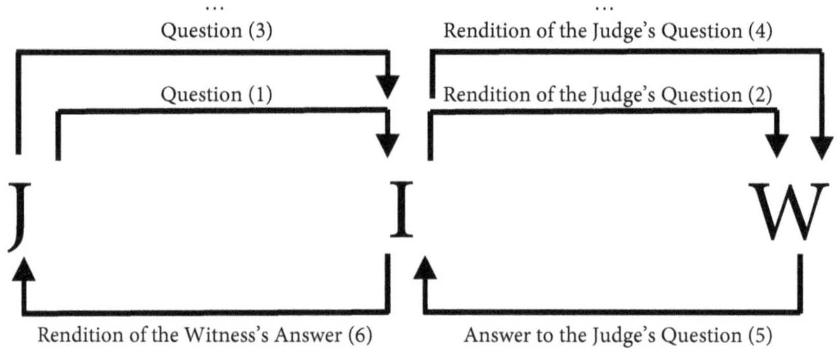

Fig. 5.1: Interaction with two-part or multi-part renditions

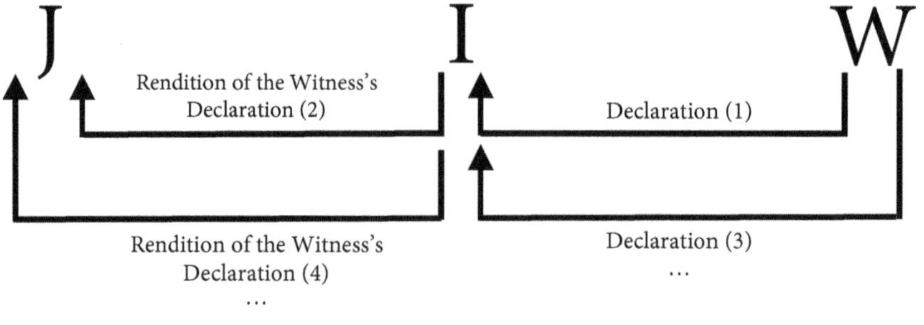

Fig. 5.2: Interaction with multi-part and close renditions

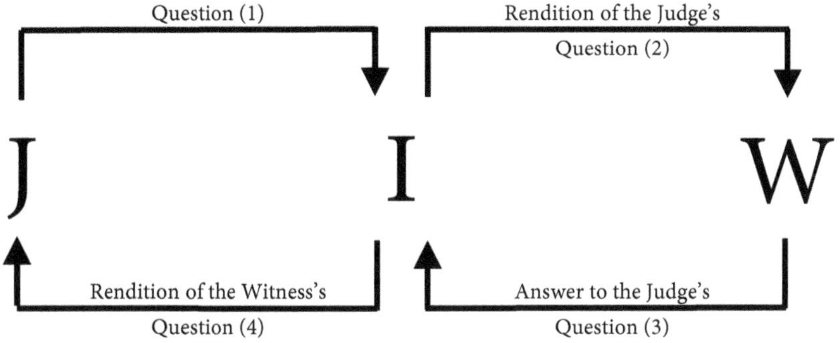

Fig. 5.3: Interaction with extended renditions

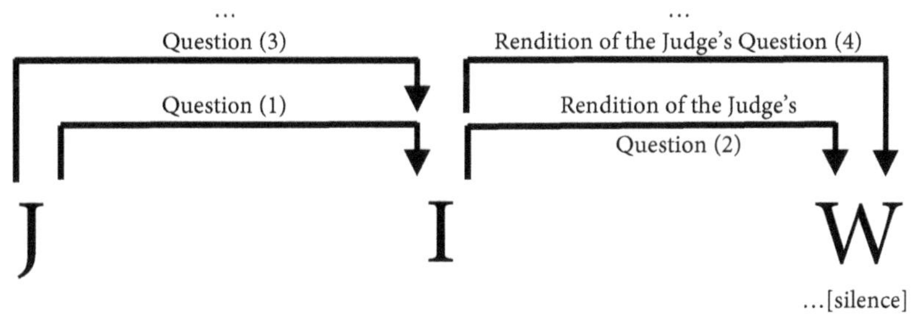

Fig. 5.4: Interaction with reduced renditions

When it comes to the episode where an extended rendition is provided (Extract 5.25), the question-rendition-answer-rendition pattern of interaction appears (Fig. 5.3):

Each utterance produced by the original speaker is followed by the interpreter's rendition.

The reduced rendition (Extract 5.26) is provided within the pattern of interaction presented in Fig. 5.4:

The judge asks the question and the interpreter renders it. However, without waiting for the witness's answer, the judge asks the next question to the witness and the interpreter renders it.

In the episode where summarized rendition is provided (Extract 5.31), the pattern as presented in Fig. 5.5 appears:

The counsels ask questions to the witness and comment on the case. The interpreter decides to choose to ask her own questions based on what the counsels are talking about. Thus, the interpreter asks questions to the witness who answers them;

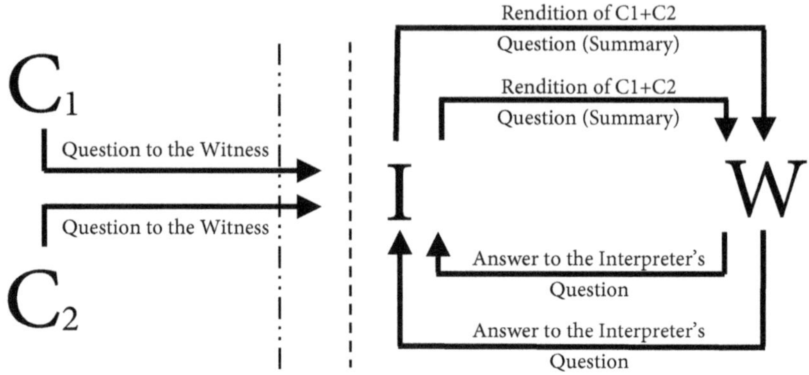

Fig. 5.5: Interaction with summarized renditions

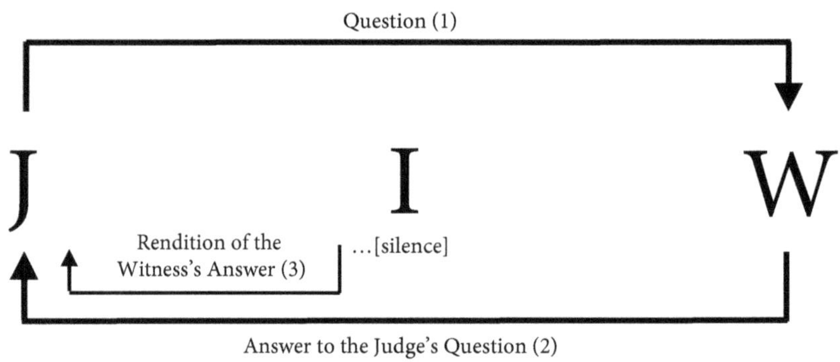

Fig. 5.6: Interaction with zero renditions

they both create a communicative circle separated from the dialoguing counsels. The communication is unidirectional: the interpreter hears what the counsels are talking about, while the counsels are not listening to the interpreter's renditions.

A zero rendition (Extract 5.30) appears when the parties follow the pattern as shown in Fig. 5.6:

The lawyers discuss the content of the questions, after which one of the lawyers transmits the question to the interpreter, who provides a rendition.

When **gaps** are concerned, alike overlaps, they can occur in either interactant's talk. When they occur in the primary party's turns, the interpreters logically do not reproduce them in their renditions. When they are produced by interpreters, they are real silences resulting from the interpreter's decision not to speak, or they are filled silences where the interpreters replace verbal with non-verbal communication. As regards the former, the interpreters remain silent in those places of interaction, where they either assume that the interpretation is unnecessary as the interlocutors understand the others' talk, or they find the main speaker's talk inappropriate as for the institutional talk (logically, such instances are zero renditions). As regards the latter, the analysis has shown that the interpreters resort to body language when they want to accelerate the pace of the communication or make it shorter, and also in order to make sure that the interlocutors know who is who in the courtroom. In other words, a non-verbal channel to communicate messages is an added value in the interaction as it contributes to making the act of communication a successful bilingual talk. There are occasions where nothing is said, but thanks to the use of gestures, the participants send and receive information. Moreover, body language is able to convey the interpreter's attitude towards the parties to the proceedings, as well as to the profession itself. For example, when the interpreter nods, she actually helps the lawyers obtain answers from the witness, who reads the head movement as a manifestation of empathy, full understanding and interest; such witness more eagerly *collaborates* with the interpreter within the interaction. Non-verbal communication covers also those instances in which the interpreter not only renders the original utterances but also e.g. presents the documents. The fact of assisting a person is praiseworthy, nonetheless, in formal encounters, and such is the case of the courtroom, such behavior assumes a particular sense; the question arises whether the interpreter blindly complies with the ethical rule of impartiality. Furthermore, it has been revealed that there are long periods of silences which constitute information gaps for the non-Polish speaking parties to the proceedings. These silences (with subsequent zero renditions) are actually talks involving all interactants but non-Polish speaking parties during which technicalities are discussed.

The gaps relate to zero renditions on the part of the interpreter, but are followed in number by non-renditions, close, and extended renditions, as illustrated in Tab. 5.2:

Overwhelmingly, the question-rendition-answer-rendition pattern of interaction is followed, where the interpreters provide close renditions (Extracts 5.40–5.42), and non-renditions (Extracts 5.45–5.46), as shown in Fig. 5.7:

Each utterance produced by the original speaker is followed by the interpreter's rendition.

When a unique episode with an extended rendition (Extract 5.43) and one of the episodes with a non-rendition (Extract 5.44) appear, the pattern of interaction is as follows (Fig. 5.8):

Tab. 5.2: Gaps

Extract	Renditions / Interactant	CR	ER	RR	SBR	SMR	TMR	NR	ZR
5.32	Lawyers	0	0	0	0	0	0	0	**1**
5.33	Witness	0	0	0	0	0	0	0	**1**
5.34	Defendant	0	0	0	0	0	0	0	**1**
5.35	Judge	0	0	0	0	0	0	0	**1**
5.36	Defendant	0	0	0	0	0	0	0	**1**
5.37	Judge	0	0	0	0	0	0	0	**1**
5.38	Respondent	0	0	0	0	0	0	0	**1**
5.39	Witness	0	0	0	0	0	0	**1**	0
5.40	Judge	**1**	0	0	0	0	0	0	0
5.41	Witness	**1**	0	0	0	0	0	0	0
5.42	Witness	**1**	0	0	0	0	0	0	0
5.43	Judge	0	**1**	0	0	0	0	0	0
5.44	Judge	0	0	0	0	0	0	**1**	0
5.45	Judge	0	0	0	0	0	0	**1**	0
5.46	Witness	0	0	0	0	0	0	**1**	0
5.47	Witness	**1**	0	0	0	0	0	0	0
5.48	Judge/Interpreter	0	0	0	0	0	0	0	**1**
Total:		**4**	**1**	**0**	**0**	**0**	**0**	**4**	**8**

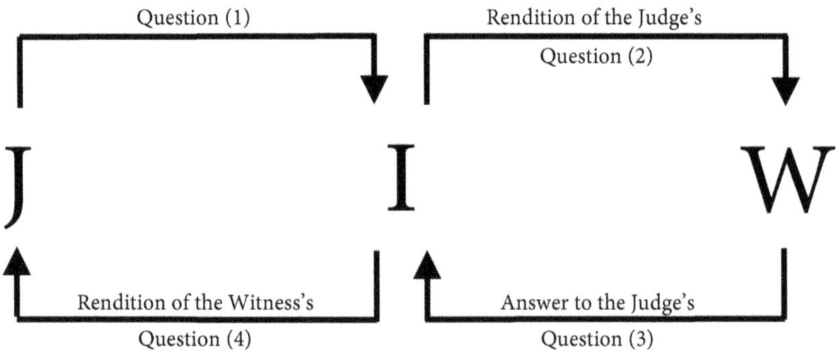

Fig. 5.7: Interaction with close and non-renditions

This interaction is typical for the judge's pre-closing requests at the end of the episode, rendered by the interpreter. However, the witness is not expected to respond, nor is the interpreter expected to provide a rendition.

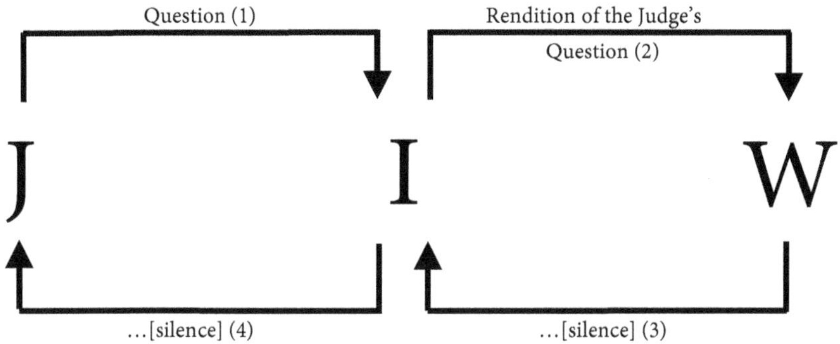

Fig. 5.8: Interaction with extended and non-renditions

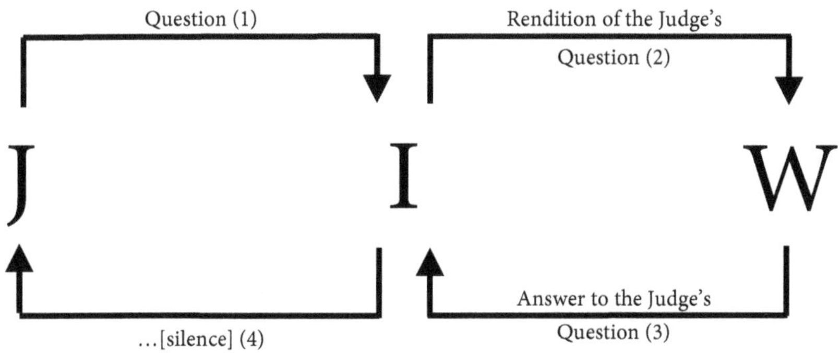

Fig. 5.9: Interaction with zero renditions

Different interaction patterns occur as far as zero renditions are concerned. In the majority of the episodes (Extracts 5.33, 5.34, and 5.36), the pattern is as follows (Fig. 5.9):

This pattern would show a question-rendition-answer-rendition order if the interpreter rendered the witness's answer to the judge's question. Nevertheless, the interpreter fails to do so under the assumption that either the judge understands the witness's utterance or the judge does not need to know what the witness is saying due to his rudeness or any other reason relating with the content of the witness's answer.

For Extract 5.35 where a zero rendition is detected the pattern is shown in Fig. 5.10:

The judge asks the question and the witness answers it. The interpreter is present but does not verbally participate in the act of communication; instead, by

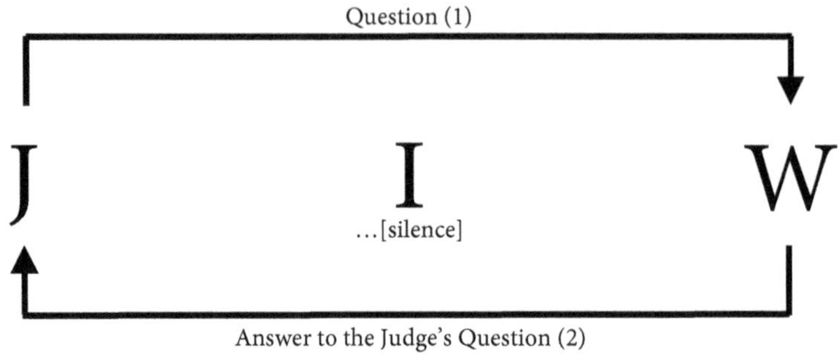

Fig. 5.10: Interaction with zero renditions

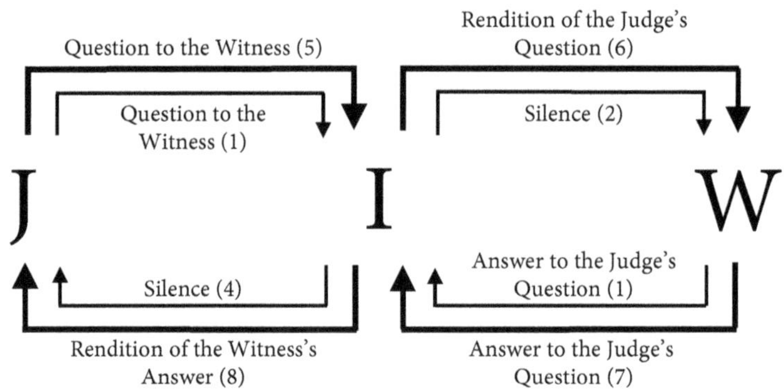

Fig. 5.11: Interaction with zero renditions

saying nothing, she is a typical non–person: all the interlocutors know that she is obliged to appear in the courtroom but they (or at least some of them) do not need her services to communicate. The situation is such when a theoretically non–Polish speaking party understands and speaks Polish.

A zero rendition is also provided in Extract 5.37 (Fig. 5.11):

This pattern would show a question-rendition-answer-rendition order in turns taken by individual interactants, however, in the first sequence, the interpreter remains silent when she is supposed to render the judge's question (the witness tries to respond by himself), and then, the witness's answer (the judge does not wait, instead, he asks the next question. Interestingly, in the second sequence the interpreter transmits the entire message.

A zero rendition as presented in Extract 5.32 shows the following pattern (Fig. 5.12):

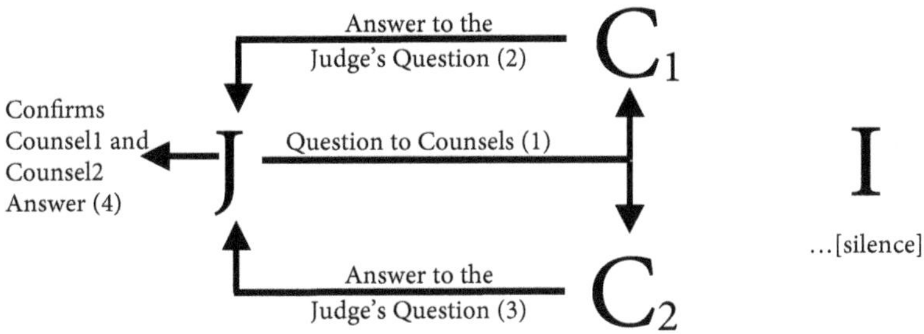

Fig. 5.12: Interaction with zero renditions

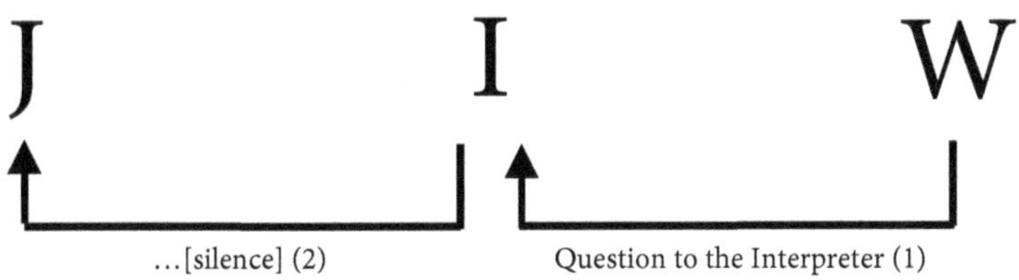

Fig. 5.13: Interaction with zero renditions

The judge asks a question to the counsels who answer the question and the judge confirms to understand the information. The whole act of communication is in Polish so the interpreter's task is to render it to the witness. Nonetheless, the interpreter remains silent, probably on the assumption that the lawyer's talk is of no importance to the witness.

In Extract 5.38 the pattern of interaction as shown in Fig. 5.13 appears:

The witness asks the question to the interpreter, but it is never transmitted to the judge.

For a zero rendition, there is also a pattern which appears in Extract 5.48 (Fig. 5.14):

The judge asks the interpreter questions and the interpreter answers these questions. In such an interaction a non-Polish speaking party is completely excluded from the act of communication.

As regards non-renditions (Extract 5.39), there is yet another pattern (Fig. 5.15):

The witness asks the interpreter a question; the interpreter, even though remaining silent, uses body language to answer this question. This episode of

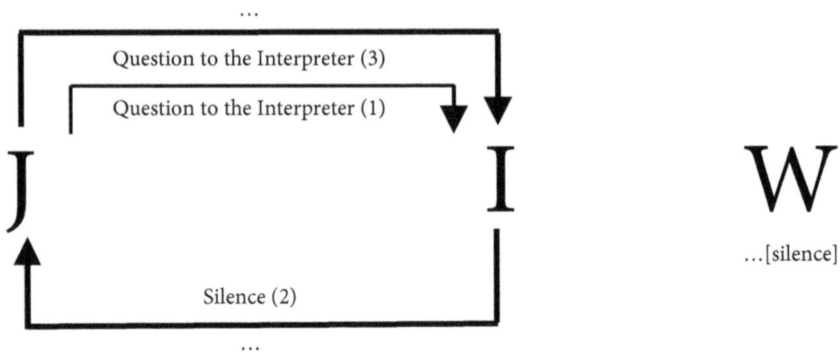

Fig. 5.14: Interaction with zero renditions

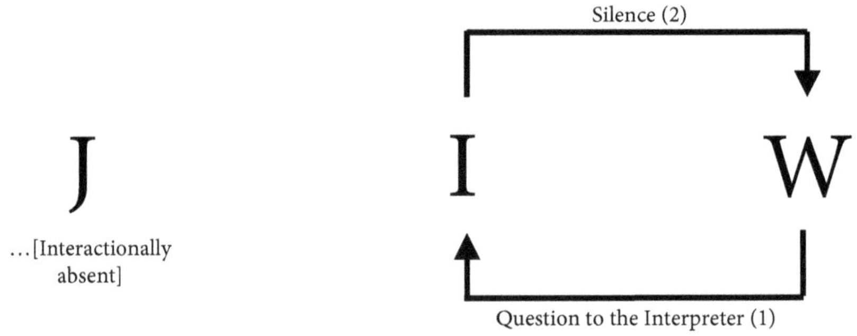

Fig. 5.15: Interaction with non-renditions

interaction is carried out off record and the judge is never informed about the content of the talk.

In general, the interpreter's attitude towards the overlaps and gaps cannot be considered as only their struggling with interactional obstacles, but also as those components of the communicative act that affect the way the interpreters are perceived as either neutral or biased interlocutors. Overlaps and gaps can also be considered as those mechanisms which have a potential to exclude the interpreter, and therefore the non-Polish speaking party, from the interaction.

6 Adjacency pairs as components of bilingual institutional talk

In this chapter, **adjacency pairs** described as basic sequences at talk (Sacks et al. 1974; Schegloff 1991; Schegloff and Sacks 1973) are analyzed. Due to characteristics of the courtroom interactions, during which adjacency pairs are naturally produced by main speakers, e.g. when the judge or the counsel asks a question, it is the recipient's obligation to respond (Heffer 2005: 46). In other words, at both casual and institutional talks, ideally, each first pair part (FPP) requires a second pair part (SPP) to ensure the flow of the talk (Schegloff and Sacks 1973). These pairs are considered as **preferred**, but also **dispreferred responses** can be produced (when, e.g. the reply is negative instead of the expected positive one). Another category of adjacency pairs is **counters**, which are produced by the speakers to announce a problem (Liddicoat 2011: 142) and may adopt a form of either asking an extra question or requesting for repeating the message transmitted by a previous speaker, or by remaining silent. **Assessments** appear when the next speaker refers to the elements of the current speaker's talk by either **upgrading** or **downgrading**, or providing the **same evaluation**.

In this analysis, the primary focus is on the following issues:

(1) who produces these components of interactions, and
(2) what renditions are provided of these components.

The analysis is aimed at determining a degree of the interpreters' active participation in the episodes of interactions, in which these components have been detected.

A preliminary analysis of the collected material has allowed to subdivide **counters** into those **created by the judge** and those **produced by the witness**. Moreover, it has been noticed that it is the judges' questions which provoke **preferred** or **dispreferred actions** on the part of the interpreters and other primary parties. Furthermore, assessments have been presented as **upgrades**, **same evaluations** and **downgrades**. As counters, all of the assessments are interpreter-created, hence it has been decided that the episodes of interaction be classified according to the primary party whose assessment is upgraded, evaluated in the same way or downgraded.

6.1 Counters in courtroom interactions

At the institutional talk of the courtroom, there are instances, where FPP needs to be repeated or elaborated on in order to make the communicative act continue.

6.1.1 Judge-created counters

In Extract 6.49 the judge produces a counter to elicit a detailed answer:

(6.49)	**Original PL/EN talk**	**Author's verbatim translation into EN**
Defendant:	I decided (.) I have better things to do with my life and I'm su::re (0.2) she does too:.	
Interpreter:	(0.2) y:::: zdecydowałem (.) że mam lepsze rzeczy do zrobienia w życiu (.) i myślę: (.) że ona <także>.	*[Yyy…I decided I have better things to do in my life and I think she does too.]*
Judge:	(0.3) jaka ona także?	*[What do you mean by she?]*
Interpreter:	(.) she? (0.3) who do you mean she?	
Defendant:	(0.2) my (0.5) my żo:na.	*[My, my wife.]*
Interpreter:	(0.2) moją żonę (0.3) mam na myśli.	*[My wife, I mean]*

The defendant describes the reasons for his decision by saying that he has better things to do with his life and he's sure she does too. The interpreter applies a close rendition when she transmits the defendant's utterances; she, in which even the pronouns *I* and *she* are preserved. Such verbatim interpretation makes the judge confused as to the identity of the *she* mentioned by the defendant, and in consequence, leads to the judge's counter: he addresses the defendant with a request to specify *what he means by she*. The interpreter consistently renders the judge's question and the defendant's answer, without any changes in pronouns; she evidently is not actively involved in the interaction, however, as regards the interpretation of the counter, an **extended rendition** is provided.

Similarly, the following example shows that the judge produces a counter:

(6.50)	**Original PL/EN talk**	**Author's verbatim translation into EN**
Witness:	Ou:h (.) X is a fan-tastic mum!	
Interpreter:	((nodding)) X jest fantastyczną matką.	*[X is a fantastic mother.]*
Judge:	co pan rozumie pod pojęciem fantastycznej matki?	*[What do you understand by fantastic mother?]*
Interpreter:	((nodding)) (0.3) what do you understand by fantastic mother?	

(6.50)	Original PL/EN talk	Author's verbatim translation into EN
Witness:	hmm: (.) she::: she i:s:: she i:s very crea:tive… she::… looks after him… she buys him special boo:ks that not every other child has... I think she gives him fantastic opportunities… she is very creative, the house is always clean. she teaches him to speak Polish very well... Ye::s, she's just a very good mother =	
Interpreter:	= jest bardzo kreatywna (.) opiekuje się nim (.) kupuje specjalne książki (.) których niektóre dzieci nie mają. Myślę (0.2) że da mu to wspaniałą możliwość (0.3) dom zawsze jest czysty. uczy go mówić dobrze po polsku... jest po prostu bardzo dobrą matką... =	*[She is very creative, she looks after him, she buys him special books that some children do not have. I think that it will give him an excellent opportunity. The house is always clean. She teaches him to speak Polish well. She is just a very good mother.]*
Witness:	= she loves him unconditiona[lly.	
Interpreter:	[i kocha go bezwarunkowo.	*[And she loves him unconditionally.]*

In the FPP the witness states that X is a fantastic mom, of which the interpreter provides a close rendition. The recipient of this information is the judge, who, however, considers the witness's answer too general and thus he reverses the FPP to prompt the witness to expand on the possible qualities of X as a fantastic mother. Such reversing is done by repeating the witness's FPP with a slight modification of the intonation. This makes the witness develop the first FPP; his second FPP is elaborated and the full of details justifying the opinion expressed in the first FPP. The witness's positive response to the judge's counter is confirmed after the interpreter completes a **close rendition**, when the witness complements the picture of X as a fantastic mother by saying that she loves her child unconditionally, which words the interpreter renders immediately, even with a reduced transition space.

The subsequent episode of interaction also includes a counter produced by the judge:

(6.51)	Original PL/EN talk	Author's verbatim translation into EN
Judge:	co według strony powodowej było celem tej umowy?	*[What was the goal of this contract according to the plaintiff?]*
Interpreter:	(0.5) what was the goal of this contract (.) according to the plaintiff?	

(6.51)	Original PL/EN talk	Author's verbatim translation into EN
Witness:	(0.2) we were contracted to provide advi::ce… to X...	
Interpreter:	(.) naszym celem było…	*[Our aim was to…]*
Witness:	0.4) if this contract could be:: hmm: (.) introduced in Poland…	
Interpreter:	(0.3) mieliśmy doradzać (.) czy ten kontrakt może być hy:::m::: wypełnio:ny (.) być zrealizowany…	*[We were to provide advice… if this contract could be… fulfilled, be executed.]*
Judge:	czy może być zrealizowany pod jakim wzglę:dem?	*[Could be executed in which aspects?]*
Interpreter:	(0.2) the settlement of (.) what (0.3) what was >your advice<? <I me::an> y::: under which >terms and conditions<?	

The judge asks the plaintiff about the aim of this contract. The interpreter provides a close rendition of the judge's question, to which the witness answers *that they were contracted to provide advice to X if this contract could be introduced in Poland.* Contrary to the rendition of the judge's question, the interpreter provides a non-rendition, which does not reflect the substance of the original message (*we were to provide advice if this contract could be fulfilled, be executed*). This provokes the judge's counter: he repeats the last TCU of the interpreter's utterance (*could be executed in which aspects?*). The counter would probably not appear should the interpreter provided a close rendition of the witness's utterances. In response to the judge's question, the interpreter provides another **non-rendition**, which means that she creates her own question in English. This example shows how a modification made by the interpreter may cause a counter and an avalanche of questions, which probably would never appear in the act of communication.

6.1.2 Primary party-created counters

The example that follows shows a counter produced by the witness who seemingly needs further information to be able to answer the judge's question:

(6.52)	Original PL/EN talk	Author's verbatim translation into EN
Judge:	a jak wygląda (0.2) jak pan widzi (.) kwestie związane z opieką nad dzieckiem przez ojca? (0.5) pan obserwował opiekę nad dzieckiem…	*[and how does how do you see the issues concerning childcare by the father? You observed the childcare]*

(6.52)	Original PL/EN talk	Author's verbatim translation into EN
Interpreter:	(.) and how do you see the childcare by the father? (.) you saw the childcare by the father?	
Witness:	when? =	
Interpreter:	= kiedy?	*[When?]*
Judge:	(0.2) przez ten cały okres czasu (.) od urodzenia dziecka.	*[During the entire period since the child was born.]*
Interpreter:	(.) during the whole period since the child was born.	

The judge asks the witness about his opinion *about the childcare carried out by the father based on the fact that the witness saw the father take care of the child*. The interpreter provides a summarized rendition of the judge's question to repair the judge's false start (*and how does how do you see the issues concerning the childcare by the father*). The witness does not answer the question; instead, he responds by asking a question (*when?*), by which he introduces a counter. Now it is the witness who asks questions to be answered by the judge. The interpreter provides a **close rendition** immediately after the witness's question, then, after an appreciable pause (0.2) answered by the judge (*during the entire period since the child was born*), and afterwards interpreted. This episode of interaction shows a reverse institutional talk initiated by the witness.

The following example shows an episode of interaction in which it is the witness who produces a counter:

(6.53)	Original PL/EN talk	Author's verbatim translation into EN
Witness:	(0.3) what was the settlement of? (0.2) in terms of? (0.4)	
Interpreter:	(.) pan chciałby <uściślić> (.) o co dokładnie wysokiemu sądowi chodzi? (0.2) jak wyglądało co w tym projekcie?	*[He would like to specify what's Your Honor specifically means? How things looked in this project?]*
Judge:	(0.5) jak wyglądała współpraca? (1.0) współpraca ze stroną zamawiającą?	*[What did the cooperation, cooperation with the contracting party look like?]*
Interpreter:	((to herself)) (0.2) °ze stroną zamawiającą° (1.0)	*[... with the contracting party...]*
Interpreter:	((to the witness)) ho:w (2.0) e:: what was the cooperation with the::: e::: client?	

It is the witness who begins this episode of interaction; instead of asking the judge to repeat the question, he addresses the interpreter directly as he does not understand the substance of the judge's question. Although the question is simple in both the language and the form of the interpreter's rendition, while transmitting the sense, it differs from the original question. The interpreter considers that she has been wrongly selected as the next speaker and decides to pass on the witness's question to the judge. Hence, instead of transmitting the witness's question (which is FPP), she replaces it with another FPP, which is an **extended rendition** of the witness's FPP. In particular, the interpreter uses indirect instead of direct speech (*He would like to specify…*), adds an address term *Your Honor*, as well as changes the level of formality. She does so by, firstly, deploying an informal style (*what do you mean specifically?*), and secondly, by quoting the judge's previous question. Such a reversing of the flow of the talk contributes to a violation of one of the rules of institutional talk providing for the right of one of the speakers to ask, and the obligation of the other to answer, the questions.

Similarly, the next example also shows that it is the witness who produces a counter:

(6.54)	**Original PL/EN talk**	**Author's verbatim translation into EN**
Prosecutor:	na co pan wydaje te pieniądze?	*[On what do you spend this money?]*
Interpreter:	how do you spend the money? =	
Witness:	= I <u>don't</u> spend the money.	
Interpreter:	(.) nie wydaję tej emerytury… (1.0) nie ruszam tej emerytury...	*[I don't spend this social security, I don't touch this social security.]*
Prosecutor:	(0.2) ehm:: a te pieniądze wpływają na konto? (.) gdzie te pieniądze są?	*[And this money is deposited to an account? Where is this money?]*

The interpreter provides a close rendition of the prosecutor's question (*on what do you spend the money?*), in response to which the witness answers with a dispreferred response (*I don't spend the money*). By doing so, the witness creates a counter, which introduces a shift from a response projected by the prosecutor who has asked a detailed question to an actual response being an answer to a general hypothetical question (*do you spend the money?*). Although the projected response would be a short *Yes, I do* (preferred) or *No, I don't* (dispreferred), the witness deploys a full S-V-O syntax to implicitly manifest his impatience and ignorance towards the prosecutor, and probably, towards the judicial system that is making him appear before the court. The interpreter provides **an extended**

rendition: in her first TCU she almost reproduces the witness's utterance (replaces *money* with *social security*), she suspends her talk, after which she produces the second TCU, where she replaces *spend* with *touch*, hence the final version of her rendition (*I don't touch this social security*). Evidently, the witness's counter has affected the interpreter's extended rendition; by producing the second TCU she attempts to divert the prosecutor's attention from the witness's counter to her longish rendition. This only makes the prosecutor ask the next question about the place the money is deposited.

As in previous examples, in Extract 6.56 it is the witness who produces a counter:

(6.55)	**Original PL/EN talk**	**Author's verbatim translation into EN**
Judge:	jaki był wynik tych spotkań? (1.0) czy:::?	*[What was the outcome of these meetings? Were…?]*
Interpreter:	what was the result of these meetings? (1.0) what was the outcome of the::: =	
Witness:	= there wasn't (1.0) was no deal (0.7) that's why we are here.	
Interpreter:	(0.2) tak naprawdę nie było żadnych uzgodnień (1.0) i dlatego tutaj jesteśmy dzisiaj (1.0) jesteśmy w tym miejscu dzisiaj (0.5) bo nie doszliśmy do porozumienia.	*[There were actually no arrangements. And that is why we are here today, we are in this place today. Because we have not reached an agreement.]*

The judge produces a TCU in which he asks about *the result of the meetings*, and then, after and appreciable pause (1.0), he begins another TCU, which is however suspended and remains uncompleted. At first, the interpreter echoes the judge's question, but then makes an appreciable pause (1.0) and makes a repair (*what was the outcome of the:::*) of her first TCU in order to provide as close a rendition as possible. Interestingly, the interpreter reproduces the judge's suspension, which finalizes both the judge's and her turn. In response to that, the witness produces a counter consisting in a false start (*there wasn't (1.0) was no deal*) and a post-expansion (*that's why we are here*) which is a justification why these court proceedings take place. The interpreter begins her rendition after an appreciable pause (0.2). She produces four TCUs separated by appreciable pauses (each lasting from 0.5 to 1.0) out of which two are repairs of the other two (*there were actually no arrangements* repaired by *because we have not reached an agreement*, *we are here today* repaired by *we are in this place today*), all of them creating an **extended rendition** of the witness's original talk.

Extract 6.56 shows a similar situation:

(6.56)	Original PL/EN talk	Author's verbatim translation into EN
Judge:	(.) proszę powiedzieć (0.2) czy:: >uczestniczył pan< w negocjacjach umowy?	*[Please tell me if you participated in the negotiations of the contract?]*
Interpreter:	(.) did you participate in negotiations of the contract? =	
Witness:	: = there was effectively no negotiation really…=	
Interpreter:	= tak naprawdę nie było negocjacji (0.2) otrzymaliśmy ofertę (.) przyjęliśmy ją.	*[There was actually no negotiation, we received an offer, we accepted it.]*

The judge requests the witness to state if he participated in negotiations of the contract. In her turn, the interpreter resigns from the pre-expansion deployed by the judge (*proszę powiedzieć, please tell me*), which makes the witness produce a counter, in which he informs the judge that *there was effectively no negotiation.* In response to that, the interpreter not only transmits the original utterance, but also, after an appreciable pause (0.2), adds an explanation to soften the original utterance, thus a **non rendition** is provided.

In Extract 6.57 the witness produces an overlapping counter:

(6.57)	Original PL/EN talk	Author's verbatim translation into EN
Judge:	krótko (0.2) pytanie >jest na razie< krótkie (0.2) czy cofa pan (.) czy pan je podtrzymuje? =	*[Briefly, the question is brief for the time being, do you withdraw or do you uphold it?]*
Interpreter:	do you withdr[a::w …	
Witness:	[it was withdrawn.	
Interpreter:	(.) pan twierdzi (.) że już to °wycofał°.	*[He states that he has already withdrawn it.]*

The judge requires that the witness shortly answer the question *whether he withdraws his demand or upholds it.* The interpreter takes a turn immediately after the judge completes his question, but the witness does not let him render the question; instead, he produces an overlapping counter to announce that *it was withdrawn*, with *was* being stressed. This counter, as all counters produced by witnesses, confirms that they are deployed by primary parties to express their impatience, as well as to delay a moment of responding to the judge's question. The interpreter's **rendition is** also **extended**, as in previous examples of this section, which proves that the interpreters find it problematic to be obliged to transmit the counters and that they need to describe, or, even to outtalk the original speakers, hence they say much more than primary parties.

6.2 Judge-initiated preferred and dispreferred responses

The episodes of interaction presented in this subchapter show the instances in which the judge as the current speaker expressly gives a choice to the next speaker as to what response (preferred or dispreferred) he will deploy. The interpreter's renditions of these instances are of main interest. The main question is whether they are close to the judge's utterances or the interpreters fail to reproduce the judges' intentions.

The example below shows the way the judge gives a choice to the witness to produce a preferred or dispreferred response:

(6.58)	**Original PL/EN talk**	**Author's verbatim translation into EN**
Judge:	czy strony obecnie mieszkają razem? (0.2) a jeśli nie (.) to gdzie?	*[Do the parties live together now, and if not, then where?]*
Interpreter:	(.) do the parties live together now (.) and if they don't (1.0) where do they live?	
Witness:	(0.2) no:: I think they don't live together from (0.3) two years?	
Interpreter:	(.) wydaje mi się (.) że nie mieszkają razem prawie <dwa lata> (0.2) °od grudnia°.	*[I think they haven't lived together for almost two years since December.]*

The judge begins this episode of interaction by asking a question as to whether the parties live together. This TCU, although completed, is followed by another TCU, in which the speaker prompts the next speaker to provide a detailed response irrespective of the answer (in either case an affirmative or a negative response, the judge wants the witness to be specific). The interpreter provides a close rendition of the question. The witness answers the question by choosing a negative response that the parties do not live together, but still, elaborates on the answer by adding a detail that the period in which they have not lived together has lasted 2 years. However, the witness expresses his hesitation as to a number of years by using a rising question-specific intonation. The interpreter evidently wants to be accurate: she reflects the witness's hesitation by adding an adverb *almost* which is to compensate the witness's lack of certainty. Nonetheless, when it comes to the other part of the information transmitted by the interpreter, she provides more details than the witness: from what she says the judge not only knows for how long the parties have not been living together (*almost two years*), but also that it was December that is the border month. Obviously, in an **extended rendition** of the witness's answer, the interpreter takes advantage of her previously acquired knowledge of the case; however, this is not the information that has been expressly made public during this particular court session.

Similarly, the example that follows shows an interaction, in which the judge wants the witness to choose the answer which reflects reality:

(6.59)	**Original PL/EN talk**	**Author's verbatim translation into EN**
Judge:	czy::: ten stan - takiego bra:ku zrozumienia uległ pogorszeniu >czy uległ poprawie<?	*[Did this condition of lack of understanding get worse or better?]*
Interpreter:	(.) did this condition of e:a:::: lack of a::::h understanding: got worse or better?	
Witness:	no (.) it got worse,	
Interpreter:	nie: (0.2) pogorszył się,	*[No, it got worse.]*
Judge:	czy pan wie (.) z jakiego względu?	*[Do you know for what reason?]*
Interpreter:	do you know (.) for what reason?	

The judge asks the witness whether *this condition of lack of understanding got worse or better*. The interpreter provides a **close rendition** of the questions. The witness chooses a negative response (*no it got worse*), again interpreted verbatim. The witness's answer makes the judge ask another question about *the reason for the condition of getting worse*. This episode of interaction confirms that at the institutional talk, the judge does not deem a certain type of a response to his question to be a preferred or dispreferred one. If the response is dispreferred, then the judge seeks a further explanation of the situation being the subject of the answer. Thus, for the judge, the dispreferred response does not pose a problem in the interaction, nor it is for the interpreter to render the judge's invitation to provide whatever response.

The next example shows that, contrary to the above two episodes, the interpreter finds it difficult to deal with the judge's invitation addressed to the witness:

(6.60)	**Original PL/EN talk**	**Author's verbatim translation into EN**
Judge:	a czy pan zamierza samodzielnie (.) się żoną opiekować (0.2) czy ewentualnie przy pomocy innych osób?	*[And are you going to look for your wife by yourself or possibly with the help of other people?]*
Interpreter:	(.) how are you going to look (0.3) to take care of your wife? (1.0) on your own or…	
Witness:	(.) no:: (.) I will (0.7) I will >get a nurse<.	
Interpreter:	(.) nie: (.) zatrudnię pielęgniarkę.	*[No, I will get a nurse.]*

The judge asks the witness whether he is going to look for his wife by himself or possibly with the help of other people. The interpreter addresses the witness with the question which evidently deviates from the original utterance (*how are you going to look to take care of your wife*). This first TCU is a detailed question which requires a detailed answer, not just a yes or no answer expected by the judge. This poses a problem to the interpreter who, in her second TCU, attempts to introduce a repair (*on your own or…*). However, as her first TCU does not need the second TCU to be answered, a **reduced rendition** is provided. In spite of these problematic instances, the witness perfectly understands what the interpreter wants to say and answers the question without any hesitation, which answer is interpreted verbatim.

In the subsequent example a similar interpreter's rendition appears:

(6.61)	**Original PL/EN talk**	**Author's verbatim translation into EN**
Judge:	czy pan jest w stanie opisać (0.3) jaka była relacja pomiędzy stronami? (2.5) czy byli zgodnym małżeństwem (0.3) czy też nie?	*[Are you able to describe the relationship between the parties? Where they a good couple or not?]*
Interpreter:	(.) are you able to say (.) what was the relationship between the parties? (1.0) were they a good marriage or…?	
Witness:	(0.7) ye::s (.) it was (0.2) ye:s (0.2) a good marriage =	
Interpreter:	= tak (0.3) byli dobrym (.) normalnym małżeństwem.	*[Yes, they were a good, normal marriage.]*

The judge asks the witness whether he is able to describe the relationship between the parties and whether they were a good couple or not. As in a previous example, the interpreter provides a **reduced rendition** by which she suspends her turn. Nonetheless, the witness answers the question. Next, when it is the interpreter's turn to provide the interpretation of the witness's answer, she unconsciously tries to compensate her previous failure to be accurate and an extended rendition is produced.

In the extract below it is the prosecutor who expects either an affirmative or a negative response on the part of the witness:

(6.62)	**Original PL/EN talk**	**Author's verbatim translation into EN**
Prosecutor:	a w Stanach (0.5) żona ma jakąś emeryturę >czy nie<?	*[And does your wife receive any social security benefits in the States or not?]*

(6.62)	Original PL/EN talk	Author's verbatim translation into EN
Interpreter:	(0.3) does your wife have any retirement pension in the US?	
Witness:	(1.0) in the US no::: (1.) because I worked myself (0.5) and when I die she gets everything what I have…	
Interpreter:	(0.4) w Stanach Zjednoczonych żona >nie ma uprawnień< emerytalny:ch (0.4) bo to ja tam pracowałem (1.0) natomiast (0.2) zadbałem o uposażenie żony na wypadek mojej śmierci.	*[In the United States my wife doesn't have any social security rights because I was the one who worked there. Nonetheless, I ensured my wife's pension in the event of my death.]*

The prosecutor asks the witness if his wife has any social security benefits in the US, which question is a completed TCU. Nevertheless, the prosecutor changes the pace of his talk, and adds *or not* with a rising intonation. By this, the witness is given an interactional choice to provide either a preferred or dispreffered reply. The interpreter omits the last element of the prosecutor's turn, hence a **reduced rendition** is provided. The witness deploys a dispreferred reply by saying that his wife does not receive any social security benefits in the US. When the interpreter renders the witness's answer, she evidently raises the style as the witness's answer consists of three TCUs, simple in form and in content. The interpreter's rendition, which also consists of three TCUs, is complex and literary. Apparently, the interpreter strives for compensating both the witness's nonchalant style with grammatical renditions and the fact the witness deploys a dispreferred reply.

6.3 Upgrades

All upgrades relate either to the judge's assessments inserted in their questions, or to the witness's or defendant's assessments included in their answers, both expressed in the turns immediately prefacing the interpreter's rendition.

6.3.1 The Judge's assessment upgraded

Extract 6.63 is the only example found in the analyzed material in which the interpreter introduces an intensifier when she renders the judge's question:

(6.63)	Original PL/EN talk	Author's verbatim translation into EN
Judge:	czy wykonawca projektu otrzymywał wszystkie informacje?	*[Did the project's contractor receive all the information?]*

(6.63)	Original PL/EN talk	Author's verbatim translation into EN
Interpreter:	(.) did the contractor with the project receive all the necessary documentation?	
Witness:	Received the information eventually that allowed to come to conclusion, yes.	
Interpreter:	Tak, w końcu dostaliśmy wszystkie konieczne materiały, żeby można było zakończyć projekt.	*[Yes, we finally received all the necessary materials to be able to complete the project.]*

The judge asks whether *the project contractor received all the information*. The interpreter adds an intensifier before the noun and thus provides an **extended rendition**. Hence, a new detail appears: the interpreter specifies what type of information was received (not any, but *all the necessary information*). Although such a modification does not significantly affect the substance of the judge's question, it can be perceived as causative for breaking the principle of the interpreter's impartiality.

6.3.2 The Witness's/Defendant's assessment upgraded

In the example that follows it is the interpreter who upgrades the assessment provided by the witness:

(6.64)	Original PL/EN talk	Author's verbatim translation into EN
Judge:	czy pan jest w stanie opisać (0.3) jaka była relacja pomiędzy stronami? (2.5) czy byli zgodnym małżeństwem (0.3) czy też nie?	*[Are you able to describe the relationship between the parties? Where they a good couple or not?]*
Interpreter:	(.) are you able to say (.) what was the relationship between the parties? (1.0) were they a good marriage or…?	
Witness:	(0.7) ye::s (.) it was (0.2) ye:s (0.2) a good marriage =	
Interpreter:	= tak (0.3) byli dobrym (.) normalnym małżeństwem.	*[Yes, they were a good, normal marriage.]*

The witness states that *it was a good marriage*. The interpreter provides an **extended rendition**: she upgrades the original utterance by adding an intensifier. Hence, according to the interpreter, the marriage referred to by the witness was not only good, but also normal. As regards the interaction, the interpreter responds to the witness's turn as any interlocutor who agrees with the witness's assessment would respond; however, and as underlined on several occasions in this book, the interpreter is ethically forbidden to take part in the talk, understood as an obligation to refrain from any kind of assessment. Otherwise the interpreter's impartiality can be questioned.

Similarly, the next example shows an upgrade of the witness's assessment:

(6.65)	**Original PL/ES talk**	**Author's verbatim translation into EN**
Judge:	czy ceny asfaltu zmieniły się w trakcie realizacji umowy? =	[Did the prices of asphalt change during the execution of the contract?]
Witness:	= mucho (0.2) muchísimo. =	*[A lot, very much.]*
Interpreter:	= bardzo (0.2) bardzo dużo (.) w bardzo dużym stopniu.	*[…a lot, very much, substantially.]*

The judge asks if the prices of asphalt changed during the execution of the contract. The Spanish-speaking witness understands the judge's question to a degree. He is able to answer the question (*much, very much*) without waiting for the interpreter's turn and her rendition. Only then does the interpreter intervene, however, she overrates the information contained in the original answer. By deploying an upgrade and providing an **extended rendition**, which intensifies the witness's answer, she apparently wants to outtalk the witness's arbitrary response.

In the subsequent Extract, the interpreter deploys non-verbal communication to upgrade the witness's assessment:

(6.66)	**Original PL/EN talk**	**Author's verbatim translation into EN**
Witness:	Ou:h (.) X is a fan-tastic mum!	
Interpreter:	((nodding)) X jest fantastyczną matką.	*[X is a fantastic mother.]*
Judge:	co pan rozumie pod pojęciem fantastycznej matki?	*[What do you understand by fantastic mother?]*

The witness is very enthusiastic when he answers the judge's question about X: he almost shouts out that *X is a fantastic mother*. The interpreter provides an **extended rendition** of the witness' statement: in her talk, an intensifier, a head movement, appears, which may mean, on the part of the interpreter, that she either confirms to understand what the witness means by what he is saying, or she agrees with the witness in what he is saying about X. If the former occurs, the gesture is understood as a sign of the interpreter's linguistic competence. In the latter case, the interpreter might be thought to proceed against an ethical rule of neutrality: by nodding she makes her mark, which, even unconsciously, may affect the judge's perception of X as a *really* fantastic mother.

Extract 6.67 also shows an episode of interaction where the interpreter produces a stronger evaluative term than the one deployed by the original speaker:

(6.67)	**Original PL/EN talk**	**Author's verbatim translation into EN**
Witness:	what was said (.) was that it was unacceptable (0.4) we >were not told< why.	
Interpreter:	(.) powiedziano (.) że:: praca przez nas wykonana jest niezadowalająca (.) ale: y:: nie podano przyczyn (.) konkretnych przyczyn.	*[It was said that the work we did was unsatisfying, but no reasons, no specific reasons, were given.]*

The witness declares that *what was said was that it was unacceptable, we were not told why*. The interpreter adds an element of emphasis by way of repeating the answer and surrounding it with an adjective (*specific*), hence providing an **extended rendition**. This might have influenced the judge's assessment of the situation: according to the witness the work was unacceptable and the reasons for that were unknown, while from what the interpreter says it results that the work was unsatisfactory but no specific reasons for that opinion were given. By adding an evaluative adjective, the interpreter shows her bias.

Extract 6.68 below presents an intensifier of the defendant's response:

(6.68)	**Original PL/EN talk**	**Author's verbatim translation into EN**
Defendant:	(.) so (.) that's what happened.	
Interpreter:	(.) to się stało (0.3) tak właśnie to było.	*[This happened. That's how it was.]*

The defendant sums up what he has already said (*so that's what happened*). The interpreter's rendition of the defendant's simple answer consists of two TCUs, each of them being a mirror reflection of the other. By doing so, the interpreter intensifies the witness's answer. Such a repetition (creating an **extended rendition**) does not change the trajectory of the act of communication, however, it may be perceived as putting an emphasis on the defendant's words, while the original utterance is rather the defendant's summary of the previous talk.

In Extract 6.69 below the interpreter upgrades the witness's answer:

(6.69)	**Original PL/EN talk**	**Author's verbatim translation into EN**
Judge:	czy podawała X jakieś przyczyny (0.2) dlaczego?	*[Did X give any reasons why?]*

(6.69)	Original PL/EN talk	Author's verbatim translation into EN
Interpreter:	(.) did X gave any reasons for termination? =	
Witness:	= only a <u>very</u> (.) very generic basis (.) not specific.	
Interpreter:	(.) były to: (.) były to uwagi bardzo ogólne (.) z tego co pamiętam (.) nie było żadnych szczegółowych wskazań (.) dlaczego umowa została wypowiedziana.	*[They were, they were very general comments, from what I remember, there was no detailed indications as to why the contract had been terminated.]*

The judge asks the witness whether X gave any reasons why, and the interpreter, when she renders the judge's elliptical question embedded in a particular act of communication, says more than original speakers; she is more precise and refers to the whole context of the talk, which is about the termination of the contract. By this, the interpreter wants to ensure that the witness is linguistically present and is following the interaction. The witness, categorically, responds (*only a very very generic basis, not specific*). When the interpreter renders the witness's answer, she adds an element of uncertainty (*from what I remember*) and again she makes reference to the termination of the contract. Although the **extended rendition** does not seriously affect the meaning of both the judge's question and the witness's answer, it is worth paying attention to the timing of the interpreter's rendition of the latter, which is much longer than the primary party's utterance. This may raise two questions: about the interpreter's credibility as a competent language expert and about her biased attitude towards the witness.

Similarly, in Extract 6.70, the interpreter upgrades the defendant's assessment:

(6.70)	Original PL/EN talk	Author's verbatim translation into EN
Defendant:	he owns a: small dog. =	
Interpreter:	= ma psa.	*[he has a dog.]*

The defendant states that *he owns a small dog*. The interpreter omits an adjective describing the animal, which might be a consequence of the interpreter's knowledge of the case hence she knows that in this particular case, the size of the dog does not matter. Nonetheless, with a **reduced rendition**, an element of evaluation appears in the interpreter's attitude (it is the interpreter who decides which element to interpret, and, which can be left without interpretation). This example can be considered trivial, but the broader context in which it appears can cast the interpreter's intervention in a different light. *A small dog* owned by a male, claimed by the defendant, and *a dog owned by a male* are images which call up different (positive and neutral to negative, respectively) associations. By upgrading an assessment, the interpreter unconsciously manifests her bias towards the judiciary.

In the example that follows, it is the interpreter who upgrades the assessment provided by the witness:

(6.71)	Original PL/EN talk	Author's verbatim translation into EN
Defendant:	I think at about nine thirty.	
Interpreter:	(.) około 21.30.	*[About 9.30 .]*

The defendant declares that *he thinks at about nine thirty*. The interpreter applies a **reduced rendition**: she ignores the defendant's hesitation expressed by a pre-expansion *I think* and renders only the second TCU (*about nine thirty*). By doing so, she upgrades the level of certainty expressed by the defendant as to the exact time of a particular event. This leads to picturing the defendant as more self-confident than he probably is.

Similarly, the episode of interaction shows an upgrade resulting from the interpreter's reduced rendition:

(6.72)	Original PL/EN talk	Author's verbatim translation into EN
Witness:	I don't know (1.0) it is between eight hundred and one thousand zlotys a month.	
Interpreter:	(0.2) pomiędzy osiemset a tysiąc złotych miesięcznie.	*[Between 800 and 1000 zlotys a month.]*

The witness states that *he doesn't know it is between eight hundred and one thousand zlotys a month*. The interpreter renders the witness's declaration as if she did not hear the hesitation included in the pre-expansion *I think* which contributes to the witness's uncertainty of the amount of money, or may be a manifestation of the witness's reluctance to respond to the judge's question. Due to a **reduced rendition**, in the judge's perception, the witness, as presented through the interpreter's rendition, is sure of the amount of money.

In the next episode of interaction, the interpreter upgrades the message while applying a reduced rendition:

(6.73)	Original PL/EN talk	Author's verbatim translation into EN
Lawyer:	czy po tym mailu (0.2) otrzymał pan jakąkolwiek (.) informację dotyczą:cą y:: tych kwestii: (.) które znajdowały się w mailu?	*[Did you receive any information after this email relating to these matters that were included in the email?]*
Interpreter:	(0.4) have you received any information in reply to this email?	
Witness:	(1.0) <concre::te> no::: (0.5) I don't remember (.) but I didn't receive any concrete answer.	
Interpreter:	(1.0) y::: nie otrzymałem konkretnej odpowiedzi.	*[yyy… I did not receive any specific answer.]*

The lawyer asks the witness if he received any information relating to the matters included in the email. The interpreter provides a close rendition of the question. When the witness responds, he is not sure of the answer: he begins speaking after an appreciable pause (1.0), stretches the vocals (*concre::te*) and deploys a vocalic filler (*no:::*); only then, after another appreciable pause (0.5), he states that *he doesn't remember but he didn't receive any concrete answer.* The interpreter begins her turn after an appreciable pause (1.0) and a vocalic filler (*y:::*) to say: I did not receive any specific answer. Thus, the interpreter provides a **reduced rendition** by omitting the witness's excuse *I don't remember*, by which she creates an impression that the witness is absolutely sure of the situation he is talking about.

In the subsequent example, the interpreter upgrades the original utterance and applies reduced rendition:

(6.74)	Original PL/EN talk	Author's verbatim translation into EN
Witness:	it wa:s e::: (0.5) I think e::: we were best friends (1.0) often (0.7) maybe sometimes once a week? (0.2) sometimes twice a week? (1.0) often.	
Interpreter:	(0.5) byliśmy najlepszymi przyjaciółmi (1.0) bywaliśmy raz w <tygodniu> (0.2) może dwa razy w tygodniu: (0.5) często…	*[We were best friends. We were there once a week, maybe twice a week, often.]*

When the witness answers the judge's question, he is hesitant, the manifestation of which are two vocalic fillers (*e:::*), five appreciable pauses (0.5, 1.0, 0.7,0.2, and 1.0), a modal verb (*maybe*) and four adverbs of frequency (*often*, *sometimes*). The interpreter provides a **reduced rendition**: she resigns from rendering the witness's lack of certainty as to the relations between the persons he is talking about; instead, she transmits an affirmative statement about a real friendship existing between the witness and the person about whom he is talking. What the interpreter preserves in her rendition is a modal verb and an adverb of frequency, while three appreciable pauses (0.5, 1.0, 0.2, and 0.5) are probably the interpreter's silences to think of the interpretation.

In Extract 6.75, the upgrade adopts a form of a shift in the intonation:

(6.75)	**Original PL/EN talk**	**Author's verbatim translation into EN**
Judge:	i do kiedy pan tam będzie przebywał? (1.0) jakie są plany?	*[And as of when will you stay there? What are the plans?]*
Interpreter:	(0.5) so >what are< your plans? (1.0) how long are you going to stay in this place?	
Defendant:	(1.0) for at least one e: year?	
Interpreter:	(,) przynajmniej przez jeden rok.	*[For at least one year.]*

The judge asks the defendant *as of when he will stay there and what the plans are*. The interpreter, after an appreciable pause (0.5) provides a close rendition. The defendant's answer is not an affirmative statement, but a question, by which the speaker expresses his hesitation or lack of confidence as to his memory. Nevertheless, the interpreter does not render this hesitation; instead, she produces a typically affirmative statement. By providing a **reduced rendition**, the interpreter conceals the real meaning of the defendant's answer that originally carries the message: *I am not sure, I think for at least one year*.

The subsequent episode of interaction presents a similar example:

(6.76)	**Original PL/EN talk**	**Author's verbatim translation into EN**
Witness:	the child lives with A (.) and B has him (1.0) I think (0.5) twi:ce? a week >for a couple of hours< and e:: every second week.	
Interpreter:	(1.0) dziecko mieszka z A (0.5) B ma je dwa razy w tygodniu zabiera:ć i chy::ba w co drugi weekend.	*[The child lives with A, and B is to take him twice a week and probably every second week.]*

The witness declares that *the child lives with A, and B is to take him twice a week and probably every second week*. The point is that the witness is not sure of the frequency of the father's visits, which is manifested by a rising intonation (*twice? a week*), which is not reproduced by the interpreter. What is more, the interpreter quite freely shifts uncertainty conveyed in the witness's *I think*, which then appears in the form of *probably* in a totally different place and meaning of the interpreter's rendition. Hence, a **reduced rendition** is provided.

Similarly, in Extract 6.77 that follows the interpreter upgrades the witness's utterance:

(6.77)	**Original PL/EN talk**	**Author's verbatim translation into EN**
Counsel:	skąd pan wie (0.5) jak śpi żona?	*[How do you know how your wife sleeps?]*
Interpreter:	0.2) how do you know how your wife <slee:ps>?	
Witness:	(0.5) she slee:ps e::: in Florida she could not sleep all night… (1.0) may be sometimes she didn't sleep all night and may be sometimes she went to bed e:: may be: at seven p.m. and then got up at may be four five o'clock a.m.	
Interpreter:	(0.5) często się zdarzało właśnie na Florydzie (.) że żona nie mogła spać w nocy (0.5) ale też równie często miała miejsce sytuacja (.) że żona kładła się spać około godziny dziewiętnastej (.) i później budziła się o czwartej nad ranem.	*[It frequently happened in Florida that my wife could not sleep at night, but equally frequently a situation also took place where my wife went to sleep at about 7:00 pm and then woke up at 4 a.m.]*

When the counsel asks the witness how he knows how his wife sleeps, the interpreter provides a close rendition. When the witness, after an appreciable pause (0.5) responds, he deploys five modal verbs and two vocalic fillers, all of them manifesting that the witness needs time to think of the answer. When the interpreter's turn comes, she needs the same length of the appreciable pause (0.5) to start interpreting. Then, from the primary speaker's modal verbs, only the meaning of *could not* is rendered verbatim, while *maybe sometimes she didn't sleep* is changed into *it frequently happened*, with all other modals completely omitted. By doing so, the interpreter upgrades the original utterance: in her **reduced rendition** the statement sounds more affirmatively, there is no uncertainty, but rather information in relation to which the witness has no doubts.

The next example shows an upgrading of the primary party's utterance who deploys a pragmatic marker *well* and a *modal*:

(6.78)	**Original PL/EN talk**	**Author's verbatim translation into EN**
Witness:	yhm::: we:ll: (0.2) we don't see him now anymore y::: (0.3) maybe just occasionally (2.0) when I saw him once (0.2) sitting in a car with his child (2.0) so::: y::: but before that y::: (0.5) Y was taking care of e::: of y:::: of e::: the child.	

(6.78)	Original PL/EN talk	Author's verbatim translation into EN
Interpreter:	już go teraz nie widujemy (0.2) czasami go widujemy (0.3) widzimy (.) jak przejeżdża (2.0) raz widziałem go y: (0.4) jak siedział w y:: samochodzie z dzieckiem podczas y:::: ale przedtem Y zajmowała się Z.	*[We don't see him now anymore, we sometimes see him, we see how he comes, once I saw him sitting in the car with the child during…, but before Y had been taking care of Z.]*

The witness starts his utterance with a vocalic filler *yhm:::* and a stretched pragmatic marker. Along with six appreciable pauses (0.2, 0.3, 2.0, 0.2, 2.0, and 0.5) separating the TCUs, another seven vocalic fillers and a modal expression *maybe just occasionally*, the witness's utterance makes an impression of being highly hesitant; evidently, for the witness it is difficult to talk about his friends' private life. In a **reduced rendition**, the discourse marker *well*, which slows down the talk to give time for the speaker to think over his answer, is not interpreted, as well as the modality *maybe just occasionally* contributing to the witness's uncertainty as to the frequency of seeing the defendant. Furthermore, the interpreter resigns from the overwhelming majority of vocalic fillers (the two remaining in her rendition are probably characteristic of her own talk). As a consequence, the utterance in TL is an affirmative statement, in which a lack of certainty of the original is lost.

6.4 Over-answering yes-no questions

A separate category of upgrades isolated from the material collected are those created mainly and specifically by interpreters who, instead of proposing a verbatim interpretation of short one-particle *yes* or *no* answers offered by the witness, provide elaborated statements. Wahlster et al. (1983: 643) denominates such upgrades as *over-answering yes-no questions* defined as "generating extended responses that provide additional information".

The example below shows an interaction in which the interpreter intensifies the witness's response to a general question posed by the judge:

(6.79)	Original PL/EN talk	Author's verbatim translation into EN
Witness:	no. =	
Interpreter:	= nie (.) nie kwestionuje.	*[No, he does not question it.]*

The witness provides a one-word response (*no*) to the judge's question. The interpreter, instead of rendering a very simple negative answer of the witness, says *no, he does not question it*, which is also true as it is an exact reproduction of the judge's question in the previous turn. However, it intensifies the witness's original response. Evidently, the witness is rather reluctant to be the subject of the examination, while the interpreter's **extended rendition** may indicate that the witness is eager to collaborate with the judge to explain the issue. Hence, the interpreter can be perceived as not being neutral in her renditions.

Similarly, Extract 6.80 provides for the interaction in which the interpreter intensifies the witness's response:

(6.80)	**Original PL/EN talk**	**Author's verbatim translation into EN**
Witness:	no.	
Interpreter:	(.) nie (.) nigdy.	*[No, never.]*

The witness provides a short answer (*no*) to the judge's question. The interpreter underlines a negativity of the witness's original answer by introducing the adverb *never*, by which she puts an emphasis on the witness's conviction as to his answer and provides an **extended rendition**. At the same time, however, as short negative answers are dispreferred at talks, the interpreter probably attempts to tone down the witness's response. Therefore, paradoxically, by upgrading the response the interpreter contributes to a weaker evaluation on the part of the judge of the witness's answer and thus, his attitude towards the judiciary.

The next episode involves intensifying the witness's affirmative response:

(6.81)	**Original PL/EN talk**	**Author's verbatim translation into EN**
Judge:	zamieszkuje pan gdzie? =	*[You live where?]*
Interpreter:	= where do you live?	
Defendant:	I live in Y.	
Interpreter:	(.) mieszkam na Y.	*[I live at Y]*
Judge:	(.) w X (.) tak?	*[In X, yes?]*
Interpreter:	(.) so you live in X (.) right?	
Defendant:	yes. =	
Interpreter:	= tak (.) mieszkam w X.	*[Yes, I live in X.]*

The interpreter renders the judge's questions verbatim, including the interjection *right*. However, when she interprets the defendant's short final answer *yes*, she decides to build it round with an affirmative statement. In this particular interaction, by using an intensifier, she actually provides a **summarized rendition** of the information the judge has been looking for and thus, restores a trajectory of the talk. As a consequence, after the interpreter's turn the judge is fully informed of the defendant's place of residence, which was the main goal of his question.

The subsequent episode shows a similar interaction in which the witness's answer is upgraded:

(6.82)	Original PL/EN talk	Author's verbatim translation into EN
Judge:	a czy pan się zapoznał osobiście z tymi raportami?	*[Did you personally read these reports?]*
Interpreter:	(.) did you see the reports yourself? (0.2) did you: read these re[ports through?	
Witness:	[yes.=	
Interpreter:	= tak (.) tak (.) zapoznałem się z tymi raportami.	*[Yes. Yes, I read these reports.]*

The judge asks the witness if he personally read the reports. The interpreter applies a specific intensifier consisting in, firstly, reproducing the primary party's question, and then, repeating the same question. Thus, the judge's question is doubled in the interpreter's **extended rendition**. In his response, the witness provides an affirmative answer (*yes*), which the interpreter intensifies by doubling the adverb *yes* and reproducing the information included in the judge's original question.

In a subsequent example the interpreter intensifies the witness's answer by deploying a part of her rendition from the previous turn:

(6.83)	Original PL/EN talk	Author's verbatim translation into EN
Judge:	ale w odniesieniu do obecnie istniejącego: e::: (.) sposobu zarządzania drogami?	*[But with reference to the currently existing manner of road management?]*
Interpreter:	(.) this fifteen percent is in comparison to what is now (0.2) let's say (.) in the [market?	
Witness:	[yes.	
Interpreter:	tak (.) w stosunku do tego: e:: co obecnie jest na rynku.	*[Yes, with reference to what is currently on the market.]*

In his question, the judge refers to a *currently existing manner of road management*. The interpreter, in her rendition, refers to the information (*this 15 percent*) which has been released during a previous stage of the trial. Although it is a detail not mentioned in the judge's original question, it helps integrate particular utterances forming the act of communication into a smooth exchange of information. When the witness briefly answers (*yes*), the interpreter renders this answer and then intensifies it by adding *with reference to what is currently in the market* (*w stosunku do tego co obecnie jest na rynku*). Hence, the interpreter deploys the content of the TCU included in her previous turn to upgrade the witness's response and provides an **extended rendition**.

Similarly, the next example shows an interaction in which the witness's answer is intensified:

(6.84)	**Original PL/EN talk**	**Author's verbatim translation into EN**
Judge:	oczywiście (.) wie pan (.) czego dotyczy sprawa? =	*[Of course, do you know what the case is about?]*
Interpreter:	= you know what the case is about? =	
Witness:	= y[es.	
Interpreter:	[tak (.) wiem.	*[Yes, I know.]*

The judge asks the question *do you know what the case is about* (*wie pan czego dotyczy sprawa*) which is preceded by a pre-expansion *of course* (*oczywiście*). By asking this question, the judge wants to check the witness's knowledge of the case. The interpreter is very zealous to render the utterance verbatim: she compensates a resignation from the judge's pre-expansion *of course* in favor of the emphasis put on the witness's response (*yes, I know*) instead of the witness's short response *yes*. In other words, interactionally, the pre-expansion deployed by the judge in his question imposes the over-answering upon the interpreter who provides an **extended rendition**.

The subsequent interaction shows an intensifier deployed by the interpreter in a similar way:

(6.85)	**Original PL/EN talk**	**Author's verbatim translation into EN**
Judge:	czy pan był prezesem spółki powoda (.) która była wcześniej pod nazwą Z?	*[Were you the president of the plaintiff's company, which was previously under the name Z?]*
Interpreter:	(.) you were the president of Z (0.4) °previous name°.	
Witness:	(.) in <u>Poland</u> (0.7) <u>ye:s</u>.	
Interpreter:	(.) tak (0.3) to prawda.	*[Yes, it's true]*
Judge:	(0.2) tak (0.3) to prawda… (1.0) byłem prezesem strony powodowej.	*[Yes, it's true, I was the plaintiff's president]*

The judge asks the witness if *he was the president of the plaintiff's company*. The interpreter provides close rendition of the judge's question. The witness answers affirmatively, but limits the territory where he was the president to Poland (*in Poland yes*). The interpreter renders the witness's answer only to the degree it is positive, however, she is not as specific as the witness in that she does not precisely state where the witness was the president. All the parties to the trial probably know that company Z carried out its activities within the territory of Poland, but it is never expressly stated during the entire court session, thus this information comes from the interpreter's knowledge of the case and not from what is really said. Instead, the interpreter provides an **extended rendition** by intensifying the witness's affirmative response (*yes it's true*). This intensified response is then repeated by the judge who dictates the witness's answer to the court recorder who is keeping the minutes; in the judge's utterance there is no specification of the place, instead, it is a reproduction of the interpreter's rendition. This fragment, however trivial, shows how the interpreter can influence the statements made by other participants' in the act of communication.

6.5 Under-answering yes-no questions

Although, as stated above in subchapter 6.4, there is an overwhelming number of episodes where it is the interpreters who over-answer the primary speakers' yes-no answers, in the material subject to the analysis for the purposes of this study, a unique example of reverse over-answering has been found:

(6.86)	**Original PL/EN talk**	**Author's verbatim translation into EN**
Witness:	I believe so: (.) yes.	
Interpreter:	(.) tak.	*[Yes.]*

In this episode of interaction the answers a general question which requires a yes or no response. However, as the witness hesitates, and is not sure of the reality concerned in the question, he begins his answer with an expression *I believe so*, and only then he creates another TCU consisting of an emphasized particle *yes*. The interpreter reads the witness's utterance as a repair: in her **reduced rendition** she completely neglects to transmit the witness's uncertainty included in the first TCU and renders only the second TCU. From the point of view of interaction, it is the witness who over-answers, but as regards the interpreter, she under-answers the witness's response, and, as a consequence, upgrades the original utterance.

6.6 Same evaluation

In this subchapter a phenomenon of the same evaluation defined as providing the same assessment by the next speaker as a response to the current speaker's assessment is discussed. The main interest focuses on the interpreter's position within the interaction where same evaluation is deployed.

6.6.1 Lawyer-interpreter same evaluation

Extract 6.87 shows the sameness of the judge's and the interpreter's assessment:

(6.87)	**Original PL/EN talk**	**Author's verbatim translation into EN**
Judge:	w jakiej odległości mieliście państwo >swój pokój z partnerem< od pokoju pani X? (0.2) w tym samym hotelu (.) na tym samym piętrze?	*[How far was you and your partner's room from Ms. X's room? Was it the same hotel, on the same floor?]*
Interpreter:	(.) how far was the room of you and your partner from the room of Mrs. X? (.) was it the same hotel (.) the same floor?	

The judge requests the witness to inform *whether his hotel room was in the same hotel and on the same floor as the respondent's room*. The interpreter deploys the same evaluation hence provides a **close rendition** of the lawyer's question.

Extract 6.88 shows the sameness of the lawyer's question and interpreter's rendition, but also the witness's response and the interpreter's rendition:

(6.88)	**Original PL/EN talk**	**Author's verbatim translation into EN**
Lawyer:	czy słyszał pan od powoda bądź stron <wspólnie> (0.2) że postanowili być razem?	*[Have you heard from the plaintiff or from the parties jointly that they decided to be together?]*
Interpreter:	(.) have you heard from the plaintiff ((the interpreter points out the plaintiff)) (0.2) or from both parties (.) that they decided >to stay together<? =	
Witness:	= yes. =	
Interpreter:	= tak.	*[Yes.]*

The interpreter provides a **close rendition** of the lawyer's question. The only difference is that the interpreter uses a pointing gesture at the plaintiff, when he perceives that the witness might not properly identify the plaintiff. It may be due to the fact that the term *plaintiff* belongs to a legal register, and the interpreter wants to avoid any confusion or possible additional questions posed by the witness as to about *whom* the lawyer has asked. The pointing gesture does not affect the assessment expressed by the lawyer. As far as the witness' short answer *yes* to the judge's question is concerned, it is reproduced without any modifications.

6.6.2 Witness-interpreter same evaluation

Extracts 6.89–6.91 show a permanent element of the trial, where the judge asks the party whose examination is beginning, about their criminal record:

(6.89)	Original PL/EN talk	Author's verbatim translation into EN
Judge:	czy był pan karany za składanie fałszywych zeznań przed sądem? =	*[Have you ever been punished for giving false testimony before the Court?]*
Interpreter:	= do you have criminal record for false testimony before the court?	
Witness:	(0.2) no. =	
Interpreter:	= nie.	*[No.]*

The interpreter provides a **close rendition** of the judge's question and the witness's answer. The judge's style has been preserved, and the witness's answer is reproduced as a one-word same response.

(6.90)	Original PL/EN talk	Author's verbatim translation into EN
Judge:	za fałszywe zeznania nie był pan <u>karany</u>?	*[You have not been punished for false testimony?]*
Interpreter:	(0.5) you have never been punished for saying <u>untruth</u> to the court? =	
Witness:	= no. =	
Interpreter:	= nie.	*[No.]*

The interpreter provides a **close rendition** of the judge's question and the witness's response. As in the previous example, the same evaluation appears in the primary parties' and interpreter's utterances.

(6.91)	Original PL/EN talk	Author's verbatim translation into EN
Judge:	czy był pan karany za składanie fałszywych zeznań? =	*[Have you ever been punished for giving false testimony?]*
Interpreter:	= have you ever been punished for false testimony? =	
Witness:	= no (.) <u>never</u>. =	
Interpreter:	= nie (.) nigdy.	*[No, never.]*

The interpreter provides a **close rendition** of both the judge's question and the witness's answer. As visible from Extracts 6.89 and 6.90, the witness's response is expanded to *no, never*, followed by a verbatim interpretation.

Extract 6.92 shows the same evaluation as regards the interpretation of an obligation:

(6.92)	Original PL/EN talk	Author's verbatim translation into EN
Witness:	X and I decided that we have to keep an eye on Y. =	
Interpreter:	= my z X stwierdziliśmy (0.2) że musimy go pilnować.	*[X and I decided that we have to keep an eye on him.]*

The witness declares that *X and he decided that they had to keep an eye on Y.* The obligation is reproduced in a **close rendition**, and the evaluation is preserved.

Similarly, in Extract 6.93 a modal *must* appear which receives same evaluation in the interpreter's rendition:

(6.93)	Original PL/EN talk	Author's verbatim translation into EN
Witness:	we must check that Y leaves with us (.) because we didn't trust him (1.0) and we took him (1.5) we took him back with us one night to the room (.) and the next morning we heard (.) that he walked circle around and spent the rest of the night with the rest of the group.	
Interpreter:	(.) ktokolwiek idzie do swojego pokoju ostatni (0.2) musi pilnować (.) że Y wrócił z nami (0.5) jednej nocy nawet (0.3) ponieważ mu nie ufaliśmy (0.2) jednej nocy nawet (.) zaprowadziliśmy go wracając (0.4) i rano dowiedzieliśmy się (.) że on zrobił kółko i <u>wrócił</u> (0.2) żeby z powrotem spędzić wieczór z pozostałymi.	*[Whoever goes to his room as the last one, we must make sure that Igor comes with us. One night even, because we didn't' trust him, one night we even took him to his room when we were going back, and in the morning we found out that he had turned back around and went back to spend the evening with others.]*

A modality expressed by the witness with the verb *must* is transmitted in the interpretation, by which the same evaluation is maintained, hence a **close rendition** is provided.

The next episode of interaction proves that sameness can be achieved by replacing modal verbs with adverbs:

(6.94)	Original PL/EN talk	Author's verbatim translation into EN
Witness:	He met her when we were on holiday in November that year. I would say probably one month, month and a half.	
Interpreter:	Poznał ją, jak byliśmy na wakacjach w listopadzie prawdopodobnie tego roku, tak, że prawdopodobnie parę miesięcy.	*[He met her when we were on holiday in November probably that year, yes, so probably a couple of months.]*

In the original answer the witness uses a modality *I would say probably* to express his uncertainty as to the exact period of time. The interpreter renders that meaning by repeating the adverb *probably* twice, where the first use is an equivalent of *I would* while the second one is a **close rendition** of the witness's words.

Similarly, in the episode below the interpreter preserves the witness's attitude towards the described reality:

(6.95)	Original PL/EN talk	Author's verbatim translation into EN
Witness:	we:ll (0.3) terms and conditions defined in the contract e:: but…	
Interpreter:	(0.3) y:::: warunki y:: były określone przez <u>kontrakt</u>…	*[… yyy… terms and conditions were set forth in the contract…]*

The witness begins his turn with a stretched pragmatic marker (*we::ll*) and an appreciable pause, after which he produces a TCU (*terms and conditions defined in the contract*). In this particular interaction, an opening *well* means *I don't know why you are asking this question, it's obvious that…* The interpreter replaces *well* with two vocalic fillers(*y::::* and *y::*) which gives the interpreter time to think of the rendition, as well as manifests her focusing on what she is to say. Also, interactionally, the interpreter follows the hesitant pattern determined by the original speaker, therefore, she provides a **close rendition**.

6.7 Downgrades

Alike upgrades, downgrades are produced by interpreters with relation to the judge's and witness's or defendants' assessments.

6.7.1 Judge's assessment downgraded

Extract 6.96 is the only episode of interaction found in the analyzed material which shows that the interpreter downgrades the judge's question:

(6.96)	**Original PL/EN talk**	**Author's verbatim translation into EN**
Judge:	czyli w związku z pana pracą <zawodową> (0.5) że pan pracuje od godziny <piętnastej> (1.0) wchodzą w grę tylko kontakty (0.5) jeśli by były (1.0) do godziny piętnastej (.) tak?	*[So in connection with your professional activity, that you work from 3.00 pm, only contacts, if there were any, until 3.00 pm, are taken into account, yes?]*
Interpreter:	(0.5) so: you::: so: (0.2) the contacts (0.2) would be sort of y::: those (0.2) >in the earlier hours<?	

The judge asks the defendant a question about possible hours of contact with his child. The judge's utterance consists of six TCUs separated with four appreciated pauses (0.5, 1.0, 0.5, and 1.0) and one micro-pause which all make an impression of a lengthy stretch proving that the judge actually does not know what he wants to ask about. This uncertainty is passed on to the interpreter; she begins her turn with an appreciable pause (0.5) and afterwards deploys tree more appreciable pauses (0.2 each), vocalic fillers an adverb *sort of* when she renders the fragment relating to the hours in which the defendant is able to see his child. What is more, *sort of* introduces the fragment of the judge's question that is **reduced** in the interpreter's **rendition**: she is not able to repeat the exact hours of contacts mentioned by the judge from memory.

6.7.2 Witness's/Defendant's downgraded assessment

In Extract 6.97 the interpreter produces a downgrade of the defendant's strong assessment included in his utterance:

(6.97)	**Original PL/EN talk**	**Author's verbatim translation into EN**
Defendant:	(.) that I found it totally enough this abu::se of my relationship with e:: (.) of (.) my child with myself.	
Interpreter:	(.) miałem już całkowicie dosyć (0.2) y::: taki:ego yh:::my::: niekorzystnego °sposobu° moich relacji z dzieckiem.	*[I was totally fed up with… y… y… such yhm… unfavorable manner of my relationship with the child.]*

The defendant is desperate about the way he is treated by his ex-wife as regards his contacts with the child. Hence, his style is rough, with emphases and exaggerations. The interpreter perceives the defendant's style as inadequate for the courtroom and introduces a downgrade: she evidently tones down the language by which she softens the message included in the original utterance (*abuse of my relationship* vs. *unfavorable manner of my relationship*). In consequence, the interpreter's **extended rendition** is a neutral answer to the judge's question, while the defendant's original style indicates his impatience and strong will to finish the proceedings as quickly as possible.

In the example that follows the interpreter downgrades the assessment provided by the witness:

(6.98)	**Original PL/EN talk**	**Author's verbatim translation into EN**
Witness:	we claimed that… =	
Interpreter:	= poniekąd składała zażalenie…	*[…she was in a way lodging a complaint]*

The witness's utterance is affirmative, short and informing that the party represented by the witness *claimed that*. The interpreter introduces an element of uncertainty as to an actual activity the witness is talking about by using a pragmatic marker *in a way* (*poniekąd*). This may be due to the fact that the interpreter is thinking of a rendition of the witness's utterance, and, not having a ready solution, e.g. an equivalent of the verb *claim*, adds a particle, which, firstly, gives her time to produce the Polish version of the witness's declaration, and, secondly, distances her from the meaning of the verb she finally suggests although she is still not sure of that. In consequence, an **extended rendition** can be identified.

The example below shows that the interpreter uses the adverb *sort of* to downgrade the witness's utterance:

(6.99)	**Original PL/EN talk**	**Author's verbatim translation into EN**
Respondent:	I want to <u>respect</u> my wife's schedule.	
Interpreter:	(0.2) chciałem jakby <u>uszanować</u> harmonogram mojej żony.	*[I wanted to sort of respect my wife's schedule.]*

When the respondent produces a TCU *I want to respect my wife's schedule*, it seems that nothing can affect the close rendition. However, what the interpreter does is that she, after an appreciable pause (0.2) foreshadowing a problem in the interaction, prefaces the verb *respect* (*uszanować*) with *sort of*. This **extended**

rendition may be due to the fact that the English verb *respect* has its equivalent in Polish (*respektować*) however used in other contexts than it is used in English; a well-rooted equivalent (*uszanować*), actually used by the interpreter, exists. Nonetheless, it does not form a collocation with the noun *schedule* (*harmonogram*). This lexical aspect affects the interpreter's downgrading of the original message.

The interpreter's deployment of the adverb *sort of* in renditions into Polish forms a separate group of downgrades, as shown in Extracts 6.100 – 6.102.

(6.100)	**Original PL/EN talk**	**Author's verbatim translation into EN**
Defendant:	she told me (.) that she needed time to reset.	
Interpreter:	(0.5) powiedziała (.) że potrzebowała czasu (.) żeby się: jakby:: (0.7) °zresetować°.	*[She told me that she had needed time to sort of reset.]*

The defendant states that *she told him that she had needed time to reset*, where the last word is emphasized. The interpreter begins his turn with an appreciable pause (0.5), after which she fluently renders the defendant's original utterance until the moment in which she deploys an adverb *sort of* which makes her stop for another appreciable pause (0.7), and only then, by saying *reset* (*zresetować*) silently, she completes an **extended rendition**. By doing so, the interpreter manifests that she does not feel comfortable with using the verb *reset* in her rendition, which may be due to the fact that this verb is considered as "permissible in games"[92] in Polish thus its use is limited to a specific area of the language.

(6.101)	**Original PL/EN talk**	**Author's verbatim translation into EN**
Defendant:	up to that day y: (0.2) all contacts y::: (1.0) all meeti::ngs to that day (0.5) were dictated by my wife.	
Interpreter:	(0.3) wszystkie spotkania do tej pory: (1.0) do tej soboty: (0.3) były jakby dyktowane przez y:::: przez y:: moją <żonę>.	*[All meetings up to that date… up to that Saturday were sort of dictated by yyy… by… yyy my wife.]*

92 dopuszczalny w grach https://sjp.pl/zresetowa%C4%87 (August 1, 2016).

The defendant states that *up to that day all contacts all meetings to that day were dictated by his wife*. He is hesitant – he deploys three appreciable pauses (0.2, 1.0, and 0.5), vocalic fillers (*y:* and *y:::*), and stretched words (*meeti::ngs*). The interpreter preserves the defendant's uncertainty, and even adds to it by using the adverb *sort of* which precedes the verb *dictated* (*jakby dyktowane*). In Polish, the verb *dictate* (*dyktować*) is regularly used in collocations meaning *writing something* (i.e. *dictate a letter*) or *dictating the conditions of the contract* (*meetings cannot be dictated*). Interestingly, the vocalic fillers in the interpreter's **extended rendition** occur just after *dictated*, which emphasizes the problematic nature of this verb.

(6.102)	**Original PL/EN talk**	**Author's verbatim translation into EN**
Defendant:	I want active (0.2) balanced (0.3) healthy contacts (0.2) where she has a mother and a father and grandparents and people in Z.	
Interpreter:	(0.4) nalegałem na to (0.3) żeby: mieć właśnie (0.2) jakby: te zdrowe (0.3) zbilansowane kontakty również z udziałem >rodziny jej< i o to mi chodziło.	*[I want active, balanced, healthy contacts where she has a mother and a father and grandparents and people in Z.]*

The respondent emphatically declares that *he wants active balanced healthy contacts*. The interpreter provides an **extended rendition**, where she includes all the elements of the original message, with the exception of the adverb *sort of* which she puts before the adjective healthy and an appreciable pause (0.3) before balanced (*jakby te zdrowe (0.3) zbilansowane kontakty*, *sort of healthy (0.3) balanced contacts*). The rendition manifests a lack of certainty on the part of the interpreter as to both (*healthy contacts* and *balanced contacts*), where the former is probably subjective of the interpreter, while the latter may result *from* a regular use of the verb *balance* (*zbilansować*) in professional registers used e.g. by accountants.

There are episodes of interaction where downgrades are multiplied by the interpreter. Such is an example of masterpiece use of pragmatic markers:

(6.103)	**Original PL/EN talk**	**Author's verbatim translation into EN**
Defendant:	so (.) I decided to protect my interests (.) and ask for oversight (.) but I did not object to examination.	

(6.103)	Original PL/EN talk	Author's verbatim translation into EN
Interpreter:	(.) yhm:: (0.5) czyli pan tutaj po prostu: chciałby jakby chronić (0.5) upewnić się (.) że jego interesy będą (.) e:: będą tutaj jakby chronione: (.) i po prostu poprosił o dodatkową y::: dodatkową osobę (0.5) czy: dodatkową opinię (0.4) >ale w żaden sposób się nie sprzeciwił< temu (.) żeby to badanie się odbyło.	*[Yhm. So he would simply sort of protect, make sure that his interest will be… eee…, will be sort of protected here and simply asked for an additional … yyy… additional person, or an additional opinion, but he in no way objected to that examination being carried out.]*

The defendant produced a fluent affirmative statement in which he announces that *he decided to protect his interests and ask for oversight but he did not object to an examination*. The only pragmatic marker used by the defendant is when he begins his turn: *so* is deployed to connect the preceding question with his response. Contrary to the original message, the interpreter's **extended rendition** is larded with pragmatic markers and other elements, such as appreciable pauses and vocalic fillers. By doing so, the interpreter downgrades the defendant's utterance. What is more, all the elements which appear in the interpreter's talk add to an impression that it is problematic for her to render the utterance.

The subsequent episode of interaction is an example, where the interpreter produces a downgrade by providing a **reduced rendition**:

(6.104)	Original PL/EN talk	Author's verbatim translation into EN
Witness:	we agreed also that this payment will be done after the winter season (0.2) because we were in October (0.3) and winter were coming (.) so:: (1.5) after the winter season (.) because of lack of cash flow.	
Interpreter:	(0.4) ze względu na przepływy pieniężne (.) czy te::ż e::: (0.2) uzgodniliśmy (.) że płatność ta nastąpi jednak dopiero po zakończeniu: y:::: sezonu zimowego (2.0) a rozmowa miała miejsce w październiku.	*[Due to cash flows or… we agreed that this payment will be made until after the end of the … yyy… winter season. And the conversation took place in October.]*

The witness declares that they agreed that the payment will be made after the winter season […] *because of lack of cash flow*, by which he expressly admits that the company he represents had financial problems. The interpreter says that *due to cash flows they agree that this payment will be made after the end of winter season.* When she omits a negation (*lack of cash flow*), she tones down the information about an actual financial situation of the company represented by the witness. The downgrade she applies can be a sign of the interpreter's bias towards the witness.

6.8 Conclusions

For the purposes of the analysis conducted in chapter 6, adjacency pairs have been divided into: counters, preferred and dispreferred responses, upgrades, same evaluations and downgrades.

As regards the **counters**, they may be produced as a response to a variety of interactional problems, one of them being a close rendition proposed by the interpreter, although from the point of view of ethics it is obviously the required interpretation. The other reason for producing a counter is a need to request the interlocutor to give further details. The counters are equally produced by the judges, who need more specific information that already provided by the examined parties (followed by extended or non-renditions), and by the witnesses, when they either ask the judge what exactly he wants to know (with subsequent close renditions), or they produce a dispreferred response, by which they manifest their arrogant attitudes towards the proceedings (extended renditions are provided). These findings are shown in Tab. 6.1:

As far as **preferred** or **dispreferred responses** are concerned, all of the examples cover the issue of initiating such actions by the judges who, in their FPPs give a choice to the recipients of their questions to respond either with a preferred or dispreferred answer. In all the examples the judge's questions have been transmitted through close, extended or reduced renditions, as illustrated in Tab. 6.2 below:

Upgrades have proven to be commonly used assessments in the interpreters' renditions. In the collected material only one episode has been detected in which the assessment included in the judge's question is upgraded (with extended rendition), while the majority of episodes involve upgrading the assessments in the witness's and defendant's utterances. Within the category of the witness's/defendant's upgraded assessment, extended renditions are provided when the upgrading is done by adding adjectives, adverbs, repeating the same information in the form of paraphrases, but also are transmitted through non-verbal channels of communication (nodding). Reduced renditions within this category are provided through omitting adjectives, verbs of thinking, and pragmatic markers, adding adverbs of frequency and adverbials of probability, as well as changing the intonation. This is shown in Tab. 6.3:

Tab. 6.1: Counters in courtroom interactions

Extract	**Renditions** / **Interactant**	**CR**	**ER**	**RR**	**SBR**	**SMR**	**TMR**	**NR**	**ZR**
6.49	Judge	0	**1**	0	0	0	0	0	0
6.50	Judge	**1**	0	0	0	0	0	0	0
6.51	Judge	0	0	0	0	0	0	**1**	0
6.52	Witness	**1**	0	0	0	0	0	0	0
6.53	Witness	0	**1**	0	0	0	0	0	0
6.54	Witness	0	**1**	0	0	0	0	0	0
6.55	Witness	0	**1**	0	0	0	0	0	0
6.56	Witness	0	0	0	0	0	0	**1**	0
6.57	Witness	0	**1**	0	0	0	0	0	0
Total:		**2**	**5**	**0**	**0**	**0**	**0**	**2**	**0**

Tab. 6.2: Judge-initiated preferred and dispreferred responses

Extract	**Renditions** / **Interactant**	**CR**	**ER**	**RR**	**SBR**	**SMR**	**TMR**	**NR**	**ZR**
6.58	Judge	0	**1**	0	0	0	0	0	0
6.59	Judge	**1**	0	0	0	0	0	0	0
6.60	Judge	0	0	**1**	0	0	0	0	0
6.61	Judge	0	0	**1**	0	0	0	0	0
6.62	Prosecutor	0	0	**1**	0	0	0	0	0
Total:		**1**	**1**	**3**	**0**	**0**	**0**	**0**	**0**

Furthermore, within a category of upgrades, a subcategory of **over-answering yes-no questions** have been isolated. It has been found out that when the primary party, be it the witness or the defendant, give a *yes* or *no* answer, then it is over-answered by the interpreter who thus intensifies a short and clear message, hence overwhelmingly extended renditions are provided, as is illustrated in Tab. 6.4:

In the analyzed material only one episode has been detected where the interpreter **under-answers** the witness's elaborated response to the judge's question. Thus, it is intuitively assumed that, taking a number of occurrences of under-answering on the part of the interpreter into account, it is a dispreferred response as regards the renditions. It is further presumed that while over-answering means creating an answer which, apart from the particle *yes* or *no* includes additional information, under-answering is technically the opposite On the basis of this

Tab. 6.3: Upgrades

Extract	Interactant \ Renditions	CR	ER	RR	SBR	SMR	TMR	NR	ZR
6.63	Judge	0	1	0	0	0	0	0	0
6.64	Witness	0	1	0	0	0	0	0	0
6.65	Witness	0	1	0	0	0	0	0	0
6.66	Witness	0	1	0	0	0	0	0	0
6.67	Witness	0	1	0	0	0	0	0	0
6.68	Defendant	0	1	0	0	0	0	0	0
6.69	Witness	0	1	0	0	0	0	0	0
6.70	Defendant	0	0	1	0	0	0	0	0
6.71	Defendant	0	0	1	0	0	0	0	0
6.72	Witness	0	0	1	0	0	0	0	0
6.73	Witness	0	0	1	0	0	0	0	0
6.74	Witness	0	0	1	0	0	0	0	0
6.75	Defendant	0	0	1	0	0	0	0	0
6.76	Witness	0	0	1	0	0	0	0	0
6.77	Witness	0	0	1	0	0	0	0	0
6.78	Witness	0	0	1	0	0	0	0	0
Total:		**0**	7	**9**	**0**	**0**	**0**	**0**	**0**

Tab. 6.4: Over-answering yes-no questions

Extract	Interactant \ Renditions	CR	ER	RR	SBR	SMR	TMR	NR	ZR
6.79	Witness	0	1	0	0	0	0	0	0
6.80	Witness	0	1	0	0	0	0	0	0
6.81	Defendant	0	0	0	0	1	0	0	0
6.82	Witness	0	1	0	0	0	0	0	0
6.83	Witness	0	1	0	0	0	0	0	0
6.84	Witness	0	1	0	0	0	0	0	0
6.85	Witness	0	1	0	0	0	0	0	0
Total:		**0**	6	**0**	**0**	1	**0**	**0**	**0**

particular example it can be set out that: 1) under-answering consists in reducing a developed answer to a sole *yes* or *no* particle; 2) it belongs to a category of upgrades as it replaces such original responses as a) **Yes, I think so**, b) **yhm**, and c) **silence/gap/pause**, or d) **non-verbal message**. Further analysis is needed to investigate whether under-answers could be categorized as downgrades, that is

Tab. 6.5: Under-answering

Extract	Renditions / Interactant	CR	ER	RR	SBR	SMR	TMR	NR	ZR
6.86	Witness	0	0	**1**	0	0	0	0	0
Total:		**0**	**0**	**1**	**0**	**0**	**0**	**0**	**0**

Tab. 6.6: Same evaluation

Extract	Renditions / Interactant	CR	ER	RR	SBR	SMR	TMR	NR	ZR
6.87	Judge	**1**	0	0	0	0	0	0	0
6.88	Lawyer	**1**	0	0	0	0	0	0	0
6.89	Witness	**1**	0	0	0	0	0	0	0
6.90	Witness	**1**	0	0	0	0	0	0	0
6.91	Witness	**1**	0	0	0	0	0	0	0
6.92	Witness	**1**	0	0	0	0	0	0	0
6.93	Witness	**1**	0	0	0	0	0	0	0
6.94	Witness	**1**	0	0	0	0	0	0	0
6.95	Witness	**1**	0	0	0	0	0	0	0
Total:		**9**	**0**	**0**	**0**	**0**	**0**	**0**	**0**

specifically in the instances where a strong original response is produced (e.g. *Yes, I am sure this is so*), and the interpreter renders such utterance with the particle *yes*. Although such examples have not been detected in the collected material, they seem to be a broad area of study within both interactional and ethical aspect of court interpreting. Tab. 6.5 shows that under-answering relates to reduced renditions:

As regards the **same evaluation**, it occurs on a regular basis in the instances of a permanent stage of the trial, where the judge asks about the criminal record of the witness who is to be examined and who gives a short *yes* or *no* answer, moreover, when modals are deployed, as well as when the interpreter renders the lawyer's question which include an assessment. In either case, close renditions are provided, as shown in Tab. 6.6:

Downgrades are deployed by the interpreters when they are not sure of what to say: either due to memory deficits (they barely remember the original utterance) or because of lexical difficulties, these being a consequence of either their uncertainty as regards their understanding of the primary speakers' talk, or a conscious use of calques which they consider not the optimal, but indeed the

Tab. 6.7: Downgrades

Extract	Renditions / Interactant	CR	ER	RR	SBR	SMR	TMR	NR	ZR
6.96	Judge	0	0	**1**	0	0	0	0	0
6.97	Defendant	0	**1**	0	0	0	0	0	0
6.98	Witness	0	**1**	0	0	0	0	0	0
6.99	Respondent	0	**1**	0	0	0	0	0	0
6.100	Defendant	0	**1**	0	0	0	0	0	0
6.101	Defendant	0	**1**	0	0	0	0	0	0
6.102	Defendant	0	**1**	0	0	0	0	0	0
6.103	Defendant	0	**1**	0	0	0	0	0	0
6.104	Witness	0	0	**1**	0	0	0	0	0
Total:		**0**	7	**2**	**0**	**0**	**0**	**0**	**0**

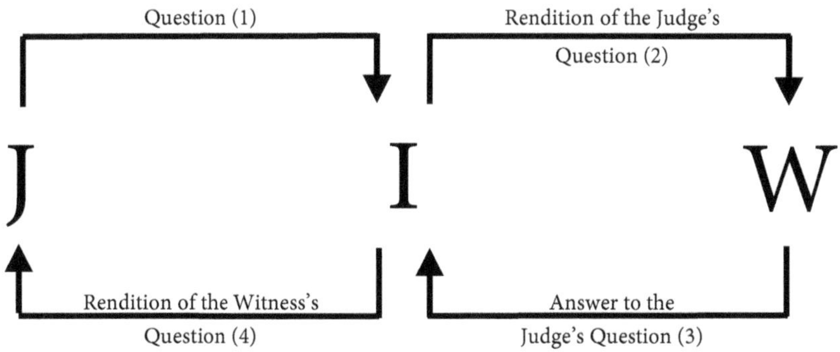

Fig. 6.1: Interaction with all types of renditions

only lexical solutions that come to their minds. A reduced rendition has been provided in only one example detected in the analyzed material of the judge's downgraded assessment. In the majority of extracts in which the witness's or defendant's downgraded assessment occur, extended renditions are provided, while in two others, it was a reduced rendition, as presented in Tab. 6.7:

As regards adjacency pairs, the pattern of interaction followed (independently of the type of rendition provided) in all—except five episodes—is as shown in (Fig. 6.1):

The interpreter's rendition comes after each original utterance: the judge asks the question, which is rendered by the interpreter to the witness, who answers the question, which, in turn, is rendered by the interpreter to the judge; the sequence

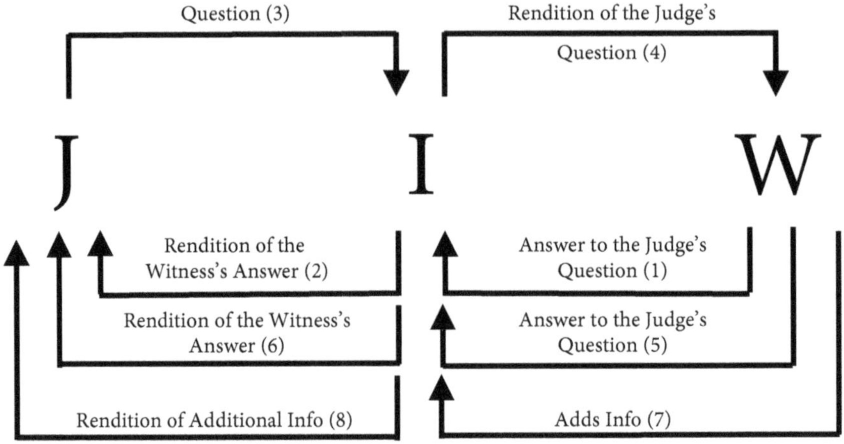

Fig. 6.2: Interaction with close renditions

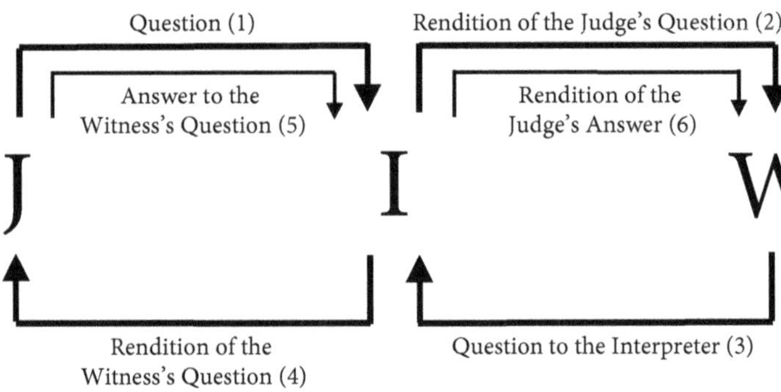

Fig. 6.3: Interaction with close renditions

may repeat. Such interactions appear obviously when the renditions are accurate but also when the interpreter introduces additions or when the interpreter deals with rude or sarcastic utterances, and finally with those renditions that are created as totally parallel statements that have nothing to do with the content of the original utterances.

Nevertheless, there are several exceptions, mostly appearing within counters, while one exceptional episode of interaction occurs in the category of upgrades.

As far as counters are concerned, three other patterns have been identified. When a close rendition is provided (Extract 6.50), the interaction is modeled as follows (Fig. 6.2):

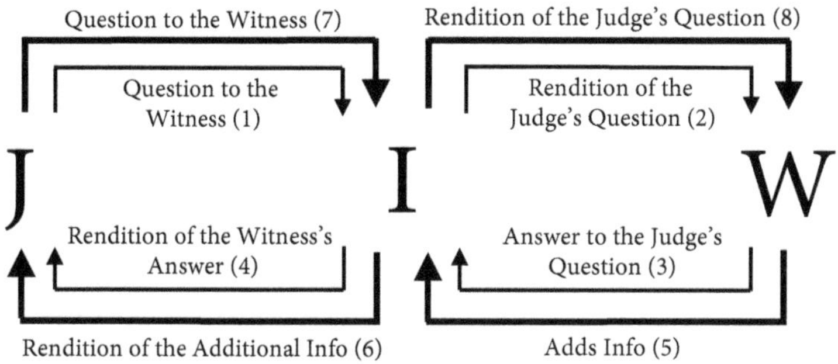

Fig. 6.4: Interaction with extended and non-renditions

The counter produced by the judge triggers out a response on the part of the witness, followed by his next TCU transmitting additional information.

Extract 6.52 presents yet another model for close renditions within counters (Fig. 6.3):

The counter is produced by the witness, whose counter is addressed to the interpreter. However, the interpreter does not answer the witness's question by herself, but instead she refers the question to the judge, who provides an answer, rendered by the interpreter.

Moreover, another model within counters, for both extended (Extract 6.49) and non-renditions (Extract 6.51), has been identified (Fig. 6.4):

Interestingly, this pattern is deployed in such an extreme episode, as when the interpreter renders the messages produced by the main speakers (Extract 6.49), and when the interpreter positions herself as the main speaker – although it seems that she renders the original utterances, she fails to do so; instead she creates her own information context. In other words, although the interaction is developed, what the primary speakers and the interpreter say are two different contents.

As far as extended renditions of upgrades are concerned, there is one more episode (Extract 6.65), which alters the picture of adjacency pairs as being unproblematic for the interpreter (Fig. 6.5):

The above pattern of bilingual interaction confirms that when a non-Polish speaking party understands Polish at least at a basic level, the question-rendition-answer-rendition interaction is disturbed by that party, who takes his turn without waiting for the interpreter's turn. However, as the answer is given in Spanish, the interpreter takes a turn after the witness in order to render the message to the judge.

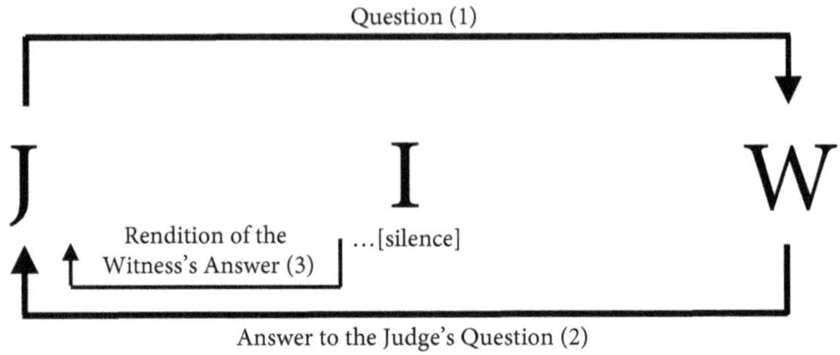

Fig. 6.5: Interaction with extended renditions

In general, adjacency pairs created by primary parties contribute to the interpreters' active participation in the communicative event. Close renditions occur when same evaluations appear, while extended and reduced renditions are provided in the majority of episodes. This leads to the conclusion that when the interaction is undisturbed by gaps or overlaps, in other words, when it is predictable to all participants, then the interpreter positions herself among these participants and feels comfortable enough to add or omit details in the transmitted messages.

7 Pre- and post-expansions in the interpreters' renditions

In this chapter **pre-expansions** and **post-expansions** as those components of the talk which are investigated. **Pre-expansions** preface the sequence (Schegloff 2007), while **post-expansions** occur after a possible completion of a sequence (Schegloff 1990).

The purpose of the analysis is to find a reply to the research questions, and in particular:

(1) to determine who (the interpreter or the main speakers) apply pre- and post-expansions,
(2) to explain the reasons for deploying pre- and post-expansions, and
(3) to discuss the interpreter's renditions of pre- and post- expansions.

To this aim, the episodes of interaction have been divided according to a participant in the talk who deploys, first, pre-expansions, and secondly, post-expansions.

7.1 Pre-expansions

Pre-expansions are divided into two groups: those, which are created by the interpreters, and the ones created by primary parties to the communicative events.

7.1.1 Interpreter-created pre-expansion

In Extract 7.105 the pre-expansion is applied to emphasize the interpreter's neutrality:

(7.105)	Original PL/EN talk	Author's verbatim translation into EN
Witness:	(.) I have friends in Poland. =	
Interpreter:	= pan twierdzi (.) że ma znajomych w Polsce.	*[He claims that he has friends in Poland.]*

The witness states that he has friends in Poland. The interpreter adds a pre-expansion (*he claims that*) and as a consequence **extended rendition** of the original message is provided. This grammatical shift consisting in changing the direct style of the primary speaker to the indirect style in the rendition into English is to identify that speaker as the original author of the information: the interpreter uses indirect style to talk about the witness's personal experience, as well as to keep distance from the reality described by him.

The indirect style is used also in the subsequent example:

(7.106)	Original PL/EN talk	Author's verbatim translation into EN
Counsel:	dlaczego strona pozwana nie zapłaciła tych faktur?	*[Why didn't the defendant pay these invoices?]*
Interpreter:	(.) can you tell why you (0.2) or °you as defendant° (0.2) didn't pay these invoices?	

In Extract 7.106 the counsel uses a direct style to ask the defendant about the reason for his having failed to pay the invoices. The interpreter uses a pre-expansion (*can you tell why you*) to attract the attention of the next speaker; this could be caused by the fact that the counsel uses a formal register (*defendant, strona pozwana*), the knowledge of which is not obligatory for the parties to the proceedings. This presupposition is confirmed by the subsequent pre-expansion (*or you as defendant*), in which the interpreter recovers the formal register used by the primary speaker. Only then does the interpreter complete her **extended rendition**.

In the example that follows, the interpreter applies a pre-expansion as an introductory comment to her rendition:

(7.107)	Original PL/EN talk	Author's verbatim translation into EN
Witness:	he drinks sometimes during a wee:k and on weeke:nds (1.0) when he drinks (0.5) he gets drunk.	
Interpreter:	(0.5) wzór był taki: (0.2) że on od czasu do czasu: e::: zdarzało mu się pić w trakcie tygodnia: (0.3) pi:ł (0.3) e::: w weekendy (2.0) jak pił (0.2) zdarzało mu się upijać.	*[The pattern was that from time to time… eee… he happened to drink during the week, he drank… eee… at weekends. When he drank, he would get drunk.]*

The witness produces an affirmative, pre-expansion free statement. The interpreter uses hedges and fillers when providing an **extended rendition**; this shows that she feels uncomfortable with the information she is to transmit. The sentence in which the defendant's addiction is revealed is preceded by the pre-expansion *the pattern was that…*, whose function is probably to mitigate both the harshness of the message and the interpreter's stress.

As distinct from previous examples, in Extract 7.108 the interpreter attempts to affect the witness's response:

(7.108)	Original PL/EN talk	Author's verbatim translation into EN
Lawyer:	czy uważał się pan za najlepszego przyjaciela obu stron w tamtym czasie?	*[Did you consider yourself the best friend of both parties at that time?]*
Interpreter:	(.) you said you considered yourself best friend of both parties at that time?	

The lawyer asks a direct question whether *the witness considered himself the best friend of both parties at that time.* The interpreter applies a pre-expansion (*you said…*), which may be a consequence of changing the order from a plain question (*did you consider yourself*) into an affirmative statement. By doing so, the interpreter provides an **extended rendition** and obviously makes a reference to the witness's possible previous answers, but at the same time she loses distance to the reality discussed during the examination; she fails to be neutral when she attempts to make the witness recall what he has said in one of his previous turns.

Furthermore, as a pre-expansion, the particle *so* is commonly deployed by interpreters.

In Extract 7.109 the interpreter uses *so* as a connector between the judge's question and her rendition:

(7.109)	Original PL/EN talk	Author's verbatim translation into EN
Judge:	((to the witness)) czy pan podpisał tę umowę?	*[Did you sign the contract?]*
Interpreter:	(0.3) so you signed this contract?	
Judge:	0.2) czy przed podpisaniem umowy w jakiś sposób weryfikował pan te y::: wysoko:ści (.) które są podane przez linie lotnicze?	*[Did you somehow verify these amounts quoted by the airlines prior to signing the contract?]*
Interpreter:	(0.2) did you verify these amounts prior to signing the contract (0.2) the contract?	

The judge asks the witness *whether he signed the contract.* The interpreter provides an **extended rendition**: she precedes her turn with the particle *so*, by which she evidently attempts to link a question–answer sequence. Therefore, the pre-expansion added by the interpreter builds up the structure of the act of communication.

In Extract 7.110 the particle *so* used as a pre-expansion plays a different role:

(7.110)	Original PL/EN talk	Author's verbatim translation into EN
Judge:	ile pan ma lat?	*[How old are you?]*
Interpreter:	(0.2) so (0.2) how old are you? =	
Defendant:	= I am forty seven.	
Interpreter:	(0.3) mam 47 lat.	*[I am forty seven.]*

The judge asks the defendant *how old he is*. The interpreter starts her **extended rendition** with *so*, which does not appear in the judge's original question. By introducing this element, the interpreter implicitly informs the interlocutor that he should focus on what she is saying. This gives the defendant time to concentrate and be prepared for providing the answers to further questions.

In Extract 7.111 the particle *so* is supposed to give time to the interpreter to think of the rendition:

(7.111)	Original PL/EN talk	Author's verbatim translation into EN
Judge:	od kiedy: e::: pan e::: y::: (0.2) przebywa na stałe w X?	*[Since when... eee... have you... yyy... stayed permanently in X?]*
Interpreter:	(0.2) so::: e:: since when did you stay permanently in X?	

The judge asks the witness *since when he has stayed permanently in Warsaw*. His question is hesitant, particular words are separated by three vocalic fillers and an appreciable pause (0.2). The interpreter deploys a particle *so* at the beginning of her **extended rendition** by which she intends to wipe out hesitations expressed by the judge that split his question and made it lengthy. In this particular context *so* is an equivalent of *to sum up* and/or *thus*, and, therefore, puts in order the original question.

Yet another way to preface the utterance with a pre-expansion is to add a pragmatic marker *yes*:

(7.112)	Original PL/EN talk	Author's verbatim translation into EN
Witness:	(.) a:nd... y:: then I take these photos (.) print them (.) providing to my friends...	

(7.112)	Original PL/EN talk	Author's verbatim translation into EN
Interpreter:	(0.2) ta:::k e: i potem pan drukuje te zdjęcia akt (.) a następnie (.) e::: (.) przedstawia je (0.2) daje do zapoznania (.) swoim (.) e::: swoim (.) *znajomym...*	*[Yes, and then he prints these photos of the files, and then, aaa..., he presents them, gives them to his, eee... his acquaintances to read...]*

The witness describes what he does with *the photos he takes* of the files: *he prints them and provides them to his friends.* The interpreter begins her turn with an appreciable pause (0.2), when she produces a stretched pragmatic marker *yes*, which in this particular context functions in the same way as *well*, that is, it appears in the interpreter's rendition for at least two reasons: to implicitly indicate the beginning of the interpreter's TCU, and to give her extra time to process the information. Afterwards, the interpreter provides an **extended rendition**.

In Extract 7.113, the interpreter produces a pre-expansion situated well in the middle of her rendition:

(7.113)	Original PL/EN talk	Author's verbatim translation into EN
Defendant:	and my experience so far well (0.2) she's already told you everything (.) you need to know (0.4) no contact (0.2) that's her wish (.) no contacts. =	
Interpreter:	= a moje doświadczenie jest takie (0.2) tak jak ona powiedziała (0.3) tłumaczę dosłownie (.) czyli tak (.) jak powiedziała (0.5) prze:d (0.2) >przede mną< (0.3) żadnych kontaktów...	*[And my experience is like she's already said, I'm interpreting literally, that is, like... she said... before... before me, no contacts...]*

In the defendant's talk the TCUs are short and they altogether create incoherent information. The interpreter attempts to provide a close rendition of the first (*and my experience is...*) and the second TCU (*like she's already said*), but facing a problem resulting from the nonchalant original message, she creates her own pre-expansion: *I'm interpreting literally, that is, like she said*, by which she, firstly, expressly informs the interlocutors that she is aware of her obligation to provide a verbatim interpretation, and secondly, gives a definition of what she means by literal interpretation: the one reflecting exactly, i.e. *repeating* what the primary party says in the target language. This pre-expansion is situated at an untypical point of the interpreter's talk: it is interlaced in-between the **extended rendition**, which is, as stated above, probably due to the style of the main speaker.

The episode below shows a similar example, where the interpreter deploys a pre-expansion which is positioned within her rendition:

(7.114)	Original PL/EN talk	Author's verbatim translation into EN
Defendant:	yes (0.2) and in fact I requested the co::urt (0.3) and my wi::fe (0.4) to release this entire medical report...	
Interpreter:	(0.2) tak (0.2) pan wie: (0.2) i tutaj prosił żonę (.) aby: <rozumiem> y::: sporządziła e:: ja:kby y::: cały::: y::: medyczny: jakby:: protokó:ł (0.2) czyli listę y: związaną z y;: chorobą X…	*[Yes, he knows, and here he asked his wife to, as I understand, prepare sort of, yyy… the whole… yyy… medical… sort of… report, that is a list concerning X's disease.]*

The defendant states that *he requested the court and his wife to release a medical report*. The interpreter begins with reproducing the original pre-expansion *yes*, but afterwards she preserves only the defendant's *wife* as one of the addressees of the request, while omitting the *court* as the other addressee. This shift in the way she renders the original message makes her create a pre-expansion (*as I understand*), by which she provides an explanation of her interpretation. Only then does she continue interpreting, however, a degree of hesitation is appreciable in her talk. As a result, an **extended rendition** is provided.

7.1.2 Primary party-created pre-expansion

In Extract 7.115 the pre-expansion is introduced by the judge to allow him to expressly identify with the institution he represents:

(7.115)	Original PL/EN talk	Author's verbatim translation into EN
Judge:	(.) sąd chciałby zapyta:ć (0.2) od kiedy pan zna pana X i panią X?	*[The judge would like to ask you since when you have known Mr. X and Mrs. X?]*
Interpreter:	(.) the court would like to ask you since when (.) you know Mr. X (.) and Mrs. X?	

The judge begins this episode of interaction; he deploys a pre-expansion *the Court would like to ask you* (*Sąd chciałby zapytać*) to enhance the level of formality of the trial and emphasize his majesty. The interpreter provides a **close rendition** of the judge's question to the degree that she interprets the Polish concept *sąd* with the English *court*[93]. In this particular example the judge refers to his official function rather than to the whole institution he represents. The interpreter's aim is to render the judge's question verbatim.

Similarly, in Extract 7.116, the judge deploys a pre-expansion to preface his question:

(7.116)	**Original PL/EN talk**	**Author's verbatim translation into EN**
Judge:	(0.2) i teraz sąd pana wysłucha w przedmiocie dwóch pana wniosków…	*[And now you will be heard with relation to your two motions.]*
Interpreter:	(.) and no:w (.) you will be heard and asked questions about your two motions…	

The judge announces that he will examine the witness (*now the court will hear you, teraz sąd pana wysłucha*). This pre-expansion is reproduced by the interpreter who, however, changes the grammatical form of the original utterance from active into passive voice. In the interpreter's **extended rendition** the emphasis is put on the activities to which the witness's is going to be submitted, while the judge underlines the majesty of the institution he represents.

In the example that follows the judge's turn comprises only pre-expansions:

(7.117)	**Original PL/EN talk**	**Author's verbatim translation into EN**
Judge:	(.) i czy dzisia:j (0.3) jeszcze ra:z (0.2) po raz trzeci (.) sąd pyta… (.) proszę powiedzieć?	*[And today once again, for the third time, the Court asks, if could you say.]*
Interpreter:	and toda:y (.) you are asked for the third time if you…	

Due to technical problems, this extract is only a short episode of longer interaction hence it is impossible to precisely determine whether the judge's turn is a pre-expansion to his own or the witness's further talk. However, based on the assumption that in CA it is difficult to unambiguously classify a particular episode of interaction as belonging to a certain group of techniques deployed by the interactants, it has been assumed accordingly that the judge is using several

93 In Polish the word *sąd* has three meanings. Firstly, it is a judicial institution established to settle disputes; secondly it is a judge or a panel of judges who hold a hearing http://sjp.pwn.pl/sjp/sad;2519448.html (September 12, 2017); and thirdly it is a building where judges examine the cases and pronounce sentences.

pre-expansions. The first (*and today once again for the third time*), second, the pre-expansion announcing that it is the judge representing the court who asks the question (*the court asks, sąd pyta*), and third, the next pre-expansion, which is a request addressed to the witness to make him speak (*could you say*). The interpreter provides a **substituted rendition** of the judge's utterances; she changes the grammatical form from an active *the court asks* to *you are asked*, as well as cuts off the other pre-expansion to *if you…*, which makes an impression of a suspended interpretation. In this example, as well as in Extract 7.116, the interpreters choose to use passive voice to get round a linguistic obstacle: in their pre-expansions the judges use a highly formal third-person singular form of introducing their questions (*the court asks*); even though the interpreters modify the grammatical content of the original utterances, the level of formality is fully preserved.

In Extract 7.118, the judge deploys a pre-expansion to expressly announce that he is going to ask a question:

(7.118)	**Original PL/EN talk**	**Author's verbatim translation into EN**
Judge:	pan przychodzi do czytelni i czyta akta (0.5) pytanie sądu jest (.) czy zna język polski w związku z tym? (0.2) proszę zapytać (.) czy pan sam czyta akta? =	*[You come to the reading room and read the files. The question of the court is if therefore he knows Polish? Please, ask, if he himself reads the files?]*
Interpreter:	= so:: (0.2) do you read the files by yourself in Polish?	

The judge deploys several pre-expansions. The first is to establish what has already been declared by the witness (*you come to the reading room and read the files, pan przychodzi do czytelni i czyta akta*) and is a repetition of the information included in the previous turn, probably either directed to the court clerk who is drawing up the minutes of the trial, or not addressed to any particular party to the proceedings and being just an element of thinking out loud on the part of the judge. The second pre-expansion is to announce the judge's question (*the question of the court is, pytanie sądu jest*) and, as well, may be directed to the next speakerin order to inform him that now it is the judge's turn to speak. In addition, the first and the second pre-expansion is separated by an appreciable pause (0.5). The third, separated from the second by an actual question about the witness's knowledge of Polish, is addressed to the interpreter (*please ask, proszę zapytać*); this situates the interpreter among the active participants in the interaction which makes her feel justified to provide a **reduced rendition** of the judge's two questions. An interesting feature of this particular episode of interaction is that even though the interpreter does not reproduce the judge's pre-expansions she begins her turn with a stretched particle *so* after which an appreciable pause (0.2) occurs. By doing so, she substitute the features of the primary party's talk with the characteristic elements composing her own talk.

In Extract 7.119 the judge's question is prefaced by the particle *so* which plays a role of the pre-expansion:

(7.119)	**Original PL/EN talk**	**Author's verbatim translation into EN**
Judge:	czyli w ocenie pana (0.2) projekt został wykonany prawidłowo?	*[So in your opinion the project was done in a proper way?]*
Interpreter:	(0.3) in your opinion (0.3) the project was done in a proper way?	
Witness:	(0.2) ye:s.	
Interpreter:	(.) tak.	*[Yes.]*

The judge asks *whether in the witness's opinion the project was done in a proper way*, this question being preceded by a pre-expansion *so* (*czyli*) which is to sum up what the previous speaker has said. The interpreter provides a **reduced rendition** of the judge's question, when she omits the pragmatic marker *czyli* (*so*), which pertains to the judge's talk: it is he who isolates his new question from what has just been said by the previous participant in the interaction. The interpreter echoes the judge, but does not render the marker as being an artificial element in her turn.

Extract 7.120 shows that it is the judge who is creating a pre-expansion:

(7.120)	**Original PL/EN talk**	**Author's verbatim translation into EN**
Judge:	chciałam zapytać świadka o <u>godność</u>, (0.3) czy ma pan jakiś dokument tożsamości? =	*[I wanted to ask the witness for their name, do you have any form of identification?]*
Interpreter:	= what is your name? do you have any <u>identification</u> document?	
Witness:	(xxx) I have got a: passport. =	
Interpreter:	= ma [paszport.	*[He has a passport.]*

The judge begins this episode of interaction by asking the witness about his name and his form of identification. The question itself is preceded by a pre-expansion *I wanted to ask the witness*. When the interpreter renders the judge's question, she omits the pre-expansion and, by deploying two TCUs, asks two direct questions about the witness's name and about his form of identification.

The witness's response is as well direct (*I have a passport*) thus it can be deduced that a **reduced rendition** on the part of the interpreter causes that the witness to provide a simple answer. Furthermore, the combination of two direct-style turns makes the interpreter increase the distance to the witness's original answer.

In the following example, the judge addresses the witness with a double pre-expansion:

(7.121)	Original PL/EN talk	Author's verbatim translation into EN
Judge:	proszę pana, chciałabym się dowiedzieć (.) jeśli chodzi o relacje (0.3) czy pan zauważył kiedykolwiek (.) że te relacje >między małżonkami się< °pogorszyły°?	*[Sir, I would like to know, as far as the relations are concerned, whether you have ever noticed that these relations between the spouses got worse?]*
Interpreter:	(.) have you ever noticed (.) that e::: the relationship of the partie:s e::: got worse?	
Witness:	ye::s (0.7) it was like h (0.2) I guess y:: a few months after their son was born.	
Interpreter:	(0.2) tak (0.2) myślę (.) że było to kilka miesięcy po narodzinach syna.	*[Yes, I think that it was a few months after their son was born.]*

The judge begins his turn with a generic pre-expansion *Sir* (*proszę pana*) the aim of which is to attract the witness's attention not as much to the fact that it is him who is being heard by the judge (this has been announced at the moment in which the judges requests the witness to approach the witness stand) but rather to make him listen to and answer the judge's questions. Immediately afterwards the judge deploys a type-specific pre-expansion *I would like to know*, which adds to the emphasis introduced by the first pre-expansion. Nevertheless, the TCUs that follow are featured with an appreciable pause (0.3), and a variable pace. This makes the judge's utterance stretch. In response, the interpreter omits the two pre-expansions (probably in order to speed up the timing of the conversation) and uses a direct style to render the judge's question. Nevertheless, although a **reduced rendition** is provided, the interpreter fails in her attempts to shorten the interpretation time: in her turn there are two vocalic fillers which prolong the rendition and add an element of hesitation. The witness, as the next speaker, reproduces the judge's and the interpreter's hesitant style, which is then repeated in the interpreter's SPP. In the witness's FPP the use of a sequence of pragmatic markers (*yes*, *it was like*, *I guess*) is noticeable; however, the interpreter rather freely transmits them: she picks up the pragmatic marker which stands at the beginning of the turn and thus is the most audible element of the original utterance, which, as can be argued, has to be rendered in order to maintain the clients' impression of an accurate interpretation.

In the same vein the next example shows an episode of interaction where the counsel deploys a double pre-expansion:

(7.122)	**Original PL/EN talk**	**Author's verbatim translation into EN**
Counsel:	proszę pana (0.2) proszę powiedzieć (0.2) czy wie pan co było przyczyną kłótni pomiędzy małżonkami (.) które obserwował w przeciągu (.) <powiedzmy> (.) ostatnich trzech lat (.) przed tym (.) zanim się powód wyprowadził?	*[Sir, could you tell me whether you know what caused the arguments between the spouses which you had been observing let's say during the last 3 years, before the plaintiff moved out?]*
Interpreter:	(.) do you know what was the reason for the arguments that you witnessed during the last three years (.) before the petitioner moved out?	
Witness:	(0.3) some yes (0.2) some no.	
Interpreter:	(.) w niektórych przypadkach tak (.) w niektórych nie.	*[In some cases yes, in others no.]*

The counsel uses a generic pre-expansion *Sir* (*proszę pana*) to begin his turn. After an appreciable pause (0.2), the counsel adds a type-specific pre-expansion *could you tell me* (*proszę powiedzieć*), which intensifies the counsel's first pre-expansion. Interestingly, the counsel increases a number of pre-expansions by adding *do you know* (*czy wie pan*). Such a multiplication of pre-expansions considerably delays the moment in which an actual question is asked; this may be due to a delicate matter being the substance of the question (arguments between the spouses). The interpreter reproduces only the last pre-expansion, being the most contiguous to the actual question, however, the **reduced rendition** is almost as long as the FPP. This probably contributes to the witness's short response: he begins with an appreciable pause (0.3) to afterwards deploy two TCUs separated by another appreciable pause (0.2). When the interpreter reduces the two silences to two micro-pauses, the witness's hesitant style is lost.

In a similar example, it is the prosecutor who is deploying a type-specific pre-expansion:

(7.123)	**Original PL/EN talk**	**Author's verbatim translation into EN**
Prosecutor:	proszę powiedzieć (0.3) czy pana żona ma jakąś <emeryturę>? =	*[Could you say whether your wife receives an old-age pension?]*
Interpreter:	= does your wife get old-age pension (0.) retirement pension?	

(7.123)	Original PL/EN talk	Author's verbatim translation into EN
Witness:	Yes, she gets from here, from Poland. Yes she gets a pension.	
Interpreter:	Tak, otrzymuje polską emeryturę budżetową.	*[Yes, she gets a Polish budgetary pension]*

The prosecutor deploys the pre-expansion *please tell me* (*proszę powiedzieć*), after which he asks an actual question concerning the witness's wife's old-age pension. The interpreter omits the pre-expansion (a **reduced rendition** is provided), but instead, she doubles the original TCU: she provides two equivalents of one Polish term (*old-age pension*, *retirement pension*, *emerytura*), which makes the timing of her rendition equal to the one of the original question. This apparently makes the witness provide a detailed answer, immediately after which the interpreter provides a close rendition into Polish. In this episode of interaction, the impression on the witness made by interpreter that she is doing her best to communicate ideas to the witness as meticulously as possible, causes the witness's answer to be, firstly, preferred (the witness responds affirmatively and clearly), and, secondly, it includes even more information than has been required.

There are instances, in which a pre-expansion is not a prelude to a question, but a confirmation of the current speaker understanding the information he has just received.

In Extract 7.124, the judge begins his turn with a type-specific pre-expansion to confirm his understanding of the witness's explanations:

(7.124)	Original PL/EN talk	Author's verbatim translation into EN
Judge:	rozumiem (2.) jak często pan <odwiedzał> swoją żonę >w tym domu w X< będąc w Polsce?	*[I understand. How often did you visit your wife in that house in X when you were staying in Poland?]*
Interpreter:	(.) how often >did you visit your wife in X<?	

The judge uses a pre-expansion *I understand* (*rozumiem*) followed by an appreciable pause (0.2), after which he asks an actual question. The interpreter provides a **reduced rendition**: she omits the pre-expansion and asks a direct question in the assumption that the pre-expansion is a confirmation of what the previous speaker (the witness) has said.

In the following episode, the judge deploys two pre-expansions to confirm that he understands what the witness has said:

(7.125)	Original PL/EN talk	Author's verbatim translation into EN
Judge:	Y:hm: (.) rozumiem (0.4) i zamieszkają państwo wtedy tutaj (0.3) w tym domu w X?	*[Yhm, I understand. And you then will be living here in the house in X?]*
Interpreter:	(.) and you will be living in X?	

The judge twice confirms his understanding of what the witness has just declared. The first pre-expansion is a pragmatic marker *y:hm* and the other, *I understand* (*rozumiem*). Afterwards there is a long pause (0.4) and only then does the judge ask the question. However, the interpreter does not render either of the judge's confirmations. This may be due to the fact that the judge's pre-expansions are manifestations of his professional involvement in the examination. As the interpreter is supposed to maintain neutrality, she provides a **reduced rendition** by omitting the two pre-expansions, by which she wants to distance from the judges' approach and implicitly inform the witness that she only transmits the questions and does not take a stance as to the content of the declarations.

The next example shows a double pre-expansion produced by the judge:

(7.126)	Original PL/EN talk	Author's verbatim translation into EN
Judge:	czyli rozumiem (.) że: (0.3) dobrze zrozumiałam? (0.2) że po pół roku jak pan wróci (0.2) to państwo zamieszkają razem w X (0.2) i pan zatrudni pielęgniarkę (.) która się będzie żoną opiekować?	*[So, I understand that… have I understood correctly that after half a year when you go back, you will be living in X and you will employ a nurse who will look after your wife?]*
Interpreter:	(.) when >you are back in June< you are going to live in X?	
Witness:	Ye:s	
Interpreter:	Tak.	*[Yes.]*

The judge begins his turn with a pre-expansion *so, I understand that* (*czyli rozumiem, że*), which requires the ending consisting of an actual question. However, the speaker makes an appreciable pause (0.3) and then, instead of asking the question, produces another pre-expansion, which is a repetition of the first one (*dobrze zrozumiałam, have I understood it correctly*). The difference between the two is that while the former is a rhetorical figure which includes a self-confirmation and thus does not need further confirmation on the part of the next speaker, the latter is addressed to the next speaker and needs his response. Nevertheless, the judge, after another appreciable pause (0.2) produces the next four TCUs, each separated from the next by two appreciable pauses (0.2 each) and one micro-pause. The interpreter provides a **reduced rendition**; she omits the two pre-expansions in her rendition, by which she eliminates the need for confirmation expressed by the judge when he shyly asks if he has understood correctly the witness's words from the information transmitted to the witness. This is intensified by changing the judge's question into an affirmative statement. Thus, in the witness's eyes the judge is sure of what he is saying and strong in his convictions; the witness's answer is affirmative and consists of one word only, so does the interpreter's rendition.

The example that follows show pre-expansions that occur in the talks of both the judge and the witness:

(7.127)	**Original PL/EN talk**	**Author's verbatim translation into EN**
Judge:	(.) zna pan przyczynę (.) dla której nastąpił taki stan rzeczy?	*[Do you know the reason why it happened?]*
Interpreter:	(.) do you know the reason why it happened?	
Witness:	(.) y:::hm (0.2) I'm not really su::re (0.2) I think tha::t (0.3) I think (.) tha:t X wasn't happy. I think he: wasn't happy with the amount of time (.) he had to:::: (.) that had to be:: dedicated to his son. =	
Interpreter:	= nie jestem pewien (.) wydaje mi się (.) że X nie był szczęśliwy z powodu tego (.) ile czasu (.) ma poświęcać swojemu syno[wi.	*[I'm not sure, I think that X wasn't happy because of the time he was to dedicate to his son.]*
Witness:	[and I thi:nk (0.2) he told us he::: (.) I think he was (.) bored (0.2) he wanted to have parties… (.) I think he felt like >that time was< over.	
Interpreter:	(.) mam wrażenie (0.2) powiedział nam (.) że był znudzony (.) nadal chciał chodzić (.) y:::: (.) wychodzić na imprezy (.) dobrze się bawić (.) i miał wrażenie y::: że ten czas się skończył.	*[I'm under the impression, he told us that he was bored, he still wanted to go… yyy… to go to parties, to have fun and had an impression that the time was up.]*

The judge begins his turn with a pre-expansion *do you know the reason* (*zna pan przyczynę*), which is preserved in the interpreter's rendition. In response to the question, the witness begins his turn with a series of pre-expansions (*y:::hm, I'm not really su::re, I think tha::t, I think that, I think he:*), each separated from the subsequent by two appreciable pauses (0.2 each), another appreciable pause (0.3), and an initial part of the answer (X wasn't happy), all of which contribute to an overall hesitation of the witness concerning the provided information. The instances of hesitation may be a result of the structure of the interaction: when the judge invites the witness to answer the question by adding a pre-expansion, he expects an affirmative response. The witness as the next speaker presumes that the preferred response would be a positive one, however, he needs to decline: thus, the interaction is not comfortable for the witness, and this is audible in his declarations. Interestingly, the interpreter reduces the number of instances of hesitation; only two pre-expansions (*I'm not sure, I think that, nie jestem pewien, wydaje mi się*) are transmitted, and the pace is higher as compared to the original response. The witness continues answering the judge's question; again, he deploys a number of pre-expansions (*I think*) interlaced with an appreciable pause (0.2) and an element of the answer. In her turn, the interpreter preserves a number of pre-expansions (*I've got an impression, he told us, he had an impression, mam wrażenie, powiedział nam, miał wrażenie*) and thus reproduces the witness's hesitancy. As a whole, a **substituted rendition** is provided.

7.2 Post-expansions

Post-expansions include two categories, one of them comprising the post-expansions created by the interpreters, and the other one covering those created by the primary parties.

7.2.1 Interpreter-created post-expansions

Extract 7.128 shows that the interpreter deploys a post-expansion to implicitly transmit additional information:

(7.128)	Original PL/EN talk	Author's verbatim translation into EN
Judge:	Jak się nazywała ta osoba, z którą pan się spotkał?	*[What was the name of the person whom you met]*
Interpreter:	What's the name (.) of eh:: that person with whom you met?	
Witness:	<u>Królikowski</u>[a]. =	
Interpreter:	= Królikowski? jeśli dobrze pan…	*[Królikowski? If well he…]*

[a] In Extract 7.128 a proper name Królikowski appears. This is not the name originally mentioned by the witness, but the substitute inserted for the purposes of this study to illustrate the difficulty to pronounce Polish names.

The judge begins the talk and asks the witness about the name of the person with whom the witness met. The interpreter provides a close rendition of the judge's question. In response to that, the witness says one word: Królikowski, that is, provides the judge with the person's name. The interpreter repeats the name with a rising question-like intonation and afterwards deploys a post-expansion *if well he…* (*jeśli dobrze pan…*) hence a **non-rendition** is provided. This post-expansion supplements the interpreter's reaction to the witness's answer: the interpreter is surprised that the English-speaking witness correctly pronounces a Polish surname. In other words, the interpreter self-appoints to evaluate the witness's linguistic competence in order to transmit an implicit message that the non-Polish speaking party might mispronounce the person's name.

In Extract 7.129, the post-expansion serves the interpreter to assess the information provided by the witness:

(7.129)	**Original PL/EN talk**	**Author's verbatim translation into EN**
Judge:	Kiedy e::: spotkał się pan z y::: panem X?	*[When did you meet Mr. X?]*
Interpreter:	(.) when did you meet Mr. X? =	
Witness:	= it was five years ago. =	
Interpreter:	= to już pięć lat temu wię:c trochę trudno:	*[It's already been 5 years now, so it's a little bit difficult…]*

The judge begins the talk by asking a question about the date when the witness met Mr. X. The interpreter provides a close rendition of the question. The witness's response is an affirmative statement (*it was five years ago*), from which it results that the witness is completely sure of his answer. The interpreter adds an adverb *already* (*już*) when rendering the witness's answer, and then a **non-rendition** is provided in the form of a post-expansion *so it's a little bit difficult* (*więc trochę trudno*). By assessing the witness's ability to recall the events which took place several years ago in this way, the interpreter shows bias towards the witness.

In Extract 7.130, the interpreter produces a post-expansion in which she assumes the competences of the judge to assess the witness' statements:

(7.130)	**Original PL/EN talk**	**Author's verbatim translation into EN**
Judge:	= tylko <u>czyta</u> po polsku?	*[He only reads in Polish?]*
Interpreter:	(.) do you <u>read</u> in Polish?	
Witness:	no, I do not…	
Interpreter:	nie: pan nie czyta eee… po polsku: (0.3) przepraszam (.) bo wcześniej pan powiedział (.) że czyta: (0.2) ale teraz mówi (.) że nie czyta.	*[No, he doesn't read eee… in Polish, I'm sorry, because before he said that he read and now he is saying that he doesn't read.]*

The judge asks the question whether the witness only reads in Polish. The interpreter provides a close rendition of the judge's question, but there is a shift in the grammatical person; the judge, by saying *he only reads in Polish*? (*tylko czyta po polsku*?) expressly addresses the interpreter whom he is asking about the witness. The interpreter modifies the grammatical form so that the question is addressed to the witness as an actual recipient. When the witness provides a negative response (*no, I do not*), the interpreter changes the grammatical person by deploying a polite and formal address term *pan*. Afterwards, an appreciated pause (0.3) occurs and the interpreter provides a **non-rendition**: she creates a post-expansion by which she informs the judge that the witness' statements are incoherent and confusing. Hence, as distinct to Extract 7.128, the post-expansion is not a linguistic comment on the part of the interpreter. Instead, by commenting on the witness' statements, the interpreter expressly becomes a component of the judiciary.

The next example shows that the interpreter uses a post-expansion to suggest the answer:

(7.131)	**Original PL/EN talk**	**Author's verbatim translation into EN**
Judge:	jak często chce pan mieć kontakty z dzieckiem (.) dopóki nie zostanie sporządzona opinia? (0.3) pan o nie wnioskuje (0.4) jak często?	*[How often do you want to have contact with the child until an opinion is prepared? You request them. How often?]*
Interpreter:	(.) how often do you have this contact? (.) until the moment that an <u>opinion</u> from this examination will be prepared? (0.3) <u>so</u> (.) how often do you like to have this contact… bu:t (0.4) like y::: (0.2) <u>temporary</u>?	

The judge asks the defendant *how often he wants to have contact with the child*. The interpreter introduces two serious modifications to the judge's original question. Firstly, the judge asks about a frequency with which the defendant wants to have contact with his child, while the interpretation loses a detail relating to the defendant's will to have these contacts and refers to the present situation (*how often do you have this contact…*). Secondly, the interpreter uses a post-expansion, in which she suggests the frequency of the contact (*like… temporary*), by which a **non-rendition** is provided.

Extract 7.132 shows that a post-expansion aimed originally at retrieving information from the witness does not produce the expected effect:

(7.132)	Original PL/ES talk	Author's verbatim translation into EN
Judge:	a jaki wysoki był ten wzrost?	*[And how high was this increase?]*
Interpreter:	(.) y cuál cuál era el nivel de esta alza? (0.2) el porcentaje? =	*[And what what was the level of this increase? The percentage?]*
Witness:	= hasta:: (0.2) si no recuerdo mal (.) se compraba por X ezlotys	*[Up to… If my memory serves me well it was bought for X zlotys.]*

The judge asks about the value of the increase. The interpreter transmits the judge's question, and provides a **non-rendition** when she produces a pre-second insert expansion (*the percentage?*) to elicit a detailed answer from the witness. Nonetheless, the witness focuses on the first question. In consequence, he answers only the judge's question, ignoring the interpreter's expansion with an added request. Extract 7.132 shows that there are occasions on which the witness does not let the interpreter take over the judge's power of lawyers.

Extract 7.133 shows that the interpreter applies a post-expansion which reveals her bias towards the judiciary:

(7.133)	Original PL/EN talk	Author's verbatim translation into EN
Judge:	sąd nie wydaje decyzji (0.6) zapoznaje się z tym (.) co jest w aktach…	*[The court does not issue decisions, it familiarizes itself with what is in the files.]*
Interpreter:	(0.2) the court do not issue any decision about this (1.5) they just make themselves familiar with this (1.0) they read this because they read <u>everything</u> in the files.	

The judge, in response to the witness's previous comments concerning the judge's attitude towards the proceedings, informs the witness that *the judge does not issue decisions, he familiarizes himself with what is in the files*. The interpreter applies a **non-rendition**, by which she adds a post-expansion (*they read this because they read everything in the files*). By doing so, the interpreter shows a bias towards the judiciary: in the knowledge that the judge loses his hierarchical position by explaining his previous decisions instead of asking questions, the interpreter feels obliged to make the judge recover that privileged position.

In Extract 7.134, the interpreter produces a post-expansion to distance from the content of the message:

(7.134)	Original PL/EN talk	Author's verbatim translation into EN
Witness:	(0.3) and we agree:d that ah::: we have to: (.) to::: (0.5) set up (0.2) ah:: settle this payment.	
Interpreter:	(0.3) uzgodniliśmy (.) że musimy: y:::: (0.2) że::: musimy rozliczyć tę <płatność> (.) że::: musimy (0.4) że musimy po prostu:: (0.2) oni muszą uiścić tę płatność.	*[We agreed that we had to, yyy… that we had to settle this payment, that we had to, that we had to simply, they had to make this payment…]*

The witness begins his turn after an appreciable pause (0.3), his talk is hesitant, with stretches (*agree:d*, *to:*, and *to:::*), vocalic fillers, and two other appreciable pauses (0.5 and 0.2), he also detects a repairable (*set up*). The interpreter provides a **substituted rendition**. She begins with an appreciable pause (0.3), after which she reproduces the witness's speaking style, including the original grammatical person *we* (*we agreed that we had to, that we had to settle this payment*). Apparently, she completes her rendition. Nonetheless, after a micro-pause, she continues speaking (*that we had to that we had to simply they had to make this payment*), where the most noticeable modification is that she applies a shift from *we* to *they*, probably owing to her subjective fear that the judge could understand the use of *we* as an express manifestation of the interpreter's partiality and forming part of the group comprised by *we-inclusive*. Therefore, she chooses to increase the distance between the interpreter and the private client.

In Extract 7.135 the interpreter uses a post-expansion to put an emphasis on the most important fragment of the original message:

(7.135)	Original PL/EN talk	Author's verbatim translation into EN
Judge:	czy jednym z elementów tego kontraktu (.) było ustalenie przez wykonawcę (0.3) czy tego rodzaju kontrakty są bardziej opłacalne?	*[Was one of the elements of the contract to determine if such contracts were more profitable by the contractor?]*
Interpreter:	(.) was the aim (0.2) one of the aims of the contract (0.3) was to settle (.) if it is more profitable to introduce this kind of settlements (.) performance in the market in Poland? (0.2) >is it more profitable<?	

The judge asks whether *one of the elements of the contract was to determine if such contracts were more profitable by the contractor*. The interpreter provides an **extended rendition**; firstly, she adds an element which specifies the place (*Poland*) where the contract is to be performed, and secondly she gives particulars regarding the nature of the contract (*introduction of this kind of settlements*). Afterwards, the interpreter produces a post-expansion (*is it more profitable?*) which summarizes the prefacing rendition and points out the main fragment of the question.

Similarly, the next example proves that the interpreter applies a post-expansion to attract the recipient's attention to a particular fragment of the question:

(7.136)	**Original PL/EN talk**	**Author's verbatim translation into EN**
Judge:	dlatego można powiedzieć (0.2) że zmarnowaliśmy rok.	*[So it can be said that we have wasted one year.]*
Interpreter:	(0.4) so we could actually say (0.2) that we wasted one year no:w (1.0) because the test cannot be issued. =	
Judge:	= ja to kieruję do pana (0.2) ale to jest do obu stron.	*[I am talking to you but it's to both parties.]*
Interpreter:	(0.2) it's not only to you (1.0) it's to both parties (2.0) the statement that you::: actually (0.5) one year was wasted (0.2) because you bo:th y::: a kind of y::: didn't like y:::: you both didn't want this examination happen.	

The judge says to the witness that *it can be said that they have wasted one year*. The interpreter adds a pragmatic marker *actually*, and then adds a post-expansion (*because the test cannot be issued*) aimed at explaining the preceding utterance. Immediately after the interpreter completes her turn, the judge adds that *he is talking to the respondent but it's to both parties*. The interpreter transmits the judge's utterance (*it's not only to you it's to both parties*), but then, after an appreciable pause (2.0), creates a post-expansion which, as in her previous turn, is to recall the history of the case and thus to justify the judge's questions. The two post-expansions are **non-renditions**, where the interpreter takes advantage of previously acquired knowledge of the case.

7.2.2 Primary party-created post-expansions

Extract 7.137 shows a post-expansion produced by the defendant, and reproduced by the interpreter:

(7.137)	**Original PL/EN talk**	**Author's verbatim translation into EN**
Judge:	teraz proszę o zabranie głosu panią adwokat…	*[Now I ask the counsel to take the floor.]*

(7.137)	Original PL/EN talk	Author's verbatim translation into EN
Interpreter:	(0.3) now the counsel will speak...	
Defendant:	(.) I understand…	
Interpreter:	(.) dobrze.	*[Good.]*

The judge asks *the counsel to take the floor*. The interpreter provides substituted rendition by telling the defendant that *now the counsel will speak*. In terms of interaction, this could be a complete episode of interaction as the judge does not expect any response to his announcement. Nonetheless, the defendant responds by saying *I understand* in order to confirm that he is following the act of communication and knows that now it is the counsel's turn to speak. This post-expansion created by the primary speaker causes the interpreter to take her turn to render it by saying *good*; thus a **close rendition** is provided. For the trajectory of the interaction the post-expansion is irrelevant: regardless of the response on the part of the defendant, the proceedings are continued.

7.3 Multiple expansions

Examples of the complex use of expansions by one or more interactants have been detected.

Extract 7.138 shows that the interpreter creates both a pre- and a post-expansion to apply her extralinguistic competences:

(7.138)	Original PL/EN talk	Author's verbatim translation into EN
Witness:	(0.2) the unique problem after that was the problem of <u>exchange</u> rate. =	
Interpreter:	= yhm? (0.4) wię:c uzgodniono (0.2) że (0.3) natomiast kwestią pozostającą do uzgodnienia (.) był kurs wymiany walut (0.3) jaki mielibyśmy przyjąć do tej korekty…	*[Yhm. So it was agreed that… Whereas an issue that still remained to be agreed upon was an exchange rate, which we were supposed to employ in this value adjustment.]*

The witness answers that *the unique problem after that was the problem of the exchange rate*. The interpreter surrounds this straightforward response with a pre-expansion (*so it was agreed that whereas an issue that still remained to be agreed upon was*) and a post-expansion (*which we were supposed to employ in this value adjustment*), hence an **extended rendition** is provided. The use of the pre-expansion is aimed at indicating that the interpreter is distancing herself from the transmitted message: the passive voice contributes to pointing out that something was agreed upon but that the interpreter did not participate in these agreements. The post-expansion is a manifestation of the interpreter's extralinguistic competences: not only does she transmit the information about the exchange rate, but also explains why this matter was discussed by the parties involved.

The subsequent example shows a **substituted rendition** of the judge's type-specific pre-expansion and ends up with the interpreter's post-expansion:

(7.139)	**Original PL/EN talk**	**Author's verbatim translation into EN**
Judge:	(.) proszę powiedzieć (0.2) czy:: >uczestniczył pan< w negocjacjach umowy?	*[Please tell me if you participated in negotiations of the contract?]*
Interpreter:	(.) did you participate in negotiations of the contract? =	
Witness:	: = there was effectively no negotiation really…=	
Interpreter:	= tak naprawdę nie było negocjacji (0.2) otrzymaliśmy ofertę (.) przyjęliśmy ją.	*[There was actually no negotiation, we received an offer, we accepted it.]*

The judge begins this episode of interaction with the pre-expansion *please tell me* (*proszę powiedzieć*). The interpreter resigns from the pre-expansion to render the actual question posed by the judge. Interestingly, when a request is omitted in the rendition, this makes the witness produce a dispreferred response (*there was effectively no negotiation really*), while the projected and preferred answer would be *yes, I did* or, only a projected one: *no, I didn't*. However, the witness does not speak about his possible participation in the negotiations, but rather about the absence of negotiations of the contract. The interpreter perceives the witness's answer as evasive, thus she adds an explanation of what the procedure consisted in: *they received an offer and accepted it* without any negotiations, which might be exactly what happened, but neither the witness nor any other party to this act of communication has ever mentioned these facts. In other words, the interpreter's direct question reverses the judge's attempts to make the witness speak which results in the interpreter adding extra elements (a post-expansion) to construct preferred response in her SPP.

7.4 Conclusions

All the episodes of interaction analyzed in this chapter have been classified as pre- or post-expansions. The analysis has shown that both categories comprise interpreter-created and primary party-created expansions.

Tab. 7.1: Interpreter-created pre-expansions

Extract	Interactant \ Renditions	CR	ER	RR	SBR	SMR	TMR	NR	ZR
7.105	Witness	0	1	0	0	0	0	0	0
7.106	Counsel	0	1	0	0	0	0	0	0
7.107	Witness	0	1	0	0	0	0	0	0
7.108	Lawyer	0	1	0	0	0	0	0	0
7.109	Judge	0	1	0	0	0	0	0	0
7.110	Judge	0	1	0	0	0	0	0	0
7.111	Judge	0	1	0	0	0	0	0	0
7.112	Witness	0	1	0	0	0	0	0	0
7.113	Defendant	0	1	0	0	0	0	0	0
7.114	Defendant	0	1	0	0	0	0	0	0
Total:		**0**	**10**	**0**	**0**	**0**	**0**	**0**	**0**

As regards **pre-expansions created by the interpreter**, they can be divided into further groups according to the function they serve. (1) Indirect speech is used to create and maintain a psychological distance between the neutral interpreter and the courtroom reality in which she is situated; (2) shifts from questions to affirmative statements are manifestations of the interpreter's bias towards one of the interactants; (3) the use of the particle *so* vary: it builds the structure of the conversation, is to attract the next speaker's attention, and gives the current speaker time to think of his utterance (in the same way another pre-expansion—*yes*—works). There are also pre-expansions produced in the middle of the interpreter's rendition, which work in a similar way to indirect speech—they are to exclude the interpreter from the described reality. As the interpreters enrich the original utterances, the application of these pre-expansions involves providing extended renditions, as shown in Tab. 7.1:

Furthermore, **primary party-created pre-expansions** assume different functions, depending on who deploys them. The judges and other representatives of the judiciary use them to expressly identify with the institution they represent, to announce the question, to request for answering the question, and to confirm their understanding of the declarations made by the examined parties. When the witness uses a pre-expansion, it is to underline that what he says is his personal opinion. In the episodes with primary party-created pre-expansions the interpreters provide typically reduced renditions, but also substituted, close and extended renditions can be identified. These findings are presented in Tab. 7.2:

Tab. 7.2: Primary party-created pre-expansions

Extract	Renditions / Interactant	CR	ER	RR	SBR	SMR	TMR	NR	ZR
7.115	Judge	**1**	0	0	0	0	0	0	0
7.116	Judge	0	**1**	0	0	0	0	0	0
7.117	Judge	0	0	0	**1**	0	0	0	0
7.118	Judge	0	0	**1**	0	0	0	0	0
7.119	Judge	0	0	**1**	0	0	0	0	0
7.120	Judge	0	0	**1**	0	0	0	0	0
7.121	Judge	0	0	**1**	0	0	0	0	0
7.122	Counsel	0	0	**1**	0	0	0	0	0
7.123	Prosecutor	0	0	**1**	0	0	0	0	0
7.124	Judge	0	0	**1**	0	0	0	0	0
7.125	Judge	0	0	**1**	0	0	0	0	0
7.126	Judge	0	0	**1**	0	0	0	0	0
7.127	Judge/Witness	0	0	0	**1**	0	0	0	0
Total:		**1**	**1**	**9**	**2**	**0**	**0**	**0**	**0**

Moreover, **interpreter-created post-expansions** serve to give additional information introducing the interpreter's personal point of view, suggesting the answer to the examined party, showing the interpreter's a bias towards the judiciary, underlining a particular fragment of the rendition, or distancing from the declarations of the examined party. On such occasions, the interpreters have first provided all of the non-renditions, but also single episodes with extended and substituted renditions have been detected, as presented in Tab. 7.3:

On the basis of only one, exceptional, as regards the analyzed material, episode of interaction with the **primary party-created post-expansion**, by which the defendant expresses his acceptance to the judge's request, addressed to the counsel, to move onto the next stage of the proceedings, is irrelevant for this particular communicative act; however, a close rendition has been provided by the interpreter (Tab. 7.4):

Moreover, a separate category of **multiple expansions** has been isolated, which proves that, firstly, one interlocutor in one turn has a potential to create pre- and post-expansions, and secondly, the pre-expansion produced by one interlocutor implies the creation of the post-expansion by another interlocutor. It confirms that pre- and post-expansions, even though function differently in the interaction, can still influence the pre- and post-expansions irrespective of

Tab. 7.3: Interpreter-created post-expansions

Extract	Interactant \ Renditions	CR	ER	RR	SBR	SMR	TMR	NR	ZR
7.128	Witness	0	0	0	0	0	0	1	0
7.129	Witness	0	0	0	0	0	0	1	0
7.130	Witness	0	0	0	0	0	0	1	0
7.131	Judge	0	0	0	0	0	0	1	0
7.132	Judge	0	0	0	0	0	0	1	0
7.133	Judge	0	0	0	0	0	0	1	0
7.134	Witness	0	0	0	1	0	0	0	0
7.135	Judge	0	1	0	0	0	0	0	0
7.136	Judge	0	0	0	0	0	0	1	0
Total:		**0**	**1**	**0**	**1**	**0**	**0**	7	**0**

Tab. 7.4: Primary party-created post-expansions

Extract	Interactant \ Renditions	CR	ER	RR	SBR	SMR	TMR	NR	ZR
7.137	Defendant	1	0	0	0	0	0	0	0
Total:		**1**	**0**	**0**	**0**	**0**	**0**	**0**	**0**

Tab. 7.5: Multiple expansions

Extract	Interactant \ Renditions	CR	ER	RR	SBR	SMR	TMR	NR	ZR
7.138	Witness	0	1	0	0	0	0	0	0
7.139	Judge	0	0	0	1	0	0	0	0
Total:		**0**	**1**	**0**	**1**	**0**	**0**	**0**	**0**

being applied by one or more interlocutors. In the case of multiple expansions, extended and substituted renditions are provided (Tab. 7.5):

Taking all the above information into account, it has been concluded that pre- and post-expansions are an important component of the interaction, and are considered as such by both primary speakers and the interpreters, the proof of which is that they are overwhelmingly rendered; there is no case of zero renditions of any of these elements detected, and no instances of summarized or two-part or multi-part renditions have been identified.

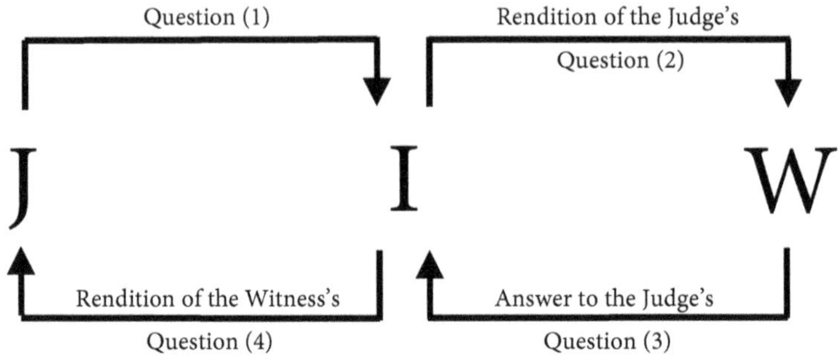

Fig. 7.1: Interaction with close, extended, reduced, substituted, and non-renditions

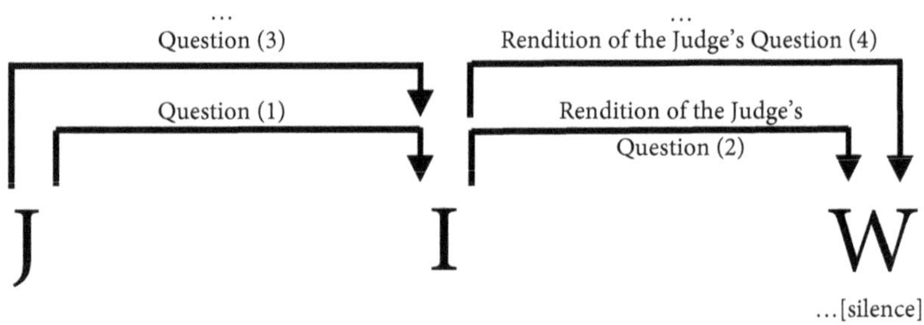

Fig. 7.2: Interaction with extended and non-renditions

In terms of interaction, the most frequent pattern, occurring with close renditions (Extracts 7.115 and 7.137), extended renditions (Extracts 7.105–7.108, 7.110–7.114, 7.116, 7.135, and 7.138), reduced renditions (Extracts 7.118–7.126), substituted renditions (Extracts 7.117, 7.134, and 7.139), and non-renditions (Extracts 7.128–7.133), is a question-rendition-answer-rendition interaction (Fig. 7.1):

The overwhelming occurrence of the above pattern proves that even though the interpreters introduce pre- or post-expansions, or they omit them in their renditions, the primary parties do not know whether they originate in the main speakers' or the interpreters' turns. Therefore, as the use of these mechanisms remains covered by apparently smooth interpretation, they do not have a potential to generate additional questions on the part of primary parties, and hence change the order of the bilingual interaction.

Moreover, two other patterns in three separate episodes have been detected. Fig. 7.2 shows the pattern of interaction with an extended rendition of an

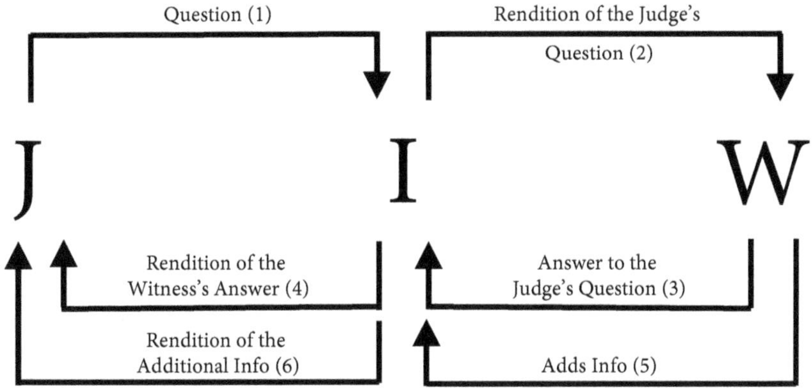

Fig. 7.3: Interaction with substituted renditions

interpreter-created pre-expansion (Extract 7.109) and a non-rendition within the interpreter-created post-expansion (Extract 7.136):

The judge asks the question and the interpreter renders it. However, without waiting for the witness's answer, the judge asks the next question (to supplement previous one) to the witness and the interpreter renders it. This makes the witness unable to take his turn as both current speakers fail to give him the opportunity to do so.

Fig. 7.3 presents the pattern of interaction with a substituted rendition of a primary party-created pre-expansion (Extract 7.126):

The above pattern shows that it is the witness who needs two subsequent turns to complete the answer to the judge's question. So does the interpreter, who renders the witness's utterances each time they occur in the interaction.

In general, pre- and post-expansions in bilingual communicative events leave the order of the interaction unmarked, that is, the question-rendition-answer-rendition pattern is deployed by the speakers. However, there are also episodes which include either simpler or more complex sequences.

8 Insert expansions in communicative events

The purpose of this chapter is to analyze the occurrence of insert expansions in bilingual interactions in order to find answers to the research questions, and in particular:

(1) to determine who (the interpreter or the main speakers) insert expansions in the communicative acts,
(2) to discuss the functions fulfilled by insert expansions, and
(3) to detect the ways the interpreters cope with these components of interaction.

To this aim, all episodes of interaction have been divided into two core groups according to the type of expansion they include: **post-first insert expansions** and **pre-second insert expansions**. Furthermore, within each group, expansions inserted by the interpreter and by the primary parties have been isolated. In addition, the third group of **multiple-insert expansions** has been formed, which includes complex insert expansions that can be produced by the interpreter alone or cooperatively by the primary parties.

8.1 Post-first insert expansions

Post-first insert expansions can be deployed by both the interpreter and the primary parties.

8.1.1 Interpreter-created post-first insert expansions

Extract 8.140 shows that a post-first insert expansion can be a repetition of the TCU included in the previous speaker's talk:

(8.140)	**Original PL/EN talk**	**Author's verbatim translation into EN**
Counsel:	kiedy? jaki alkohol? w jakim wieku byli nieletni? (.) którym >powód rzekomo< proponował alkohol?	*[When, what alcohol, how old were the minors whom the Defendant allegedly offered alcohol to?]*
Interpreter:	(.) when? (.) what was the age of the minors? (0.2) what kind of alcohol?	
Witness:	(.) the age: e::: fourteen (0.3) >it was two< (.) two teenagers (0.2) fourteen years old >and it was vodka<. =	
Interpreter:	= <u>fourteen</u> years [old?	
Witness:	[ye:s…	

(8.140)	Original PL/EN talk	Author's verbatim translation into EN
Interpreter:	(.) wiek czternaście lat (.) dwoje nastolatków (.) chłopak i dziewczyna (.) i wódka.	*[Age: fourteen years old, two teenagers, a boy and a girl and vodka.]*

The counsel asks about *the kind of alcohol and the age of the minors whom the alcohol was offered to*. The interpreter omits the information of *the alleged offer*. The witness answers by giving all the required details. However, the interpreter has a problem with either understanding or memorizing all the data, and thus deploys a post-first insert expansion—addressed to the witness—by repeating one detail of the witness's response (*fourteen years old*). When the witness confirms the age, the interpreter transmits all the information included in the witness's answer. What is more, the interpreter adds a new element not referred to in the proceedings to that moment: she says that there were *two teenagers, a boy and a girl*, while this does not appear in the witness' statement. It may result from the fact that the interpreter knows the case; nevertheless, she exceeds her power to speak in that she becomes yet another voice in the talk. Moreover, the syntax of the interpreter's rendition is significant: the underneath information provided by the interpreter is that she is sure that the counsel shares her knowledge of (even hypothetical) situations between fourteen years old teenagers where drinking alcohol is involved. On the whole, the interpreter provides a **summarized rendition**. In terms of ethics, the interpreter's impartiality can be questioned: she attracts the counsel's attention to the issues she deems crucial. This shows that the use of post-first insert expansions which assume the form of a repetition has the power to induce the speakers (including the interpreter) to forge the details that are not based on reality.

The next example shows a post-first insert expansion created by the interpreter to complete her rendition:

(8.141)	Original PL/EN talk	Author's verbatim translation into EN
Judge:	od kiedy pan (0.4) y::::: (0.2) przebywa na stałe w X?	*[Since when have you… yyy... been staying permanently in X?]*
Interpreter:	(.) so::… since when did you (0.2) stay permanently in X?	
Defendant:	(0.3) december nineteen two thousand and ten	
Interpreter:	so (0.2) dwa tysiące drugi rok.	*[So, two thousand and two]*
Interpreter:	((to the defendant)) december… (0.2) december…=	

(8.141)	Original PL/EN talk	Author's verbatim translation into EN
Defendant:	= december nineteen.	
Interpreter:	dziewiętnastego grudnia…	*[December 19.]*

The defendant provides the exact date of an event about which the judge has asked. The interpreter renders (however wrongly) the year of the event, but, in the knowledge that she does not remember the day of the event, she deploys a post-first insert expansion addressed to the witness, in which she repeats *December, December…* to elicit a cue from the witness. When the witness responds to her expansion, only then does the interpreter complete a **summarized rendition**. In other words, the interpreter cooperates with the defendant to obtain the information from him that might have been lost in translation if the defendant is not asked to repeat the date. However, two issues are to be observed: firstly, as in Extract 8.140, the interpreter does not inform the judge that she needs to ask a question to the defendant; and, secondly, probably the judge's exclusion from the talk results in the interpreter not verifying her incorrect rendition of the date (2002 instead of 2010).

Similarly, the subsequent example shows the interpreter who, by deploying a post-first insert expansion, seeks a repair on the part of the witness:

(8.142)	Original PL/EN talk	Author's verbatim translation into EN
Witness:	And then I'll be back in May or June […]	
Interpreter:	Więc… you're going to be back in… in…?	*[So… you're going to be back in… in…?]*
Witness:	June… or May…	
Interpreter:	Zamierzam wrócić w maju albo w czerwcu.	*[I'm going back in May or June.]*

It is probably the interpreter's short-term memory capacity, which makes her forget the exact months in which the witness is going back; thus she addresses the witness with a post-first insert expansion: *you're going to be back in… in…?* to encourage the witness to complete the question. What is more, the interpreter is evidently upset with her failure to render the witness' statement correctly: she starts her expansion with the Polish discourse marker *więc* (*so*). The witness adds the required information (*June or May*), and only then does the interpreter transmit it to the judge. As in previous examples, the expansion contributes to providing a **summarized rendition**.

As in previous examples, Extract 8.143 shows that the interpreter produces a post-first expansion to elicit information from the witness:

(8.143)	Original PL/EN talk	Author's verbatim translation into EN
Judge:	jakiego rzędu oszczędności miały być?	*[What level of savings would it be?]*
Interpreter:	(.) what level of savings would (0.5) >would it be<?	
Witness:	(.) from memory (0.4) it was fifteen percent. =	
Interpreter:	= fifteen… =	
Witness:	= fifteen (0.2) one-five (.) yea:h.	
Interpreter:	Yhm:, (.) z tego co pamiętam (.) to było <około> piętnaście procent.	*[Yhm. From what I remember, it was about 15 percent.]*

When the judge asks the witness about an approximate level of savings, the interpreter transmits the question to the witness who answers that *as far as he remembers it was fifteen percent.* In the next turn, the interpreter transmits the numeral fifteen and applies an open-end intonation to make the witness repeat the information. When the witness repeats the detail twice (*fifteen one-five*), it proves that he has considered the interpreter's request for help as a manifestation of the lack of understanding of the witness's utterance. Only then does the interpreter take a turn and provide a **summarized rendition** (*from what I remember it was about fifteen percent*).

In the next example it is also the interpreter who initiates a post-first insert expansion:

(8.144)	Original PL/ES talk	Author's verbatim translation into EN
Witness:	básicamente no porque el contrato se preparó para Eurocopa.	*[Basically no because the contract was prepared for Euro.]*
Interpreter:	((to the witness)) (0.3) ppara…? =	*[For…?]*
Witness:	= para eurocopa.	*[For Euro.]*
Interpreter:	(.) euro: y:hm,	*[Euro... yhm.]*
Witness:	Y entre 2011–2012 los precios subieron porque subió la demanda.	*[And between 2011–2012 the prices went up because the demand went up]*

The witness responds to the judge's question. When it is the interpreter's turn to render the witness's answer, she fails to provide an interpretation. Due to either hearing deficits or, most probably, the interpreter's not knowing what *Eurocopa* is, she deploys a post-first insert expansion to elicit a repetition of the FPP from the witness. She wants to establish the meaning of the concept by repeating a preposition directly preceding the problematic term (*for…?*) and then, deploying a suspending and question-like intonation. The witness reads the interpreter's signaling of the problem appropriately and repeats the last two words of the FPP, in the belief that the interpreter cannot hear what he is saying. The interpreter, however, repeats only a part of the term (*Euro*) after the witness, but a **zero rendition** is provided. In this case the communication fails: the judge is kept linguistically absent. He is aware of the fact that the interpreter is talking with the witness outside the main trajectory of the interrogation, but still, is not provided with the expected information.

8.1.2 Primary party-created post-first insert expansions

Extract 8.145 shows that the witness's initiative to insert an expansion is provoked by the interpreter's reduced rendition:

(8.145)	**Original PL/ES talk**	**Author's verbatim translation into EN**
Judge:	a jaką ogólnie stratę poniósł? (03.) w jakiej wysokości?	*[And what loss did he suffer in general? In what amount?]*
Interpreter:	(.) y cuál era la pérdida?	*[And what was the loss?]*
Witness:	(.) no está todavía cerrado el contrato (.) pero la pérdida está pues en torno a un millón.	*[The contract has not been terminated yet, but the loss is well about 1 million.]*
Interpreter:	(.) o:ke:y... un millón… =	*[OK. 1 million.]*
Witness:	= pero todavía no está cerrado el contrato.	*[But the contract has not been terminated yet.]*
Interpreter:	(.) ale jeszcze nie zamknęliśmy tego kontraktu (0.2) to znaczy (.) że nie otrzymaliśmy wszystkiego od inwestora.	*[But we have not terminated the contract yet. It means that we have not received everything from the investor.]*

The judge begins the interaction by asking about *the amount of the loss suffered by the party*. The interpreter transmits the question to which the witness answers by providing a rough amount which was lost (*about one million*). However, the witness's response is preceded by a pre-expansion: in the first TCU the witness makes a reservation that *the contract has not been terminated yet* (so the exact amount of the loss has probably not been calculated yet), and in the next TCU another pre-expansion occurs—a discourse marker *well*, which contributes to a delay in revealing the amount lost. The interpreter renders only the latter TCU, prefaced by a pre-expansion *okey*, which is to confirm her understanding of the witness's response. This is an implicit post-first insert expansion: the interpreter has either not heard, or has not memorized the witness's first TCU, or does not deem it necessary to render it to the judge, or yet, as the interpreter's open-ended intonation suggests, she has not completed her talk while the witness initiates his insert-expansion. Either way, the Spanish-speaking witness supplements the interpreter's rendition: he repeats the first TCU from his previous turn that *the contract has not been terminated yet*. By doing so, the witness attempts to repair the talk, but also contributes to the **extended rendition**: the interpreter joins the witness in the repairing; she states that *we have not terminated the contract yet.* Furthermore, she adds explanatory information, which is absent from the talk between the parties: neither the judge nor the witness mention that *we have not received everything from the investor.*

Similarly, Extract 8.146 shows interactants who cope with a problem which arises in the FPP produced by the interpreter:

(8.146)	Original PL/EN talk	Author's verbatim translation into EN
Judge:	Yhm, rozumiem. I zamieszkają państwo wtedy tutaj w tym domu w X?	*[Yhm, I understand. And then you will be living here in the house in X?]*
Interpreter:	And you will be living in X?	
Witness:	What?	
Interpreter:	Are you going to live in X?	
Witness:	yes	

The interpreter renders the judge's question as an FPP. The witness indicates that there is a problem: he reacts to the question by initiating an insert sequence (*what?*) which aims at repairing the conversation. The interpreter, instead of rendering the witness's question, repeats her first utterance hence, a **zero rendition** is produced. Only then the witness, in his SPP, briefly answers the question. From the point of view of the act of communication, such an insert sequence is comprehensible as it is required to maintain the conversation. Nonetheless, the judge is kept uninformed when the interpreter repeats the question to the witness who evidently could not hear what the judge has said.

The next episode also shows that a post-first insert expansion has the potential to encourage the interpreter to provide a zero rendition of the original statements made by the parties to the proceedings:

(8.147)	Original PL/EN talk	Author's verbatim translation into EN
Judge:	Ile pan ma lat?	*[How old are you?]*
Interpreter:	how old are you? (.) how old are you?	

(8.147)	Original PL/EN talk	Author's verbatim translation into EN
Witness:	((to the interpreter)) (.) wha[t?	
Interpreter:	[how old are you? =	
Witness:	= seventy nine. =	
Interpreter:	= mam siedemdziesiąt dziewięć lat.	*[I'm 79.]*

The interpreter renders the judge's question concerning the witness's age. However, the witness's problem with hearing, resulting from his advanced age, makes it impossible to react to that question even though the interpreter repeats it twice. The witness needs to ask a question (*what?*) to give a signal to the interpreter that she is expected to repeat the question. The witness's question is a post-first insert expansion, by which the witness attempts to inform the interpreter of the communication problem. This turn is counted as an FPP, of which the interpreter provides a **zero rendition**. Instead, she starts the repair (being an SPP) as an overlap with the witness's FPP: she repeats the question. It is only then that the witness is able to produce his SPP to answer the question. The post-first insert expansion serves as an initiation of the repair necessary to make the communication between the parties possible. Moreover, it is noticeable that, firstly, although the interpreter provides a close rendition, the problem lies in the interaction, and secondly, neither the judge nor any other representative of the judiciary who ask questions are parties to the insert sequence. This is carried out between the witness and interpreter, while the lawyers (although only for a while) are excluded from the communicative act.

Similarly, Extract 8.148 shows a post-first expansion inserted by the witness who requests for the question to be repeated:

(8.148)	Original PL/EN talk	Author's verbatim translation into EN
Judge:	rozumiem (.) że jest pan emerytem (0.2) ta::k?	*[I understand that you are retired, yes?]*
Interpreter:	(.) you are on retirement?	
Witness:	(0.2) what? =	
Interpreter:	= you are on retirement…	
Witness:	(.) ye:s (0.3) for fifteen years. =	
Interpreter:	= już od piętnastu lat (.) jestem na emeryturze.	*[I've been retired for already 15 years now.]*

The judge seeks confirmation on the part of the witness that he is retired. The interpreter provides close rendition of the question, but the witness, instead of responding, initiates a post-first insert expansion due to his not having heard the question, of which a **zero rendition** is provided. The interpreter repeats the question, although the intonation is different from the one deployed in her first rendition: this time she uses an affirmative-sentence intonation, probably in order to elicit the witness's response as quickly as possible. Only then the witness answers that he has been retired for fifteen years. The interpreter renders all the information provided by the witness, however, she adds the adverb 'already', which implicitly attracts the judge's attention to, firstly the fact that the witness is advanced in years, secondly, he might have nothing to live on, and thus, thirdly, the judge's attitude towards him should be special. This is a manifestation of a lack of neutrality on the part of the interpreter who, probably due to her empathy towards an elderly witness, attempts to influence the judge's view of the situation.

The subsequent episode is another example of the witness's post-first insert expansion:

(8.149)	**Original PL/EN talk**	**Author's verbatim translation into EN**
Judge:	rozumiem (0.3) jak często pan odwiedzał swoją żonę w tym domu w Y będąc w Polsce? =	*[I understand. How often did you visit you wife in that house in Y when you were visiting Poland?]*
Interpreter:	= how often >did you visit your wife [in Y<?	
Witness:	((to the interpreter)) [how often?	
Interpreter:	((to the witness)) (.) yes. =	
Witness:	= almost every day (0.3) I:: had to take a taxi and go back by bus. =	
Interpreter:	= praktycznie codziennie (.) za wyjątkiem <weekendów> ponieważ tutaj nie mam samochodu (.) więc jechałem w tamtą stronę taksówką a wracałem autobusem.	*[Practically every day, except weekends because here I don't have a car, so I went there by taxi and came back by bus.]*

The judge asks the witness about a frequency of his visits. The interpreter provides a reduced rendition of the judge's question (the information that the judge asks about the witness's visits in Poland is omitted). The witness has not heard the question and thus he addresses the interpreter with a post-first insert expansion, in which he reproduces the beginning of the question (*how often…?*) and suspends his voice to wait for a clue. The interpreter provides a **zero rendition** of the witness's question; instead, she shortly confirms by answering *yes* which is sufficient for the witness to respond (*almost every day…*) and provide further details of the visits. Evidently, the interpreter gains complete power over the conversation: the witness does not address the judge with his question and answer, but the interpreter to whom he reveals the information.

8.2 Pre-second insert expansions

Pre-second insert expansions are overwhelmingly deployed by the interpreter and sporadically by the primary parties.

8.2.1 Interpreter-created pre-second insert expansions

Extract 8.150 presents a pre-second insert expansion created by the interpreter:

(8.150)	**Original PL/EN talk**	**Author's verbatim translation into EN**
Interpreter:	((to the judge)) (0.2) czy tu szczegóły jakieś poprosimy?	*[Are we asking for some details here?]*

Due to a short failure of the recording system, it was possible to transcribe this episode of interaction starting only from the interpreter's FPP, in which she addresses the judge by asking him to provide some details. This FPP refers to the previous turn in which the judge has asked a question which, even though probably rendered by the interpreter, is still unclear to a non-Polish speaking defendant. Hence, by applying a **non-rendition**, the interpreter asks for further information as a pre-condition for the defendant to produce an SPP. From the point of view of the interaction, the interpreter's request is justified, it sounds tone-downed by the use of *we-inclusive*, by which the interpreter implicitly informs the judge that the question is not hers because she understands what the judge is saying, but comes from the non-Polish speaking client for whom the judge's original question might have been confusing. Nevertheless, the interpreter takes over the judge's privilege to begin the talk – it is now the interpreter who addresses the judge as if she were interrogating him.

In the next episode of interaction, the interpreter expressly informs the judge that she is going to ask the witness an additional question:

(8.151)	**Original PL/EN talk**	**Author's verbatim translation into EN**
Interpreter:	((to the judge)) chciałam tylko doprecyzować kwestię Beaty (.) [Betty...	*[I just wanted to clarify the issue of Beata, Betty...]*
Judge:	[((nodding))	
Interpreter:	((to the witness)) Hmh::: just to be more <precise> about Betty (.) Beata...	

The interpreter wants to prompt the witness to reveal more information to her about Betty. Thus, in her FPP, the interpreter asks the judge for permission to ask the witness about that woman. She understands the judge's nodding as his consent. She does not wait for further judge's TCU and addresses the witness with the question about Betty. This is an example of a **non-rendition**, where the interpreter suspends the main trajectory of the examination managed by the judge in order to provide a close rendition of the witness's utterance.

Similarly, Extract 8.152 shows a pre-second insert expansion produced by the interpreter:

(8.152)	**Original PL/EN talk**	**Author's verbatim translation into EN**
Defendant:	I went to my (0.2) my friend's house initially...	
Interpreter:	(.) na początku przyjechałem do domu przyjaciela. =	*[Initially I went to my friend's house...]*
Interpreter:	((to the defendant)) = male or female? =	
Defendant:	= female.	
Interpreter:	(0.3) y::: (.) przyjaciółki.	*[...yyy... girlfriend.]*

The defendant in his FPP tells the judge that *he went to his friend's house*. The interpreter transmits the defendant's utterance, but immediately afterwards, she addresses the witness with a question about the mentioned friend's sex (*male or female?*), hence a **non-rendition** is provided. Only when the defendant determines the friend's sex (*female*), is the interpreter able to correct her original rendition. In other words, the interpreter's linguistic competence makes her change the trajectory of the interaction: instead of allowing the judge to select him as the next speaker, she self-selects herself with the pre-second insert expansion in order to provide an accurate interpretation.

As in previous example, in Extract 8.153 the interpreter deploys a pre-second insert expansion to obtain information from the witness:

(8.153)	**Original PL/EN talk**	**Author's verbatim translation into EN**
Judge:	(0.2) w jaki sposó:b (0.2) świadek dowiedział się e:m::: o tym fakcie?	*[How did the witness come to know about this fact?]*
Interpreter:	(.) how did you know about this?	
Witness:	(.) we received a message.	
Interpreter:	was it a letter? =	
Witness:	= email =	
Interpreter:	= aha: (.) w tej wiadomości elektronicznej (0.2) w tym mailu...	*[Aha, in this electronic message, in this email...]*

The judge asks the witness about *the way he came to know about the fact.* The interpreter provides a close rendition, to which the witness says that *they received a message.* For the interpreter the answer seems to be too general thus she asks the witness, on her own, about the form of the message (*was it a letter?*). Only when she receives the answer does she address the judge with the detailed information (*in this electronic message, in this email*). By deploying the expansion, the interpreter takes over the judge's privilege to ask questions and requests detailed responses on the part of the witness. As in the previous example, the interpreter's close rendition of the judge's FPP makes it necessary for her to create a pre-second insert expansion and hence to a **non-rendition**.

Extract 8.154 shows that the interpreter's pre-second insert expansions are a consequence of rendering the TCU which does not occur immediately before the interpreter's current turn:

(8.154)	**Original PL/EN talk**	**Author's verbatim translation into EN**
Public Prosecutor:	jeszcze jedno pytanie... (0.3) kto opłaca koszty pobytu pana małżonki w X? (0.2) jaka to jest suma?	*[One more question. Who pays the costs of your spouse's stay in X? What amount is it?]*
Interpreter:	(.) who pays the bill for X? =	
Witness:	= me (.) all the bills.	
Interpreter:	(.) tak (.) ja płacę wszystkie rachunki...	*[Yes, I pay all the bills.]*
Interpreter:	[to the witness] (.) how much is it?	

The public prosecutor begins this episode of interaction. His FPP is composed of three TCUs: a pre-expansion *one more question*, after which there is an appreciable pause (0.3), and two questions: *who pays the cost of your spouse's stay in X* and *what amount is it* separated by an appreciable pause (0.2). In her turn, the interpreter ignores the pre-expansion and provides a close rendition of the question concerning *the person who pays the bills.* Only when she receives the answer from the witness and transmits it to the public prosecutor, does she ask another question about *the amount of money paid.* Therefore, by splitting the FPP, she provides a **two-part rendition**. In terms of interaction, she needs to create this pre-second insert expansion to elicit all the information from the witness required by the public prosecutor. Also, the interpreter's rendition is more straightforward than the prosecutor's original utterance, by which a shade of harshness on the part of the public prosecutor is added.

In the subsequent example the interpreter uses a pre-second expansion to suggest an answer:

(8.155)	Original PL/EN talk	Author's verbatim translation into EN
Witness:	for this we agreed a calendar to pay.	
Interpreter:	(.) ugodniliśmy kalendarz płatności (.) <ponieważ>, =	*[We agreed on a payment calendar because…]*
Interpreter:	((to the witness)) = to split the payment to smaller amounts? =	
Witness:	= ye:s (0.2) to split the payment to smaller amounts. =	
Interpreter:	= rozdzieliliśmy tę płatność (0.2) rozbiliśmy tę płatność na mniejsze kwoty (0.3) na mniejsze płatności miesięczne.	*[We split this payment, this payment to smaller amounts, to smaller monthly payments.]*

When the interpreter renders the witness's utterance (*for this we agreed a calendar to pay*), she uses a conjunction *because* (absent from the witness's statement), which syntactically needs to be supplemented by an explanation. Thus, the interpreter thinks of an ending of her rendition and hence, she produces a pre-second insert expansion (a **non-rendition**) by addressing the witness with a suggestion (*to split the payment into smaller amounts?*) being a possible justification for having agreed on a payment calendar. The witness submits himself to the interpreter's proposal and, after an affirmative *yes*, he repeats the interpreter's FPP (*to split the payment to smaller amounts*). Immediately after that, the interpreter renders the witness's statement. The expansion that occurs in the interpreter's talk on the one hand facilitates to elicit more details from the witness, on the other hand however is used to suggest the answer to the witness.

8.2.2 Primary party-created pre-second insert expansions

The example below shows a pre-second insert expansion produced by the judge:

(8.156)	Original PL/EN talk	Author's verbatim translation into EN
Judge:	w tej sprawie (.) że przez pół roku pana nie będzie w <Polsce> (.) tak?	*[In this matter that you will not be in Poland for half a year, yes?]*
Interpreter:	(.) you are >in GB yes<? =	
Witness:	((partially in Polish)) = tak (0.2) in January (.) February (0.3) January or February… =	*[Yes, in January, February..., January or February…]*
Interpreter:	= tak (.) wyjeżdżam na pięć lub sześć miesięcy (.) wracam w styczniu albo w lutym.	*[Yes, I'm leaving for five or six months, I'm coming back in January or in February.]*
Judge:	(0.2) yhm… =	

(8.156)	Original PL/EN talk	Author's verbatim translation into EN
Witness:	= because I'm going to have rehabilitation. =	
Interpreter:	= no::: czeka mnie rehabilitacja.	*[Well... I 'm going to have physical therapy.]*

The judge asks the witness whether he *will not stay in Poland for half a year*. The interpreter makes use of her knowledge of the case, thus the rendition of the judge's question is extended; more than an interpretation, it is an attempt to make the question more understandable for the witness and to obtain a clear answer (*you are in GB yes?*). The witness seems to feel comfortable with the interpreter's approach: he probably wants to show his friendly attitude towards the interpreter when he starts answering the question by using the Polish *tak* (*yes*), and then mentions the two months in which he will probably arrive back in Poland (*in January February in January or February*). Evidently, the interpreter adjusts the style to the projected expectations of the judge who gets involved in the interaction: he produces a pre-second insert expansion (*yhm...*), which, even though a **zero rendition** is provided, encourages the witness to continue speaking (*because I'm going to have physical therapy*). What the judge gains is that the witness reveals more information than he has been asked in the judge's original question.

8.3 Multiple-insert expansions

At institutional talks in the courtroom there are episodes of interaction in which interlocutors deploy multiple insert expansions, which all together create the communicative act of the courtroom.

8.3.1 Interpreter-created multiple-insert expansions

In Extract 8.157, the post-first insert expansion is at the same time of the pre-second insert expansion:

(8.157)	Original PL/EN talk	Author's verbatim translation into EN
Witness:	that's the reason (.) we are asking for compensation.	
Interpreter:	(0.2) i z tej przyczyny właśnie prosimy tutaj o rekompensatę (0.2) y::: (0.2) pozostałej kwoty... =	*[... and for this reason precisely we are asking here for compensation...yyy ... of the remaining amount...]*

(8.157)	Original PL/EN talk	Author's verbatim translation into EN
Interpreter:	((to witness)) = of the remaining amount? =	
Witness:	= ye:s (.) two hundred thousand...	
Interpreter:	(.) pozostałej kwoty (.) i ta pozostała kwota wynosi dwieście tysięcy dolarów amerykańskich.	*[... of the remaining amount and this remaining amount is 200 thousand American dollars.]*

The witness says that *that's the reason we are asking for compensation*. The interpreter provides close rendition, with one exception; she wants to add information about the amount of the compensation claimed by the witness which has not yet been revealed. Thus, she needs to elicit the detail from the witness. Her pre-second insert expansion is a type of a post-expansion: the rendition she provides (*and for this reason precisely we are asking here for compensation*) could be a sufficient interpretation of the witness's statement. However, she wants to supplement the information with a detail concerning the amount of the compensation (*of the remaining amount*), with which she then addresses the witness who informs about the amount. Only then does the interpreter repeat the first part of the already transmitted information and adds a full sentence containing the detail she has asked for, hence an **extended rendition** is provided. This extract shows that it is thanks to the interpreter's post-first insert question aimed only at confirming the information about the ending of the statement (whether the witness has said *of the remaining amount* or something else), the witness provides information about an exact amount, which is not actually the detail the witness has been asked by the judge. Thus, the post-first insert expansion *of the remaining amount* becomes the pre-second insert expansion.

8.3.2 Primary party-created multiple-insert expansions

Extract 8.158 shows that the post-first insert expansion has the power to cause the pre-second insert expansion to appear:

(8.158)	Original PL/EN talk	Author's verbatim translation into EN
Witness:	(.) a::nd (0.3) when I take these photos (.) print them (.) providing to my friends... =	
Interpreter:	= tak (1.0) i potem pan drukuje te zdjęcia a:kt (.) a następnie (0.2) a::: przedstawia je (0.2) daje do zapoznania swoi::m (.) e::: swoi:m znajomym...=	*[Yes, and then he prints these photos of the files, and then, aaa..., presents them, gives them to his, eee... his acquaintances to read...]*

(8.158)	Original PL/EN talk	Author's verbatim translation into EN
Witness:	= helpers... =	
Judge:	((gazing at the interpreter)) = swoim znajomym (.) którzy są dwujęzyczni? =	*[To his acquaintances who are bilingual?]*
Interpreter:	= <u>tak</u>.	*[Yes.]*

The witness continues telling the judge that *he takes the photos, prints them and provides them to his friends*. The interpreter immediately begins her turn by saying that *he prints these photos of the files and then presents them, gives them to read to his acquaintances*. Evidently, the interpreter has interrupted the witness's FPP: the witness interjects with additional information (*helpers*), which is a post-first insert expansion (he could not complete his FPP). The judge seems not to pay attention to the witness's expansion and, by deploying a pre-second insert expansion, asks the question (*to his acquaintances who are bilingual?*). In response to that, the interpreter answers affirmatively (*yes*). It is the interpreter who answers the judge's question addressed to the witness without transmitting the question to the witness. She does so probably on the basis of her knowledge of the case. In the interaction, although the witness's expansion occurs first, it is the judge's expansion, which meets a reaction, while the witness's interjection remains unnoticed. The judge's expansion is so strong that the interpreter feels obliged to respond immediately, thus providing a **non-rendition**.

8.3.3 Multi-party multiple-insert expansions

In Extract 8.159, an expansion produces the next expansion:

(8.159)	Original PL/EN talk	Author's verbatim translation into EN
Judge:	Rozumiem. A jakie jest stanowisko... wobec tego, że to jest... sprawa dotyczy... yeh... wniosku o ubezwłasnowolnienie małżonki Pana? To jakie jest stanowisko Pana? Czy Pan uważa, że małżonkę... eee... należy ubezwłasnowolnić tak jak chce tego córka czy też generalnie czy ta pani jest w stanie samodzielnie funkcjonować?	*[I understand. And what is a position... in relation to the fact that it is... the case concerns... yeh... a request for the incapacitation of your spouse? So what is your position? Do you think that your spouse... eee... should be incapacitated as her daughter wants it or generally is she able to function independently?]*
Interpreter:	Is your wife able...?	
Witness:	She functions.	
Interpreter:	She is OK, yes?	

(8.159)	Original PL/EN talk	Author's verbatim translation into EN
Witness:	She is OK.	
Interpreter:	Żona jest w porządku. Stan zdrowia nic nie dolega.	*[My wife is OK. Health is not a problem.]*
Judge:	No rozumiem, czyli generalnie przyłącza się do stanowiska żony, tak?... że, tak, tak, mogę go zrozumieć, tak? Że że że wnosi o oddalenie wniosku o ubezwłasnowolnienie?	*[I understand, so generally he joins the position of his wife, yes?... that, I can understand him in this way, in this way, yes? That that that he claims that the motion for incapacitation should be dismissed.]*

The judge asks a complex question, which is however incoherent: the judge begins a TCU but does not complete it – he suspends his voice to start speaking again. Hence, the interpreter selects the information included in the judge's talk and reduces it to a simple *is your wife able…?* with a suspended question-like intonation. This makes the witness respond shortly (*she functions*), but for the interpreter the answer is not exhaustive enough. Hence, she deploys an insert expansion to make sure that she has understood the witness's answer properly, as well as to encourage the witness to elaborate on his response. Therefore, the interpreter's expansion works as both a post-first and a pre-second expansion because it not only refers to the previous turn, but also is oriented towards the next turn. Nevertheless, the witness does not grasp the interpreter's intention and persists in giving laconic answers. This makes the interpreter to stop producing the next expansion, but she needs to compensate the witness's answer as to the content and the length: she produces two TCUs. The first TCU is a close rendition of the witness's TCU (*wife is okey*), but the second is the interpreter's addition based on her own overview of the situation. The judge does not protest against the talk between the interpreter and the witness, instead, as a consequence of the interpreter's expansions, the judge himself starts treating the interpreter as a partner in the interaction: his next turn (*I understand, so generally he joins the position of his wife, yes?*) is entirely addressed to the interpreter. On the whole, a **summarized rendition** is provided.

Similarly, Extract 1.160 shows that a number of multiple insert expansions that occur in the interpreter's talk can be endless:

(8.160)	Original PL/EN talk	Author's verbatim translation into EN
Counsel:	jak zrozumiał…?	*[How did he understand…?]*
Interpreter:	(.) how did you understand…?	

(8.160)	Original PL/EN talk	Author's verbatim translation into EN
Interpreter:	((to the counsel)) (.) maybe he means that he already paid the amount (.) tak tak tak tak tak tak tak (.) rozumiem	*[yes, yes, yes, yes, yes, yes, I understand]*
Interpreter:	((to the witness)) (.) this is some kind of opposite info, (0.) to jakby nie jest spójne.	*[This is sort of incoherent.]*

This episode of interaction begins with the counsel's post-first insert expansion pertaining also to a previous episode of interaction; the lawyer asks a question whether the witness understood the information being the subject of the questionning. The interpreter starts transmitting the question, but suddenly she suspends her voice. After that she produces only **non-renditions**. She addresses the counsel with the explanations (in English) by speculating what the witness might mean when he provides a particular detail. By doing so, she replaces the witness who is an actual recipient of the question and the one who is supposed to provide a repair in the conversation. Suddenly, the interpreter begins the subsequent TCU (in Polish), still looking at the counsel (*yes, yes, yes, yes, yes, yes, I understand*), but apparently commenting on her own understanding of the witness's explanations. Immediately afterwards, the interpreter begins her next TCU addressed to the witness (this is some kind of opposite info, expressed in English and then reproduced in Polish). She totally confuses who she is talking to and in what language. Moreover, the remarks concerning the information she receives adversely affect the interpreter's image as a neutral professional.

8.4 Conclusions

The analysis of the material has allowed for a confirmation that both post-first and pre-second insert expansions can appear in the talk of the interpreter and that of the primary parties. Nonetheless, the detected number of episodes with inserted expansions varies depending on a particular group of expansions, and on the interaction creating such expansions. Also, the types of renditions provided by the interpreter are different and random.

The interpreters create **post-first insert expansions** to elicit information from non-Polish speaking parties to the proceedings. As a consequence, overwhelmingly summarized renditions are provided, or zero renditions, in the event the interpreter fails to obtain the required information. If the primary parties insert post-first expansions, it is because they understand Polish to the degree that they are able to monitor the communicative act (extended

Tab. 8.1: Post-first insert expansions

Extract	Interactant \ Renditions	CR	ER	RR	SBR	SMR	TMR	NR	ZR
8.140	Witness	0	0	0	0	**1**	0	0	0
8.141	Defendant	0	0	0	0	**1**	0	0	0
8.142	Witness	0	0	0	0	**1**	0	0	0
8.143	Witness	0	0	0	0	**1**	0	0	0
8.144	Witness	0	0	0	0	0	0	0	**1**
8.145	Witness	0	**1**	0	0	0	0	0	0
8.146	Witness	0	0	0	0	0	0	0	**1**
8.147	Witness	0	0	0	0	0	0	0	**1**
8.148	Witness	0	0	0	0	0	0	0	**1**
8.149	Witness	0	0	0	0	0	0	0	**1**
Total:		**0**	**1**	**0**	**0**	**4**	**0**	**0**	**5**

Tab. 8.2: Pre-second insert expansions

Extract	Interactant \ Renditions	CR	ER	RR	SBR	SMR	TMR	NR	ZR
8.150	Judge	0	0	0	0	0	0	**1**	0
8.151	Judge	0	0	0	0	0	0	**1**	0
8.152	Defendant	0	0	0	0	0	0	**1**	0
8.153	Witness	0	0	0	0	0	0	**1**	0
8.154	Public Prosecutor	0	0	0	0	0	**1**	0	0
8.155	Witness	0	0	0	0	0	0	**1**	0
8.156	Judge	0	0	0	0	0	0	0	**1**
Total:		**0**	**0**	**0**	**0**	**0**	**1**	**5**	**1**

renditions of such expansions are provided), or they request the interpreter to repeat her utterance (with the subsequent zero renditions). The results are presented in Tab. 8.1:

Pre-second insert expansions, shown in Tab. 8.2, appear in the interpreter's talk when she needs to request an additional detail to be revealed by the primary party (non-renditions or two-part renditions are involved). Only one episode of interaction with the judge who inserts a pre-second expansion has been detected in the collected material; by deploying an insert expansion, the judge encourages the witness to provide more information than originally meant, even though a zero rendition is provided.

Tab. 8.3: Multiple-insert expansions

Extract	Renditions / Interactant	CR	ER	RR	SBR	SMR	TMR	NR	ZR
8.157	Witness	0	1	0	0	0	0	0	0
8.158	Judge/Witness	0	0	0	0	0	0	1	0
8.159	Witness	0	0	0	0	1	0	0	0
8.160	Counsel	0	0	0	0	0	0	1	0
Total:		**0**	1	**0**	**0**	1	**0**	2	**0**

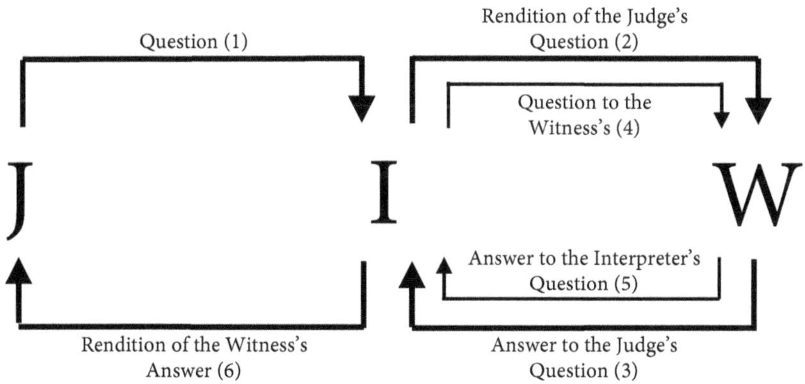

Fig. 8.1: Interaction with extended, summarized, two-part, zero and non-renditions

As regards **multiple-insert expansions**, presented in Tab. 8.3, they can be created by interpreters, when they need further explanations on the part of the primary speaker, and these are fundamental for elaborating on the collected data (thus an extended rendition is provided). Also, they can be deployed by the primary parties collaboratively (with a summarized rendition), and finally, it is the interpreter and the representatives of the judiciary, who alternatively insert expansions (with non-renditions).

In terms of interaction, the findings prove that the most commonly occurring pattern, where extended (Extracts 8.145 and 8.157), summarized (Extracts 8.140–8.143 and 8.159), two-part (Extract 8.154), non-renditions (Extracts 8.152, 8.153, and 8.155), and zero renditions (Extract 8.146) is as shown in Fig. 8.1:

The interpreter renders the judge's question and receives the witness's answer but decides to ask an additional question to the witness; only when the witness answers the interpreter's question, does she render the witness's answer to the judge.

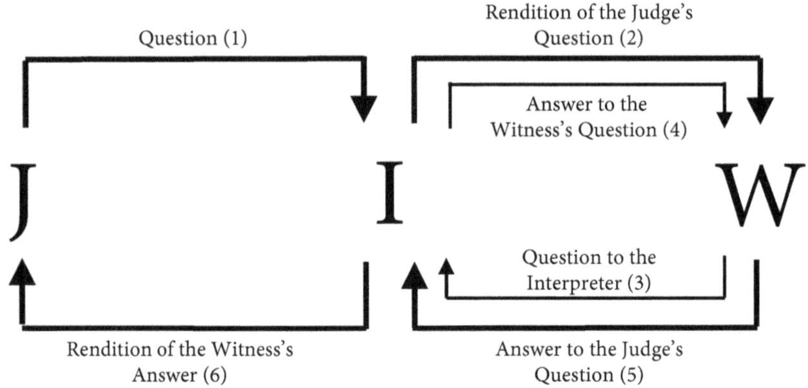

Fig. 8.2: Interaction with zero renditions

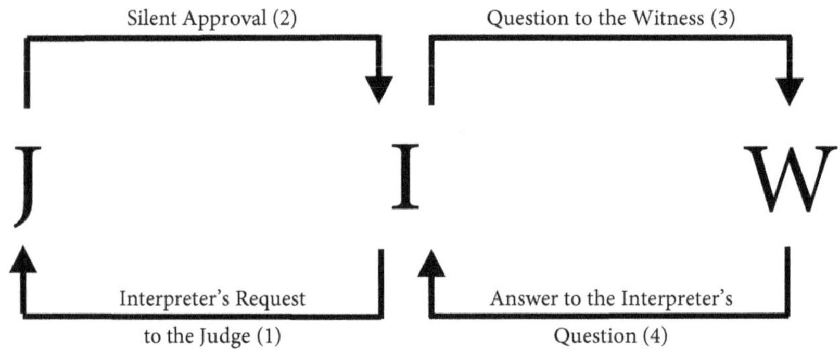

Fig. 8.3: Interaction with non-renditions

The second in number pattern (Extracts 8.147–8.149), in which zero renditions appear, is as shown in Fig. 8.2:

The question-rendition-answer-rendition sequence of turns (where after each original utterance the interpreter's rendition comes) is interrupted. When the interpreter renders the judge's question, the witness asks the interpreter for an explanation, to which the interpreter answers; only then does the witness answer the judge's question, and the interpreter renders his answer.

Furthermore, as for non-renditions, there are three more different patterns for three episodes. When the interpreter produces a pre-second insert expansion (Extract 8.151), the pattern is as shown in Fig. 8.3:

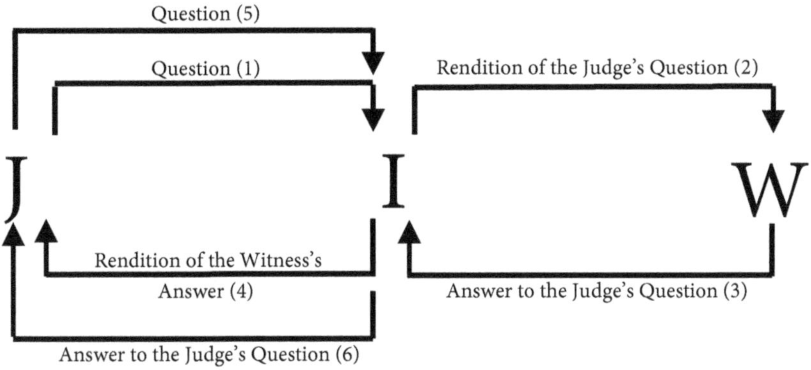

Fig. 8.4: Interaction with non-renditions

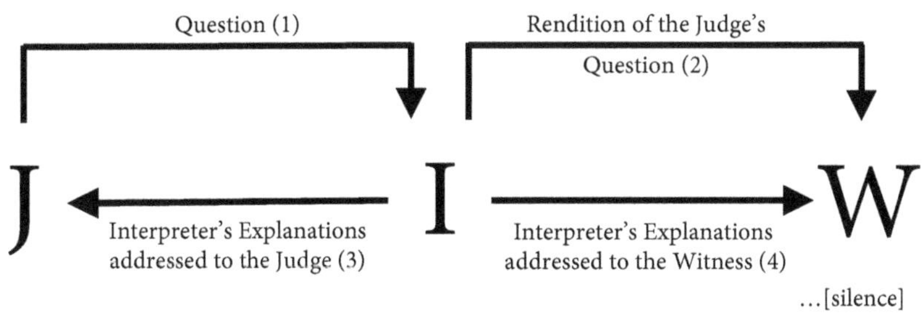

Fig. 8.5: Interaction with non-renditions

It is the interpreter who begins the episode by addressing the judge with the request to which the judge gives his silent consent. Only then does the interpreter ask the question to the witness, who gives explanations.

With multiple-insert expansions, a non-rendition (Extract 8.158) is situated within the pattern as shown in Fig. 8.4:

The interaction is question-rendition-answer-rendition in pattern until the second question asked by the judge, when the interpreter decides to provide the answer to the question without rendering it to the witness.

Moreover, a non-rendition (Extract 8.160) can be illustrated with Fig. 8.5:

The interpreter renders the judge's question to the witness, but, without waiting for his answer, she addresses both the judge and the witness with her own comments and explanations (that may relate to a variety of issues).

Furthermore, when it comes to zero renditions, there are two patterns. As for the post-first insert expansion (Extract 8.144), it is presented in Fig. 8.6:

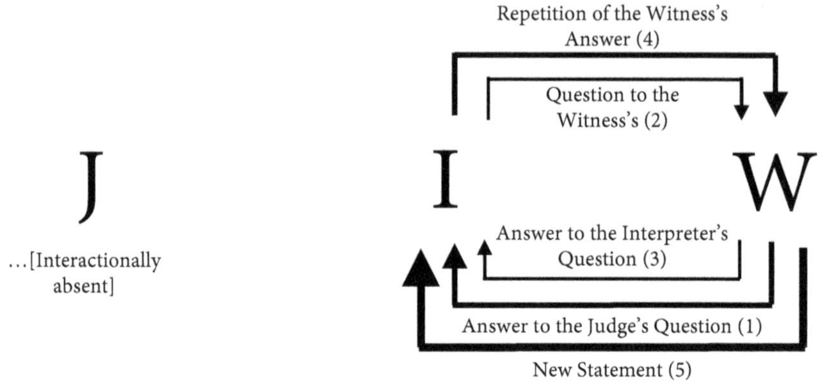

Fig. 8.6: Interaction with zero renditions

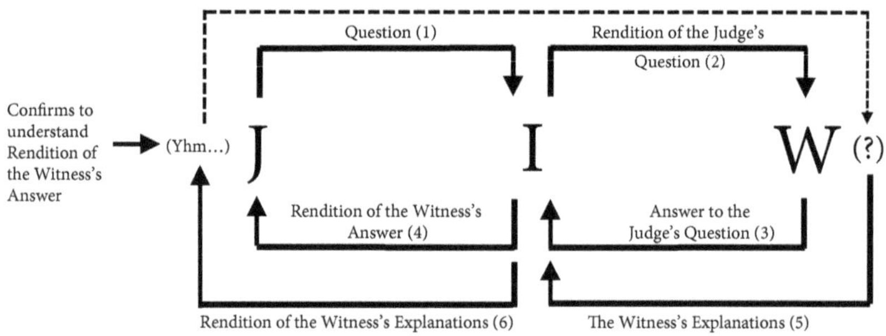

Fig. 8.7: Interaction with zero renditions

The judge is excluded from this episode of interaction. When the witness produces his utterance, the interpreter does not transmit it to the judge; instead, the interpreter prompts the witness to repeat his answer. However, when the witness does so, the interpreter still does not render the message to the judge. In response to the interpreter's indolence, the witness begins a new episode of interaction.

The pre-second insert expansion followed by a zero rendtion (Extract 8.156) is shown in Fig. 8.7:

In the above pattern, until the moment the interpreter renders the witness's answer the interaction follows a question-rendition-answer-rendition order. However, when the judge hears the rendition, he confirms to understand the message by applying a pragmatic marker *Yhm...*, which the witness perceives as the judge's request for further explanations on the part of the witness. Thus the witness continues answering and the interpreter renders the answer.

In general, the analysis has shown that insert expansions are indispensable for bilingual communicative acts as they contribute to a flow of information between the interlocutors. Although overwhelmingly two patterns of interaction have been detected, there are also instances, where the communicative act develops according to other orders.

9 Repairs as responses to problems in bilingual interactions

This chapter deals with repairs that are applied by the interactants as they detect problems which make it impossible to develop the communicative acts to which they are parties. The aim of the analysis is to reflect on the interpreters' active participation in producing repairs, and in particular:

(1) to find out who—the interpreter or the primary parties—produces a problem in the interaction which needs to be repaired,
(2) to analyze such problems, depending on who—the interpreter or the primary speakers—identifies and repairs them, and
(3) to categorize the repairs, either made by the interpreter or the main speakers, according to the rendition provided by the interpreter.

To this end, all episodes of interaction analyzed in this chapter are presented according to the type of repair they include: **self-initiated self-repair**, **self-initiated other-repair**, **other-initiated self-repair**, and **other-initiated other-repair**. For the purposes of this analysis, it has been assumed that the use of **self-** indicates that the repair has been either identified (**self-initiated**), or provided (**self-repair**) by the interpreter, while **other-** implies the repair either initiated (**other-initiated**) or made (**other-repair**) by the primary speaker.

9.1 Self-initiated self-repair

As stated above, for the purposes of this study, self-initiated self-repair is understood as a repair both initiated and provided by the interpreter. Such repairs are a consequence of either the interpreter-created or the primary party-created problem in the conversation.

9.1.1 Interpreter-created problem in conversation

In Extract 9.161, the interpreter makes a false start, identifies the repairable item and makes a repair:

(9.161)	**Original PL/EN talk**	**Author's verbatim translation into EN**
Judge:	czy również był wykonany ten projekt (0.2) zgodnie ze standardem określonym przez y::: <u>Bank</u> Światowy	*[Was this project also run according to the standard established by the World Bank?]*

(9.161)	Original PL/EN talk	Author's verbatim translation into EN
Interpreter:	(0.7) and also was this project concluded according to:: the standards of e:: the Bank (1.0) World Bank?	

The judge asks the question whether *this project also was run according to the standard established by the World Bank*. When the interpreter renders the judge's question, she produces a TCU in which she fails to provide an exact denomination of the *bank*. She needs an appreciable pause (1.0) to identify a problem, after which she introduces a repair (*World Bank*). By so doing, she provides a **close rendition**.

Extract 9.162 includes a false start which involves syntax:

(9.162)	Original PL/EN talk	Author's verbatim translation into EN
Judge:	(0.3) y:: było to: (.) umówione spotkanie (.) za pośrednictwem pana żony? proszę szczegółowo opowiedzieć sądowi (.) przebieg tego spotkania...	*[It was a meeting arranged through your wife? Please, give the court the details about the course of that meeting.]*
Interpreter:	(.) was the meeting? (.) it was arranged with your wife… (0.2) please describe this meeting to the court.	

The judge asks the witness for *the details about the meeting and whether it was arranged through the witness's wife*. As soon as the interpreter says *was the meeting*, she makes a micro-pause (.), after which she changes the form of her **close rendition** from a question to an affirmative statement. Hence, it is only the interpreter who identifies the beginning of her rendition as a false start and considers it necessary to introduce a repair.

Similarly, in Extract 9.163 below, the interpreter introduces a repair when a false start appears in her rendition:

(9.163)	Original PL/EN talk	Author's verbatim translation into EN
Judge:	a czy jakieś uwagi (0.5) w trakcie realizacji tamtego kontraktu były zgłaszane? (1.0) przez stronę pozwaną?	*[And were any remarks reported in the course of the performance of that contract … by the defendant?]*
Interpreter:	(1.0) whether (1.0) <u>what</u> (1.0) e:: and e:: (.) what were the remarks (0.5) >brought by the defendant<?	

The judge asks a general question if *there were any remarks were reported in the course of the performance of that contract by the defendant*. The interpreter needs an appreciable pause (1.0) to start interpreting, after which she deploys a conjunction *whether* characteristic for indirect questions, which probably is due to the fact that this exact conjunction is used in Polish to begin general questions. Then, the interpreter makes another appreciable pause (1.0) followed by a wh-question with which she attempts to repair a false start. Even with the repair, a **reduced rendition** is produced: the original question is general, while the interpreter's question assumes that *remarks were made* and focuses on *what those remarks were.*

Similarly, Extract 9.164 below shows a repair detected and introduced by the interpreter:

(9.164)	**Original PL/EN talk**	**Author's verbatim translation into EN**
Counsel:	czy świadek uczestniczył e:: w odbieraniu przez powoda (.) dziecka (0.2) z mieszkania obecnej partnerki?	*[Did the witness take part in picking up the child by the plaintiff from the present partner's flat?]*
Interpreter:	(.) did you take pa::rt y::: (0.5) were you present (.) in picking up the child (.) from the present partner's flat?	
Witness:	= ye:s. =	
Interpreter:	= tak.	*[Yes.]*

The counsel asks the witness whether *he took part in picking up the child by the plaintiff from the present partner's flat*. The interpreter repeats the first part of the counsel's question (*did you take part*), followed by a vocalic filler *y:::* and an appreciable pause (0.5), which shows that she has identified a problem. Evidently, the interpreter considers her rendition as to close to the counsel's original question hence she decides to make a repair (*were you present in picking up the child from the present partner's flat?*). Interestingly, the repair is made after the first TCU has been produced and it is this TCU which is subject to the repair. Nonetheless, in this particular place the interaction is unproblematic hence the repair has not been necessary. Even though the repair has been provided, the **rendition** is **reduced**: the interpreted has failed to specify that the question concerns the picking up of the child *by the plaintiff*.

Extract 9.165 below shows two repairs on the part of the interpreter:

(9.165)	**Original PL/EN talk**	**Author's verbatim translation into EN**
Judge:	(0.5) jak wyglądała <u>współpraca</u>? (1.0) współpraca ze stroną zamawiającą?	*[What did the cooperation, cooperation with the contracting party look like?]*

(9.165)	Original PL/EN talk	Author's verbatim translation into EN
Interpreter:	((to herself)) (0.2) °ze stroną zamawiającą° (1.0)	*[...with the contracting party...]*
Interpreter:	((to the witness)) ho:w (2.0) e:: what was the cooperation with the::: e::: <u>client</u>?	

The judge asks *what the cooperation with the contracting party looked like.* When the interpreter's turn comes, she firstly shadows the final part of the judge's question (*with the contracting party*), and only then begins the next TCU, in which she switches into the interpretation into English. This results in a false start in the rendition: the interpreter's first attempt to transmit the judge's question begins with the *how* question, which is a verbatim translation of the Polish interrogative pronoun *jak* used by the judge. It may mean that the interpreter, striving to provide a **close rendition**, tries to interpret the judge's question verbatim. However, she identifies a problem and after an appreciable pause (2.0) she makes a repair (*what was the cooperation*), after which a vocalic filler *the::: e:::* occurs, which manifests her hesitation and is a sign of looking for an English term *client* or *contracting party* (equivalent of the Polish term *strona zamawiająca*).

In Extract 9.166 the repair is introduced when the interpreter is looking for a proper equivalent of a single verb:

(9.166)	Original PL/EN talk	Author's verbatim translation into EN
Witness:	we agreed for the amount (.) of ...	
Interpreter:	(.) rozmawialiśmy: wówczas o kwocie (1.0) czy:: (0.4) <u>uzgodniliśmy</u> kwotę...	*[We then were talking about the amount, or we agreed on the amount...]*

The witness says that *they agreed on the amount.* At first, the interpreter deploys a neutral verb *talk*, by which she generalizes the information and conveys only the message that there was communication between the primary parties. Nonetheless, she notices that *talking* is not the activity the witness is referring to; therefore, she needs an appreciable pause (1.0) to introduce a repair. This is done at two levels: lexical, where she changes a verb, and pitch, when she employs a stressing intonation on the verb *agreed*, which is understood as pointing out the correct part of a **close rendition**.

Extract 9.167 shows that the interpreter repairs the entire TCU:

(9.167)	Original PL/EN talk	Author's verbatim translation into EN
Judge:	to dlaczego doszło do wypowiedzenia tej umowy?	*[So why was this contract terminated?]*
Interpreter:	(.) >so why< this agreement was terminated (0.5) this contract (.) was terminated?	
Witness:	((throwing up his hands)) (1.) we:ll e:: the X wanted to terminate it - not us.	
Interpreter:	(.) to X chciała go wypowiedzieć (0.3) nie my. =	*[X wanted to terminate it, not us.]*
Witness:	= so (.) >I think I can't say<.	
Interpreter:	(0.2) więc nie bardzo mogę na to pytanie odpowiedzieć (2.0) nie umiem na to pytanie odpowiedzieć.	*[So I can't really answer this question. I am not able to answer this question.]*

The judge asks *why the contract was terminated.* At first, the interpreter chooses to render the question as *to why this agreement was terminated*, but evidently she detects a problem. This is the reason she makes an appreciable pause (0.5) needed to think about a possible repair. Only then does she produce another TCU (*this contract was terminated*). The interpreter uses the same procedure when the witness says *I think I can't say*: she needs an appreciable pause (0.2) to start interpreting. When she renders the witness's utterance, she pauses (0.2) to look for another Polish equivalent of *I can't*, although both of her choices (*I can't, I'm not able*) are correct. The witness's answer is very short; he communicates that *to his knowledge he can't say*, by which his lack of certainty achieves a high degree. The interpreter renders this statement twice: for the first time, as *I hardly can* and then as *I can't.* Such a repetition leaves an impression that the interpreter is in a constant search for a proper meaning of the modal *can't* or she simply is not satisfied enough with her first, **close rendition**.

Extract 9.168 below shows that repeated false starts and repairs affect the interpreter's credibility and power of language:

(9.168)	Original PL/EN talk	Author's verbatim translation into EN
Witness:	and that's all... (2.) so the problem was coming from this difference between euro and dollar.	
Interpreter:	(0.4) a więc (1.0) reasumując y:: (0.5) ten problem wyniknął z różnicy kurso – (1.0) z::: (0.4) z::: (0.2) z różnicy (1.0) ze zmieniających się w czasie kursów Y:: (0.3) czy też stosunku kursów euro do dolara.	*[So, to sum up…, this problem resulted from the exchange rate difference, from… from… from… the differences of exchange rates varying with time or the rate of the euro in relation to the dollar.]*

The witness expresses a clear message: *the problem was coming from this difference between [the] euro and [the] dollar*. The interpreter has visible problems with rendering the witness's technical statement relating to exchange rate differences: she needs an appreciable pause (0.4) to begin interpretation, and then she deploys a pragmatic marker *so* separated by another appreciable pause (1.0) from the next pragmatic marker *to sum up*. After a vocalic filler *y::* and an appreciable pause (0.5) she produces an uncompleted TCU (*this problem resulted from the difference in exchange ra-(te)*) followed by subsequent pauses and repairs. The false starts and repairs manifest that the interpreter is looking for the best equivalent to render the witness's utterance. However, by repeating the information and introducing the conjunction *or*, she implicitly suggests that the linguistic choice be made by her clients. In other words, she lets the clients choose the interpretation they deem is the most appropriate, which means that she implicitly agrees to lose ground to the primary speakers: it is not she who is imposing the meanings. Interestingly, in spite of the false starts and repairs, the interpreter provides a **close rendition** of the original utterance.

The following example shows a repair consisting in producing an additional TCU:

(9.169)	**Original PL/EN talk**	**Author's verbatim translation into EN**
Witness:	ye::s (0.3) the bank >didn't have< any objections to our work at all,	
Interpreter:	(.) ta:k (0.2) bank nie miał żadnych zastrzeżeń (1.0) do naszej pracy.	*[Yes, the Bank didn't have any objections. To our work.]*

The witness declares that *the bank didn't have any objections to our work at all*. The interpreter attempts to provide a close rendition of the declaration, although the pauses reveal that she applies a repair to achieve this end. She says that *the bank didn't have any objections*, which is a completed TCU. Then, she makes an appreciable pause (1.0) during which she evidently recalls that the TCU she has produced needs to be supplemented if all the information is to be transmitted. Only then does she produce another TCU, by which she adds a missing detail (*to our work*), hence a **two-part rendition** is provided. Should she not repair her utterance, the message would be a generalization and could refer to any activities to which the bank did not have any objections.

The following example shows a repair which makes the interpreter's rendition sound natural in the target language:

(9.170)	Original PL/EN talk	Author's verbatim translation into EN
Defendant:	she is a Polish scientist.	
Interpreter:	(0.3) ona jest Polką… (0.4) naukowcem…	*[She is a Pole, a scientist.]*

The defendant states that *she is a Polish scientist*. The interpreter, after an appreciable pause (0.3) provides an apparently close rendition of the defendant's answer. However, she splits the sentence: firstly, she says only *she is a Pole*, and only then, after an appreciable pause (0.4), does she complete the TCU by adding *a scientist* which contributes to providing a **two-part rendition**. What is more, the repair contributes to a natural flow of the Polish language: should the verbatim word order be maintained in the rendition, it would sound artificial and too formal as compared to the witness's original utterance.

9.1.2 Primary party-created problem in conversation

The following repair initiated and introduced by the interpreter is of a grammatical nature:

(9.171)	Original PL/EN talk	Author's verbatim translation into EN
Counsel:	jak zrozumiał pan tę część?	*[How did you understand that part?]*
Interpreter:	(.) how do you understand that part?	

The counsel asks the witness *how he understood that part*. The interpreter provides a **close rendition**, although a grammatical modification is applied; this shift consists in that the counsel asks his question using the past tense, while the interpreter makes it present. Evidently, the repair may only mean that the interpreter, being set in the context, knows that the question does not refer to the past, but to the present; thus her decision to use the historical present.

In Extract 9.172, it is the interpreter who detects a repairable and provides a repair:

(9.172)	Original PL/EN talk	Author's verbatim translation into EN
Judge:	(0.2) czasami jest zaburzo:na… (0.2) a to znaczy: (.) co pan ma na myśli mówiąc).) że czasami jest zaburzona?	*[She is sometimes confused… Does it mean, what do you mean, by saying she is sometimes confused?]*
Interpreter:	(0.2) what do you mean by saying (.) she is sometimes confu:sed?	

(9.172)	Original PL/EN talk	Author's verbatim translation into EN
Witness:	(0.3) people at her (.) you kno:w (.) age (0.3) not always think clearly (0.4) yes…	
Interpreter:	(.) ludzie w jej wieku już nie zawsze myślą jasno…	*[People her age do not always think clearly…]*

The judge asks the witness *what he means by saying that she is sometimes confused*, and the question is prefaced by a TCU, which is evidently addressed to a court clerk who is preparing the minutes of the examination. The interpreter identifies this TCU as a repairable fragment, hence she does not include it in her rendition. The witness begins his turn after an appreciable pause (0.3), which means that he needs time to think of the response. After that he states that *people at her age do not always think clearly*, where between the word *her* and *age* a pragmatic marker (*you know*) appears, which is used probably to soften the message. The interpreter identifies the marker as a repairable item and does not reproduce it in her rendition. By doing so, she makes the **reduced rendition** far more straightforward than the original utterance.

The repairs can be forced by the structure of the institutional talk:

(9.173)	Original PL/EN talk	Author's verbatim translation into EN
Judge:	(0.2) okazuje paszpo:rt… (.) wiek pana i zawód?	*[He presents a passport… Your age and profession?]*
Interpreter:	(.) your age and your profession?	
Witness:	(.) yhm: fifty six [and (I'm a)…	
Interpreter:	[mam pięćdziesiąt sześć lat =	*[I am fifty six years old.]*
Witness:	[civil engineer…	
Interpreter:	(.) jestem inżynierem...	*[I am an engineer.]*

The judge asks the witness about his age and profession; the style applied is clerical (*your age and profession*). The interpreter renders the judge's question verbatim, preserving the style. The witness's answer is short (*fifty six*), but he cannot complete his TCU as the interpreter renders the answer (*I am fifty six years old*). Only then is the witness able to supplement the information (*civil engineer*), interpreted as *I am an engineer*. The style used by both the judge and the witness is equally laconic, while the interpreter's renditions of the utterances produced by both primary speakers vary depending on whose utterance is rendered. As regards the judge's question, a **close rendition** is provided. After the witness responds, the interpreter applies extended renditions in which a repair is introduced consisting in changing the style into fully grammatical sentences. As a consequence, the judge receives a round and polite message but, as regards the style, far from the witness's original answers.

Extract 9.174 proves that it is the interpreter who assesses whether or not to initiate and deploy a repair:

(9.174)	**Original PL/EN talk**	**Author's verbatim translation into EN**
Judge:	lat pan ma?	*[Your age?]*
Interpreter:	what's your age?	
Witness:	(0.2) forty four.	
Interpreter:	(.) czterdzieści cztery.	*[Forty four.]*
Judge:	z zawodu pan jest?	*[Your occupation?]*
Interpreter:	(.) your occupation?	
Witness:	(.) colorist.	
Interpreter:	(0.4) hm::: °kolorysta°...	*[Hmmm, colorist...]*

The judge asks the witness how old he is, however, his talk style (*your age*, *lat pan ma*) manifests that he is positioning himself higher in the hierarchy. The interpreter provides a **close rendition** as to the content of the question, but ignores the judge's style (*what's your age?*), which means that it has been the problem in the interaction that she deemed necessary to detect and repair. Interestingly, when the witness answers the question (*forty four*) his style reflects the judge's style, and, what is more, the interpreter reproduces the witness's style (*forty four*). Furthermore, when the judge asks another question, this time concerning the witness's occupation, the interpreter does not identify it as a problem, and again reproduces the main speaker's style. When the witness informs about his occupation (*colorist*), the interpreter needs an appreciable pause (0.4) and a vocalic filler to consider whether there is a problem. Even though she produces a close rendition, she lowers her voice which manifests that she is still not sure of the appropriate equivalent. This episode of interaction shows that interpreters are capable of withdrawing from a repair even at the stage of initiating such a technique.

Extract 9.175 shows that the interpreter identifies and repairs problems relating to the nonchalant speaking style of the primary parties:

(9.175)	**Original PL/EN talk**	**Author's verbatim translation into EN**
Defendant:	((to the Judge, very impatiently)) Okey (0.5) may I say something?	
Interpreter:	(.) czy może pan co[ś powiedzieć?	*[Could he say something?]*
Defendant:	[I'm aware of cultural issues in Poland...	
Interpreter:	((addressing the judge)) (xxx)	

The defendant impatiently addresses the judge. The interpreter detects two problems in the defendant's talk: first, that the defendant is not in a position to speak to the judge in an aggressive style, and second, that she cannot reproduce the grammatical form (*I*) in which the defendant expresses his individual emotions. These two elements make the interpreter introduce repairs. In a **reduced rendition**, she omits the pragmatic marker *okey* in her rendition as it does not correspond to the formal style which should be preserved by the speaker. She also expressly emphasizes the fact of not being a party to the court proceedings, to which aim she changes the grammatical form of the original utterances from the first to the third-person singular. By doing so, she indicates that it is not she, but the defendant, who would like to say something. This may be due to the fact that the *I* form is reserved to the witness's utterances, while all other parties to the court proceedings and the interpreter should use the third-person singular. In other words, the two repairs serve as a tool to present a strong feeling of the interpreter's own identity.

As in a previous example, the interpreter considers all categorically sounding announcements produced by primary parties as a repairable:

(9.176)	**Original PL/EN talk**	**Author's verbatim translation into EN**
Judge:	pan przychodzi do czytelni i czyta akta (0.5) pytanie sądu <u>jest</u> (.) czy zna język polski w związku z tym? (0.2) proszę zapytać (.) czy pan <u>sam</u> czyta akta? =	*[You come to the reading room and read the files. The question of the court is if therefore he knows Polish? Please ask, if he himself reads the files?]*
Interpreter:	= so:: (0.2) do you read the files by yourself in Polish?	
Witness:	<u>no:::</u> (.) what I do is <u>this</u> (0.2) I take a smartphone (.) I take <u>pictu::res</u> (.) ye:s… ((gazes at the interpreter)) (1.0) <u>I want this on protocol</u>.	
Interpreter:	(.) czyli pan chciał (.) żeby to było zapisane w protokole y:: (.) że pan robi zdjęcia akt (.) robi zdjęcia akt.	*[So he wants to have it recorded in the minutes that he takes photos of the files, takes the photos of the files.]*

The witness, addressing the judge, begins his turn with an emphasized *no:::* and states that *he takes a smartphone and takes pictures*. As soon as he completes his turn, he addresses the interpreter to declare that *he wants this on protocol*. The interpreter deploys a grammatical shift from first to third-person singular to repair a problem detected in the defendant's talk: the use of a short negative sentence (*No, what I do is this*), and a short affirmative sentence (*I want this on protocol*) that sounds like an imperative, make the witness's answer blunt and show the witness's restlessness. What is more, although it is the judge who is the target recipient of the witness's answers, the interpreter may find herself in an uncomfortable position due to the fact that when the witness says *I want this on protocol*, he expressly turns his head to the interpreter. It is thusshe who is delegated a responsibility to communicate this message to the judge. Hence, the interpreter unconsciously attempts to distance herself from the message; she does so by applying the grammatical shift, as well as by using a pragmatic marker *so*, which functions as a separator of the interpreter's **reduced rendition** from the witness's utterance.

Extract 9.177 shows that the interpreter's repairs can adopt the form of a **zero rendition**:

(9.177)	**Original PL/EN talk**	**Author's verbatim translation into EN**
Judge:	ale >nie mówi< pan po polsku?	*[But you don't speak Polish?]*
Interpreter:	but you <don't> speak Polish? =	
Witness:	= I wish I did.	
Interpreter:	(.) nie (.) nie mówi pan po polsku. =	*[No, he doesn't speak Polish.]*
Judge:	= tylko czyta po polsku?	*[He only reads in Polish?]*
Interpreter:	(.) do you read in Polish?	

The judge begins this episode of interaction by seeking a confirmation that the witness does not speak Polish, which is interpreted verbatim. In response to that, the witness sarcastically says *I wish I did*. From the interpreter's rendition it results that she perceives the witness's entire answer as inappropriate for the institutional talk. Hence, the response is completely lost in the interpretation: the interpreter states that he does not speak Polish, thus the judge is not informed about the witness's attitude to the proceedings. As a result, the judge poses the next question, which is rendered by the interpreter. This example proves that a repair may lead to creating the judge's false impression not only as regards the party's self–confidence, but also his general approach to the court proceedings.

Extract 9.178 shows that the interpreter initiates and provides a repair to compensate her failure to provide an accurate interpretation of the previous turns:

(9.178)	**Original PL/ES talk**	**Author's verbatim translation into EN**
Judge:	jaką pan pełnił funkcję przy realizacji kontraktu między: e:: (0.2) firmą X a firmą Y? z dnia 1 kwietnia 1999 roku?	*[What office did you hold during the performance of the contract between a company X and a company Y? of April 1, 1999?]*

(9.178)	Original PL/ES talk	Author's verbatim translation into EN
Interpreter:	(1.0) qué pape:l (0.5) qué función desempeñaba?	*[What role, what office did you hold?]*
Witness:	(.) jefe del proyecto	*[Project Manager]*
Interpreter:	(0.4) byłem szefem projektu.	*[I was a Project Manager.]*

The interpreter renders only the first part of the judge's question *about the office that the witness held in the performance of the contract*, while providing a reduced rendition of the second part of the question in which the judge specifies what contract he is referring to. Interestingly, when the witness answers by giving only the name of the office he was holding (project manager), the interpreter provides an extended interpretation (*I was a Project Manager*). This compensation in interpreting contributes to a **substituted rendition** of the information transmitted in the entire episode.

9.2 Self-initiated other-repair

In self-initiated other-repair it is the interpreter who initiates a repair, but only the next speaker responds to the interpreter's initiative and provides a repair.

9.2.1 Interpreter-created problem in conversation

In Extract 9.179, the interpreter projects a failure in her turn, indicates the repairable, and requests the interactants to provide a repair:

(9.179)	Original PL/ES talk	Author's verbatim translation into EN
Witness:	subió el precio de áridos...	*[The price of aggregate went up.]*
Interpreter:	(0.2) °áridos° son?	*[Aggregate is…?]*
Witness:	(.) e:::: áridos (.) po polsku [jest…	*[Aggregate in Polish is…]*
Attorney-at-law	[kruszywo…=	*[Aggregate…]*
Interpreter:	= aha::: (0.2) >czyli ceny< <kruszy::wa:>… =	*[… so the prices of aggregate…]*
Witness:	= el precio de ace:ro… =	*[… the price of steel…]*
Interpreter:	= (0.2) sta:li…	*[… steel…]*

The witness states that *the price of aggregate went up…* but cannot complete his TCU; the interpreter interrupts his turn as she is not able to provide a lexical equivalent of the term *aggregate*. Hence she initiates a repair by asking a question about the meaning of the word. Two speakers respond to her question: firstly, the Spanish-speaking witness who probably speaks Polish (*aggregate in Polish is…*) but still is not able to provide an equivalent, and secondly, the attorney-at-law who provides a Polish equivalent. Only then does the interpreter render the witness' statement. Immediately afterwards, the witness completes his first TCU in which he evidently wants to specify more products than just *aggregate* (*steel*). In this episode of interaction it is all three speakers who work towards providing a repair. The interpreter eagerly *uses* the services spontaneously offered by both the witness and the lawyer, hence providing a **summarized rendition.** In casual conversations such repair initiatives occur when interlocutors give one another hints as to the ideas. However, in formal talks assisted by experts, each in a different field, every party assumes responsibility for their own area of expertise.

9.3 Other-initiated self-repair

Other-initiated self-repair is provided by the interpreter, but a need to introduce a repair has been detected by the primary party. In other words, it is a current speaker who initiates a repair, and the interpreter who responds to that speaker's initiative by correcting the rendition given in her previous turn.

9.3.1 Interpreter-created problem in conversation

In the episode below it is the judge who initiates a repair:

(9.180)	Original PL/EN talk	Author's verbatim translation into EN
Judge:	czy doświadczenie z innych krajów było wymogiem w ogóle przystąpienia do składania ofert? (0.2) czy tego w ogóle oczekiwała X od oferentów?	*[Was experience from other countries a requirement in general to proceed to tender? Was it generally what X expected from tenderers?]*
Interpreter:	(0.1) was any experience needed or >one of the demands< that the XY wanted while making the bid? =	
Judge:	= doświadczenie z innych krajów… =	*[Experience from other countries…]*
Interpreter:	= experience from different markets (1.0) was the condition of the offer? =	
Judge:	= czy X oczekiwała jak gdyby tego?	*[Did X sort of expect that?]*
Interpreter:	(0.2) did the X wanted the company to have (.) such an experience from the different market? (1.0) was it anywhere stated?	

The judge asks *if experience from other countries was a requirement in general to proceed to tender*. The interpreter renders the judge's question but omits a detail to which the judge refers: *experience from other countries*. The judge, who follows the interpreter's rendition, and in the knowledge that his question is long and complex, thus it may be difficult to interpret, initiates a repair by self-selecting as the next speaker to provide the fragment omitted in the interpreter's rendition. The interpreter reacts to this initiative: she renders the judge's interjection (*experience from different markets was the condition of the offer*). Interestingly, a successful initiative to indicate a repairable, makes the judge take another turn in order to repeat another fragment of his original question (*did X sort of expect that?*), which is transmitted by the interpreter. This Extract proves that the judge feels responsibility for both levels of the courtroom interaction: mainly, for the examination, and secondly, for the act of communication. Therefore, he implicitly *cooperates* with the interpreter to eliminate any possible problems in the communicative act. As a consequence, a **summarized rendition** is provided.

In Extract 9.181, it is the counsel who initiates a repair:

(9.181)	**Original PL/EN talk**	**Author's verbatim translation into EN**
Counsel:	czy pamięta pan może? (0.2) ile miało to dziecko?	*[Do you happen to remember how old the child was?]*
Interpreter:	(0.3) do you remember (.) how old the child was? =	
Counsel:	= mniej więcej…	*[More or less…]*
Interpreter:	(0.2) more or less…	
Witness:	(1.0) he was like (0.5) y::: one month (1.0) one month e::: one year (.) and two three months…	
Interpreter:	(.) rok i dwa trzy miesiące. …	*[One year and two three months…]*

The counsel asks the witness *whether he happens to remember how old the child was*. The interpreter omits a modality and asks a straightforward question *if the witness remembers how old the child was*. By doing so, she deprives the counsel's question of softness in addressing the witness. However, immediately after the interpreter's rendition, the counsel self-selects as the next speaker and interferes with *more or less* which means that he does not need precise information of the child's age. The interpreter provides a close rendition after an appreciable pause (0.2). The witness answers hesitantly as he is not sure of the child's age; his utterance resembles thinking aloud where the witness makes every effort to recall a particular detail. In her next turn, the interpreter omits the information, which she thinks is redundant, by which, again, a **reduced rendition** is provided: the interpreter transmits only the final message, which may be due to her intention to reduce the time dedicated to her turn and to clear up the act of communication.

9.3.2 Primary party-created problem in conversation

The example that follows shows a repetition produced by the judge and repaired by the interpreter:

(9.182)	Original PL/EN talk	Author's verbatim translation into EN
Judge:	jak wygląda teraz opieka nad dzieckiem? Kto się opiekuje dzieckiem?	*[What does the childcare look like now? Who takes care of the child?]*
Interpreter:	(0.2) who takes care of the child?	

The judge asks the witness twice about the childcare: the former question is general (*what does the childcare look like now?*), while the latter is specific (*who takes care of the child?*). The interpreter treats the second TCU as a repair; she decides to interpret only the second question, hence she provides a **reduced rendition**. Thus, the witness receives a clear message concerning what information he is supposed to provide.

Similarly, in Extract 9.183, the interpreter provides a repair initiated by the judge:

(9.183)	Original PL/EN talk	Author's verbatim translation into EN
Judge:	czy umowa była wykonywa – (1.0) czy::: była::: y:::: umowa wykonywana y:: zgodnie z zapisami tej umowy? (1.0) czy wszystkie czynności były wykonane?	*[Was the contract executed… was… the contract executed according to the terms and conditions of the contract? Were all the activities carried out?]*
Interpreter:	(0.2) was the contract conformed according to <all terms> of the contract?	

The judge begins this episode of interaction by asking a question in an interrupted style, with unfinished words, two appreciable pauses (0.2 each), stretches and vocalic fillers. The interpreter's turn begins with an appreciable pause (0.2), after which she provides a reduced rendition: although there are no characteristics of the judge's hesitant style, still the rendition suffers from the lack of all details; the judge asks not only about the *execution of the terms and conditions of the contract*, but also *whether all the activities were carried out*. The interpreter's **reduced rendition** covers only the first part of the original question.

In the example that follows the judge's initiative to repair is reproduced by the interpreter:

(9.184)	Original PL/EN talk	Author's verbatim translation into EN
Judge:	jak <stro:na>... (0.2) strona (.) <wykonawca> (0.3) jak wykonawca eh:: interpretował zapisy umowy (0.2) odnośnie płatności?	*[How did the party, party, the contractor, how did the contractor interpret the terms and conditions of the contract relating to payment?]*
Interpreter:	(0.3) what was the interpretation of the contractor (0.2) concerning the remuneration (0.2) payment of remuneration?	

The judge commits a false start in his question concerning the denomination of the subject: firstly, he denominates him as the *party*, and then makes a repair and deploys the noun *contractor*. The interpreter provides a repair in his turn by eliminating the false starts and hesitations; by doing so, the interpreter changes the judge's style and presents him as an unequivocal representative of justice. What is more, the interpreter provides a repair in her own turn: as soon as she says the *remuneration*, she pauses (0.2) and makes a repair (*payment of remuneration*). Nonetheless, both versions are **substituted renditions** as the judge asks about *payment* in general without specifying the type of the payment.

Extract 9.185 is an example of a repair initiated by the judge and provided by the interpreter:

(9.185)	Original PL/EN talk	Author's verbatim translation into EN
Judge:	((nods towards and gazes at the witness's wife)) ojciec pani...	*[Your father]*
Interpreter:	(.) your father–in–law...	

The judge, when producing the utterance, nods towards and gazes at the witness's wife, by which the interpreter perfectly understands that the judge is referring to the witness's wife's father who in turn, is the witness's father-in-law. Therefore, it is a non-verbal communication deployed by the judge which contributes to initiating a repair. As far as the interpreter's rendition is concerned, it is not only the primary speaker's body language, but also the social context of the courtroom which enables her to provide a **close rendition** of the original utterance.

Paradoxically, the literal meaning of what the judge is saying (*your father*) does not reflect the actual meaning of his utterance. Only the interpreter situated within the interaction is able to latch on to a real sense of what is being said.

Extract 9.186 shows that the counsel expressly announces that a repair is needed in his talk, but it is the interpreter who provides such repair:

(9.186)	**Original PL/EN talk**	**Author's verbatim translation into EN**
Counsel:	proszę pana? (1.0) czy świadkowi coś wiadomo? (0.2) e::: (1.0) powiem ina:czej (2.0) przepraszam (1.0) czy świadek był (0.2) y:::::: (.) uczestniczył (1.0) czy słyszał >coś o kłótni stron<?	*[Sir, does the witness know anything, eee…, I'll put it differently, sorry, was, did the witness, yyy…, participate or hear anything about the argument between the parties?]*
Interpreter:	(.) were you involved (1.0) did you hear anything (.) any arguments between the parties?	

The counsel's question is tangled, interrupted with appreciable pauses, vocalic fillers and false starts. The interpreter strives for extracting the content from the counsel's question so that the witness is clear on what the counsel is asking him about. **A reduced rendition** is evident proof of the necessity, on the part of the interpreter, to look at the original utterances from a bird's eye. Only then is it possible to understand the primary speaker's talk.

Yet another example shows that it is only the interpreter who is able to perceive the primary speaker's initiative to provide a repair as such:

(9.187)	**Original PL/EN talk**	**Author's verbatim translation into EN**
Judge:	a żona ma jakieś schorzenia neurologiczne?	*[And does your wife have any neurological conditions?]*
Interpreter:	(.) does your wife suffer from some e:: neurological disease?	
Witness:	(.) yes (0.5) y:: (.) no! she is sometimes confused. =	
Interpreter:	= nie: (0.2) po prostu czasami jest zaburzona...	*[No, she is simply disturbed sometimes.]*

The judge asks the witness *whether his wife has any neurological conditions*, which is followed by close rendition into English. To answer the judge's question, the witness firstly says yes, and then produces an appreciable pause (0.5) and a vocalic filler (*y::*). By doing so, he gains time to consider his original response, proof of which is his emphasized *no* followed by a post-expansion, in which he elaborates on his answer. The interpreter chooses to render only a *no*-version as he knows it is actually a repair initiated by the main speaker—only such a response can be followed by the post-expansion the witness has applied. On the whole, a **close rendition** is provided.

The following example shows that the interpreter repairs the problems which appear in both the judge's and the witness's TCUs:

(9.188)	**Original PL/EN talk**	**Author's verbatim translation into EN**
Judge:	czy::: według pana uczestnika (0.2) bo rozumiem (.) że tutaj chce zatrudnić opiekunkę:: (0.2) czy żona: (0.4) czy potrzebna jest opieka nad żoną (.) i dlaczego? (1.0) dlaczego żona nie jest w stanie samodzielnie funkcjonować? =	*[According to Mr. participant, because I understand that here he wants to employ a carer, does your wife…, is care for your wife necessary and why? Why is your wife not able to function independently?]*
Interpreter:	= do you think that is taking care of your wife necessary? (.) and if so (0.3) why is it necessary? (1.0) is your wife able to live independently according to you?	
Witness:	(0.5) not independent.	
Interpreter:	(0.2) żona >nie jest w stanie funkcjonować< samodzielnie.	*[My wife is not able to function independently.]*

There are two instances in this episode of interaction in which the interpreter introduces repairs consisting in altering the styles used by the original speakers. In order to make the utterance concise and comprehensible for the interlocutor, the interpreter shortens the judge's questions by omitting the two principal TCUs (*according to Mr participant, because I understand that here he wants to employ a carer*). Interestingly, another problem is implicitly signalized by the witness who produces a very short answer (*not independent*) as compared to an elaborated question (*do you think that is taking care of your wife necessary and if so why is it necessary, is your wife able to live independently according to you?*). As a repair, the interpreter changes the witness's response into a fully grammatical statement (*wife is not able to function independently*). As regards both repairs, the interpreter embellishes the participants' styles and, furthermore, casts them in a different light: in the interpreter's **substituted renditions** the judge is sure of what he is asking about and the witness is eager to respond before the court.

In Extract 9.189 the witness signalizes the problem and attempts to provide a repair:

(9.189)	Original PL/EN talk	Author's verbatim translation into EN
Witness:	ye:s (.) because (.) as they we::re (2.0) they were like a cou:ple. (2.0) yes (0.3) we were best friends for both of them. =	
Interpreter:	= ta:k (0.2) dla nas byli parą (1.5) byliśmy najlepszymi przyjaciółmi ich obojga.	*[Yes, for us they were a couple, we were best friends for both.]*

The witness hesitates when he answers the judge's question: repetitions (*they were... they were*), stretches (*we::re, cou:ple*) and appreciable pauses (2.0, 2.0, and 0.3) occur in his talk. All of them prove that he is attempting to make repairs to create a coherent utterance; this aim is achieved by the interpreter who eliminates the repetitions, although appreciable pauses still occur, hence a **close rendition** is provided.

In Extract 9.190 the witness initiates a repair in his talk and the interpreter continues the repair:

(9.190)	Original PL/EN talk	Author's verbatim translation into EN
Judge:	sąd chciałby zapytać (2.0) od kiedy pan zna pana X i panią X?	*[The judge would like to ask for how long you have known Mr. X and Mr. X?]*
Interpreter:	(1.) the court would like to ask you (0.2) since when you know Mr. X and Mrs. X?	
Witness:	(2.0) eh::: fro::m (2.0) ((to the interpreter)) from New Year's Eve 2008/2009. =	
Interpreter:	= od Sylwestra 2008/2009.	*[From New Year's Eve 2008/2009.]*

The judge begins this episode of interaction by *asking since when the witness has known Mr. X and Mr. X*. The interpreter renders the judge's question verbatim. When, after an appreciable pause (2.0), the witness responds, a vocalic filler and a false start appears (*eh::: fro::m*) followed by another appreciable pause (2.0). After that, the witness answers that *from New Year's Eve 2008/2009*. The interpreter provides a **close rendition** of the witness's answer, eliminating however the witness's false start, this being a consequence of a change of recipients of that response: at the beginning the witness addresses the judge, but then starts talking to the interpreter as the person to whom he actually transmits the message. Thus the witness logically repeats the first part of his answer, and the interpreter, following the same logic, repairs the witness's talk.

In Extract 9.191 the witness detects a problem and the interpreter makes a repair, but attempts to preserve the primary party's style:

(9.191)	**Original PL/EN talk**	**Author's verbatim translation into EN**
Judge:	(0.2) czy pan wie (.) z jakiego względu?	*[Do you know for what reason?]*
Interpreter:	(.) do you <u>know</u> (.) for what reason?	
Witness:	(0.5) ye::s (.) yhm:::: I think that X became mo:re e:::: I think yh y:: he was limited about his son (1.0) I think that e:: X was limited with what he could do.	
Interpreter:	(0.2) ta:k (0.2) myślę (.) że było to z powodu jego syna: (0.6) X był ograniczony w tym (.) co mógł robić…	*[Yes, I think that it was because of his son. X was limited in what he could do.]*

The judge begins this episode of interaction asking about the reason for a particular situation, and the interpreter provides a **close rendition** of the question. When the witness starts talking after an appreciable pause (0.5), he stretches the vocalic fillers (yhm:::) and deploys a false start (*I think that X became more… I think he was…I think that X was limited…*). The interpreter does not reproduce these false starts, but still a hesitating style, as well as the meaning of the witness's declaration is preserved: the interpreter stretches the affirmative particle (ye::s), uses a discourse marker (*I think*), and slows down the talk by using an appreciable pause (0.6).

The subsequent example shows a repair consisting in combining short statements:

(9.192)	**Original PL/EN talk**	**Author's verbatim translation into EN**
Witness:	yes (1.0) she gets from <u>here</u> (0.5) from <u>Poland</u> (1.0) ye:s (0.2) she gets a pension.	
Interpreter:	(.) tak (0.2) otrzymuje polską emeryturę budżetową	*[Yes, she gets a Polish budgetary pension.]*

The witness chaotically responds to the judge's question: at first he provides an affirmative answer (*yes*) followed by an appreciable pause (1.0), after which he begins another TCU (*she gets from here*), interjects an appreciable pause (0.5), another TCU (*from Poland*) followed by the thirds appreciable pause (1.0). Afterwards, he reaffirms his first TCU (*yes*), followed by an appreciable pause

(0.2) and a new TCU (she gets a pension). Thus, the witness repeats the information twice. The interpreter repairs the witness's turn by combining all the details to create a grammatical statement and providing a **close rendition**.

9.4 Other-initiated other-repair

An other-initiated other-repair is provided when it is not the interpreter who is the only party to the courtroom interaction who establishes the meanings and possibly corrects herself, but a lawyer, a person from the public, or any other participant who knows or pretends to know the language of a non-Polish speaking party to the proceedings.

9.4.1 Interpreter-created problem in conversation

Extract 9.193 shows a repair initiated and provided by the judge:

(9.193)	**Original PL/EN talk**	**Author's verbatim translation into EN**
Witness:	ye:s (1.0) we've got a condominium in X… =	
Interpreter:	= tak (0.3) mamy kondominium [w X.	*[Yes, we have a condominium in X…]*
Judge:	[°mieszkanie°…	*[An apartment…]*
Interpreter:	((gazes at the judge)) (silence)	

The witness declares that *they've got a condominium in X*. The interpreter renders the witness's answer verbatim but an English word *condominium* and a Polish *kondominium* are false friends; a *condominium* is "a building or complex of buildings containing a number of individually owned apartments or houses"[94] while in the Polish language *kondominium* is used to designate "a territory governed by the joint control of two or more states, or the joint control over such territory"[95]. However, when in Polish the term *condominium* and not *kondominium* is deployed, it is more and more frequently used as a jargon equivalent in the same meaning it is used in English[96]. The judge, probably in the

94 https://en.oxforddictionaries.com/definition/condominium (October 1, 2017).

95 terytorium podlegające wspólnym rządom dwóch lub kilku państw; też: rządy sprawowane w ten sposób http://sjp.pwn.pl/szukaj/kondominium.html (October 1, 2017).

96 https://www.infolinia.com/2012_03_08_condominium_czyli_mieszkanie_wlasnosciowe (October 1, 2017).

assumption that the interpreter uses an incorrect calque, gets involved in rendering the real meaning by mentioning *an apartment…* en passant. By doing so, the judge initiates a repair, which however is not continued by the interpreter whose turn is silent (a **zero rendition** is produced), although she is aware of the judge's initiative for repair.

In Extract 9.194, it is the counsel who indicates the repairable in the interpreter's rendition and provides a repair:

(9.194)	Original PL/EN talk	Author's verbatim translation into EN
Witness:	we're ready to consider compensation of unpaid… =	
Interpreter:	= yhm? (0.2) w tym mailu jest mowa o tym (0.3) y::: że pan X deklaruje gotowość spółki Y do zrekompensowania (.) czy do kompensa[ty.	*[Yhm. In this mail it is said that, y… that Mr. … declares the readiness of the company… to indemnify, or to compensate.]*
Counsel 1:	[consider (0.5) rozważenia… =	*[consider…consider]*
Counsel 2:	= wysoki sądzie (1.0) ja bym prosił (0.2) żeby strona nie sugerowała (0.3) i wręcz nie <tłumaczyła>…	*[Your Honor, I would like to ask the party not to suggest or, plainly, to translate…]*
Interpreter:	(0.4) e::: (0.3) deklaruje gotowość do::: rozważe:nia: (0.4) do:brze:: (0.3) deklaruje gotowość do tego (0.2) aby wziąć pod uwagę zrekompensowanie (xxx) niewypłaconych (0.2) niezapłaconych…	*[… eee… declares that he is ready to… consider… OK… declares that he is ready to consider compensating… unpaid, unpaid…]*

The witness answers the judge's question by declaring that they *are ready to consider compensation of unpaid…*after which he suspends his voice, apparently in search of a proper word. The interpreter does not allow the witness complete his TCU and starts interpreting. However, she hesitates, is obviously unsure of how to interpret the witness's statement, and, finally, confuses the verbs (*consider* vs. *declare*), to which one of the counsels reacts by prompting the interpreter with an adequate meaning of the word used by the witness. By doing so, the counsel both initiates a repair and repairs the previous speaker's talk. In response to the repair, the other counsel protests against such behavior of his counterpart and asks *not to suggest or even to interpret the witness's statements*. The interpreter seems not to take note of the exchange of ideas between the counsels; she continues to use the verb *declare* instead of *consider*, but deploys a syntactic figure to intersperse her rendition with the concept of *considering* or *taking into account* suggested by one of the lawyers. This means that the interpreter is aware of her error and the need to repair it; she listens carefully to the lawyers' comments, and draws conclusions; as a result, an **extended rendition** is provided.

The subsequent episode shows that an unknown speaker can initiate and provide a repair:

(9.195)	**Original PL/ES talk**	**Author's verbatim translation into EN**
Witness:	y nosotros hemos pagado >el IVA< en su totalidad.	*[And we have paid VAT in full]*
Interpreter:	(.) zapłaciliśmy całość.	*[We have paid in full.]*
?:	((whispering from the public)): °I-VA (0.3) VAT°...	
Interpreter:	(0.3) zapłaciliśmy całą kwotę VAT...	*[We have paid VAT in full...]*

The witness states that they *have paid VAT in full*. The interpreter renders the statement as they *have paid in full*. It is a voice from the public who initiates a repair: he helps the interpreter to establish the meaning of the lost detail (the witness is talking about Value Added Tax and not any payable amount), which makes the transmitted message complete. Only then does the interpreter introduce a repair leading to a **close rendition**. Therefore, not only participants in the proceedings, but also third persons theoretically not involved in the interaction, become active participants in the act of communication. It is actually they who monitor the interpreter's renditions although they are not the direct interlocutors.

In Extract 9.196 in the course of the interaction, someone from the public takes a turn:

(9.196)	**Original PL/EN talk**	**Author's verbatim translation into EN**
Interpreter:	(xxx)	
?:	nic nie sły-chać	*[I can't hear a thing]*
Interpreter:	((without addressing any particular person, but gazing at the public)) (.) nic na to nie poradzę	*[I can't help it]*
Judge:	(0.3) po prostu (.) proszę się >przysunąć trochę<...	*[Simply please move a little closer]*
Interpreter:	(0.2) dobrze, (.) oczywiście...	*[Good, of course]*

The interpreter's utterances are inaudible, which causes complaints from the public. This makes the interpreter self-select as the next speaker. Evidently, she personally feels unfairly attacked. As she is more than convinced that the inaudibility is caused by a technical failure of the microphone, she immediately responds to the anonymous comment. By doing so, she makes the judge self-select as the next speaker; he asks the interpreter to move closer to the microphone in order to improve the sound quality. As the judge expressly reacts to the inaudibility problem in which the interpreter is involved, she understands that she is a recipient of the judge's advice, thus she confirms to the judge that she understands, agrees, and is going to do what the judge tells her to do. This episode of interaction shows a **non-rendition**, where the interpreter focuses on the judge's words addressed to her, hence it is impossible for her to provide an interpretation thus her decision not to involve the witness in technical issues.

9.5 Conclusions

The analysis has shown that in bilingual interactions repairs are a common mechanism used by both the interpreters and the primary speakers.

As regards the problems from which **self-initiated self-repairs** originate, they are either interpreter- or primary party-created. The first category includes the interpreter's false starts (being a consequence of applying SL syntax to the TL, using an inappropriate equivalent, deploying hypernyms), repetitions, and splitting the utterances into two parts. These problems are repaired immediately after they appear, by providing close, reduced, or two-part renditions. The second category comprises the use of tenses, the overuse of pragmatic markers, applying terms unknown to the interpreter, and deploying an overly formal or overly informal style. The problem in the primary party's talk is repaired in the interpreter's turn directly following the turn in which such a problem has occurred – by providing close, reduced, or zero renditions. Incidentally, the occurrence of complex problems in conversation has been detected, where, on the whole, the interpreter has provided a substituted rendition of the judge's question and the next speaker's utterance. The results are presented in Tab. 9.1:

Based on only one episode of interaction of a **self-initiated other-repair** found in the analyzed material (Extract 9.179)—where a problem is reported by the interpreter, but it is the primary party who provides a repair—occurs, it can be estimated that such a technique is uncommon and deployed by the interpreter only as a last resort in the knowledge that she is not able to provide a rendition of the original talk. The problem is interpreter-created and results from her inability to come up with an appropriate lexical equivalent of a particular term ("failure to lexicalize", Shlesinger 1991b: 5). In the discussed episode of interaction, as a consequence of the repair, a summarized rendition has been provided, as shown in Tab. 9.2:

Tab. 9.1: Self-initiated self-repair

Extract	Renditions / Interactant	CR	ER	RR	SBR	SMR	TMR	NR	ZR
9.161	Judge	**1**	0	0	0	0	0	0	0
9.162	Judge	**1**	0	0	0	0	0	0	0
9.163	Judge	0	0	**1**	0	0	0	0	0
9.164	Counsel	0	0	**1**	0	0	0	0	0
9.165	Judge	**1**	0	0	0	0	0	0	0
9.166	Witness	**1**	0	0	0	0	0	0	0
9.167	Judge	**1**	0	0	0	0	0	0	0
9.168	Witness	**1**	0	0	0	0	0	0	0
9.169	Witness	0	0	0	0	0	**1**	0	0
9.170	Defendant	0	0	0	0	0	**1**	0	0
9.171	Counsel	**1**	0	0	0	0	0	0	0
9.172	Witness	0	0	**1**	0	0	0	0	0
9.173	Judge	**1**	0	0	0	0	0	0	0
9.174	Judge/Witness	**1**	0	0	0	0	0	0	0
9.175	Defendant	0	0	**1**	0	0	0	0	0
9.176	Witness	0	0	**1**	0	0	0	0	0
9.177	Witness	0	0	0	0	0	0	0	**1**
9.178	Judge/Witness	0	0	0	**1**	0	0	0	0
Total:		**9**	**0**	**5**	**1**	**0**	**2**	**0**	**1**

Tab. 9.2: Self-initiated other-repair

Extract	Renditions / Interactant	CR	ER	RR	SBR	SMR	TMR	NR	ZR
9.179	Witness	0	0	0	0	**1**	0	0	0
Total:		**0**	**0**	**0**	**0**	**1**	**0**	**0**	**0**

As far as **other-initiated self-repair** defined as the one initiated by the primary party and provided by the interpreter, both interpreter- and primary party-created problems in conversation have been found, however the former occur only in two episodes of interaction, while the latter is commonly present. When the primary speakers identify a problem in the interpreter's talk, they do so under the following circumstances: firstly, the problem is detected in the interpreter's renditions into English, secondly, they understand the renditions, and thirdly, they do not criticize the interpreter for an uncompleted interpretation, but rather want to help her transmit the whole original utterance, thus, their initiative for a repair consists in

Tab. 9.3: Other-initiated self-repair

Extract	**Interactant** / **Renditions**	**CR**	**ER**	**RR**	**SBR**	**SMR**	**TMR**	**NR**	**ZR**
9.180	Judge	0	0	0	0	**1**	0	0	0
9.181	Witness	0	0	**1**	0	0	0	0	0
9.182	Judge	0	0	**1**	0	0	0	0	0
9.183	Judge	0	0	**1**	0	0	0	0	0
9.184	Judge	0	0	0	**1**	0	0	0	0
9.185	Judge	**1**	0	0	0	0	0	0	0
9.186	Counsel	0	0	**1**	0	0	0	0	0
9.187	Witness	**1**	0	0	0	0	0	0	0
9.188	Judge/Witness	0	0	0	**1**	0	0	0	0
9.189	Witness	**1**	0	0	0	0	0	0	0
9.190	Witness	**1**	0	0	0	0	0	0	0
9.191	Witness	**1**	0	0	0	0	0	0	0
9.192	Witness	**1**	0	0	0	0	0	0	0
Total:		**6**	**0**	**4**	**2**	**1**	**0**	**0**	**0**

prompting the interpreter with the necessary details. As a repair, the interpreters provide either a summarized or a reduced rendition. The problems identified by the primary speakers in their own talk include, as regards the judges and other representatives of the judiciary: false starts (looking for an appropriate term), completing the TCU with additional information, figurative meanings; as regards the witness: false starts (looking for an appropriate term), using laconic style, as well as overuse of vocalic fillers and stretched words. In order to repair the problems signalized by the judges and other lawyers, the interpreters provide reduced, substituted and close renditions, while the problems identified in the witnesses' utterances, close renditions are provided. These findings are illustrated in Tab. 9.3:

In the event of **other-initiated other-repair**, where a problem in conversation is both detected and repaired by the primary party, the problems occur in the interpreter's talk. These problems are a consequence of too close a rendition (where a calque is applied), extended rendition (although the interpreter transmits a lot of information, she fails to deploy an appropriate equivalent in TL), a non-rendition (when the interpreter speaks with her own words), and a zero rendition (when the interpreter fails to convey the whole original message), as shown in Tab. 9.4:

Within the mechanism of repairs, the question-rendition-answer-rendition pattern of bilingual interaction prevails however, there are considerable

Tab. 9.4: Other-initiated other-repair

Extract	Renditions / Interactant	CR	ER	RR	SBR	SMR	TMR	NR	ZR
9.193	Judge	0	0	0	0	0	0	0	1
9.194	Lawyers	0	1	0	0	0	0	0	0
9.195	Public	1	0	0	0	0	0	0	0
9.196	Public	0	0	0	0	0	0	1	0
Total:		1	1	0	0	0	0	1	1

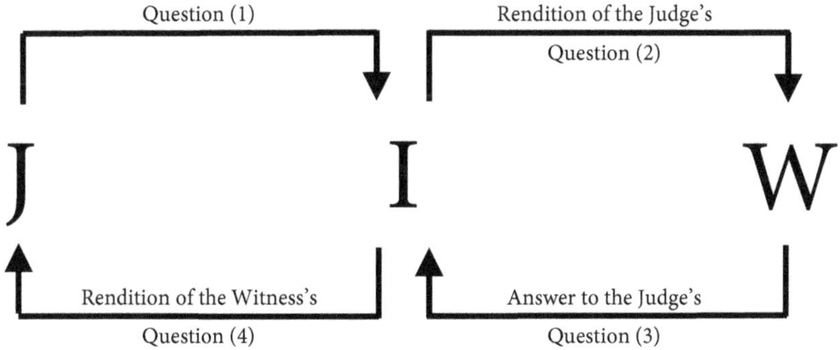

Fig. 9.1: Interaction with close, reduced, substituted, summarized and two-part renditions

exceptions. Interestingly, this pattern occurs only with self-initiated self-repairs (Extracts 9.161–9.166, 9.168–9.172, 9.174, 9.176, and 9.178) where close, reduced, substituted and two-part or multi-part renditions are provided, as well as with other-initiated self-repairs (9.182–9.192) when close, reduced, substituted, and summarized renditions appear (Fig. 9.1):

The interpreter's rendition comes after each original utterance: the judge asks the question, which is rendered by the interpreter to the witness, who answers the question, which in turn is rendered by the interpreter to the judge; the sequence may repeat. Such interactions appear obviously when the renditions are accurate but also when the interpreter introduces additions or when the interpreter deals with rude or sarcastic utterances, and finally with those renditions that are created as totally parallel statements that have nothing to do with the content of the original utterances.

The overwhelming deployment of the above interaction within self-repairs, be it self- or other-initiated, proves that self-repairs do not pose problems in bilingual interaction.

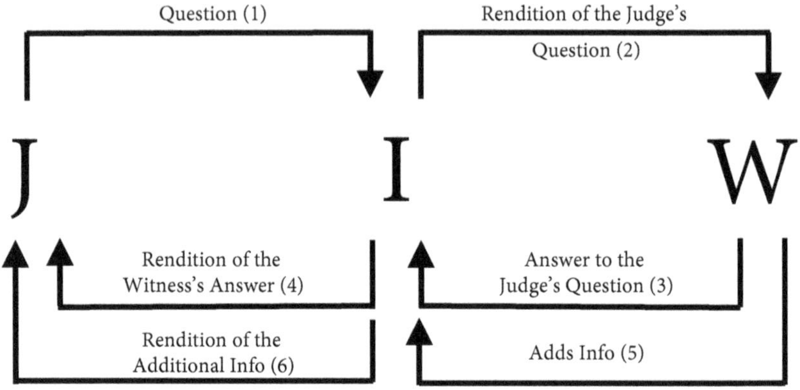

Fig. 9.2: Interaction with close renditions

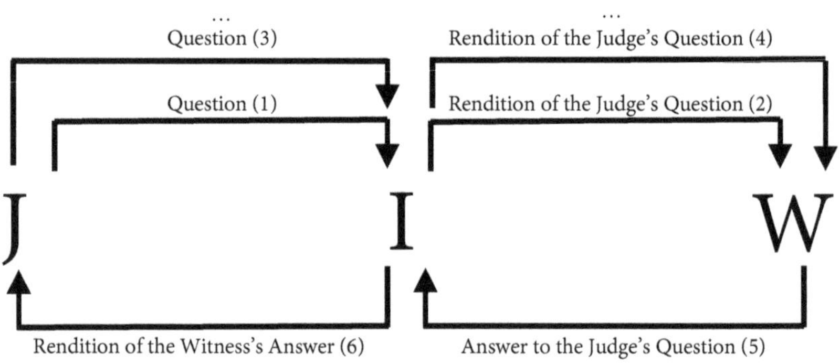

Fig. 9.3: Interaction with reduced and zero renditions

Another pattern of interaction has appeared in two episodes within self-initiated self-repairs where close renditions have been provided (Extracts 9.167 and 9.174) (Fig. 9.2):

This pattern is like the question-rendition-answer-rendition one, but only until the moment the interpreter has finished her rendition. Then, the witness immediately adds information to supplement his previous utterance, and thus the interpreter provides a rendition of this additional information.

A similar pattern occurs in the same category of self-initiated self-repairs where a zero rendition (Extract 9.177) is provided and within the category of other-initiated self-repair, where the interpreter provides a reduced rendition (Extract 9.181), as shown in Fig. 9.3:

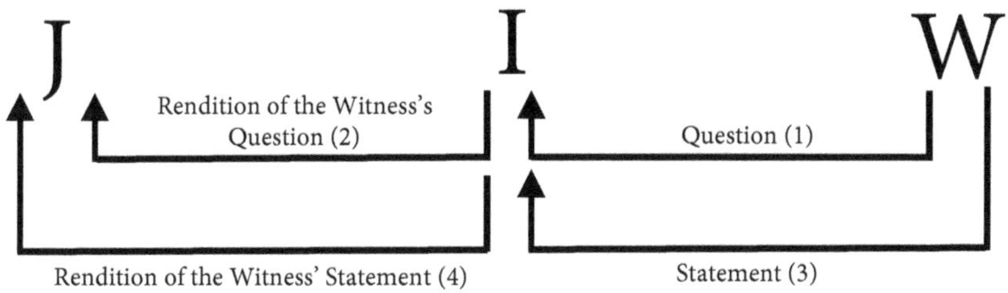

Fig. 9.4: Interaction with reduced renditions

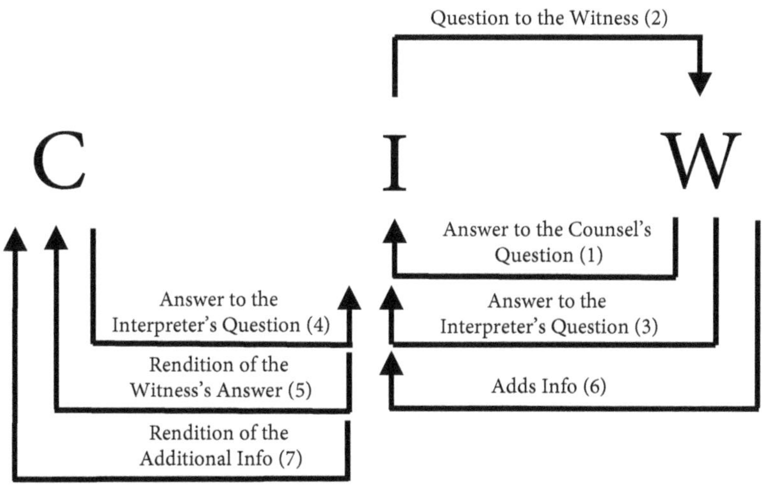

Fig. 9.5: Interaction with summarized renditions

Interestingly, the pattern should be read in two different ways, depending on the episode. As far as Extract 9.177 is concerned, it illustrates additional questions posed by the judge who reacts to the witness's answer, while in Extract 9.182 the judge asks an additional question before the witness answers his first question.

Yet another pattern, with a single occurrence within self-initiated self-repairs and with a reduced rendition (Extract 9.175), is as follows (Fig. 9.4):

The interpreter renders all utterances produced by the witness, be it the witness's answer or statement.

The only example of a self-initiated other-repair found in the analyzed material (Extract 9.179) where a summarized rendition is provided can be illustrated as in Fig. 9.5:

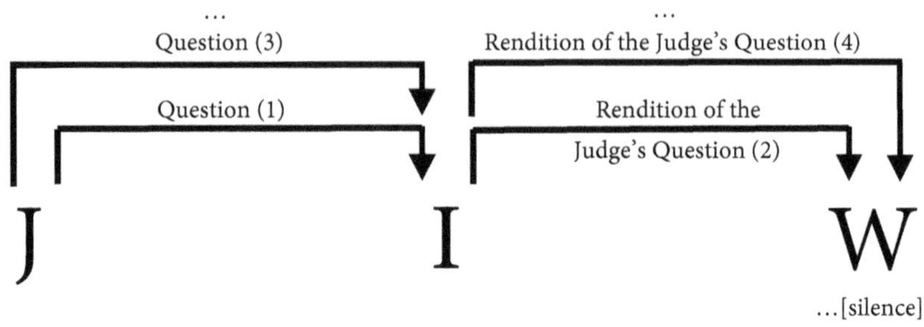

Fig. 9.6: Interaction with summarized renditions

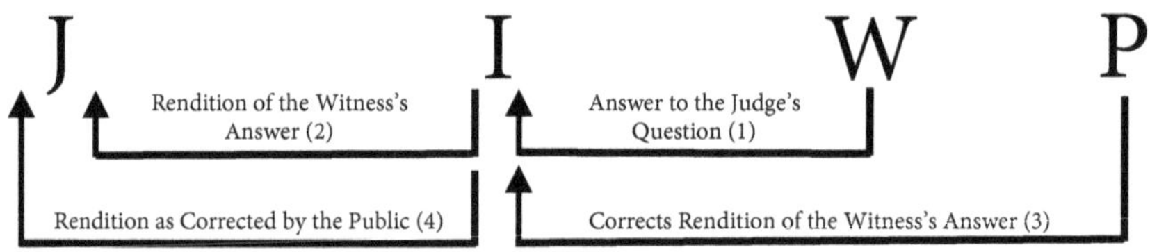

Fig. 9.7: Interaction with close renditions

Such a complex interaction is carried out when the interpreter has terminological problems and cannot be a communicative liaison between the parties. Interestingly, on such instances other participants start positioning themselves as interpreters.

Moreover, for summarized renditions, and as regards other-initiated self-repairs (Extract 9.180), there is yet another exceptional pattern of interaction (Fig. 9.6):

The judge asks the question and the interpreter renders it. However, without waiting for the witness's answer, the judge asks the next question to the witness and the interpreter renders it. Such a pattern can be carried out until the moment the judge decides not to supplement his questions with additional details.

Furthermore, within the mechanism of repairs, the category of other-initiated other-repair is the most heterogeneous of all, which is due to the fact that these repairs have a potential to be initiated and carried out by any participant or non-participant in the communicative act of the courtroom. Hence, in all four episodes comprised by this category, four different patterns of interaction appear. When it comes to a close rendition (Extract 9.195), the following pattern has been identified (Fig. 9.7):

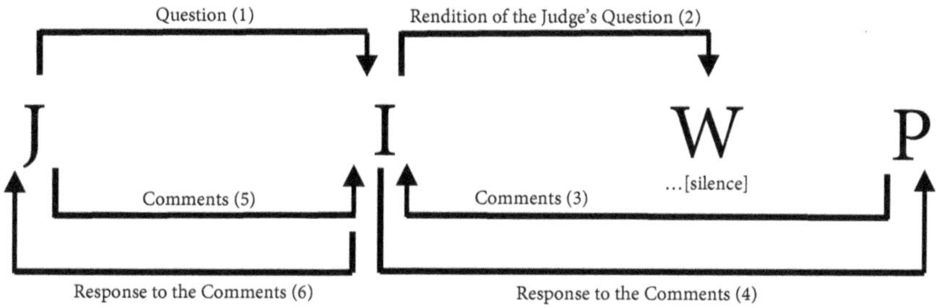

Fig. 9.8: Interaction with non-renditions

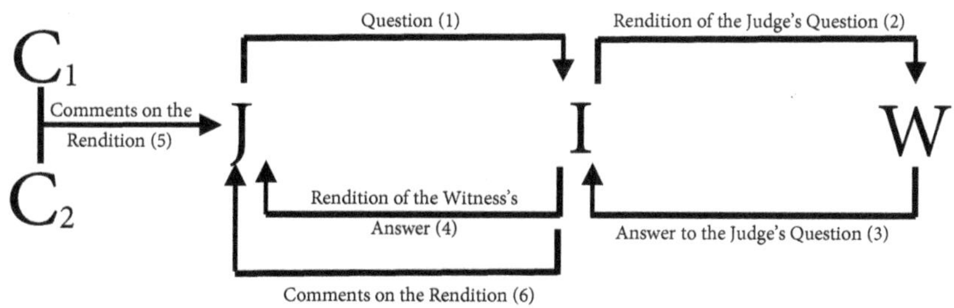

Fig. 9.9: Interaction with extended renditions

At a certain moment of interaction, the voice from the public corrects the interpreter's rendition, and, what is more, the interpreter takes into account the whispered information and corrects her rendition.

Another pattern, in which the public is involved, appears with non-rendition (Extract 9.196) (Fig. 9.8):

The voice from the public disturbs the flow of bilingual communication and makes the interpreter begin a new episode of interaction—with both the public and the judge.

As far as an extended rendition is concerned (Extract 9.194), the following pattern of interaction appears (Fig. 9.9):

At the beginning, the interaction follows the question-rendition-answer-rendition pattern. Then, however, the counsels start commenting on the interpreter's rendition. The interpreter reacts by joining the talk.

As regards a zero rendition (Extract 9.193), the following pattern appears (Fig. 9.10):

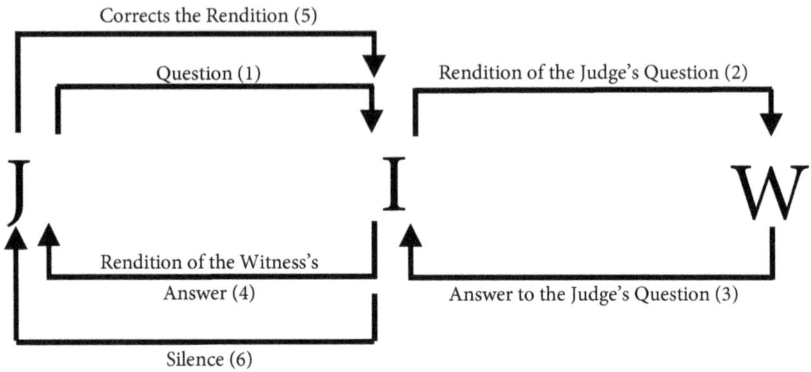

Fig. 9.10: Interaction with zero renditions

The interaction is question-rendition-answer-rendition in terms of the turn-taking system deployed in bilingual interactions, but the judge interrupts the pattern by correcting the interpreter's rendition. The interpreter behaves as if she has not heard the judge's utterance and remains silent.

In general, repairs are mechanisms deployed not only by all participants in the interaction, but also by non-participants (the public). The above discussed examples show that the interpreters cope equally with the interactants who are either directly or indirectly involved in communicative events.

10 Discussion on the results and recommendations for further research

The aim of this study has been to fulfill the neglected area of descriptive research into court interpreting in Poland based on "real-life interpreted-mediated encounters" (Wadensjö 1995: 50), involving the Polish-English and (to a lesser degree and thus for illustrative purposes) Polish-Spanish language pairs.

This research has been embedded in the sociological theory of interaction (Garfinkel 1967, Goffman 1956, 1967) and undertaken on the assumption that court interpreters, as active participants in the communicative event (Shlesinger 1991a; Wadensjö 1995, 1997, 1998, 2012; Gentile, Ozolins, and Vasilakakos 1996; Fenton 1997; Fowler 1997; Roberts 1997; Hale 1997a, 1997b, 2001, 2003, 2004, 2007, 2008; Mason 1999; Kadrić 2000; Jacobsen 2002, 2003, 2004; Rudvin 2002; Valero Garcés and Dergam 2003; Biernacka 2008a, 2008b, 2009, 2010a, 2010b, 2014a, 2014b, 2016; Nartowska 2013a, 2013b, 2015; Stawecka 2010; Tryuk 2010) form part of the trilogue comprising the court stakeholder, the court's private client and the interpreter (Roy 1990; Malheiros-Poulet 1995; Taylor Torsello 1997; Kang 1998; Tryuk 2006; Pöchhacker 2008; Shisheng and Shuang 2012; Biernacka 2014a).

Hence, the research questions have been aimed to refine the picture of the court interpreter as an interlocutor within a bilingual communicative event. In particular, the following issues have been submitted to the analysis:

(1) the interpreter's co-acting, at both interactional and linguistic level, with the primary parties in order to perform the act of communication;
(2) the types of renditions of the original utterances produced by primary speakers provided by the interpreters;
(3) the renditions as manifestations of complying, on the part of the interpreters, with the ethical principles of accuracy and impartiality required in the bilingual communicative events of the courtroom;
(4) the possible patterns in deploying interpreting techniques, depending on a particular interaction mechanism to which the interpreter is a component.

The naturally occurring data have served as a point of departure for proposing an integrated study comprising the following components: Conversation Analysis of the episodes of interaction, discussion concerning the interpreters' renditions, and assessment of these renditions from the point of view of ethical principles.

For the purposes of this study, qualitative research has been conducted. Therefore, the main characteristics of the methodological design have been as follows:

(1) a small sample size (Hale 2001, 2003, 2004; Dörnyei 2007; Torstensson and Gawronska 2009; Nartowska 2013a, 2013b, 2015; Biernacka 2014a; Creswell 2014);
(2) flexibility of the design (Dörnyei 2007; Creswell 2014);
(3) exploratory nature of the research (Dörnyei 2007); and
(4) particularity of data (Creswell 2014).

As regards a small sample size, this has been due mainly to confidentiality observed by the courts, obliged to protect the sensitive data obtained in the course of the trials. The size of the collected material has been a pre-limitation of the study in terms of defining the research as qualitative, while leaving an idea of conducting quantitative or mixed research. Nonetheless, flexibility of the design has made it possible to adjust the research questions to the material actually collected at the preliminary stage; in other words, the research has been narrowed to the interactions performed in the civil and economic divisions of the court. The research has been then redesigned to an exploratory in nature, which has been intended to detect irregularities and hence, find new areas of both interpreter-mediated interactions and possible future academic investigations. Furthermore, particularity of data has had its implications for the non-quantification of the results however it has contributed to carrying out an in-depth analysis (Creswell 2014) of the episodes of interaction thus helping get a non-statistical picture of the courtroom communicative events as interpreter-mediated interactions.

The analysis of interpreter-mediated communicative events of the courtroom conducted within the proposed methodological design shows the following features of the bilingual talk:

(1) all interactants, be it primary speakers or interpreters, intervene on an equal basis in the turn-taking system. It means that the judge, or another representative of the judiciary, is not the one who has the exclusive right and privilege to select the next speaker by addressing a particular party with a question or a request. Thus, similarly to casual conversations and contrary to the findings concerning monolingual court talks (Atkinson and Drew 1979; Atkinson 1982; Rzeszutko 2003; Heffer 2005; Bednarek 2014a), if the interpreter contributes to creating the communicative triangle, the turn-taking system can be infringed. This occurs in the events where the interpreter produces a non-rendition by asking the judge to repeat the question,

or where the non-Polish speaking parties self-select to speak, without observing the orderliness of the institutional talk – as a consequence, on such occasions the interpreter is expected to take a turn, although, as shown, she regularly chooses to provide a zero rendition;

(2) contextual organization of the bilingual courtroom talk has been noted, which confirms one of the assumptions of CA, namely, that the talks are context-shaped (Heritage 1984; Jacobsen 2002, 2008) and that the contexts are formed from both the situation and the language used in that situation (Lyons 1972). This can be observed in the episodes of interaction, in which the interpreters provide reduced, extended or substituted renditions. In these instances the interpreters resort to their knowledge of the case; this confirms that *one topic* (Atkinson 1982), as the characteristic of institutional talk, makes the interpreters contextualize the primary parties' utterances. Moreover, the sequential organization of the talk (Heritage 1984) contributes to the interpreters' and the primary parties' understanding of the episodes of interaction constructed during the whole talk without need for a verbatim interpretation (Hale 2007, 2008);

(3) a question-rendition-answer-rendition pattern of interaction – understood as the one, in which after each primary party's turn the interpreter speaks to render the original utterance – prevails within all mechanisms, and, interestingly, allows for a range of renditions: from close renditions to non-renditions, which appear within gaps, counters and post-expansions. It means that these three mechanisms, when deployed in a bilingual interaction, have the potential to take cover and make an impression as if no such elements occurred in the communicative act. This finding – that a question-rendition-answer-rendition interaction does not impose only close renditions – confirms Kempiński's opinion that smooth communication between the parties does not equal providing accurate interpreting (1986);

(4) the second – in number of occurrences – pattern of interaction is the one which follows a question-rendition-answer-rendition sequence, however, after the witness answers the judge's question, the interpreter, instead of transmitting it to the judge, asks an additional question to the witness. This pattern is naturally characteristic for insert expansions (which impose summarized renditions), but there are single occurrences within the mechanism of the next speaker being selected by the current speaker, and the next speaker being self-selected. This finding confirms the results of the studies carried out by Berk-Seligson (1990/2002), Hale (2003), Jacobsen (2003), Tryuk (2004, 2006), and Biernacka (2014a) which underline that the

interpreter's interventions consisting in asking for explanation or repetition constitute a constant element of triadic exchanges;

(5) within adjacency pairs, two opposite groups—over- and under-answering—have been identified. Over-answering has been noted in the episodes of interaction, in which short yes-no answers are provided by the primary parties. This mechanism, implemented within the interpreters' extended renditions, has proven to be widely deployed by the court interpreters in this study. Although only one example of under-answering—provided within the interpreter's reduced rendition—has been identified in the collected material, it can serve as a solid basis for the intuition that what is an exception in this study, may be more broadly exemplified in further research. Both over- and under-answering provide additional information as compared to the original utterance which confirms the findings of Wahlster et al. (1983), Pomerantz (1984) and Jacobsen (2003);

(6) close renditions, highly recommendable by the code of ethics as accurate interpretations, constitute a margin of the interpreters' interventions; interestingly, interpreters never provide close renditions of insert expansions, probably considering them as additional and unnecessary components of the communicative act. A scarce occurrence of close renditions confirms the findings of Wadensjö (1997, 1998), Jacobsen (2004, 2008, 2009), Hale (2004, 2007, 2008) and Biernacka (2014a) that the interpreters do not consider the original utterances only as talk-as-text, but rather talk-as-action. Therefore, in order to make the participants in conversation understand and be understood, the interpreters modify their utterances, thus apply other types of renditions than close ones. Where close renditions dominate—within four categories: gaps, self-initiated and other initiated self-repairs, as well as, naturally, the same evaluations of adjacency pairs—a question-rendition-answer-rendition pattern of interaction is pursued, which proves that these mechanisms are conducive to achieving accuracy in interpretation;

(7) zero renditions are provided when the next speaker self-selects and addresses the parties to the interaction in a way the interpreter perceives as inappropriate. In such instances one of the interpreter's clients is linguistically absent (as opposed to "linguistically present", Gentile, Ozolins, and Vasilakakos (1996));

(8) non-renditions are provided within the category of post-first insert expansions, where the interpreter gives explanations to a non-Polish speaking party, without asking the judge for permission to do so. Non-renditions have a potential to occur when a question-rendition-answer-rendition pattern of interaction is pursued, but also within other patterns with a single occurrence.

The appearance of non-renditions in the interpreter's talk reaffirms the findings of Shlesinger (1991a), Malheiros-Poulet (1995), Wadensjö (1995, 1997, 1998, 2012), Gentile, Ozolins, and Vasilakakos (1996), Fenton (1997), Fowler (1997), Roberts (1997), Hale (1997a, 1997b, 2001, 2003, 2004, 2007, 2008), Taylor Torsello (1997), Mason (1999), Kadrić (2000), Jacobsen (2002, 2003, 2004, 2008, 2009), Rudvin (2002), Valero Garcés and Dergam (2003), Pöchhacker (2008, 2012), Biernacka (2008a, 2008b, 2009, 2010a, 2010b, 2014a, 2014b, 2016), Nartowska (2013a, 2013b, 2015), Stawecka (2010), Tryuk (2004, 2006, 2010), and Shisheng and Shuang (2012) concerning the interpreter's active participation in the communicative event;

(9) the interpreters' active participation in the courtroom interactions has been identified not only on the basis of the instances, in which they mediate between the primary parties, but also where they are addressed by the primary party with requests or questions, which reaffirms the findings of Berk-Seligson (1990/2002), Mason (1999), and Kenigson Kristy (2009/2010), or where they become primary parties (e.g. when the lawyers discuss the rendition provided by the interpreter, or when the interpreter informs the judge that she has to go out). This last example shows that the interpreter's zero renditions have a potential to refer not only to a particular episode of interaction, but also to the entire communicative event assisted by the interpreter;

(10) basically, a particular mechanism of bilingual conversations does not allow for a large number of patterns of interaction. Therefore, the mechanisms are rather homogeneous as regards the order of sequences and turns taken by individual interlocutors. However, two mechanisms—gaps and overlaps—are exceptional as regards the complexity of interactions, which proves that they are especially problematic for the court interpreters in this study. These results, as far as overlaps are concerned, allow to confirm the findings presented elsewhere (Roy 2000: 85). As regards gaps, understood as the interpreters' "unspoken activity turns" (Atkinson and Drew 1979: 194), they prove that court interpreters are empathic observers of, and active participants in, non-verbal communication. In general, the more problematic the communicative event, the more complicated pattern of interaction is involved;

(11) as regards gaps and overlaps, their occurrence contradicts the description of institutional talk as the one, in which spontaneous reactions of the parties to the utterances produced by another parties do not appear (Atkinson and Drew 1979; Atkinson 1982; Heffer 2005);

(12) it is impossible to propose one model of bilingual interactions of the courtroom, which is due to the complex nature of the communicative events

with the participation of interpreters in this study. This reaffirms earlier comments concerning monolingual communication in the courtroom (Heffer 2005);

(13) the interpreters make ethical sacrifices in order to pursue the goal of communication. In other words, it can be argued whether, at least some of the interpreters' verbal and non-verbal expressions satisfy the requirements of impartiality and/or neutrality or not. This confirms Schegloff's (1991) findings concerning monolingual talks that the right to communicate supersedes the strict ethical requirements. It only proves that even originally highly ritualized contexts, as it is undoubtedly in the event of the courtroom, give way to the interaction; this being the rule binding upon all interlocutors in interpreted events.

(14) there are instances, in which the interpreters show a biased approach towards either the institutional or private stakeholder that is not a consequence of the interpreters' submission to the interaction mechanisms. Contrary to that, in such instances the interpreters infringe the turn-taking system and produce a non-rendition, in which they repeat the primary party's opinion thus attract the other primary party's attention to the fragment of the original utterance which would be neglected if not the interpreter. This lack of neutrality cannot be described as the interpreter's expressing her own opinion on the primary party's recent utterance (as raised by Ostarhild 2001; Framer 2005), but certainly needs consideration as contrary to the ethical recommendations as discussed by Edwards 1995 and Hale 2007.

An awareness of the fact that it has been impossible to analyze all aspects of bilingual interactions of the courtroom has been underlined, and that, if the discussed episodes of interaction do not show certain characteristics, it does not mean that interpreter-mediated communicative acts exclude such features. Quite the opposite, it only indicates that further research is necessary in the field of court interpreting.

Taking the methodological pre-limitations of the study as discussed in methodological Chapter 3 of this book, as well as the above findings into account, a comprehensive follow-up investigation can be recommended, and in particular:

(1) an extended analysis of interpreter-mediated communicative events with a biased sample size with Polish-English and Polish-Spanish language pairs represented, in order to conduct a comparative study of bilingual interactions;

(2) an analysis of communicative events where other than Polish-English and Polish-Spanish language pairs are represented, in order to identify potential differences and similarities as they may appear between these interactions;
(3) in-depth qualitative research of both verbal and non-verbal communication channels, in order to conduct a multimodal analysis of specialized discourse of the courtroom;
(4) a more comprehensive study, for which a more extensive in size (number of hours and of interpreters involved) material would be collected in a large number of courts, and in other (e.g. criminal, family law) sections – in order to carry out mixed (both qualitative and quantitative) research.

In general, the results obtained draw attention to a **multidirectionality** of interactions during interpreter-mediated encounters, understood as communication carried out in multiple directions (a) by all the speakers (including the interpreter) at the same time (thus overlaps occur), or (b) by one speaker (including the interpreter) having a potential to speak to any other interactant, be it the institutional or private stakeholder, or the interpreter, depending on a particular episode of interaction. This means that the turn-taking system of the monolingual courtroom in which certain order of speaking is observed (Atkinson and Drew 1979; Atkinson 1982; Rzeszutko 2003; Heffer 2005; Bednarek 2014a) is disobeyed. This contributes to a **deritualization** of institutional talk, but there are also other manifestations of this phenomena, such as the shifts in address forms (Zieliński 1999; Zgółka and Zieliński 2003), underlining the hierarchy of the courtroom (Jopek-Bosiacka 2006) which occur in both the primary speakers' and the interpreters' talk. Furthermore, it has been noted that the court interpreters are not only active participants in the interaction, but also, in the instances where they become primary parties speaking with their own voice, **independent participants** in the communicative events.

Hope is expressed that this naturally occurring data based study has shown that not only prescriptive approach, well-rooted in the Polish scholarly tradition (Jopek-Bosiacka 2006, 2010, 2014; Kierzkowska 1991, 2005, 2007/2008, 2011; Kościałkowska-Okońska 2010; Matulewska 2014), needs to be developed, as the one helping identify actual performances of court interpreters. The descriptive approach as adopted for the purposes of this study has a potential to contribute to the further development of product-based, bottom-up research into court interpreting, hence providing for a better understanding of the profession: implementation of the requirement of the specialist training in bilingual interpreting and a narrow specialization in the field of court interpreting, as well as a discussion on its ethical constraints.

Bibliography

Abel, Laura. 2009. *Language Access in State Courts*. New York: Brennan Center for Justice, New York University School of Law. https://www.brennancenter.org/publication/language-access-state-courts (March 21, 2018).

Allen, Katharine. 2014. "Note-taking for public service interpreters: towards a sector-specific teaching model." In *(Re)Considerando ética e ideología en situaciones de conflicto. (Re)Visiting Ethics and Ideology in Situations of Conflict*, edited by Carmen Valero Garcés, 232–239. Alcalá de Henares: Servicios de Publicaciones Universidad de Alcalá.

Alonso, Icíar, and Gertrudis Pàyas. 2008. "Sobre alfaqueques y nahuatlatos: nuevas aportaciones a la historia de la interpretación." In *Investigación y práctica en traducción e interpretación en los servicios públicos. Desafíos y alianzas. Research and Practice in Public Service Interpreting and Translation. Challenges and Alliances*, edited by Carmen Valero Garcés, 39–52. Alcalá de Henares: Servicios de Publicaciones Universidad de Alcalá.

Anderson, Bruce. 1976/2002. "Perspectives on the Role of Interpreter." In *The Interpreting Studies Reader*, edited by Franz Pöchhacker and Miriam Shlesinger, 209–217. London and New York: Routledge.

Angelelli, Claudia. 2000. "Interpretation as a Communicative Event: A Look through Hymes' Lenses." *Meta* 45(4): 580–592.

Angelelli, Claudia. 2003. "The Interpersonal Role of the Interpreter in Cross-Cultural Communication. A Survey of Conference, Court and Medical Interpreters in the US, Canada and Mexico." In *The Critical Link 3: Interpreters in the Community. Papers from the Third International Conference on Interpreting in Legal, Health, and Social Service Settings, Montreal, Quebec, Canada, 22–26 May 2001*, edited by Louise Brunette, Georges Bastin, Isabelle Hemlin, and Heather Clarke, 15–26. Amsterdam/Philadelphia: J. Benjamins.

Angelelli, Claudia. 2004. *Revisiting the Interpreter's Role*. Amsterdam/Philadelphia: J. Benjamins.

Angelelli, Claudia. 2007. "Assessing Medical Interpreters: The Language and Interpreting Testing Project." *The Translator* 13(1): 63–82.

Angelelli, Claudia. 2010. "A professional ideology in the making: Bilingual youngsters interpreting for their communities and the notion of (no) choice." *Translation and Interpreting Studies* 5(1): 94–108.

Angelelli, Claudia. 2012. "Coordinating Participation in Dialogue Interpreting." In *Coordinating Participation in Dialogue Interpreting*, edited by Claudio Baraldi and Laura Gavioli, 251–268. Amsterdam/Philadelphia: J. Benjamins.

Apfelbaum, Birgit. 2004. *Medical Interpreting and Cross-cultural Communication*. Cambridge: Cambridge University Press.

Apostolou, Fotini. 2009. "Mediation, manipulation, empowerment: Celebrating the complexity of the interpreter's role." *Interpreting* 11(1): 1–19.

Atkinson, J. Maxwell. 1982. "Understanding Formality: The Categorization and Production of 'Formal' Interaction." *The British Journal of Sociology* 33: 86–117.

Atkinson, J. Maxwell, and John Heritage. 1984. "Preference organization." In *Structures of Social Interaction*, edited by J. Maxwell Atkinson and John Heritage, 53–56. Cambridge: Cambridge University Press.

Atkinson, J. Maxwell, and Paul Drew. 1979. *Order in Court. The Organisation of Verbal Interaction in Judicial Settings*. Atlantic Highlands, New Jersey: Humanities Press.

Bahadir, Şebnem. 2001. *The Empowerment of the (Community) Interpreter: The Right to Speak with a Voice of One's Own*. http://www.criticallink.org/cli-3/(August 25, 2017).

Baker, Mona. 1993. "Corpus linguistics and translation studies: Implications and applications." In *Text and Technology: In Honour of John Sinclair*, edited by Mona Baker, Gill Francis, and Elena Tognini-Bonelli, 233–250. Amsterdam/Philadelphia: J. Benjamins.

Baraldi, Claudio. 2009. *Dialogue in Intercultural Communities: From an educational point of view. (Dialogue Studies, DS 4)*. Amsterdam/Philadelphia: J. Benjamins.

Baraldi, Claudio, and Laura Gavioli. 2012. *Coordinating Participation in Dialogue Interpreting*. Amsterdam/Philadelphia: J. Benjamins.

Bartłomiejczyk, Magdalena. 2004. "Strategies of simultaneous interpreting and directionality" *Interpreting* 8(2), 149–174.

Bartłomiejczyk, Magdalena. 2016. *Face Threats in Interpreting. A Pragmatic Study of Plenary Debates in the European Parliament*. Katowice: Wyd. Uniwersytetu Śląskiego.

Bednarek, Grażyna Anna. 2014a. *Polish vs. American courtroom discourse: inquisitorial and adversarial procedures of witness examination in criminal trials*. New York/Basingstoke: Palgrave Macmillan.

Bednarek, Grażyna Anna. 2014b. "Polish vs. American courtroom discourse: inquisitorial and adversarial procedures of witness examination in penal trails. What court interpreters need to know about witness examination in criminal trails under disparate legal systems to provide high level interpreting services in the light of the Directive 2010/64/EU of the European Parliament and of the Council of 20 October 2010?" *Comparative Legilinguistics. International Journal for Legal Communication* 19: 77–115.

Bednarek, Grażyna Anna. 2015. "Prolegomena to a new criminal trial procedure in Poland following the amendment of the Code of Criminal Procedure of 27.09.2013: from inquisitorial towards adversarial procedure of witness examination in criminal trials." *Comparative Legilinguistics. International Journal for Legal Communication* 24: 47–80.

Berk-Seligson, Susan. 1988. "The Impact of Politeness in Witness Testimony: The Influence of the Court Interpreter." *Multilingua* 7(4): 411–439.

Berk-Seligson, Susan. 1990/2002. *The Bilingual Courtroom. Court Interpreters in the Judicial Process.* Chicago: University of Chicago Press.

Berk-Seligson, Susan. 1999. *"The impact of court interpreting on the coerciveness of leading questions."* Forensic Linguistics 6(1): 30–56.

Biagini, Marta. 2012. "Data collection in the courtroom: challenges and perspectives for the researcher." In *Breaking Ground in Corpus-Based Interpreting Studies*, edited by Sergio F. Straniero, and Caterina Falbo, 231–255. Berlin: Peter Lang.

Biel, Łucja. 2014. *Lost in the Eurofog: The Textual Fit of Translated Law.* Frankfurt am Main: Peter Lang Edition.

Biernacka, Agnieszka. 2008a. "Intérprete jurídico como intérprete comunitario: Intento de polémica con el Código de traductor jurado polaco a la luz de tres juicios con la participación del intérprete jurídico de español." In *Encuentros. Volumen I. Encuentros de Lingüística, traducción y enseñanza de la lengua española*, edited by Joanna Wilk-Racięska and Jacek Lyszczyna, 177–189. Katowice: Oficyna Wydawnicza WIN.

Biernacka, Agnieszka. 2008b. "Intérprete en el contexto sociológico de la sala de audiencias." In *Investigación y práctica en traducción e interpretación en los servicios públicos. Desafíos y alianzas. Research and Practice in Public Service Interpreting and Translation. Challenges and Alliances*, edited by Carmen Valero Garcés, 298–313. Alcalá de Henares: Servicios de Publicaciones Universidad de Alcalá.

Biernacka, Agnieszka. 2009. "Retos de la interpretación ante los tribunales." In *Encuentros de lingüística II*, edited by Beata Brzozowska-Zburzyńska, 175–186. Lublin: Wyd. UMCS.

Biernacka, Agnieszka. 2010a. "Intérpretes ante los tribunales de Polonia: entre las normas codificadas y el acto comunicativo." In *Modos y formas de la comunicación humana*, edited by Rosario Caballero Rodríguez and María Jesús Sanz, 1187–1192. Cuenca: Ediciones de la Universidad Castilla–La Mancha.

Biernacka, Agnieszka. 2010b. Funkcje tłumacza w rozprawie sądowej. Ph.D. Thesis. Warsaw: University of Warsaw.

Biernacka, Agnieszka. 2014a. Tłumacz w rozprawie sądowej. Warszawa: Studi@ Naukowe, http:://www.sn.iksi.uw.edu.pl/documents/7732735/0/SN+16+Agn ieszka+Biernacka+Tłumacz+sądowy.pdf Accessed May 23, 2017.

Biernacka, Agnieszka. 2014b. "Precisión de interpretación vs. el yo del intérprete." In *(Re)Considerando ética e ideología en situaciones de conflicto. (Re)Visiting Ethics and Ideology in Situations of Conflict*, edited by Carmen Valero Garcés, 169–176. Alcalá de Henares: Servicios de Publicaciones Universidad de Alcalá.

Biernacka, Agnieszka. 2016. "Quality in Court Interpreting vs. (?) Role(s) of Court Interpreters." In *Interchange between Languages and Cultures: The Quest for Quality*, edited by Jitka Zehnalová, Ondřej Molnár, and Michal Kubánek, 89–102. Olomouc: Palacký University.

Bolden, Galina. 2000. "Toward understanding practices of medical interpreting: Interpreters' involvement in history taking." *Discourse Studies* 2(4): 387–419.

Borg, James. 2011. *Body Language: How to know what's REALLY being said.* Harlow: Pearson Education Limited.

Cal-Meyer, Pilar. 2013. "Clarifying Pragma-Linguistic Incongruences When Conveying Meaning Between Sociocultural Words/Worlds." *Proteus* 22(1). www.najit.org/proteus (May 21, 2014).

Colin, Joan, and Ruth Morris. 1996. *Interpreters and the Legal Process.* Winchester: Waterside Press.

Corsellis, Ann, and Leandro F. Fernández. 2001. "Code of Ethics and Conduct and Guidelines to Good Practice." In *Aequitas. Access to Justice across Language and Culture in the EU*, edited by Erik Hertog, 77–87. Antwerp: Departement Vertaler-Tolk, Lessius Hogeschool.

Creswell, John W. 2014. *Research Design. Qualitative, Quantitative, and Mixed Methods Approaches.* London, Los Angeles, New Delhi, Singapore and Washington D.C.: SAGE Publications.

Cronin, Michael. 2006. *Translation and Identity.* London and New York: Routledge.

Davidson, Brad. 2000. "The interpreter as institutional gatekeeper: The social-linguistic role of interpreters in Spanish-English medical discourse." *Journal of Sociolinguistics* 4(3): 379–405.

Davidson, Brad. 2002. "A model for the construction of conversational common ground in interpreted discourse." *Journal of Pragmatics* 34: 1273–1300.

Dąmbska-Prokop, Urszula. 2000. *Mała Encyklopedia Przekładoznawstwa*. Kielce: Wyd. WSU im. Stanisława Staszica.

Davitti, Elena. 2012. *Dialogue Interpreting as Intercultural Mediation: integrating talk and gaze in the analysis of parent-teacher meetings*. Ph.D. Thesis. Manchester: University of Manchester.

de Jongh, Elena. 1992. *An Introduction to Court Interpreting. Theory and Practice*. Lanham, New York, London: University Press of America.

Lukić Decision. 2007. *Decision on Lukić motion to compel Registry to provide verbatim transcript of* proceedings, http://www.icty.org/x/cases/milutinovic/tdec/en/070927b.pdf Accessed July 4, 2018.

Diamond, Julie. 1996. *Status and Power in Verbal Interaction. A study of discourse in a close-knit social network*. Amsterdam/Philadelphia: J. Benjamins.

Díaz-Campos, Manuel, Kimberly L. Geeslin, and Laura Gurzynski-Weiss. 2017. Introducción y Aplicaciones Contextualizadas a la Lingüística Hispánica. Hoboken, NJ: Wiley-Blackwell.

Diriker, Ebru. 2004. *De-/Re-Contextualizing Conference Interpreting. Interpreters in the Ivory Tower?* Amsterdam/Philadelphia: J. Benjamins.

Donald, Dominick. 2003. "Neutral Is Not Impartial: The Confusing Legacy of Traditional Peace Operations Thinking." In *Armed Forces and Society* 29(3). http://journals.sagepub.com/doi/abs/10.1177/0095327X0302900306?journalCode=afsa (December 10, 2017).

Dörnyei, Zoltán. 2007. *Research Methods in Applied Linguistics. Quantitative, Qualitative, and Mixed Methodologies*. Oxford: Oxford University Press.

Drew, Paul and John Heritage. 1992. "Analyzing talk at work: An introduction." In *Talk at Work*, edited by Paul Drew and John Heritage, 3–65. Cambridge: Cambridge University Press.

Dybiec-Gajer, Joanna. 2013. "Tłumacz profesjonalista. Między etyką zawodową a etyką tłumaczenia w świetle kodeksów dla tłumaczy." In *Tłumacz i przekład – wyzwania współczesności*, edited by Maciej Ganczar and Piotr Wilczek, 259–283. Katowice: Wyd. Śląsk.

Edwards, Alicia B. 1995. *The Practice of Court Interpreting*. Amsterdam/Philadelphia: J. Benjamins.

Fenton, Sabine. 1997. "The Role of the Interpreter in the Adversarial Courtroom." In *The Critical Link 1: Interpreters in the Community. Papers from the First International Conference on Interpreting in Legal, Health, and*

Social Service Settings, Canada, June 1–4, 1995, edited by Silvana E. Carr, Roda P. Roberts, Aideen Dufour, and Dini Steyn, 29–34. Amsterdam/ Philadelphia: J. Benjamins.

Fijałkowski, Tadeusz. 2001. *Kodeks postępowania cywilnego. Orzecznictwo sądowe, komentarz*. Warszawa: Artman.

Ford, Cecilia E., and Sandra A. Thompson. 1996. "Interactional units in conversation: syntactic, intonational, and pragmatic resources for the management of turns." In *Interaction and Grammar*, edited by Elinor Ochs, Emanuel A. Schegloff, and Sandra A. Thompson, 134–184. Cambridge: University Press.

Fowler, Yvonne. 1997. "The Courtroom Interpreter. Paragon and Intruder?" In *The Critical Link 1: Interpreters in the Community. Papers from the First International Conference on Interpreting in Legal, Health, and Social Service Settings, Canada, June 1–4, 1995*, edited by Silvana E. Carr, Roda P. Roberts, Aideen Dufour, and Dini Steyn, 191–200. Amsterdam/Philadelphia: J. Benjamins.

Framer, Isabel. 2005, "*Interpreters as Officers of the Court: Scope and Limitations of Practice.*" Proteus 14(2): 3–5.

Gaiba, Francesca. 1998. *The Origins of Simultaneous Interpretation: The Nuremberg Trial*. Ottawa: University of Ottawa Press.

Gamal, Muhammad Y. 2009. "Court Interpreting." In *Routledge Encyclopedia of Translation Studies*, edited by Mona Baker and Gabriela Saldanha, 63–67. London and New York: Routledge.

Garber, Nathan, and Louise A. Mauffette-Leenders. 1997. "Obtaining Feedback from Non-English Speakers." In *The Critical Link 1: Interpreters in the Community. Papers from the First International Conference on Interpreting in Legal, Health, and Social Service Settings, Canada, June 1–4, 1995*, edited by Silvana E. Carr, Roda P. Roberts, Aideen Dufour, and Dini Steyn, 131–143. Amsterdam/Philadelphia: J. Benjamins.

Garber, Nathan. 2000. "Community Interpreting: A Personal View." In *The Critical Link 2: Interpreters in the Community. Papers from the Second International Conference on Interpreting in Legal, Health, and Social Service Settings, Vancouver, Canada, 19–23 May 1998*, edited by Roda P. Roberts, Silvana E. Carr, Diana Abraham, and Aideen Dufour, 9–20. Amsterdam/ Philadelphia: J. Benjamins.

Garfinkel, Harold. 1967. *Studies in Ethnomethodology*. Englewood Cliffs, New Jersey: Prentice-Hall, Inc.

Gavioli, Laura. 2012. "Minimal responses in interpreter-mediated medical talk." In *Coordinating Participation in Dialogue Interpreting*, edited by Claudio Baraldi and Laura Gavioli, 201–228. Amsterdam/Philadelphia: J. Benjamins.

Gavioli, Laura. 2016. "Conversation analysis." In *Researching Translation and Interpreting*, edited by Claudia Angelelli and Brian James Baer, 185–194. London and New York: Routledge.

Gentile, Adolfo. 1991. "Working with professional interpreters." In *Cross-cultural Communication in Medical Encounters*, edited by Anne Pauwels, 26–48. Melbourne: Monash University.

Gentile, Adolfo, Uldis Ozolins, and Mary Vasilakakos. 1996. *Liaison Interpreting*. Melbourne: Melbourne University Press.

Giambruno (Miguélez), Cynthia. 2008. "The role of the interpreter in the governance of sixteenth- and seventeenth-century Spanish colonies in the «New World». Lessons from the past for the present." In *Crossing Borders in Community Interpreting. Definitions and Dilemmas*, edited by Carmen Valero Garcés and Anne Martin, 27–49. Amsterdam/Philadelphia: J. Benjamins.

Giddens, Anthony. 1984. *The Constitution of Society. Outline of the Theory of Structuration*. Berkeley and Los Angeles: University of California Press.

Gile, Daniel. 1995. *Basic concepts and models for interpreter and translator training*. Amsterdam/Philadelphia: J. Benjamins.

Goffman, Erving. 1956. *The Presentation of Self in Everyday Life*. Edinburgh: University of Edinburgh Social Sciences Research Centre.

Goffman, Erving. 1967. *Interaction Ritual – Essays on Face-to-Face Behavior*. Garden City, New York: Doubleday.

Goffman, Erving. 1981. *Forms of Talk*. Philadelphia: University of Pennsylvania Press.

González, Roseann D., Victoria F. Vásquez, and Holy Mikkelson. 1991. *Fundamentals of Court Interpretation: Theory, Policy and Practice*. Durham, NC: Carolina Academic Press.

Goodwin, Charles 1981. *Conversational Organization. Interaction between Speakers and Hearers*. London: Academic Press.

Goodwin, Charles, and Marjorie Harness Goodwin. 1992. "Assessments and the construction of context." In *Rethinking Context: Language as an Interactive Phenomenon*, edited by Alessandro Duranti, and Charles Goodwin, 151–189. Cambridge: Cambridge University Press.

Grbič, Nadja. 2015. "Profession." In *Routledge Encyclopedia of Interpreting Studies*, edited by Franz Pöchhacker, 321–326. London, New York: Routledge.

Gumul, Ewa. 2010. "Explicitating Political Discourse." In *Political Discourse, Media and Translation*, edited by Christina Schaeffner, 94–115. Cambridge: Cambridge Scholars Publishing.

Gumul, Ewa. 2015. "Explicitation." In *Routledge Encyclopedia of Interpreting Studies*, edited by Franz Pöchhacker, 156. London, New York: Routledge.

Hale, Sandra. 1997a. "The Interpreter on Trial. Pragmatics in Court Interpreting." In *The Critical Link 1: Interpreters in the Community. Papers from the First International Conference on Interpreting in Legal, Health, and Social Service Settings, Canada, June 1–4, 1995*, edited by Silvana E. Carr, Roda P. Roberts, Aideen Dufour, and Dini Steyn, 201–211. Amsterdam/Philadelphia: J. Benjamins.

Hale, Sandra. 1997b. "The Treatment of Register Variation in Court Interpreting." *The Translator* 3(1): 39–54.

Hale, Sandra. 2001. "How are Courtroom Questions Interpreted? An Analysis of Spanish Interpreters' Practices." In *Triadic Exchanges. Studies in Dialogue Interpreting*, edited by Ian Mason, 21–50. Manchester: St Jerome Publishing.

Hale, Sandra. 2003. "*Some Questions Answered About Court Interpreting.*" *The Critical Link – A Quarterly Journal Dedicated to Interpreting in the Social, Health Care and Legal Sectors* 1: 20–24.

Hale, Sandra. 2004. *The discourse of court interpreting. Discourse practices of the law, the witness and the interpreter.* Amsterdam/Philadelphia: J. Benjamins.

Hale, Sandra. 2007. *Community Interpreting.* Houndmills, Basingstoke, Hampshire: Palgrave Macmillan.

Hale, Sandra. 2008. "Controversies over the role of the court interpreter." In *Crossing Borders in Community Interpreting. Definitions and Dilemmas*, edited by Carmen Valero Garcés and Anne Martin, 99–121. Amsterdam/Philadelphia: J. Benjamins.

Hardy, Matt. 2004. "From the Prosecutor's Point of View: Ten Tips on Using Court Interpreters in Child Witness Cases." *Proteus* 13(2): 4–5.

Harris, Brian. 1995. Foreword: A Landmark in the Evolution of Interpreting. In *The Critical Link 1: Interpreters in the Community. Papers from the First International Conference on Interpreting in Legal, Health, and Social Service Settings, Canada, June 1-4, 1995*, edited by Silvana E. Carr, Roda P. Roberts, Aideen Dufour, and Dini Steyn, 1–3. Amsterdam/Philadelphia: J. Benjamins.

Hearn, Johnny. 1981. *The Unrecognized Professionals.* Melbourne: Education Research and Development Committee.

Heffer, Chris. 2005. *The Language of Jury Trial. A Corpus-Aided Analysis f Legal-Lay Discourse.* New York/Basingstoke: Palgrave Macmillan.

Heimerl-Moggan, Kirsty, and Vanessa Ifeoma John. 2007. *Note-taking for Public Service Interpreters.* Altrincham: Interp-Right Training Consultancy Ltd.

Heritage, John. 1984. *Garfinkel and Ethnometodology.* Cambridge: Polity.

Heritage, John. 1995. "Conversation analysis: Methodological aspects." In *Aspects of Oral Communication*, edited by Uta M. Quasthoff, 391–414. Berlin: Mouton de Gruyter.

Hertog, Erik. 2016. "Legal Interpreting Competences in Civil Justice and Mediation." In *Understanding Justice. An enquiry into interpreting in civil justice and mediation*, edited by Brooke Townsley, 51–89. London: Middlesex University.

Hewitt, William E. 1995. *Interpretation: Model Guides for Policy and Practice in the State Courts*. Williamsburg. VA: National Center for State Courts.

Horváth, Ildikó. 2012. *Interpreter behaviour. A psychological approach*. Budapest: Hang Nyelviskola Bt.

Inghilleri, Moira. 2012. *Interpreting Justice: Ethics, Politics and Language*. New York: Routledge.

Izydorczyk, Jacek, and Paweł Wiliński. 2004. *Międzynarodowy Trybunał Karny*. Kraków: Zakamycze.

Jacobsen, Bente. 2002. *Pragmatic meaning in court interpreting: an empirical study of additions in consecutively interpreted question-answer dialogues*. Ph.D. Thesis. Aarhus: Aarhus School of Business.

Jacobsen, Bente. 2003. "Pragmatics in Court Interpreting: Additions." In *The Critical Link 3: Interpreters in the Community. Selected papers from the Third International Conference on Interpreting in Legal, Health, and Social Service Settings, Montreal, Quebec, Canada, 22–26 May 2001*, edited by Louise Brunette, Georges L. Bastin, Isabelle Hemlin, and Heather Clarke, 223–238. Amsterdam/Philadelphia: J. Benjamins.

Jacobsen, Bente. 2004. "Pragmatic Meaning in Court Interpreting: An empirical study of additions in consecutively interpreted question-answer dialogues." *Hermes. Journal of Linguistics* 3: 237–249.

Jacobsen, Bente. 2008. "Interactional pragmatics and court interpreting. An analysis of face." In *Interpreting, Special Issue: Doing Justice to Court Interpreting*, edited by Miriam Shlesinger and Franz Pöchhacker, 128–158. Amsterdam/Philadelphia: J. Benjamins.

Jacobsen, Bente. 2009. "The Community Interpreter: The Question of Role." *Hermes. Journal of Language and Communication Studies* 42: 155–166.

Jefferson, Gail. 1983. *Issues in the Transcription of Naturally Occurring Talk: Caricatures versus Capturing Pronunciational Particulars*. Tilburg: Tilburg University.

Jefferson, Gail. 1986. "Notes on 'latency' in overlap." *Human Studies* 9: 153–183.

Jefferson, Gail. 1987. "On exposed and embedded correction in conversation." In *Talk and Social Organization*, edited by Graham Button and John Lee, 86–100. Cleveland and Philadelphia: Multilingual Matters.

Jefferson, Gail. 2004. "Glossary of transcript symbols with an Introduction." In *Conversation Analysis: Studies from the first generation*, edited by Gene H. Lerner, 13–23. Philadelphia/Philadelphia: J. Benjamins.

Jopek-Bosiacka, Anna. 2006. *Przekład prawny i sądowy.* Warszawa: Wyd. Naukowe PWN.

Jopek-Bosiacka, Anna. 2010. *Legal communication: a cross-cultural perspective.* Warszawa: Warsaw University Press.

Jopek-Bosiacka, Anna. 2014. "Poland: Court Interpreters' and Legal Translators' Training at the Institute of Applied Linguistics of the University of Warsaw." In *New tasks for legal interpreters and translators in the enlarged Europe*, edited by Danuta Kierzkowska, 199–208. Warszawa: TEPIS.

Kaczmarek, Łukasz. 2008. "Proposing a model of community interpreting competence." In *Investigación y práctica en traducción e interpretación en los servicios públicos. Desafíos y alianzas. Research and Practice in Public Service Interpreting and Translation. Challenges and Alliances*, edited by Carmen Valero Garcés, 240–254. Alcalá de Henares: Servicios de Publicaciones Universidad de Alcalá.

Kadrić, Mira. 2000. "Interpreting in the Austrian Courtroom." In *The Critical Link 2: Interpreters in the Community. Papers from the Second International Conference on Interpreting in Legal, Health, and Social Service Settings, Vancouver, Canada, 19–23 May 1998*, edited by Roda P. Roberts, Silvana E. Carr, Diana Abraham, and Aideen Dufour, 153–164. Amsterdam/Philadelphia: J. Benjamins.

Kalina, Sylvia. 1992. "Discourse processing and interpreting strategies – an approach to the role of teaching of interpreting." In *Teaching Translation and Interpreting. Training, Talent and Experience*, edited by Cay Dollerup and Anne Loddegaard, 251–257. Amsterdam/Philadelphia: J. Benjamins.

Kang M. Agnes. 1998. "Strategies of inclusion: Addressee(s) in triadic exchanges." *Text* 18(3): 383–416.

Katschinka, Liese. 2000. *What is Court Interpreting?* Last modified 2015. https://aiic.net/page/239/what-is-court-interpreting/lang/1 (February 17, 2017).

Katschinka, Liese. 2013. "EU Directive 2010/64 on the right to interpretation and translation in criminal proceedings – a major step forward to ensure fair trials." *Biuletyn TEPIS* 79: 7–9.

Keating, Michelle. 2005. *The International Criminal Court: An Introduction.* Last modified 2013. http://aiic.net/page/1660/

the-international-criminal-court-an-introduction/lang/1 (February 22, 2017).

Kelly, Arlene. 2000. "Cultural Parameters for Interpreters in the Courtroom." In *The Critical Link 2: Interpreters in the Community. Papers from the Second International Conference on Interpreting in Legal, Health, and Social Service Settings, Vancouver, Canada, 19–23 May* 1998, edited by Roda P. Roberts, Silvana E. Carr, Diana Abraham, and Aideen Dufour, 131-148. Amsterdam/ Philadelphia: J. Benjamins.

Kempiński, Zbigniew. 1986. "Pojęcie błędu w tłumaczeniu ustnym." In Problemy translatoryki i dydaktyki translatorycznej, edited by Franciszek Grucza, 49-60. Warszawa: Wyd. UW.

Kenigson Kristy, Judith. 2009/2010. "Language and Litigation. What judges and attorneys need to know about interpreters in the legal process." *Proteus* 18(4): 3–4.

Keselman, Olga, Anna-Christin Cederborg, and Per Linell. 2010. "That is not necessary for you to know! Negotiation of participation status of unaccompanied children in interpreter-mediated asylum hearings." *Interpreting* 12(1): 83–104.

Kierzkowska, Danuta. 1991. *Kodeks tłumacza sądowego.* Warszawa: Wyd. TEPIS.

Kodeks karny. 2005. Warszawa: Park Prawo.

Kierzkowska, Danuta. (ed.) 2005. *Kodeks tłumacza przysięgłego z komentarzem.* Warszawa: Wyd. Tepis.

Kierzkowska, Danuta. 2007/2008. "Preskryptywny charakter Kodeksu tłumacza przysięgłego." In Rocznik Przekładoznawczy. Studia nad teorią, praktyką i dydaktyką przekładu Vol. 3/4, edited by Ewa Kościałkowska-Okońska and Lech Zieliński, 95–104. Toruń: Wyd. UMK.

Kierzkowska, Danuta. (ed.) 2011. *Kodeks tłumacza przysięgłego*. www.tepis.org.pl (July 4, 2018).

Kopczyński, Andrzej. 1984. "Problems of quality in conference interpreting." In *Contrastive Linguistics: prospects and problems*, edited by Jacek Fisiak, 283–300. Berlin: Mouton Publishers.

Koskela, Merja, Kaisa Koskinen, and Nina Pilke. 2017. "Bilingual formal meeting as a context of translatoriality." *Target* 29(3): 464–485.

Kościałkowska-Okońska, Ewa. 2010. "Interpreters in the courtroom: the importance of competence and quality." *Comparative Legilinguistics. International Journal for Legal Communication* 2: 39–47.

Kubacki, Artur D. 2012. *Tłumaczenie poświadczone. Status, kształcenie, warsztat i odpowiedzialność tłumacza przysięgłego.* Warszawa: LEX.

La Traductrice. 2006. Directed by Elena Hazanov. Switzerland/Russia: Ventura Film.

Labov, William. 1972. *Sociolinguistic Patterns*. Oxford: Blackwell.

Lane, Chris. 1985. "Miscommunication in Cross-Examinations." In Cross-Cultural Encounters Communication & Miscommunication, edited by John Pride, 196–211. Melbourne: River Seine.

Lang, Ranier. 1978. "Behavioral Aspects of Liaison Interpreters in Papua New Guinea: Some Preliminary Observations." In *Language, Interpretation and Communication*, edited by David Gerver and H. Wallace Sinaiko, 231–244. New York and London: Plenum Press.

Laster, Kathy. 1990. "Legal interpreters: conduits to social justice?" *Journal of Intercultural Studies* 11(2): 15–32.

Laster, Kathy, and Veronica Taylor. 1994. *Interpreters and the Legal System*. Sydney: The Federation Press.

Liber, Katarzyna. 2012. "Tłumacz jako niewerbalny kłamca? Problem niewerbalnej wiarygodności tłumacza jako nadawcy komunikatu." *Lingua ac Communitas* 22: 137–168.

Liddicoat, Anthony J. 2011. *An Introduction to Conversation Analysis*. London, New York: Continuum.

Linell, Per. 1997. "Interpreting as Communication." In *Conference Interpreting: Current Trends and Research*, edited by Yves Gambier, Daniel Gile, and Christopher Taylor, 49–67. Amsterdam/Philadelphia: J. Benjamins.

Lowney, Robert. 2005. "Federal Judiciary Accomplishments and Challenges for the Future." *Proteus* 14(3): 9–11.

Łyda, Andrzej, and Ewa Gumul. 2008. "Błąd w tłumaczeniu ustnym." In *Błąd językowy w perspektywie komunikacyjnej*, edited by Małgorzata Kita, Maria Czempka-Wewióra, and Magdalena Ślawska, 103–116. Katowice: Wyższa Szkoła Zarządzania Marketingowego i Języków Obcych w Katowicach.

Lyons, John. 1972. "Human Language". In *Non-Verbal Communication*, edited by Robert A. Hinde, 49–85. Cambridge: Cambridge University Press.

Maley, Yon, and Rhondda Fahey. 1991. "Presenting the Evidence: Constructions of Reality in Court." In *International Journal for the Semiotics of Law* 4(10): 3–17.

Malheiros-Poulet, Maria-Eugênia. 1995. "Le rôle de l'intermédiaire linguistique dans les situations de contacts interculturels." In *Le trilogue*, edited by Catherine Kerbrat-Orecchioni and Christian Plantin, 134–160. Lyon: Presses Universitaires de Lyon.

Marcjanik, Małgorzata. 2007. *Grzeczność w komunikacji językowej*. Warszawa: Wyd. Naukowe PWN.

Martin, Anne and Isabel Abril Martí. 2008. "Community interpreter self-perception." In *Crossing Borders in Community Interpreting. Definitions and Dilemmas*, edited by Carmen Valero Garcés and Anne Martin, 203–230. Amsterdam/Philadelphia: J. Benjamins.

Martin, Anne, and Juan Miguel Ortega Herráez. 2010. *Nuremberg in Madrid: the role of interpreting in the Madrid train bomb trial*. Last modified 2016. https://aiic.net/page/3548/nuremberg-in-madrid-the-role-of-interpreting-in-the-madrid-train-bomb-trial/lang/1 (March 30, 2017).

Mason, Ian. 1999. "Introduction." In *Dialogue Interpreting. Special Issue of The Translator: Studies in Intercultural Communication*, edited by Ian Mason, 147–160. Manchester: St. Jerome Publishing.

Mason, Ian, and Miranda Stewart. 2001. "Interactional Pragmatics, Face and the Dialogue Interpreter." In *Triadic Exchanges. Studies in Dialogue Interpreting*, edited by Ian Mason, 51-70. Manchester: St. Jerome Publishing.

Matulewska, Aleksandra. 2014. "Horrory tłumaczeniowe czyli tłumacze z piekła rodem? Czyli kilka słów o efektywności komunikacji interlingwalnej." In *Scripta Neophilologica Posnaniensia Vol. 14*, edited by Stanisław Puppel, 101–118. Poznań: Wyd. Wydziału Neofilologii UAM.

Maynard, Douglas W., and Steven E. Clayman. 1991. "The Diversity of Ethnomethodology." *Annual Review of Sociology* 17: 385–418.

Mikkelson, Holy. 1999. *Verbatim Interpretation: an Oxymoron*. https://acebo.myshopify.com/pages/verbatim-interpretation-an-oxymoron (July 30, 2017).

Mikkelson, Holy. 2004. "The professionalization of community interpreting" http://aiic.net/p/1546/ (January 31, 2017).

Mikkelson, Holy. 2008. "Evolving views of the court interpreter's role: Between Scylla and Charybdis." In *Crossing Borders in Community Interpreting. Definitions and Dilemmas*, edited by Carmen Valero Garcés and Anne Martin, 81–97. Amsterdam/Philadelphia: J. Benjamins.

Mikkelson, Holy. 2010. "*Verbatim Interpretation Revisited*." *Proteus* 19(1): 2–4.

Miles, Matthew B., and A. MichaelHuberman. 1994. *Qualitative Data Analysis*. Thousand Oaks, California: SAGE Publications.

Morris, Ruth. 1993. "The interlingual interpreter – cypher or intelligent participant?" *International Journal for the Semiotics of Law* 6(18): 1–21.

Morris, Ruth. 1995. "The Moral Dilemmas of Court Interpreting." *The Translator* 1(1): 25–46.

Morris, Ruth. 2008. "Missing stitches. An overview of judicial attitudes to interlingual interpreting in the criminal justice systems of Canada and Israel." In *Interpreting, Special Issue: Doing Justice to Court Interpreting*, edited by Miriam Shlesinger and Franz Pöchhacker, 34–64. Amsterdam/ Philadelphia: J. Benjamins.

Morris, Ruth. 2015. "Courtroom interpreting." In *Routledge Encyclopedia of Interpreting Studies*, edited by Franz Pöchhacker, 91–93. London, New York: Routledge.

Moser-Mercer, Barbara. 1997. "Process models in simultaneous interpretation." In *Machine Translation and Translation Theory*, edited by Christa Hauenschild and Susanne Heizmann, 3–18. The Hague: Mouton de Gruyter.

Nagao, Hiromi. 2005. "Sprawa z Melbourne: niewłaściwe tłumaczenie przyczyną oskarżenia o niepopełnione przestępstwa." *Lingua Legis* 13: 3–7.

Najarro Smith, Nadia. 2005. "Resolving Ethical Dilemmas for Court Interpreters." In *Traducción como mediación entre lenguas y culturas. Translation as Mediation or how to Bridge Linguistic and Cultural Gaps*, edited by Carmen Valero Garcés, 161–167. Alcalá de Henares: Servicios de Publicaciones Universidad de Alcalá.

Nartowska, Karolina. 2013a. "Tłumacz i działanie translatorskie w sądzie." *Comparative Legilinguistics. International Journal for Legal Communication* 13: 115–126.

Nartowska, Karolina. 2013b. "Etyka tłumacza sądowego na sali sądowej?" *Comparative Legilinguistics. International Journal for Legal Communication* 14: 159–168.

Nartowska, Karolina. 2015. "The role of the court interpreter: a powerless or powerful participant in criminal proceedings?" In *The Interpreters' Newsletter. Dialogue Interpreting No. 20*, edited by Cynthia Jane Kellett, 9–32. Trieste: EUT.

Niemants, Natasha. 2013. "From role-playing to role-taking: Interpreter role(s) in healthcare." In *Interpreting in a Changing Landscape: Selected Papers from Critical Link 6*, edited by Christina Schäffner, Krzysztof Kredens, and Ivonne Fowler, 305–319. Amsterdam/Philadelphia: J. Benjamins.

Obenaus, Gerhard. 1995. "*The Legal Translator as Information Broker*." In *Translation and the Law*, edited by Marshall Morris, 247–259. Amsterdam/ Philadelphia: J. Benjamins.

Ostarhild, Edda. 2001. "*Linguistic standards for legal interpreters and translators at Diploma or Fist Degree Level and at MA level*." In *Aequitas. Access to Justice across Language and Culture in the EU*, edited by Erik Hertog, 21–72. Antwerp: Departement Vertaler-Tolk, Lessius Hogeschool.

Pasquandrea, Sergio. 2011. "Managing multiple actions through multimodality: Doctor's involvement in interpreter-mediated interactions." *Language in Society* 40 (4): 455–481.

Pieńkos, Jerzy. 1999. *Podstawy juryslingwistyki. Język w prawie – Prawo w języku.* Warszawa: Muza SA.

Pomerantz, Anita. 1984. "Agreeing and disagreeing with assessments: some features or preferred/dispreferred turn shapes." In *Structures of Social Interaction*, edited by J. Maxwell Atkinson and John Heritage, 57–101. Cambridge: Cambridge University Press.

Pomerantz, Anita. 1987. "Description in legal settings." In *Talk and Social Organization*, edited by Graham Button and John Lee, 226–243. Cleveland and Philadelphia: Multilingual Matters.

Poznański, Janusz. 2007. *Tłumacz w postępowaniu karnym*. Warszawa: Wyd. Translegis.

Pöchhacker, Franz. 2000. "The Community Interpreter's Task: Self-Perception and Provider Views." In *The Critical Link 2: Interpreters in the Community. Papers from the Second International Conference on Interpreting in Legal, Health, and Social Service Settings, Vancouver, Canada, 19–23 May 1998*, edited by Roda P. Roberts, Silvana E. Carr, Diana Abraham, and Aideen Dufour, 49–66. Amsterdam/Philadelphia: J. Benjamins.

Pöchhacker, Franz. 2001. "Quality Assessment in Conference and Community Interpreting." *Meta* 46(2): 410–425.

Pöchhacker, Franz. 2002. "Researching interpreting quality. Models and methods." In *Interpreting in the 21st century: Challenges and opportunities*, edited by Giuliana Garzone and Maurizio Viezzi, 95–106. Amsterdam/Philadelphia: J. Benjamins.

Pöchhacker, Franz. 2008. "Interpreting as mediation." In *Crossing Borders in Community Interpreting. Definitions and Dilemmas*, edited by Carmen Valero Garcés and Anne Martin, 9–26. Amsterdam/Philadelphia: J. Benjamins.

Pöchhacker, Franz. 2012. "Interpreting participation. Conceptual analysis and illustration of the interpreter's role in interaction." In *Coordinating Participation in Dialogue Interpreting*, edited by Claudio Baraldi and Laura Gavioli, 45–69. Amsterdam/Philadelphia: J. Benjamins.

Pöchhacker, Franz. 2015. "Interpreting studies." In *Routledge Encyclopedia of Interpreting Studies*, edited by Franz Pöchhacker, 201–206. London, New York: Routledge.

Proclamation of the Fundamental Principles of the Red Cross. www.icrc.org (December 10, 2017).

Pym, Anthony. 1999. "'Nicole Slapped Michelle'. Interpreters and Theories of Interpreting at the O.J. Simpson Trial." In *Dialogue Interpreting. Special Issue of The Translator: Studies in Intercultural Communication*, edited by Ian Mason, 265–283. Manchester: St Jerome Publishing.

Rancew-Sikora, Dorota. 2007. *Analiza konwersacyjna.* Warszawa: Wyd. Trio.

Rapley, Tim. 2007. *Doing Conversation, Discourse and Document Analysis.* London, Los Angeles, New Delhi, Singapore and Washington D.C.: SAGE Publications.

Reddy, Michael J. 1979. "*The Conduit Metaphor: A Case of Frame Conflict in our Language about Language.*" In *Metaphor and Thought*, edited by Andrew Ortony, 284–324. Cambridge: Cambridge University Press.

Repa, Jindra. 1991. "Training and Certification of Court Interpreters in a Multicultural Society." Meta 36(4): 595–605.

Riccardi Alessandra. 1998. "Interpreting Strategies and Creativity". In translator's Strategies and Creativity, edited by Ann Beylard-Ozeroff, Jana Kralová and Barbara Moser-Mercer, 171–179. Amsterdam/Philadelphia: J. Benjamins.

Roberts, Roda. 1990. "Interlingual Communication in Legal Settings." In *Proceedings of the Northeast Conference on Legal Interpretation and Translation*, edited by Angela M. Aguirre, 5–16. Jersey City, New Jersey: The Consortium of Educators in Legal Interpretation and Translation at Jersey City State College.

Roberts, Roda P. 1997. "Community Interpreting Today and Tomorrow." In *The Critical Link 1: Interpreters in the Community. Papers from the First International Conference on Interpreting in Legal, Health, and Social Service Settings, Canada, June 1–4, 1995*, edited by Silvana E. Carr, Roda P. Roberts, Aideen Dufour, and Dini Steyn, 7–26. Amsterdam/Philadelphia: J. Benjamins.

Roy, Cynthia. 1990. "Interpreters, Their Role and Metaphorical Language Use." In *Looking Ahead. Proceedings of the 31st Conference of the American Translators Association*, edited by Leslie Wilson, 77–86. Medford New Jersey: Learned Information.

Roy, Cynthia. 2000. *Interpreting as Discourse Process.* Oxford: Oxford University Press.

Rudvin, Mette. 2002. "How Neutral is 'Neutral'? Issues on Interaction and Participation in Community Interpreting." In *Perspectives on Interpreting*, edited by Maurizio Viezzi and Giuliana Garzone, 217–233. Bologna: CLUEB.

Rzeszutko, Małgorzata. 2003. *Rozprawa sądowa w świetle lingwistyki tekstu.* Lublin: Wyd. Uniwersytetu Marii Curie–Skłodowskiej.

Rzeszutko, Małgorzata. 2004. "Rozprawa sądowa jako odmiana gatunkowa tekstu." In *W kręgu weirnej mowy*, edited by Maria Wojtak and Małgorzata Rzeszutko, 349–360. Lublin: Wyd. Uniwersytetu Marii Curie–Skłodowskiej.

Sacks, Harvey, Emanuel Schegloff, and Gail Jefferson. 1974. "A Simplest Systematics for the Organization of Turn-taking for Conversation." *Language* 50: 696–735.

Schegloff, Emanuel. 1990. "On the organization of sequences as a source of "coherence" in talk in interaction." In *Conversational Organisation and its Development*, edited by Bruce Dorval, 51–77. Norwood, New Jersey: Ablex, 51–77.

Schegloff, Emanuel. 1991. "Issues of relevance for discourse analysis: Contingency in action, interaction and co-participant context." In *Computational and Conversational Discourse*, edited by Eduard H. Hovy and Donia R. Scott, 3–35. Berlin: Springer-Verlag.

Schegloff, Emanuel. 1993. "Reflections on quantification in the study of conversation." *Research on Language and Social Interaction* 26: 99–128.

Schegloff, Emanuel. 1995. "Discourse and an interactional achievement III: The omnirelevance of action." *Research on Language and Social Interaction* 28(3): 185–211.

Schegloff, Emanuel. 2007. *Sequence Organisation in Interaction*. Cambridge: Cambridge University Press.

Schegloff, Emanuel, and Harvey Sacks. 1973. "Opening up closings." *Semiotica* 7: 289–327.

Schegloff, Emanuel, Harvey Sacks, and Gail Jefferson. 1977. "The preference for self-correctionin the organization of repair in conversation." *Language* 53: 361–382.

Shackman, Jane. 1984. *The Right to be Understood: A Handbook on Working With, Employing and Training Community Interpreters*. Cambridge: National Extension College.

Shisheng, Lü and Li Shuang. 2012. "The role shift of the interpreter to a cultural mediator. From the perspective of cultural orientations and contexting." *Babel. International Journal of Translation* 58(2): 145–163.

Shlesinger, Miriam. 1991a. "Interpreter Latitude vs. Due Process. Simultaneous and Consecutive Interpretation in Multilingual Trials." In *Empirical Research in Translation and Intercultural Studies: Selected Papers of the TRANS-SIF Seminar, Savonlinna 1988*, edited by Sonja Tirkkonen-Condit, 147–155. Tübingen: Hunter Narr.

Shlesinger, Miriam. 1991b. "Lexicalization in Translation: an Empirical Study of Students' Progress." Paper presented at the Annual Meeting of the First

Language International Conference (Elsinore, Denmark, May 31–June 2, 1991), https://eric.ed.gov/?id=ED333752 (March 20, 2018).

Shlesinger, Miriam and Franz Pöchhacker. 2008. "Introduction. Doing justice to court interpreting". In *Interpreting. Special Issue: Doing Justice to Court Interpreting*, edited by Miriam Shlesinger and Franz Pöchhacker, 1–7. Amsterdam/Philadelphia: J. Benjamins.

Shuy, Roger W. 1996. *Language crimes: the use and abuse of language evidence in the courtroom*. Oxford: Blackwell Publishers Ltd.

Silverman, David. 2000. *Doing qualitative research: A practical handbook*. Thousand Oaks, New Delhi: Sage Publications of London.

Silverman, David. 2001. *Interpreting Qualitative Data. Methods of Analysing Talk, Text and Interaction*, 2nd edition. Thousand Oaks, New Delhi: Sage Publications of London.

Skorek, Marta. 2014. "Apprenticeship: The Value of Hands-on Experience in Court Interpreter Training." In *New tasks for legal interpreters and translators in the enlarged Europe*, edited by Danuta Kierzkowska, 258–266. Warszawa: Wyd. TEPIS.

Solová, Regina. 2013. *Norma i praktyka w przekładzie tekstów skonwencjonalizowanych*. Wrocław: Oficyna Wydawnicza Atut – Wrocławskie Wydawnictwo Oświatowe.

Stawecka, Aleksandra. 2010. "Ustny przekład sądowy w Polsce. Normy zawodowe a praktyka." In *O tłumaczach, prawnikach, lekarzach i urzędnikach. Teoria i praktyka przekładu środowiskowego w Polsce*, edited by Małgorzata Tryuk, 65–110. Warszawa: BEL Studio Sp. z o.o.

Takeda, Kayoko. 2007. *Sociopolitical Aspects of Interpreting at the International Military Tribunal for the Far East (1946–1948)*. Unpublished Ph.D. Thesis. Tarragona: Universitat Rovira i Virgili.

Takeda, Kayoko. 2015. "Tribunal interpreting." In *Routledge Encyclopedia of Interpreting Studies*, edited by Franz Pöchhacker, 424–425. London, New York: Routledge.

Tate, Granville, and Graham H. Turner. 1997/2002. "The Code and the Culture. Sign Language Interpreting – In Search of the New Breed's Ethics." In *The interpreting studies reader*, edited by Franz Pöchhacker and Miriam Shlesinger, 373–383. London/New York: Routledge.

Taylor Torsello, Carol. 1997. "Linguistics, Discourse Analysis and Interpretation." In *Conference Interpreting: Current Trends and Research*, edited by Yves Gambier, Daniel Gile, and Christopher Taylor, 167–186. Amsterdam/Philadelphia: J. Benjamins.

The Interpreter. 2005. Directed by Sydney Pollack. USA/United Kingdom/ France/Germany: Universal Pictures.

Tomaszkiewicz, Teresa. 1993. *Les opérations linguistiques qui sous-tendent le processus de sous-titrage des films*. Poznań: Wyd. Naukowe UAM.

Torikai, Kumiko. 2009. *Voices of the Invisible Presence*. Amsterdam/ Philadelphia: J. Benjamins.

Torstensson, Niklas, and Barbara Gawronska. 2009. "Discourse disfluencies in bilingual court hearings." *Comparative Legilinguistics. International Journal for Legal Communication* 1: 60–72.

Trosborg, Anna. 1995. "Statutes and contracts: An analysis of legal speech acts in the English language of the law." *Journal of Pragmatics* 23: 1–5.

Trosborg, Anna. 1997. *Rhetorical Strategies in Legal Language: Discourse Analysis of Statutes and Contracts*. Tübingen: Narr.

Tryuk, Małgorzata. 2004. *L'interprétation communautaire. Des normes et des rôles dans l'interprétation*. Warszawa: Wyd. TEPIS.

Tryuk, Małgorzata. 2006. *Przekład ustny środowiskowy*. Warszawa: Wyd. Naukowe PWN.

Tryuk, Małgorzata. 2007. *Przekład ustny konferencyjny*. Warszawa: Wyd. Naukowe PWN.

Tryuk, Małgorzata. 2010. *Tłumaczenie sądowe. Od teorii do praktyki*, In *O tłumaczach, prawnikach, lekarzach i urzędnikach. Teoria i praktyka przekładu środowiskowego w Polsce*, edited by Małgorzata Tryuk, 15–64. Warszawa: BEL Studio Sp. z o.o.

Tryuk, Małgorzata. 2012a. *Ty nic nie mów, ja będę tłumaczył. O etyce w tłumaczeniu ustnym*. Warszawa: UW.

Tryuk, Małgorzata. 2012b. "Tłumacz przed sądem. Międzynarodowe Trybunały Karne." In *Tłumacz: sługa pośrednik, twórca?*, edited by Małgorzata Guławska-Gawkowska, Krzysztof Hejwowski, and Anna Szczęsny, 45–60. Warszawa: ILS UW.

Tryuk, Małgorzata. 2015. *On Ethics and Interpreters*. Frankfurt am Main: Peter Lang.

Valero Garcés, Carmen, Adriana Dergam. 2003. "¿Mediador social = mediador interlingüístico intérprete? Práctica, formación y reconocimiento social del intérprete en los servicios públicos." In *La evaluación de la calidad en interpretación: Docencia y profesión*, edited by Ángela Collados Aís, María Manuela Fernández Sánchez, E. Macarena Pradas Macías, Elisabeth Stévaux, and Concepción Sánchez Adam, 257–266. Granada: Editorial Comares.

Wadensjö, Cecilia. 1992. *Interpreting as Interaction: On dialogue-interpreting in immigration hearings and medical encounters.* Linköping: Linköping University.

Wadensjö, Cecilia. 1995. "Recycled Information as a Questioning Strategy: Pitfalls in Interpreter-Mediated Talk." In *The Critical Link 1: Interpreters in the Community. Papers from the First International Conference on Interpreting in Legal, Health, and Social Service Settings, Canada, June 1-4, 1995*, edited by Silvana E. Carr, Roda P. Roberts, Aideen Dufour, and Dini Steyn, 35–52. Amsterdam/Philadelphia: J. Benjamins.

Wadensjö, Cecilia. 1997. "The Right to Lie: On Interpreter-Mediated Police Interrogations." In *Conference Interpreting: Current Trends and Research*, edited by Yves Gambier, Daniel Gile, and Christopher Taylor, 202–205. Amsterdam/Philadelphia: J. Benjamins.

Wadensjö, Cecilia. 1998. *Interpreting as Interaction*. London and New York: Longman.

Wadensjö, Cecilia. 2001. "Interpreting in crisis: The interpreter's position in therapeutic encounters" In *Triadic exchanges: Studies in Dialogue Interpreting*, edited by Ian Mason, 71–85. Manchester: St. Jerome Publishing.

Wadensjö, Cecilia. 2012. "Foreword." In *Coordinating Participation in Dialogue Interpreting*, edited by Claudio Baraldi and Laura Gavioli, xi–xii. Amsterdam/Philadelphia: J. Benjamins.

Wahlster, Wolfgang, Heinz Marburger, Anthony Jameson, and Stephan Busemann. 1983. "Over-answering yes-no questions: Extended Responses in a NL Interface to a Vision System." Proceedings of the Eighth International Joint Conference on Artificial Intelligence. Natural language 3: Generation-theoretical, including semantics, IJCI-83(2), 643–646.

Wilensky Harold L. 1964. "The professionalization of everyone?" The American Journal of Sociology 70 (2), 137–158.

Worth, John. 1821. *The trial of the Queen of England in the House of Lords. 1820*. London: T. Kelly.

Yates, Lyn. 2003. "Interpretive claims and methodological warrant in small-number qualitative, longitudinal research." *International Journal of Social Research Methodology* 6 (3), 223–232.

Zaragoza, Jeanette. 2015. *The search for a Mendi-court intepreter in The Amistad Case in order to challenge the institution of slavery*. https://www.researchgate.net/publication/318529058_The_search_for_a_Mendi-court_interpreter_in_The_Amistad_Case_in_order_to_challenge_the_institution_of_slavery (February 21, 2018).

Zgółka, Tadeusz and Maciej Zieliński. 2003. "Perswazja w języku prawnym i prawniczym." In *Język perswazji publicznej*, edited by Katarzyna

Mosiołek-Kłosińska and Tadeusz Zgółka, 182–189. Poznań: Wyd. Poznańskie.

Zieliński, Maciej. 1999. "Języki prawne i prawnicze." In *Polszczyzna 2000. Orędzie o stanie języka na przełomie tysiącleci*, edited by Walery Pisarek, 50–74. Kraków: Ośrodek Badań Prasoznawczych UJ.

Zimman, Leonor. 1994. "Intervention as a Pedagogical Problem in Community Interpreting." In Teaching Translation and Interpreting 2: Insights, Aims and Visions, edited by Cay Dollerup and Annette Lindegaard, 217–224. Amsterdam/Philadelphia: J. Benjamins.

Internet resources

Canadian Social Enterprise CISOC (Cultural Interpretation Services for Our Communities) cisoc.net (December 13, 2017).

Charter of Fundamental Rights of the European Union (2000/C 364/01) http://www.europarl.europa.eu/charter/pdf/text_en.pdf (September 4, 2017).

European Convention for the Protection of Human Rights and Fundamental Freedoms of 4 November 1950 http://www.coe.int/en/web/conventions/full-list/-/conventions/rms/0900001680063765 (September 4, 2017).

Directive 2010/64/EU of the European Parliament and of the Council of 20 October 2010 on the right to interpretation and translation in criminal proceedings http://eur-lex.europa.eu/legal-content/EN/TXT/?uri=celex:32010L0064 (January 10, 2017).

Directive 2012/13/EU of the European Parliament and of the Council of 22 May 2012 on the right to information in criminal proceedings http://eur-lex.europa.eu/legal-content/EN/TXT/?qid=1503417979735&uri=CELEX:32012L0013 (May 22, 2017).

Directive 2012/29/EU of the European Parliament and of the Council of 25 October 2012 establishing minimum standards on the rights, support and protection of victims of crime http://eur-lex.europa.eu/legal-content/EN/TXT/?uri=CELEX%3A32012L0029 (May 22, 2017).

Proclamation of the Fundamental Principles of the Red Cross https://www.icrc.org/eng/resources/documents/misc/fundamental-principles-commentary-010179.htm (December 10, 2017).

Rozporządzenie Ministra Sprawiedliwości w porozumieniu z Ministrem Skarbu z dnia 7 sierpnia 1920 r. w przedmiocie wynagrodzenia świadków, znawców i tłumaczów w postępowaniu karnem (Dz. U. z 1920 r. Nr 67, poz. 453) http://isap.sejm.gov.pl/DetailsServlet?id=WDU19200750515 (May 21, 2017).

Rozporządzenie Ministra Sprawiedliwości z dnia 24 grudnia 1928 r. o tłumaczach przysięgłych (Dz. U. z 1928 r. Nr 104, poz. 943) http://isap.sejm.gov.pl/DetailsServlet?id=WDU19281040943 (July 22, 2016).

Rozporządzenie Ministra Sprawiedliwości z dnia 9 grudnia 1953 r. w sprawie tłumaczów przysięgłych (Dz. U. z 1953 r. Nr 51, poz. 256) http://dziennikustaw.gov.pl/du/1953/s/51/256 (July 22, 2016).

Rozporządzenie Ministra Sprawiedliwości z dnia 19 sierpnia 1968 r. w sprawie tłumaczy przysięgłych. (Dz. U. z 1968 r. Nr 35, poz. 244) http://isap.sejm.gov.pl/VolumeServlet?type=wdu&rok=1968&numer=035 (July 22, 2016).

Rozporządzenie Ministra Sprawiedliwości z dnia 8 czerwca 1987 r. w sprawie biegłych sądowych i tłumaczy przysięgłych (Dz. U. z 1987 r. Nr 18, poz. 112) http://isap.sejm.gov.pl/DetailsServlet?id=WDU19870180112 (July 22, 2016).

Rozporządzenie Ministra Sprawiedliwości z dnia 24 stycznia 2005 r. w sprawie szczegółowego sposobu przeprowadzenia egzaminu na tłumacza przysięgłego http://isap.sejm.gov.pl/DetailsServlet?id=WDU20050150129 (January 11, 2017).

http://tepis.org.pl/the-polish-society-of-sworn-and-specialized-translators/ (January 5, 2017).

http://www.tepis.org.pl/index.php/tepis-o-sobie/dzialalnosc-pt-tepis/the-polish-society-of-sworn-and-specialized-translators (May 22, 2017).

Universal Declaration of Human Rights of 10 December 1948 http://www.ohchr.org/EN/UDHR/Documents/UDHR_Translations/eng.pdf (September 4, 2017).

Ustawa o zawodzie tłumacza przysięgłego z dnia 25 listopada 2004 r. (Dz.U. z 2015 r. Nr 487) https://bip.ms.gov.pl/pl/rejestry-i-ewidencje/tlumacze-przysiegli/ (October 28, 2017); transl. by Setkowicz-Ryszka available at: http://www.mc-tlumaczenia.pl/files/file/PolishSwornTranslator Act%2827_1_2005%29.pdf) (October 20, 2017).

eulita.eu (March 2, 2018).

EULITA Code of Professional Ethics http://www.eulita.eu/sites/default/files/EULITA-code-London-e.pdf (November 6, 2017).

ISO 13611:2014 Interpreting – Guidelines for community interpreting https://www.iso.org/standard/54082.html (October 1, 2017).

ISO/DIS 20228 Interpreting services – Legal interpreting – Requirements https://www.iso.org/standard/67327.html (October 1, 2017).

ISO/DIS 20228 Interpreting services – Legal interpreting – Requirements https://dgn.isolutions.iso.org/obp/ui#iso:std:iso:20228:dis:ed-1:v2:en (July 4, 2018).

BBC News. 2009. "Demjanjuk tried for Nazi crimes", http://news.bbc.co.uk/2/hi/europe/8385577.stm (October 28, 2017).

http://en.oxforddictionaries.com/definition/trial (December 10, 2017)

https://www.infolinia.com/2012_03_08_condominium_czyli_mieszkanie_wlasnosciowe (October 1, 2017).

https://sjp.pl/zresetowa%C4%87 (October 1, 2017).

http://sjp.pwn.pl/sjp/sad;2519448.html (September 12, 2017).

http://www.zztp.pl (December 15, 2017).

Index

Studies in Language, Culture and Society

Edited by Łucja Biel, Andrzej Kątny and Piotr Ruszkiewicz

The editors of this series invite books addressing the nexus between language, culture and society. Contrastive studies are welcome in particular, whether of a synchronic or diachronic orientation. Various perspectives on language / communication are of interest: grammatical, pragmatic, sociolinguistic, discursive and semiotic. A wide range of theoretical and methodological positions is accepted: cognitive / anthropological / corpus linguistics, as well as pragmatics, interactional sociolinguistics, (specialized) genre analysis, and critical discourse studies.

The cutting edge of the series is to publish innovative research elucidating the processes of *inter-* and *intra*-language variation and change, and - at the same time - relating them to flows *in* and *across* cognate categories of culture, community and society.

The series publishes monographs and edited volumes reporting on data-driven research that carries a potential for application in translation studies, language teaching, multilingual (multicultural) education, and interdisciplinary critical discourse studies.

The languages of publication are English and German, yet book proposals in other major languages will also be considered, if centrally contributive to the main aim of the series.

Vol. 1 Ewa Kucelman: Self-based Anaphora in Early Modern English. 2013.

Vol. 2 Łucja Biel: Lost in the Eurofog: The Textual Fit of Translated Law. 2014.

Vol. 3 Marek Kuźniak / Agnieszka Libura / Michał Szawerna (eds.): From Conceptual Metaphor Theory to Cognitive Ethnolinguistics. Patterns of Imagery in Language. 2014.

Vol. 4 Grzegorz Kowalski: Claim-making and Claim-challenging in English and Polish Linguistic Discourses. 2015.

Vol. 5 Małgorzata Tryuk: On Ethics and Interpreters. 2015.

Vol. 6 Anna Duszak / Grzegorz Kowalski (eds.): Academic (Inter)genres: between Texts, Contexts and Identities. 2015.

Vol. 7 Alicja Witalisz: English Loan Translations in Polish. Word-formation Patterns, Lexicalization, Idiomaticity and Institutionalization. 2015.

Vol. 8 Agnieszka Kampka / Katarzyna Molek-Kozakowska (eds.): Rhetoric, Knowledge and the Public Sphere. 2016.

Vol. 9 Maria Załęska / Urszula Okulska (eds.): Rhetoric, Discourse and Knowledge. 2016.

Vol. 10 Łucja Biel: Lost in the Eurofog: The Textual Fit of Translated Law. Second Revised Edition. 2017.

Vol. 11 Karolina Broś / Grzegorz Kowalski (eds.): Discourse Studies - Ways and Crossroads. Insights into Cultural, Diachronic and Genre Issues in the Discipline. 2017.

Vol. 12 Iga Lehman: Authorial Presence in English Academic Texts. A Comparative Study of Student Writing across Cultures and Disciplines. 2018.

Vol. 13 Katarzyna Stachowiak: Phonology Matters in Interpreting. 2018.

Vol. 14 Agnieszka Biernacka: Interpreter-Mediated Interactions of the Courtroom. A Naturally Occurring Data Based Study. 2019.

www.peterlang.com

www.ingramcontent.com/pod-product-compliance
Ingram Content Group UK Ltd.
Pitfield, Milton Keynes, MK11 3LW, UK
UKHW041447071026
15587UKWH00010B/532